Edited by Al Sarrantonio

THE NATIONAL LAMPOON TREASURY OF HUMOR

A FIRESIDE BOOK

Published by Simon & Schuster

New York, London, Toronto, Sydney, Tokyo, Singapore

OTHER FIRESIDE
BOOKS BY AL SARRANTONIO

FIRESIDE TREASURY OF GREAT HUMOR (EDITOR)
FIRESIDE TREASURY OF NEW HUMOR (EDITOR)

Fireside
Simon & Schuster Building
Rockefeller Center
1230 Avenue of the Americas
New York, New York 10020

Copyright © 1991 by Al Sarrantonio and NL Communications, Inc.
Copyright © 1971, 1972, 1973, 1974, 1975, 1976, 1977, 1978, 1979, 1980, 1981, 1982, 1983, 1984, 1985, 1986, 1987, 1988, 1989 National Lampoon, Inc.

FIRESIDE and colophon are registered trademarks
of Simon & Schuster Inc.

Designed by Liney Li
Manufactured in the United States of America

10 9 8 7 6 5 4 3 2 1

Library of Congress Cataloging in Publication Data
The National lampoon treasury of humor/edited by Al Sarrantonio.
    p.   cm.
    "A Fireside book."
    1. American wit and humor. I. Sarrantonio, Al. II. National lampoon.
PN6162.N372   1991
817'.5408—dc20   91-17788
                                                 CIP

ISBN 0-671-70833-3

"More to Come" by Michael O'Donoghue, copyright © 1972 by National Lampoon, Inc.
Reprinted by permission of the author.
"Beat the Meatles" by Chris Miller, copyright © 1977 by National Lampoon, Inc.
Reprinted by permission of the author.

Acknowledgments

My heartfelt thanks to the folks at the National Lampoon for all their help, especially George Agoglia, Howard Jurofsky and Ginger Ernano. And to Dominick Abel, who guided the agent's rudder on this one. And, of course, to the Simon & Schuster bunch, Ed Walters, David Dunton and Liz Cunningham, who, thank God, like to laugh.

Contents

Introduction by Al Sarrantonio

What you now hold in your hands (or on your lap, or with your feet if you're weird or have no hands) is a lot of the very best prose from twenty years of America's funniest magazine, the *National Lampoon*.

Yipes! Has it really been twenty years?

Do you know how long twenty years is?

Do you realize that in 1970, when the first issue of *National Lampoon* appeared, Madonna was less than ten, Christian Slater was a diaper-soiling one-year-old, and most of the New Kids on the Block weren't even egg and sperm? That Hitchcock was still making movies? That Charlemagne had just been crowned? God, they didn't even have *cars* back then, or beer, or ink. The first issues were sold orally, and, after paying in scrip or crops, the entire magazine was read into your ear by a member of the *National Lampoon* staff. A horrible experience, believe me.

But time marched on. Ink was invented. Charlemagne stopped making movies. Hitchcock discovered the car.

The *National Lampoon* kept publishing great prose.

A lot of it was gathered together so you could hold it with your feet and read it.

A word about the organization of this book. A cursory examination, or an electron microscopic analysis of the edge of page 49, paying particular attention to the genetic recombinant data obtained from the speck of weevil snout crushed with the pulp of whatever they're making paper out of these days, will reveal that this volume is arranged as close as possible to a giant issue of *National Lampoon* magazine. Why did I do it that way? Beats me. I just threw all the stuff I had up in the air, and that's the way it came down. But I did want to say that the front part of the magazine, consisting of an editorial (sometimes dealing with the issue at hand and sometimes having nothing in the world to do with it), the Letters section and various columns, such as "Mrs. Agnew's Diary" (written ostensibly in the hand of the eventually-disgraced vice president's wife, but actually by Doug Kenney, who suddenly changed it in early 1974 to "Baba Rum Raisin"), has always been special. Other columns, examples of which are included in this book, were authored by various people: "Sports Column" by Sean Kelly, John Weidman and the editors; "Canadian Corner" by Canadian expatriates Sean Kelly, Ted Mann, Bruce McCall and Brian Shein; "Generally Speaking" by Ted Mann; "Tell Debby" by Brian McConnachie; "International Date Line" by Doug Kenney and P. J. O'Rourke; "The Smart Set" by John Hughes.

If you want to, think of this as the thickest—and, hopefully, funniest—issue of *National Lampoon* ever.

If you don't want to, the hell with you. You're probably the one using your feet anyway.

This isn't a history of the *National Lampoon*. It's a collection of great prose stuff from it. If you want to know a little of the history of the magazine, who punched whom where, who slept with the goat when, there are other sources, such as Tony Hendra's *Going Too Far*, which should satisfy you.

A final word. I'm an interloper here, an archeologist. I've dug through twenty years of an extremely funny publication, one that has succeeded in offending everyone equally, to cull, I pray, the very funniest. The job has been a pleasure. And I wanted to make sure you know why:

On the acknowledgments page, I didn't mention any of the writers who penned the words in this anthology. That's because nobody reads acknowledgment pages except the people who are mentioned. I want to make sure you know how unique, and funny, these people are. Without them, there wouldn't have been any *National Lampoon* magazine. Or this book.

Even if they do all use their feet.

Al Sarrantonio
September, 1990

EDITORIAL

AS A PUBLIC SERVICE, we are presenting in this space the Abbreviated Delaware Standard Psychological Test. The pressures, frustrations, and emotional instabilities which drive men to commit wanton acts of violence, even mass murder, are shrouded in the impenetrable mysteries of the chemistry of the brain, but extensive research has made it possible in many cases to identify individuals with a potential psychopathic personality before their latent psychoses erupt into episodes of uncontrollable blood-lust. The ADSPT is by no means perfect, but it can at least give a "storm warning." We urge all readers to take it, and then, if the easy-to-tabulate results indicate the presence of possible mental disequilibrium, to seek qualified professional help.

Directions: Complete the following sentences with the word or phrase that best suits your personality. Even if none of the alternatives seem entirely satisfactory, you must choose one.

1. I would most like to be:
   (A) a male nurse
   (B) an interior decorator
   (C) a dressmaker
   (D) a butcher
2. If someone asked me what I thought of a lamp they had bought, I would say it was:
   (A) darling
   (B) just the cutest thing
   (C) too, too sweet
   (D) good for hitting people over the head with
3. Of the following sports, my favorite is:
   (A) maypole dancing
   (B) field hockey
   (C) hoop spinning
   (D) rugby
4. Of the following foods, the one I prefer is:
   (A) ladyfingers
   (B) truffles
   (C) tiny little tea cakes
   (D) good red meat
5. Of the following words, I would be most likely to use:
   (A) faience
   (B) chiaroscuro
   (C) andante
   (D) thud
6. If I had to choose among these books, I would read:
   (A) *Ten Steps to a More Satisfying Homosexual Life*
   (B) *A Layman's Guide to Unnatural Love*
   (C) *Faggot! Confessions of a Homosexual*
   (D) *Pork Chop Hill*
7. When I see a gun, I think:
   (A) what a cunning lamp it would make
   (B) how much fun it would be to kill someone with it

Directions: Choose the statement which most expresses your feelings. Even if neither statement is entirely satisfactory, you must choose one.

8. (A) I like to suck things.
   (B) I like to kill things.
9. (A) When I go to parties, I like to be ignored and made fun of.
   (B) I would like to maim a woodland animal.
10. (A) Sentimentality makes me puke.
    (B) I like the sight of blood.
11. (A) I would like to stay home and fiddle with sachets.

(B) I would like to go out on the town with the boys and get into a brawl.
12. (A) Sometimes I feel like the top of my head is going to fly off.
(B) Sentimentality makes me puke.
13. (A) I like the sight of blood.
(B) The sight of pus isn't half bad either.

To determine whether you have antisocial tendencies and suffer from the "Involuntary Violence Syndrome," turn this page upside down, and give yourself 5 points for each one of the "symbolic hostility" answers listed below. If your "psychotic profile" score exceeds 30, arrange for an interview with an experienced psychiatrist without delay. If it exceeds 60, have a friend or loved one strap you to a bed or chair IMMEDIATELY.

Questions 1-6: All "D" answers indicate hostility.
Questions 7-13: All "B" answers indicate hostility.
Questions 8-13: All "A" answers indicate hostility.

A GUEST EDITORIAL

FROM THE VICE PRESIDENT OF THE UNITED STATES

TO BEGIN WITH, let me just say, *MAD* magazine has always been a favorite . . .

To begin with, let me just say, *National Lampoon* has always been a favorite of mine. And when the executive editor, Mousy Slopoke, asked me, as my first official act in office, to author the editorial, I said, "Excuse me?" because instead of pushing the speaker button on my phone, I had pushed the mute button instead. But then, after I figured everything out, a week later, I said sure, especially seeing as how I'm not allowed outside where humans might see me and I'm not allowed in any of the meetings with the other fellas. They say it's just because they don't like me. I think it's because of that stupid Silly Putty incident. Boy, was everyone peeved. You see, I was playing with my Silly Putty at the president's desk (yes, I know I'm not allowed to play there!) when I saw these great color pictures of some lasers. And I thought, WOW! I bet these lasers would reproduce swelly (is "swelly" a word?) on my Silly Putty. So I tried it and it did. That night, at a state dinner, I showed it to everyone. They were all impressed. In fact, the East German ambassador asked if he could play with my Silly Putty. Of course I said sure, because it's always fun to share. But then, what with me spilling my milk all over Marilyn, I guess I forgot to get it back. Anyway, everyone was *très* upset.

Okay, Mousy sent me a list of what's in the issue. Let's see what we have here.

We have an ad. That looks very nice.

We have a contents page. Great! Contents pages are my favorite part of any magazine, because I'm one of those people who love lists. I'm a list person. I make lists of everything: the names of my family members, the acting credits of Ken Berry, what's in my desk . . . Hey, there's an idea. Let's see what's in my desk. Hmmm, I have a pencil. I can use that to make a list with. Oh, look, my lunch—an Indiana Whiz Baloney, my favorite! Yum! An Indiana Whiz Baloney is like a Philadelphia cheese steak but better for you. You take a nice fillet of baloney, place it on a slab of white bread, and spread a carpet of Cheez Whiz on it. Then place it in a toaster oven. Eat with a glass of milk and a large smile.

What else is in my desk? . . . A file that says TOP SECRET. Hmmm . . . I'll just throw out these papers and keep the file to put my lists in.

Back to the issue. We have an editorial. Never read 'em myself. It's all words. I like pictures. I guess that's why I like this Stick Figure piece in this issue so much. It's a retrospective of stick figure art through the ages, so you know you're gonna get the best darn stick figures they could muster up.

Oh, look, there's a twelve-page Mediocrity section. And I'm the star! Well, howdy-do! Finally, some recognition. After years of writers foaming at the mouth over the Pyramids or the Grand Canyon or even crying at the sight of famine and war, it's nice to see someone focusing on those subjects that are important to folks like you and me, such as Winnebagos and 16" × 14" coolers.

Uh-oh, the Indiana Whiz Baloney oozed all over my desk and papers. I'll just lick this up. . . . OOOOWWWWWW. . . . Just stapled my tongue. I'm all right. I'll just put some Scotch tape on it, it'll stop bleeding soon. Geez, this tastes terrible. Someone oughta invent cherry-flavored Scotch tape so if you're ever in the position of having to put Scotch tape in your mouth, it won't taste so . . . so . . . mediocre.

Here's an article called "Who Screwed Roger Rarebit." Now, why would anyone do that? I love rabbits, especially in a thick mushroom gravy. I hunt rabbits, not with rifles, but with my hands. I strangle them. It's much more manly that way. What I do is, I place an Indiana Whiz Baloney on the ground, then, when a rabbit's adorable little nose twitches as the smell tickles its nostrils in expectation of a cheesy delight, that's when I jump out from behind a tree, grab it by the neck, and choke the life out of it. Of course, I usually let it have a few bites before crushing its tiny esophagus, 'cause the Indiana Whiz Baloney *is* so tasty. And, after all, it's the rabbit's last meal. Marilyn says I'm a softy. I say, what's right is right.

What's this—"The Olde Sandusky Lard Barn." It's a cheese catalog! Any Cheez Whiz logs? No? Well, then, this isn't much of a cheese catalog, is it?! You just can't go around calling yourself a cheese catalog and not have Cheez Whiz logs. You'll go out of business in two days!

What the heck is this—"How to Enjoy the Depression of the Nineties." That's dangerous talk. Besides, we're in charge now and nothing like that will ever happen. I know, because Mr. Sununu told me, and he's an important man. I know he's important because every time he comes into the room I'm told to "get the hell out." Sununu—what a funny name. I sometimes call him Mr. Funnyname. He, in turn, sometimes wraps his arm around my neck until I pass out.

Ooops, the cheese from my Indiana Whiz Baloney just dripped into the electric pencil sharpener and shorted it out. Let me just take a second to put out the flames here. This is one of the dangers of an Indiana Whiz Baloney. It's a free-spirited sandwich, one that doesn't cotton well to being manhandled until it's well past your tonsils.

Back to the issue. Here's something called "The Assassination of St. Geraldo." Why don't they go after a real doodyhead—like Rather—and leave the true journalists alone!

Oh, my . . . now I did it. The flames are really spreading now. I ought to call someone. But first I'll stick my sandwich into the flame and toast it a little.

"Duke's Diner." This is a feature about Michael Dukakis running a diner. Dukakis. I know that name. Gee, is this what happened to him? So devastated he had to open a diner? That's sad. That's so sad. That's so so sad. That's so so so sad. That's so so so so so so so so so so so so so so so so so so so so so so so so so sad . . . . tee-hee.

Oh, well. I better be going. It's getting pretty hot in here and, as that great Republican Harry Truman once said to a chicken he was flicking, "If you can't stand the heat, get out of your office."

So see you next issue, when I'll be writing my very own personal column with no help from anyone (except with spelling) called "What I Did Today."

Until then, this is your vice president saying,

This is your vice president.

LETTERS

Sirs:

Listen, you bunch of f--king homos, last night I caught that c--ks--king son-of-a-b--ch kid of mine reading your s--t-eating magazine again. I grabbed the little pr--k by his cr--ch and beat the c--p out of the little c--thead until he about p--d in his pants. The *next* time I catch that little m----rf--ker with it, I'm going to ream his s---y little r---g with a can opener and take his h---ing p--g and make him g---y f-----m it until the tr--d runs out of his dr---p and his r--k t--bs j-ks revolve like a rusty crankshaft.

> Noah Webster
> Cambridge, Mass.

Sirs:

Slowly he neared her moonlit silhouette, standing naked but for a small chemise made transparent against the French doors. Without a word, his strong brown hands encircled her downy flesh and he kissed her breast with an urgency that surprised him as much as it startled her. Frantically, his need growing uncontrollably within him, his fingers probed her tender, secret places, heeding only the insistent throbbings of his straining loins. "Hey, baby," he murmured as he sought to probe even further, "it's hard to believe you're only a turkey."

"Gobble?" she asked, drawing away suddenly, hurt and questioning.

"I said, you're not bad, for a turkey, I mean," he said, sensing he had said something wrong.

Suddenly a shot rang out and a series of loud, angry squawks filled the boudoir. "Oh nuts," he gasped, "it's your father!"

Well, that's as far as I've gotten on chapter one, but I thought I'd send it along anyway, knowing that if I don't sell the movie rights now, I'll be hounded all next fall when I want to spend some time with Dave and Arlene.

Love to Stephen, but tell him I won't take a penny less than ten percent of the gross.

> Florence Nesbitt
> Montreal, Canada

1971

Sirs:

I'm gonna sit right down and write myself a letter.

> Smith Corona
> Harrisburg, Penn.

1972

Messieurs:

I em zorry to bosser you, but as I go to meelk zee moo-cows on my farm zees morneeng, I find zee British aeroplane all ovair zee field, smish-smash! Zen, when I am lookeeng for zee aeroplane drivair, I find in zee pasture zee pile of zee how-you-say beef goulash wearing zee pilot's uniform. *Tres* seeckeneeng, *n'est-ce pas?* But zat ees nut all. *Zut!* Inzide zee pilot's parachute, I find zee copy of zee *National Lampoon*! *Qu'est-ce qui se passe,* anyway?

> Jacques Batard
> Dunkirk, France

1973

Sirs:

He clasps the crag with crooked
    hands:
Close to the earth in lonely lands,
Ringed with the azure world, he
    stands.

The wrinkled sea beneath him
    crawls;
He watches from the mountain
    walls,
And like a thunderbolt, he farts.

                Al Tennyson
          Westminster Abbey
           London, England

Sirs:

Anyone for Tennyson?

As you can see, I am no stranger to an occasional jape myself, but I am puzzled by the preceding letter. Has a slip of the pen found its way into your generally fine transcription of "The Eagle" printed above?

As a critic lauded for my encyclopedic scam on all the big name rhymsters from Keats to Yeats and—if I may be allowed to briefly plunk my own academic twanger—perhaps *the* seminal influence on the young T. S. Eliot? (You may remember him—the skinny kid with the sharp clothes who'd say "*ek*tually" for "actually" and stirred his tea with his tool when no one was looking.) Anyhow, I have a literary bone to pick with you fellows.

I will admit that there have been some divergent readings of "The Eagle"; Abrams and Wolfe favor "crooked hands" while earlier anthologists prefer "hornèd hands," for example. Me personally, I have always harbored a clandestine fondness for "come-covered," a popular variation I came across (no pun intended) on a men's room wall at Jack's —a favorite literary hangout of mine on Mass. Ave.

But, unless I am very much mistaken, I am unfamiliar with any authoritative text reading "and like a thunderbolt he farts

(*sic*)"! I believe the correct reading is "he *falls*" (italics my own). I mean, have I blown my valves or what?

              I.A. Richards
            Cambridge, Mass.

Sirs:

As Public Relations Director for the American Audubon Society, I was disturbed to note in your fine publication a blatant ornithological fiction—namely an *Aquila heliaca* gifted with audible flatulence. Also, there is no species of eagle, at least to the Society's knowledge, that comes (no pun intended) equipped with "hands." Most species have claws or, more properly, talons.

Could Mr. Tennyson possibly be confusing his remarkable eagle with the common ground-roasted twit? This cuddly little scavenger is also found in rocky, sea-bordered biomes such as Tennyson describes, is fond of power dives, and, it has been reported, farts like a Gatling gun.

Could this be the bird of your fancy?

              T.R. Ralston
     American Audubon Society
          Washington, D.C.

Sirs:

Scree greech scrawk. Twee grackle toweech grackle krawk "and like a thunderbolt he farts"?! Cree gawrk foowee!

              Don Eagle
           Hayfork, Calif.

Sirs:

I hear where you fellas been jabbering about them there fartin' eagles. Well, some say they exist and some say they don't. But all *I* know is that me an' my kids used to spend whole dang Saturday afternoons blowin' the noisy critters off powerlines with a twelve-gauge. I mean, hell, they'd just *squat* up there lookin' at you kind of cross-eyed until you're about three maybe four yards away and then *blammo* you knock their assholes up around their collars for 'em. Something to see, I hope to tell you. Feathers and little hollow bones all over the place like confetti. Yahoo.

L. Bird Johnson
LBJ Ranch, Texas

Sirs:

Success is counted sweetest by those who ne'er succeed. Pimples can be tasty, if first you let 'em bleed.

Emily & Wiley Post
Fresno, Calif.

Sirs:

Louder and funnier.

H. Keller
Carson City, N. Mex.

Sirs:

Marcel Marceau
Paris, France

Srs:

Rdr's Dgst
Elkhart, Ind.

1974

Sirs:

You wanna know why Lee Harvey Oswald acted alone? Because he could never remember his lines.

Lee Strasberg
New York, N.Y.

1975

Sirs:

Broken arms
Can come true
It can happen to you
When you get in my way.

Frank Sinatra
Palm Springs

Sirs:

Right on, Frank.
For what is a man?
What has he got?
If not his goons,
Then he has not!!!

Sal and Vic
Everything East of Newark

Sirs:

This dance called the Latin Hustle is nothing more than a crude and suggestive parody of the Central European mazurka. There is nothing dirty about the mazurka, even though it derives from a bestial hoedown practiced in the court of Olaf the Hemophiliac. The cleaned-up version is based on the Greek legend of Mocus and Hysterektome, star-crossed lovers. Mocus (the male dancer) wears a toga made of seasoned hominy husks. Hysterektome wears less than a jaybird as she capriciously toots on a medieval woodwind called the *dildino*. Meanwhile, the drummer beats a mournful knell on bongos, cowbell, and bullclap. Only a dolt would lump this time-honored dance with the silly twists, prods, and thrusts of contemporary pop hoofing.

Caressa di Royalballs
Bunnihaupt, Hungary

Sirs:

Do you know how you can tell which housewives shopping in the supermarket are into women's lib? By the haircurlers under their arms! If you print this, can I still use it in my giant book about a family of Irish kikes who stab each other in the tits with pen knives?

Norman Mailer
Apt. 3B
Tudor Sedan Towers
Passaic, New Jersey

1976

Sirs:
Knock! Knock!
(You say), "Who's there?"
Kojak.
(You say), "Kojak who?"
Kojak off in your hat!

Eric Sevareid
New York, N.Y.

Sirs:
We're a pack of wild
dogs.
A pack of wild dogs
are we.
We run through the
hills
Bereft of job skills,
And we don't care
where we pee.

A Pack of Wild Dogs
The Hills

Sirs:
What's bloody, monthly, and sings? Give up? *The New Christy Menstruals!* Now, do you still think women aren't funny?

Some Women
Stuck at Home with the Kids

Sirs:
Living here in our little village is a wealthy merchant who during the war was a German corroborator. People would say that they were German, and this man would come up and say, "Yep, they're German, all right." He has never been prosecuted.

Jean La Feet
Merde, France

Sirs:
From here to *where*?!

James Jones
Quibly's Funeral Parlor
Sagaponach, N.Y.

Sirs:
My colleagues and I have been studying the question, "If Gloria Steinem and a full-grown sewer rat leaped off the Empire State Building at the same time, who would strike the earth first?" After many hours of thought, and with the aid of the computers at the lab here in Pasadena, we have determined that the answer would be, "Who cares?"

Carl Sagan
Pasadena, Calif.

1977

Sirs:
I got La Machine for Christmas. Two days later I cut off La Finger in the fucking thing.

Craig Claiborne
c/o The Food Section
The Times

Sirs:
Do you know what we call saddle sores in Argentina? Gaucho Marx!

Eva Peron

1978

Sirs:
I was in the hospital for two weeks, and you know what? I think some goddamn stupid intern switched bodies on me. I swear I'm in the wrong body. I never had

a bald spot on the top of my head. And I sure as heck didn't have this small a penis, and I never had trouble getting it "up" before. Also, where the heck do you suppose all this fat around my waist came from?

What I'd like to know is, how often does this happen? How many of us aren't who we really are?

Frank Flagston
Kansas City, Kan.

Sirs:

Why, Ah nevah will forget the day Ah had *forty* gentlemen callers, yes forty. Why, Ah had to borrow chairs from the neighbors to accommodate them all, and Ah made *gallons* of lemonade, and, oh my, but they were fine, handsome men, real gentlemen, not the kind of *common* man you see these days, and Ah said to them all—oh, I was in a *state*—Ah said, how can Ah evah repay y'all for your kind attentions? And they just said, "Tom, write a play." So Ah did. Ah have been writing that same play evah since.

Tennessee Williams
The Waterfront
New Orleans

Sirs:

You know what I found out? It took almost five years, but I discovered that when I do shows on a sexual topic, the women grab the microphone and hold it in suggestive ways—all unconsciously. I've even seen them run their fingers up and down the Shure A-50. Sometimes they even play with the head, where the switch is. I swear it's true because I've looked at the videotapes, which I could send you if you want.

Phil Donahue
WGN–TV

1979

Sirs:

As part of my program to toughen up the moral fiber of the English nation, I will be introducing strong measures to ensure that the British accent becomes even more incomprehensible to other English-speaking peoples than it is now. England of late has become soft, lax, and undisciplined, and some of our accents are almost like those of you Yanks. This will not be allowed to continue. Britain, after all, rose to greatness and dominated the world by speaking in such a way that no one, not even other Englishmen, could understand. We will do so again. This is the last intelligible communication you will receive from our brave little island. Ahll roight?

Margaret Thatcher
Proime Min'ster, Englahnd

Sirs:

Women are always complaining about menopause and menstruation and saying that men don't care about their problems. Well, I got news for them. Us men, we got a lot of problems ourselves. Like getting kicked in the nuts. You ever hear of a woman getting kicked in the nuts? Or getting a hard-on at the swimming pool in front of your fifteen-year-old niece, the one with the big knockers? Or when you go to a ball game and drink too much beer and have to piss in one of those giant troughs and there's always a guy with a huge schlong standing right next to you smirking at your puny little dick?

So what's the big deal about a little blood once a month?

Sylvester Stallone
Philadelphia, Pa.

Sirs:

My brother Dave was walking across the suspension bridge at the Milko Chocolate World of Fun when suddenly for no reason it collapsed. He and all the others on the bridge fell to their deaths in the Valley of Dinosaurs below. Dave hadn't done anything wrong. If there is a God, why didn't he let my brother land on someone, instead of on the Triceratop's spikes?

Velva Snapper
Tulane

Sirs:

As attorneys for the Vatican we are pleased to respond to the letter you forwarded to us from Ms. Velva Snapper of Tulane.

In the death of this man Dave Snapper we have been able to prove just and clear cause for divine vengeance. Please see enclosed letter.

Pesto Cappaletti
Cappaletti, Olivetti, and Schifoso
Vatican City

Dear Mr. Cappaletti:

There was, as you suspected, good reason for the death of Mr. Dave Snapper. Our records show we arrested Dave Snapper last year. He had been involved in mail-fraud activities, running in the newspapers advertisements for "men over seventy interested in high-paying, exciting work as human cannonballs." He would force these men, many of whom were senile, to pay him a $100 application fee. We were unable to successfully prosecute due to the influence of his prominent father, Victor Snapper, the Tulane drain tile magnate.

Stosh Ranowski
Chief of Police, Tulane

Sirs:

Husband of I and me just moved to your country from Spain. No sooner are we here than a bridge collapse of kingdom of magic dinosaurs and my husband is flung at his death on the ground below. I would say your country is a bowl of goat splatterings.

Mrs. Niko Oil
Tulane

Sirs:

A little research will tell you that Mrs. Oil's husband Niko was one of the most ferocious of Franco's aides. I know, as he once cut my cock off and threw me into a volcano. If a passing Basque shepherd had not heard my cries, I would probably be dead.

Anonymous
Tulane

Sirs:

It should be pretty obvious to everyone with the brains God gave geese that the collapse of the suspension bridge over the Milko Chocolate Valley of the Dinosaurs was no disaster but a great and long overdue come-uppance for people who, in despite of signs forbidding it, will swing or rock suspension bridges.

Xavier Mollar, President
Douchebag Suspension Bridge Ltd.
Tulane

Sirs:

We got a grievance down here at the station you might be able to help us with. We're ambulance attendants, see? The other week it was about the end of our shift and we get a call for a disaster out at the Milko Chocolate World of Fun. I says to the captain, "Hey, we're supposed to be off shift in ten minutes. So what the fuck? We drive out there and back, it's gonna be two hours minimum!"

Do you think he cares? He says, "None of your yappin', Kaminski; you and Marcello get in the wagon and get your butts out there."

I'm telling yous, I was pissed. And when we get out there, what do you think we find? Just about seventy-five people busted up all over a shitload of dinosaurs under some fuckin' bridge. Christ, I seen a lot of things, but when I seen that, I did a projectile puke, you know. It took me and Marcello three hours to get up the first load in, and by that time the fuckin' traffic was all jammed up on the parkway and we had to sit out the fuckin' rush for an hour. When we got back to the shop, Nichols and Michelson are sittin' around havin' coffee and laughing at us.

"What are you complainin' about?" says Michelson. "You're gettin' overtime."

That really got me pissed, so I told him we left his kid out there on a dinosaur's nose, 'cause I figured he would want to pick him up himself.

That really burned his ass.

Anyway, when I went to the union to complain, they told me the fucking supervisor had the right to send us out even near the end of the fuckin' shift. But the union rep said he thought it was a real shitty trick just the same.

I'm tellin' you, the captain and the supervisor got no idea of justice at all. Isn't that always the way? Tell me this is supposed to be a free country!

Pete Kaminski
Ambulance Attendants Local 451
Tulane

Sirs:

Had the dinosaurs in the Milko Chocolate Valley of the Dinosaurs been made of plastic, they would not have been so seriously damaged when the bridge above collapsed and they were subjected to a hail of falling bodies. Unfortunately, as most of the dinosaurs were either wood or metal, many were seriously damaged by the falling people. In particular a small Megalodon was crushed beneath a pair of obese twin sisters.

If the administrators of Milko Chocolate World thought to use our inflatable dinosaurs, they could simply have been patched and reinflated, and the attraction would have been restored by the next day.

Norman Snout
Vice President, Sales
Flate-O-Saur Ltd.
Sliver, Delaware

Sirs:

The Milko Chocolate amusement park bridge plunge was no accident. I looked at the cables afterward and they were pretty near rusted through. The way it was done was that a terrorist group took turns visiting the bridge every day for twenty years or so and dropped a few drops of water every day on the cable to rust it through. They doubtless used rainwater, which would leave no traces. They're smart, these people. They think they can get away with anything. They can, unless we as Americans join together to fight them.

Send five dollars today to: Fight the Terrorists, c/o The Milko Chocolate Amusement Park, Tulane, Alabama 10089. For extra fast attention, write "Mental Defective" in big letters on the outside of your envelope.

Richard Milko
Milko Chocolate Corp.
Tulane

Sirs:

We have two unclaimed bodies left over. The bodies were recovered last month from the site of the Milko Chocolate amusement park disaster. One is that of a twelve-year-old dog, the other that of a Megalodon or possibly an overweight middle-aged woman with a serious skin disease. Relatives or others wishing to claim same may do so by writing to us at the address below. This notice appears as a matter of record only.

Baltic Peoples' Funeral Home
Tulane

Sirs:

Please do not make jokes about the Milko Chocolate bridge disaster. My dog was on that bridge.

Marguerite Snuffheiser
Tulane

Sirs:

Whoops! I went to hell.

Jean-Paul Sartre

Sirs:

There's one commandment I forgot: Never read the Bible on the toilet.

God
Heaven

1980

Sirs:

Why don't we manufacture cars out of water? Such a move would reduce maintenance costs incredibly: you just add water. In the event of accidents, repairs to these cars would also be extremely cheap: just add more water. And, because we'd use "soft" water, fatalities would be greatly reduced. Except for a few possible drownings. And, with the money saved, we could build an improved drainage system to take away the extra water. This would mean better gutters for our drunks to lie in. Are you with me? Down with the multinational oil companies!

A slightly confused junior
at MIT

Sirs:

One of these days I'm really going to crack up. I'll saw my agent up into little pieces, and I'll stash her in one of those goddamned plastic bags and try to take her out and throw her in the garbage, and the fucking bag will break, I just know it.

The Man from Glad
Tired, Tired, Tired
Hollywood

Sirs:

To understand the monumental difficulties facing a poet in the late twentieth century, we need only recall the last words of that great, hard-drinking poet the late John Berryman before he plunged from the bridge into that ecstatic final icy meeting of poet and all-encompassing sea. "Hold the bottle, Allen," he said to me, "while I step over to the side here and see how far I can pee. . . ." He was a great poet, a wonderful drunk, and a sensational distance pisser, but—and I say this although I was his friend—he could not swim worth beans. A poet cannot be all things.

Allen Ginsberg
New York

Sirs:

I like to fart on airplanes. The big soft seat cushions (which also double as emergency flotation gear) absorb the noise, and most of the smell, too. Movie-theater seats are also good, especially during action movies when there's lots of noise up on the screen. Church pews are not so good, although sometimes you can rock to the side and squeeze one off in the opposite direction from your wife. But the absolute worst place in the world to fart is on a metal folding chair—Christ, it sounds like you're doing duck calls in Echo Canyon!

Supreme Court Justice
Thurgood Marshall
Washington, D.C.

1981

Sirs:

The real reason we don't want to sell you any of our oil is because we need it for our hair.

José Lopez Portillo
Mexico City

Sirs:

Hey, kids! What time is it? *It's the best of times, it's the worst of times!*

Howdy Dickens
Television City
London, England

Sirs:

I'm sure you realize that Chinese restaurants have the lowest hygiene standards this side of Calcutta, and that what you call a household pet we consider hearty soup base. The food is really greasy and gooey and it leaves you feeling nauseous and dizzy. But less than an hour later you want more, and you keep going back for it, week after week. Know why? We put opium in the food. Ah-hahahahaha!

Wo Fat
Chinatown

Sirs:

Boy, I'll bet you print some letters just to fill up space.

John Doe
Anytown, USA

Sirs:

To rent: attractive little green house. Located on Saint James Place. Free parking. RR both nearby. Rent: $16/month, more for hotel. Apply:

PARKER BROTHERS
Atlantic City, N.J.

Sirs:

Neil Armstrong here. You remember me, the first man on the moon? Sure you do. Perhaps you may be wondering why you've never heard a peep out of me since. Well, I'll tell you why: it's because I'm still on the moon! Those fuckers took off without me. Why, I've probably lost billions of dollars in commercial fees by now. Goddammit.

NEIL ARMSTRONG
Sea of Tranquility

1982

Sirs:

I had a taping system in the White House, too, and I used to listen to country music on it all the time.

Gerald Ford
38th President of the United States

Sirs:

Boy, you city folks sure know your plays! The road-show production of that *Whose Life Is It, Anyway?* just came to the Knoxville Civic Center and, oh boy, it sure was moving! It moved all over the place! That Charlie Callas feller is a nut! One scene he says, "It's a miracle, I can walk," and he gets outta bed and starts wobblin' all over the place like his legs are made out of rubber! I nearly busted a gut. Then another time he pulls up the sheets and says, "Oh my God. Not only am I a quadriplegic, but I've turned into Paul Williams," and I don't know how he did it, but all of a sudden he was three feet tall! When they say that Broadway is the entertainment capital of the world, they ain't kidding!

Bobby Joe Overalls
Knoxville, Tenn.

Sirs:

In the interest of safety, the following changes will be made in our upcoming circus tour: The high-wire team is to perform its delicate balancing act at a height of no more than five feet above the ground. Instead of using a whip, the lion tamer will be permitted to carry a gun. Also, all the clowns are to be tranquilized.

Barnum & Bailey
Big Top, Fla.

Sirs:

One of the questions asked of me is what to do if, when dining at a friend's home, you discover a bug in your food. You're put in a delicate position; you've lost your appetite, yet you don't want to hurt the host's feelings by not eating. Probably the best way to deal with such an occurrence is to excuse yourself from the table, as if you need to use the bathroom, then sneak out the back door and run like crazy.

Miss Manners
Rude Awakening, Pa.

Sirs:
Well, well, well! You finally got smart and saved yourselves all the embarrassment. After all, we've been pronouncing our planet Uranus "YOUR-inus" for eons, while you folks were flushing and giggling while saying "Your Anus." Well, sorry to spoil the fun, but we all just got together and voted to change our name. Hope you can salvage some dignity and pronounce this one correctly!

The Inhabitants of
the Planet Fuckface

Sirs:
Okay, I've got a good one for you: What do Leonard Woodcock and Pinocchio have in common? Think about it.

Gepetto
Nambla, Mass.

Sirs:
Every cabdriver in New York will tell you about all the celebrities he's had in his backseat if you give him half a chance. But do they ever ask fishermen? Heck. I've caught 'em all. Sal Mineo on Pullet Bay. Kept on thrashing around, had to stab him with a scaling knife. Bob Crane up on Boulton Lake. He was a feisty bugger, had to smash him over the head a few dozen times with an oar to keep him from tipping the boat over. Totie Fields, cut her leg off and watched her die. I could go on and on.

Ol' Tom the Fisherman
Starfish, N.H.

1983

Sirs:
There's a small animal over by that tree. There's a big brown one. That one over there seems to be eating, wouldn't you agree?

A Tour Guide Who Doesn't
Know Very Much
Wild National Park

Sirs:
Scientists at my university have refuted the bogus theory of evolution once and for all: they have unearthed fossil remains that definitely prove Jesus had a pet dinosaur. It wore a studded leather collar three feet in diameter with the name "Bowser" on its tag.

You atheists have been dealt a stunning defeat.

Bob Jones, President
Bob Jones University
Bob Jones, N.C.

Sirs:
You shouldn't have so much of that crude material in your magazine. Now take the *Reader's Digest* as an example: they have lots of humorous items without having to resort to bad language, dirty pictures, and lies. We'd like to help you get off to a brand-new start, so Ernest (my husband) and I would like to give you a joke that is funny and wholesome and really happened, too. It's yours to use with our blessing. Here it is: Ernest was pouring himself a glass of milk (he's forty-nine) and I said to him, "Ernest, you know, you really shouldn't drink milk over forty. It's not good for you." And Ernest said, "I'll say. It would be terribly sour at that age." We're taking out a year's subscription to your magazine and look forward to a bright new change in your format.

Connie and Ernest Crackhead
Friendship, Maine

Sirs:

Just a note to you lovers of sports trivia: wacky comic Jonathan Winters broke Gale Sayer's collegiate rushing record while wearing a cake-shaped masquerade outfit. Actual quote: "Easy as pie if you hit the holes right."

Bill Kisler
Cheyenne, Wyo.

Sirs:

Know how Japanese pilots get their kicks? We just replace all the passenger windows on our 747's with a hundred Sony flat-screen TV sets hooked up to a VCR in the cockpit. Next we play a tape of the jet taking off so that when the passengers look out of their "windows" everything seems normal. Then halfway over the Pacific the pilot shoves a new tape into the Betamax and announces, "Ladies and gentlemen, we are now passing the spot where KAL Flight 007 was shot down." All the passengers start rubbernecking out of what they think are windows when all of a sudden they see a whole squadron of SU-15 jet interceptors firing missiles at them. We usually manage fifteen or twenty heart attacks per trip, and one time some nut actually opened the pressurized rear door, sucking all two hundred passengers out into the Sea of Japan. All in all, it's almost as much fun as Pearl Harbor.

Captain Hideo Video
Japan Air Lines

1984

Sirs:

We here in Duluth think that calling your city "The Big Apple" is a great way to encourage popular empathy and tourism. We have thought up a few more nicknames for other cities to follow in your illustrious footsteps. How about "Birmingham, the Big Watermelon" or "San Francisco, the Big Cucumber" or maybe "Miami, the Big Coca Plant"? And how's this—"Detroit, the Big Lemon"? Hope you appreciate all this work.

The Duluth Citizens Group for
Nicknaming America's Cities and Towns
Duluth "The Big Jello Mold," Minn.

Sirs:

If you're goin'
Ta New York City
Wear a Panzer helmet
In your hair.

The Holy Lefrak Rounders
Pelham Bogs, N.Y.

Sirs:

After twenty years on the route, if I hear "Wait a minute! Wait! Mister, please wait" one more time I'm gonna back my damn truck up and flatten all you little suckers. And no, you can't owe me a nickel for an éclair until Thursday. Go ask Tom Carvel for credit.

The Good Humor Man
Right down the block

Sirs:

We're locked in here fourteen stories underground. We're horny and pissed and if we don't get two women in the next half hour, we're going to launch one of these fuckers! One half hour, starting now.

Lieutenant Dave Wetherill
and Captain Joe Marinelli
Missile Silo #48
Big Star, Mont.

Sirs:

What has a mustache, leads a band, and died for our sins?
Give up?
Saviour Cugat!
Cootchie, cootchie!

Charo
Las Vegas, Nev.

Sirs:

Don't stop me now! I'm on a roll!

The Pillsbury Dough Boy
Dairy Case, U.S.A.

Sirs:

Chet's nuts roasting by an open fire,
Jack Frost nipping at your hose,
Tiny twats with their pies all aglow,
Merry Christmas, fuck you.

Rat King Cole
Not in heaven

1985

Sirs:

The porno film industry has its own
stars and even its own terminology. "Animated shorts," for instance, refers to a
director with crabs.

Pauline Kael
New York, N.Y.

Sirs:

Would someone please put in a new box
of baking soda?

Walt Disney
Frigidaire, Calif.

1986

Sirs:

I stand behind a podium because every
time an overweight blonde from Canoga
Park tells what vegetable her husband's
bottom looks like, I spring a stiffie.

Bob Eubanks
Newlywed, Calif.

Sirs:

Have you ever noticed that all assassins
have three names, like Lee Harvey Oswald or James Earl Ray?

Sirhan Sirhan
San Quentin, Calif.

Sirs:

I'm here. You can't see me. But I'm
here.

A Booger
The Egg Salad
Burger King salad bar

Sirs:

My favorite movies?
Oh, *Friday the 13th, Halloween, Prom
Night,* anything that shows a lot of teen-
agers getting killed.

Mom
At home

Sirs:

Okay, like we all have trouble talking to
girls, right? Okay. Well, like here's a line
that I use to get started. Okay. And it goes
like this: "Baby, you've really got some
pair of tits. And I don't mean that in a
crude, cheap way—I mean it in a loving,
gentle way. 'Cause in this crazy world of
ours, we have to find reasons to live anywhere we can. And I'm lookin' at two of
them right now. So when I say I want to
do a pork job on you, I'm not saying it
because I want to *use* you. I'm simply expressing my sexuality in a natural, joyous
way." Never fails.

Leo Buscaglia, Ph.D.
Singles Bar Symposium

Sirs:

Mekka lekka hi mekka hini ho. Mekka
lekka hi mekka chonni ho. Mekka lekka la
la la la la la

National Security Council
Washington, D.C.

1987

Sirs:

You just can't beat the bustle and energy
of a busy supermarket. Crowded aisles.

Stacks of canned goods. Peaceful Muzak. And a million ways to cop a feel.

Mr. Whipple
Roaming the dairy section

1988

Sirs:

Now here's an item that I must admit I've been looking forward to telling you about all night. It's a great gift idea for the people you love the most. YES, it has the cubic zirconia; YES, it has the *adorable* baby-blue elephant string quartet; YES, it even has a quartz digital readout, but the most exciting thing about this item, Lot #33459, is that it also wipes clean with one swipe of this handy semi-chamois rag embossed with the *adorable* likeness of everyone's favorite clown, Red Skelton! But HOLD ON, because that's only the beginning of the value of this *incredible* product. . . .

The Hypnotic Drone of the
Home Shopping Network After You
Have Stumbled Home at 4:00 A.M.

Sirs:

. . . Real mother-of-pearl handles that keep you from spilling the precious liquids that no doubt you'll be storing right here in this *quaint* storage pouch in the pink kangaroo's pouch. . . .

4:30 A.M.

Sirs:

. . . Turn the Little Drummer Boy upside down . . . and PRESTO! You've got yourself an industrial-strength beef garrote! Now I know what you're thinking: what about spillage, right? Well, that's what Gertrude the Washerwoman is for! Yes, this handcarved pottery mug with the face of a broken-down German washerwoman will gladly hold any of the blood

and gore you're sure to have after the garrote has done its work!

5:00 A.M.

Sirs:

Now normally this FANTASTIC item sells for the retail price of ninety-five dollars and fifty cents, but tonight on the Home Shopping Club . . . for our first fifteen callers . . . I'm prepared to offer this product . . . Lot #33459 . . . for the incredible HSC price of . . . FIFTY-NINE CENTS!!! Yes, that's right. . . .

5:30 A.M.

Sirs:

All right, let's move on to our second item this morning. You might think it's a great value as a combination video trolley/snakebite kit, but wait . . .

Please Tell Me You're Asleep By Now

Sirs:

So foul and fair a day I have not seen
With invigorating skies favoring no man's
dreams.
The melancholy eve and stringent moon
Doth break spasmodic to an impetuous
noon.
Oh, the vehemence, the RAGE of turbulent
skies
Sequesters the languor of our lives!
Will the Rampaging Heavens VOUCH-
SAFE FORSAKE?!
. . . periodically, with temperatures lower
near the lake. . . .

Unemployed Actor Sir Laurence Olivier
in His Debut on the Weather Channel

Sirs:

Jesus, that little bastard smells. No wonder they call him Pooh Bear.

Christopher Robin
Candyland

Sirs:

Women!

You can't live with 'em, and you can't live without 'em.

Ted Bundy
Hell

Sirs:

Do you have any idea . . . Uh . . . ohhhh. you know. the . . . the . . . No. nope. I've completely forgotten what I was going to say.

Anonymous
Address withheld

1989

SPORTS COLUMN

by Red Ruffansore

There's just one way to pitch the Babe,
Says Hubbell (and I quote'm).
You wait until he digs in good,
Then fire one at his scrotum.

—Old Red's Rhythmic Rhymes

THE AUTUMN CLASSIC. The World Series. Words that conjure up a bat bag full of memories—shoestring catches, pinchhit homers, Gillette blue blades, and Coogan's Bluff. Old Red remembers every game and every pitch. Old Red was there.

Old Red was there in '57 when Lew Burdette won three big games and beat the Yankees single-handed. Lew mixed his pitches like a pro. First a fast ball, then a slider, a curve that broke just like a shot glass falling off a bar. There was a lot of talk about that curve, and some allowed as how it looked like Lew was throwing spitters, smearing lungers on the ball before he cut it loose. I asked Burdette about it in the locker room after the seventh game, but cagey Lew just smiled a funny smile. "You want to see my spitter? Here it comes," and then he hawked one right in Old Red's face. I should have punched the crazy bastard in the nose, but what the hell, he'd just made series history, and I figured that he'd earned his little joke.

And then there was the '55 series, the first one that the Dodgers won. Old Red was pulling into the carpark outside Ebbets Field when the parking lot attendant told Don Newcombe that he'd choked, and got his face punched for a tip. Big Newk was the meanest guy who ever played pro ball, and a sonofabitch to interview. Back in the clubhouse he used to beat reporters senseless. One day, after he dropped a two-to-one game to Philadelphia, he kicked my tail into the trainer's room and tried to drown me in the whirlpool bath. He was a hell of a competitor.

And how 'bout 1954? The Giants and the Indians. Old Red was there when Willie made that famous over-the-shoulder "catch" off Vic Wertz, running full tilt toward the bleachers. Old Red says "catch" because he's one guy who was wise to Willie's secret—the good old hidden ball trick. Willie's instincts were supposed to be so sharp that when a drive was hit to center, all the fans would follow Willie and forget about the ball. So Willie used to stuff his uniform with baseballs, and when he'd run to where he thought the ball might drop, he'd pull one out and pop it in his glove. Sometimes, during batting practice, he'd hide a couple in the outfield grass, in case he had to make a shoestring catch. In '54 I watched him through binoculars. Just as Wertz's shot was sailing toward the stands, Willie smiled, spit a baseball in his glove, then tipped his hat as 60,000 fans went wild. The greatest catch in history. The guy was a regular Houdini.

Redhots: Don King, look out! Now that you're flashing a big roll, some of your ex-cellmates are looking for you. . . . Where are they now? Remember Emlen Tunnell, N.Y. Giants all-pro linebacker who still holds the record for most career interceptions? He's dead . . . Red's rumor mill reports Portland Trailblazers about to finalize trade dealing lanky illiterate Bill Walton to the Atlanta Hawks for $99 and a hot dog vendor to be named at a later date. . . . What's the fuss about New Zealand's John Walker running a 3.50 mile? Some jungle bunny grabbed my wallet on Seventy-ninth Street in New York and headed north on foot. I followed him in a cab and clocked him at three minutes flat before he disappeared into the park. . . . Big League Boffs: How come Mickey Mantle taped his legs before each game? Because he wanted a record of what they sounded like!

Damned If I Know: (Answer to last month's quiz: Beats me!) Who holds the record for the longest runback of a fumbled punt return off a third down quick kick following a fifteen-yard offensive holding penalty during the final two minutes of play of the second period of an American Football League exhibition game played at night on artificial turf in a state west of the Mississippi?

That's it for this month. Pick your pitch, and don't let 'em brush you back.

CANADIAN CORNER

Far to the north where the seals give birth
There's little but frozen sod
The natives stink and are given to drink
And make mock of America's God.

—Robert W. Servicestation
The Dying Politician's Son

DRIVEN TO XENOPHOBIA by climatic conditions, Canada has recently made several attacks on what American historians all agree is the greatest country in the world—America. Though perhaps an unlettered visitor from Africa might dismiss these conflicts as sibling rivalry, deep-thinking board members of rival intellectual concerns have been unable to do so.

"Americans," says Lawrence Lemur, writing in the literary magazine *Elements*, "are fat, obnoxious persons in bermuda shorts who want to strip-mine Indian graveyards, turn ancient and weathered Baptist churches into all-night discos, and erect a sewage treatment plant on every trout stream that doesn't already have one of their nuclear reactors dripping mutated rat chromosomes into the city drinking water."*

Many Canadian creative types feel, like Lemur, that Canada is culturally dominated by Americans. Stars and stripey novels, poetry, and music are consumed by the Canadian public, which fails to distinguish between the two cultures. This irks Canada's artists and writers, who turn out all manner of anti-American works, bringing them into direct competition with the country's tourist bureaus, which turn out twice as much on better paper, encouraging Americans to come north and shoot Eskimos if they feel like it. In the end, there could be but one answer. Since Canadians can't tell the high quality home product from the imperialist foreign stuff, a protective tariff must be enacted to safeguard Canadian culture.

Time magazine was told it must have at least 80 percent Canadian content or Canadian companies would not be able to deduct advertising as a business expense. The impact of this threat was horrific. *Time* left the country, and their boardroom boys are sweating out a few martinis right now, hoping the

This would result in the death of bespectacled brook Trout.

stockholders won't notice the extra twenty-nine dollars in the liabilities column of this year's annual report.

Things don't look much better in the music industry. The right wing wants more Canadian songs, the left wing wants all Canadian songs. In Vancouver, the Canadian broadcasting Corporation just built a new complex. They couldn't justify making it large enough to get lost in, but to insure it was impressive, they built corridors that go nowhere, put hundreds of extra buttons in the thirty-six elevators descending to the eleven-car garage in the basement, and painted doors every six feet down the walls.

Many of America's enemies in Canada are anticonsumption, antigrowth. It is not surprising that a lot of these people do not themselves produce enough to feed and house a family of field mice. It has been argued that poverty entitles people to many things, but a superior moral position is not among them.

"Americans are like . . . fascists, man. Like Hitler, you know what I mean? Taking over the big rich countries like *Vietnam* . . . but they got beaten, man . . . like by the people, man. If we all got our heads together, we could nationalize everything, wow . . . it might mean a long-term shortage of venture capital, a precipitous drop in the standard of living, death by starvation, and probably atomic war, but Gordon Lightfoot might come home."

So it is a huge wave of Canadian nationalism threatens to rise up and overwhelm America. I, for, one, shall not be caught without my rubber duck feet.

Remember the Bricklin.

MRS. AGNEW'S DIARY

Dear Diary,

Spiggy is off at a Boy Scouts awards dinner (he thinks they may surprise him with The Golden Marshmallow); the apartment is quiet; and I must admit to being the teensiest bit bored and listless. To occupy these solitary hours, I have taken to rereading some of the previous entries I made in you, starting way back in Volume One (May, 1942–June, 1945) the night Spiggy and I were married! That first entry I made on our wedding night (well, I didn't actually make it *in* the diary because I had locked myself in the hotel bathroom, and the only writing materials I had was a Maybelline pencil and the cover of a *Pageant* magazine, which I Scotch-taped in later) tickles me now, being so full of naïve, girlish illusions about Life, and particularly, ess ee ex. I never even finished that entry, dear Diary, because the hotel manager finally got the door off the hinges and Spiggy charged in like the raging, lusty buck he is (well, was). Needless to say, that first night of fiery bliss was probably a memorable one—I say "probably" because just before they broke down the door I had, in my childish panic, swallowed the contents of every container in the medicine cabinet, including a Family Size bottle of Romilar CF cough syrup, and, needless to say, my recollections of that Magic Night are somewhat hazy.

Moving on to more recent entries, I found myself giggling in spite of myself at the little trials that befell us all on Inauguration Day.

The night before, Dick, Spiggy, and Mr. Graham had had a little "victory nip" in our rumpus room while Mr. Graham was supposed to be composing the Invocation on his portable tape recorder for the next day, and the next morning when Dick listened to it, all it was was a lot of cackling and parts of a rather risk-ay story Mr. Graham knew about the Pope and Jack Kennedy trapped in a girls' school. Well, of course, Dick had to get him to redo it, but first he and Spiggy had to wake Mr. Graham up, which, I can assure you, was no easy task, particularly since it took the better part of an hour to even *find* him (he was asleep in the clothes hamper under Randy's soiled quilt). Finally, he was all dressed and waking up a little when the phone rang and it was Tricia saying that Pat had been up rather late herself practicing her smile in the mirror (she sometimes has trouble getting one or the other of her lips back over her teeth at the same time) and had had a little tipple herself and now she and Julie couldn't get her to stand up either. Dick was a little flustered at this, but Spiggy, who was still trying to get Mr. Graham's pants on over his shoes, told Dick to have them stick that hat rack with casters on the base up the back of her dress and we could roll her to the ceremony. Dick gave Spiggy a sharp look, as I recall, and said he would remember that the next time Hank Kissinger asked to have Spiggy's office space in the White House (he did), but at that point Spiggy had Mr. Graham all dressed and standing up, sort of. Dick then told me to force-feed him some cottage cheese and ketchup to get his blood circulating, but all it did was make Mr. Graham gag and make a mess down the front of his pants, which Spiggy had just spent so much time getting on in the first place.

Well, dear Diary, I won't relate what Dick said then, but I think to this day that no one at the ceremony ever noticed that there were two people on the platform with little casters behind their shoes, and somebody else was wearing black shoe polish on his legs instead of trousers. (Spiggy had a grudge, and a cold, which lasted for three weeks after, and I think maybe that's when he started making up all those little jokes about Dick's breath.)

But so much for the past. Nostalgia is a thing for those who are too afraid to face the present (that's what Dick told Mr. Kai-shek, anyway, the night he called from Taiwan threatening to attack California with suicide sampans), and I should count my blessings, I know.

There *have* been little rays of sunlight for me these past few months, like the time Spiggy and I went to welcome Pat back from her African tour and Martha Mitchell made such a fuss about the wonderful ceremonial mask Pat had brought back as a souvenir and it turned out that it wasn't a mask at all: we had arrived a little too early (although on the phone she had *said* Hawaiian Punch at 5:30) and had caught Pat before she had had time to put on her makeup.

What a giggle we girls had at that one.

That same day Pat told us what wonderful people the Africans were and shouldn't we help them with their unemployment problem by seeing if TV needed any more Flip Wilsons (she said she saw *hundreds* that looked just like him) and maybe send them some of our old banjos and Pullman cars, which prompted Hank Kissinger's famous comment about where Pat was when God had passed out His briefings.

And I must say, having the children home *was* a treat, even if Kim did say that awful thing about what her high-school sorority sisters (I think they call themselves the "Third Bases" or "Out of This Worlders" or something like that) thought of Spiggy's joke he made on TV about what Mr. Lindsay should do about the welfare problem in New York and how the ASPCA should start pulling its own weight anyway. However, I am obliged to note that it was *not* necessarily a treat having Dick's children over for that pajama party Pat insisted upon (it seems that her brood has been in Washington five times in the last year, and I have had to give one for them each time—which makes me stop and think, now that I think about it). The Eisenhower boy is never really any trouble as long as I can keep him, the kitten, and the electric toothbrush in separate rooms, and he *does* so love his blue naval uniform. As a matter of fact, he once kept me up the whole night telling me about how much fun it was to fight the Commies with his missile ship, and he obviously was having such a good time I didn't have the heart to tell him that Dick had the Navy rig up a special control panel on board, especially for David, that was only connected to a screen that showed reruns of *Victory at Sea*.

As for Tricia, well, I must say that that poor Cox boy must want that appointment to the Supreme Court next year very, very badly. No wonder he——

Dear Diary, *who do I think I'm kidding?* I can fool Spiggy, and I can fool everyone else and their wives from the office, but I *know* I can't fool you. These last few months have been so terribly . . . well, the people Spiggy must work with and who I have to smile at and chatter with . . . the whole f——

Oops! That was the phone. Spiggy just called to say that the Boy Scout dinner was canceled because some I.R.A sympathizer called up and said there was an exploding potato on one of the plates and anyway he had to rush right away and would I whip up some grub quick for him and Dick and Mr. Howard Hughes because if that emergency loan didn't come off tonight, Dick was going to be in it up to here when the papers find out why the Budget was so out of whack this year and hadn't Spiggy warned him in the first place about playing the market with other people's money and giving all those Defense contracts to Hammacher Schlemmer that night Dick had a few too many with Mel Laird and Bill Buckley and maybe I'd better order out from the Chinese restaurant since Mr. Hughes is supposed to be a picky eater and we wouldn't want to risk another one of my casseroles when so much is at stake, would we, sugarbuns?

Well, I'd better phone the restaurant, dear Diary, because they'll be here any minute. I lost my train of thought anyway, but that's the way it is in this anything-can-happen-and-usually-does world I seem to be immersed in, I guess. First, though, I'm going to see if there's anything in the medicine cabinet for this cough I bet I'm coming down with.

All for now,

Judy

BABA RUM RAISIN

My Wrigglies,

Greetings from your only Baba and the wide open spaces of His teeth and Nebraska—birthplace of the very famous Mr. Johnny Carson and the increasingly less so Mr. Dick Cavett! Hu.

As your little old truth vendor deftly aims His India-red Turbo-Carrera Porsche, this very flat amount of aptly-named "the Midwest" rushes by unbroken save for an occasional blurred A & W root beer stand or snatch of denim thumbing away from home.

Not for nothing is Nebraska known among top gurus as the Land of the Perpetual Dragstrip—an excellent opportunity to wind out fine German iron and, upon misoccasion, Baba's turban, which billows behind Isadora Duncanlike as a gay thankyou to police escort even now diminishing in Baba's bullet-shattered rearview. (*Corner softly, but drive with a lead sandal*—B. Raisin.)

And indeed, so excellently does this turban-careener's rack-and-pinion steering grip this changeless 500-mile stretch that one entire hand may be set aside for this long overdue *Newsletter,* while yet another may be devoted to fine tuning of the internationally-expensive-yet-fun Ms. Julie Christie, who, your Baba is in no way distressed to relate, now sits nextward on her finely-bucketed seat. (At the speaking of which, Ms. Christie has just now informed Baba that the finely-crafted bucket featured in the *Shampoo* party sequence was in fact not Mr. Warren Beatty's, but, upon cameraman's special request, Ms. Christie's, as it proved superior both in firmness and bounce to cinematic ounce. You hear it first from Baba, no lie yes?)

This superior auto, you may now peep up, *how did it fall into Thy humble grasp, oh Baba?*

In the facts, the Porsche belongs to Mr. Uri Geller, my babies, whom Baba will one day show the secret of *duplicating* keys. As for Ms. Christie, she belongs only to herself, and, she teases her own Baba to add, occasionally to the world, yes no?

Now, as the Lip that raised a thousand flags replaces Linda Ronstadt in the fine Blaupunkt tapedeck with the more spiritually nutritious "Beachboys' Greatest Hits," Ms. Christie further agrees to handle Baba's stick shift as He types, providing indeed good vibrations for all concerned.

Now, as Ms. Christie performs her deft double clutch, your spiritual ambassador without balanced portfolio brings you yet another "Dear Baba" column, free of charge to all fan clubbers in good standing. (It is warned that all *not* in good standing—by which Baba means those sitting on their *dues*—these must *not* read the following or become star of own fright movie *Yaws*. This is not an idle threat, Mr. Timmy Mayer of 2234 Locust Drive, Burlington, Vt.! At least in no manner as idle as certain gurupies have been in their pittance remittance!)

What many of you cagier young people may be wishing to learn is how came this fine auto, this bullet-spitting pursuit? It began when the phone rang at Ms. Christie's Plaza suite (with excellent view of Central Park and a majority of the corpses) and the noise at the other end proved to be the top assistant to the very fine Tom Snyder "Tomorrow Show." The noise issued from a female person of a variety often found about such men as these—adept both at talking quickly and—it Baba's ears were not mistaken—cracking cashews with a portion of her anatomy more often associated with soup than nuts. Fish soup if you catch Baba's humble drifting.

Would Baba appear with Mr. Uri Geller tonight? Would He bring some spoons and keys? Would He bring own carfare and Cremora? Would He be sure to wear a clean blue *dhoti*?

Remembering manager Mr. Morty Taumicbaum's belief that "The only bad publicity is your obit," Baba accepted, and, parking pedicab with large youths outside NBC building who then ate same, ran. Inside, Baba and Ms. Christie were greeted by the noise person who indeed emitted a pungent fragrance not unlike pecan chowder and led Him to the make-up room where Mr. Geller already sat having his hair bent into shape while he occupied the remainder of his person melting girders with *schpritzes* from his fine boutonnière. Also did he carefully Q-Tip tiny dentist mirrors grafted in his fine ears for reasons of ESP.

While we awaited Mr. Snider, Mr. Geller and Baba passed the time guessing each other's weight and checking balances. (Mr. Geller was accurate save in the correct color of ink.) In addition, Mr. Geller attempted to guess the contents of Baba's coin purse while distracting Baba with a Vocal Projection technique known only to those familiar with the advertisements in early *Superman* comical booklets.

Before Baba could utter the Curse of 10,000 Dingleberries upon Mr. Geller's business end, Ms. Soup-of-the-Month announced air time and we were intro-duced to Mr. Slymer (Slymer Spyder Snydly what is his name?) who, similarly to Mr. Geller, enjoys a hairdo not unlike certain unsuccessful 1940s attempts at sportscar design behind the Iron Curtain. If this be a fib, Baba humps unripened figs.

As the questions began themselves, Mr. Geller immediately upped the stag-ing of Baba by bending numerous objects, including paper clips, licorice whips, and obviously-tampered-with Flay-vor Straws. All this much to do the delight of Mr. Snotter who, being an ardent Catholic, has seen many such miraculous events is this not the case? Baba Himself, Baba regrets to report, was treated with less than due respect—an unfortunancy early indicated by His introduction by Mr. Sneaker as a pile of undone laundry.

Baba, displeased, offered to bend both their necks wrongwards by means of physical force alone (a method Baba has observed in many Tibetan drunk-tanks) but was interrupted by Mr. Shyster's interesting anecdote concerning a mystical experience he enjoyed himself by means of a confessional and for-merly clean handkerchief.

During a commercial break when Mr. Geller and Mr. Stymie exchanged compliments on their reusable Beatleboots, Baba winked at Ms. Christie who, when the camera lights again themselves winked red, appeared off camera bumping and bouncing totally without her clothing almost as if by prearrange-ment. In their astonishments, both Mr. Israeli Hotcomb and Mr. Ardent Leg-crosser were unable to restrain the instantly-produced slime serpents that rose and bounced in time inside their interestingly styled, matching UFO slackwears.

It was now that Baba, thanks to delighted stage crew, commanded a close-up and proceeded to rebend these bounding phenomenobs by the chanting of Purification Mantra #6 (employed for the preservation of continence during dull-but-healthful sex fasts preceding traditional Penicillin Festivals). The an-cient Sanskrit prayer—roughly translated as *Hookworms, cancer, pus and yaws/ I saw Mommy rimming Santa Claus*—went immediately to the twin on-camera trouble spots and diminished their drumming dangledowns to their original resemblance to a length of yesterday's fettucine Alfredo.

As Mr. Geller angrily refilled his squirting blossom and Mr. Ardent Wastepile (what is his name?) sought in his UFOs the source of the short-lived unidentified throbbing object, Baba, Ms. Christie, and the majority of her garments taxied swiftly Plazawards where we enjoyed again the much-bleeped interview to-gether with a generous portion of Ms. Christie's fine smoking salmon.

As Baba anticipated, the censors omitted many of Baba's important pro-nouncements including new album release ("Baba Live at Ellis Island"—Decca) and special T-shirt offer, but failed to erase post-hypnotic suggestiveness of drooping-dangle chant. Thus, Baba regrets to say, all those who viewed Baba's appearance last evening (including, apparently, the fine prowl car psychopaths now behind and again gaining) must be afflicted with languid lingams until Baba's next therapeutic guest shot on Mr. Merv Griffin sometime after New Year's. With 20 million viewers so afflicted, the end-to-end poot melons that might have under proper conditions stretched coast to coast will, until then, reach perhaps only from Manhattan to Yonkers Raceway.

Sad news for Mr. Geller's many fine stewardesses yes no? No news for the very fine *Mrs.* Tom Speidel, however, writes Baba soliciting kindly further agreement.

However, Baba offers special relief for His fave Bent Key Club Members! This fine new nonprofit additional organ-ization (not to be correctly confused with not-so-fine and highly competitive Universalist Life Church) guarantees life-after-social-death to you boys and girls presently afflicted with sad inability to get it on, up, or damp.

Do not delay or delay must wait until after New Year's, if this may serve as a small but instructive pun.

And now, my wiggly-whangies, your Baba must return both hands to the

---

Free!

Yes Baba! Although I enjoyed your much-bleeped program, I wish, both in moderation and according to Baba's Rules of Fun, to follow the path of moral erectitude. Please send sure-fire magic T-shirt and free 45 rpm "Kama Sutra Polka" starring Baba Rum Raisin and famous dead rock guitarist reincarnated as funny noise in background. Here is as much money as I can buy stamps for! Rush!

Name _____

Address _____

How much $$$ _____

Where I live _____

---

wheel, first airing nontyping one briefly out window, as Ms. Christie observes they are now aiming at Mr. Geller's expensive Michelin radials. Is it not paradoxical that such unwise hotrodding directly results from insufficient cold showering?

And remember, babies, coupon coupon! Or on you your dates will poop on, and by this Baba does not mean a brand of mustard.

Ciao,

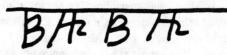

GENERALLY SPEAKING

by General Alexander Meigs Haig, Jr., U.S. Army, Ret.

FORMERLY I WAS A fellow who held the post of secretary of state. Upon my resignation (which shocked and saddened a nation), I did not cease to be a fellow. That is not the sort of fellow I am. No. I became a different sort of fellow. A fellow of the prestigious Hudson Institute.

Does this mean I gained three hundred pounds, acquired chronic curvature of the spine, and took to reading Bulgarian newspapers while eating huge unmanageable oil-soaked sandwiches at a tin desk overlooking the Hudson River like the other fellows I could name?

It does not. My spinal disks are still as neatly stacked as any soldier's. I continue to work in a uniform and not unlaundered wool pajamas with pockets full of cooling Tiparillo ashes.

Yet there are many fellows of the type described to be found at the prestigious Hudson Institute. How a corporate client could entrust a ten-year economic-stability prognostication to a fellow with a tinkling mass of greasy squab bones in his beard or a monstrous load like Herman Kahn, whose belt still makes him look like a segmented insect when it's let out to the last notch, I will not understand until I have had more time and money to study the question.

I have been running my brain in Washington on behalf of the prestigious Hudson Institute. I have been running it pretty hard, too. In much the same way a body consumes more and more calories the harder it works, a brain has got to consume more and more money in order to keep working at top efficiency. That is just one sample of the many very powerful thoughts I have had vis-à-vis the world while working here. Yes, it is pretty much axiomatic to a fellow who has given the matter the kind of particle-beam-power study I have that I need a huge big fat increase in my retainer.

Naturally, I have bound my conclusions up in a blue polyethylene presentation folder bearing the blazon of the prestigious Hudson Institute and forwarded them to Herman Kahn. A man of his girth and brainpower will doubtless recognize the super-irrefutable nature of my logic and saw me off another big presto log of cash retainer, suitable to the maintenance of my larger-than-average brain.

Naturally, there is not enough processed pulp on hand in the Western world for me to set down all the thoughts I have had since I have been working here. In fact, the ramifications of two of my thoughts alone, were they printed and bound and only ten copies distributed by conventional methods, would absorb Crown Zellerbach's paper-milling capacity for two years. This extraordinary productivity alone justifies my request for an increased retainer. If not, then the inaccuracy of Herman Kahn's Super Bowl prognostications (which cost me my whole retainer) should. If it were to become widely known that this megalo-brain had the fucking Dolphins winning by fourteen points, he would lose all his long-term overview credibility with the major corporate criminals of the world and get no more respect than that pontificating pile of Crisco, Orson Welles, and less money.

People have long been asking me, "General Alexander Meigs Haig, Jr., just when are you going to run for president?" My answer is a simple one. I don't think it would be fair to the president we have now for me to run while he is still in office. He was elected for four years, and despite the shame, disgust, and regret of the American people for the terrible mistake they made in electing this man and the enormous growing groundswell of my popularity, I think I should wait at least until the next election.

Let me tell you, the Dow Jones average would have to sink well below 950 before I would even begin to comtemplate seizing the reins of power, declaring martial law, working out a feasible emergency powers act, and acceding to the will of the overwhelming majority of the people in naming myself Supremo-for-life.

Incidentally, those of you readers with reasoning abilities anywhere beyond those of hand-held calculators will know that it is necessary for a man to be named Supremo-for-life. For example, pick any Spic nation—say, Taco Rico. Now, the goddamn Supremos down there are always grabbing the reins of government or the joystick of authority or the paddle controls of the revenue and taxation bureau like a bunch of fat kids fighting over a bag of M&M's in the back of a bus. Naturally, we could never allow such Iberian behavior in our great nation, so if—and I'm only saying if—it becomes necessary for me to snatch power I will do everything possible to ensure a similar event can never again occur, even if it means blowing a few national-security advisers and so forth out the torpedo tubes to fool the enemy and my wife.

Leaving the preservation of democracy aside for the moment, let me now address the topic of my campaign fund or, if necessary, my coup d'etat fund. Contributions have not been coming in at the rate I expected, even with the employee contributions by checkoff from our defense contractors. Can it be that the people of the United States wish me to run for president in cheap shiny-elbowed suits? Do the American people really want their future leader to spend fifteen minutes punching codes into a little MCI code box every time he wants to make a long-distance call? Does this mighty democracy want its Supremo-to-be wasting valuable thinking time arguing with Mrs. Daugherty from Visa Card about how much he may or may not be over his credit limit this month? I have gone to the people, and the people have said, "No." The

American people (and as a general who has sent them to be killed in battle I think I know the American people better than you), the American people want to be able to say to Frogs and Spics and Russkies, "Our Supremo could buy and sell your Supremo twenty times over." Or "Our Supremo has a solid-gold cabochon-encrusted Rolex watch, waterproof to six hundred feet, what kind of watch does your Supremo have?" Imagine the effect it will have on the morale of our people when they see me riding through the slums of Bombay scattering expensive pecan-loaded fruitcakes from Corsicana, Texas, amongst the starvelings of the Indian slums. What a crushing blow, too, to the pride of that left-leaning land's governing grandmother.

Well, I think I've spelled things out in sufficiently large block letters for even dairy animals to get a sense of my meaning, but in closing I would like to remind you to send money or any spare thoughts you may have to me at the Hudson Institute. I also need some black shoe polish.

General Alexander Meigs Haig, Jr.
Hudson Institute
Quaker Ridge Road
Croton-on-Hudson, N.Y.

Dear General: I sure hope you are our nation's next Supremo. I have enclosed

☐ money
☐ some thoughts
☐ black shoe polish

to help you with your efforts. I understand this is illegal.

NAME _____

ADDRESS _____

CITY _____

STATE _____ ZIP _____

TELL DEBBY

Dear Debby: I am a twenty-six-year-old mother who is about to come to her wit's end. It's because of our two boys, ages four and six. They are almost unbearable to live with. They won't do a thing I tell them and they are, by degrees, wrecking our house. And our nerves along with it. They pour honey on all of the doorknobs; they steal the food from the icebox and bury it in the backyard; they find animals that have been run over and put their bodies in our bed; when they're in crowds, they pull down their clothes and *mess*. I'm absolutely lost for a solution. I've walloped them until I thought my hand would break. And when their father comes home, he wallops them, but it never does any good.

Last week, as a final resort, my husband and I sat them down and told them that if they didn't behave, we were going to send them to an orphanage in Rangoon. For a while it seemed to work. They minded what they were told. I was so relieved and that's when I made the mistake and let down my guard. I was taking a shower and my mind was empty of all this turmoil. I thought I heard something but I didn't pay it any attention. Then in one instant, through the shower curtain I saw an enormous silhouette of a man. The curtain was pulled back and a huge carving knife was arched over me. I collapsed shrieking into the corner. It was the two boys. One on the other's shoulders. I took out after them, Debby, and I grabbed a breadboard on the way. I beat them with that breadboard until I dropped from exhaustion.

I just don't know what to do.

Doris Richards
Bluefield, W.V.

How very unpleasant.

Dear Debbie: My parents fight all the time and it makes me very unhappy. I love them both so much. They used to just fight when my daddy would come home from work but now my daddy is home all the time because his boss punched him in the eye. My daddy is very sick and has to take a lot of medicine and it makes him act funny. My mommy must have caught what my daddy has because I see her take a lot of daddy's medicine.

Every night when I say my prayers I pray to God to make my mommy and daddy all better so they will stop fighting. I love them both and it is awful when they fight.

Timmy Nurock
Denver, Colorado

Young man, you spelled my name D-e-b-b-i-e. My name is spelled D-e-b-b-y.

Dear Debby: My married sister, and only relative, was killed in a tragic car accident one month ago. The only thing to be thankful for, it seems, is that she and her husband didn't have any young ones. The funeral was quite an ordeal but my brother-in-law took it bravely, and held up remarkably well. He gave me comfort when I thought it should be the other way around.

Two weeks after the funeral, I got the shock of my life. My brother-in-law remarried. It was tasteless enough not bothering to wait a respectable amount of time, but compounded to that, he married a woman who could only be described as an ill-tempered slut. I know it's a strong thing to say about somebody, but it's the only word I can find to aptly define her. She walks around the house all day in her underwear, she's put mirrors on *all* of the ceilings, she's always eating candy, she uses language that would make a sailor cringe, and she's taken all of my late sister's McMullen blouses and cut them up so they can show all of her cleavage. It's disgraceful. I just can't understand my brother-in-law. It makes me sick.

Alice Poster
Southampton, New York

That's quite unfortunate.

Dear Debby: I am a homosexual. I am neither ashamed nor proud. It is simply what I am. I don't foster my preferences on other people and I don't want them to foster theirs on me. I am quite content. I have as many "straight" friends as I do "gay" friends. If you were to meet me, you would see nothing in my speech or manner that would indicate to you that I am a homosexual. And this, I guess, is where my problem comes in. I have a very good civilian job as an engineer on an Army installation. I enjoy my work and get along well with everyone there. Especially my supervisor. We have become close friends over the past years. He doesn't know that I am a homosexual, and consequently, he and his wife are always trying to "fix" me up with single girls they know. It's not a comfortable situation. I feel obliged, naturally, to follow through by asking the girls out a few times. Then I have to make up some excuse to him about "things not working out." I feel we are good enough friends that I could tell him the truth and that he would understand. But if I do, it might somehow change *our* relationship.

I have no one I can turn to for advice, so that's why I'm turning to you.

Name Withheld Upon Request

Debby does not withhold names upon request. Your name is David Shapiro and you live at 5645 Richmond Court, Baltimore, Maryland.

Confidential to All Washed Up: *Dame Fortune certainly isn't smiling on you, is she?*

Is something troubling you? Then don't hesitate to "Tell Debby" in care of this magazine.

ASK DR. CIPHER

by Dr. Hugh Flesch

Send your mysterious communications, incomprehensible missives, coded dispatches, secret messages, and unintelligible cryptograms to Dr. Cipher, world's foremost authority, care of this magazine.

Mrs. R. C. Colak of Germaine, Wisconsin, here is your husband's final message:

VIF	IB	BSFL
COME	AT	ONCE
POBLE	**TOR**	**DPNF**
UNABLE	TO	SPELL

For Miss Nancy Claywell, a registered nurse here in New York, Leo wishes to privately convey the following:

RDTW	YGE
CANNOT	FIND
GXLJ	**QISMPI**
READING	GLASSES

Here is an interesting message from a recent college graduate:

TFU	BUPLD	GPS
I	LOVED	YOUR
RRNBS	**ABT**	
MOTHER	FIRST	

Mrs. B. F. Grackle of Teaboro, Massachusetts, your note was one of the easiest to unravel:

RPM	IOU
RECORD	OWES
DNA	**FDR**
MOLECULE	DIME

Incidentally, I'm sure you have a very nice boardinghouse. What would be the harm in letting the boys play cards out in the open?

Mrs. Maggie Weston of Wellington, Pennsylvania, your husband says:

SAFETY PINS READY FOR DIAPER HON

Playfully, he goes on:

SAFETY PINS MAKE WILLING PARTNERS

Then concludes:

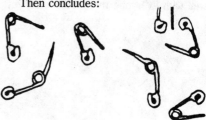

I	DROPPED	THE	SAFETY	PINS

Lee-Ann, your classmates' conversation went like this:

Willy:	OMECAY	OVERWAY
	YOU	ARE
	OTWAY	**YMAY**
	A	LATIN
	OUSEHAY	
	PIG	

Tom:	IXNAY	CURVAY
	NO	I'M
	OUSEHAY	
	NOT (A LATIN PIG)	
Willy:	SI	YMAY
	YES	YOU
	OUSEHAY	
	ARE (A LATIN PIG)	
Tom:	PUGILAY	LACKBAY
	RAISE	YOUR
	EYEWAY	
	DUKES	

I put in the part about the dukes myself, but it's obvious that that's where they were headed, Lee-Ann. Give the note to your teacher.

Dorothy Billings of Friendship, Connecticut, no, your husband doesn't believe your version of the car accident. He says:

I DOT THAT

VERY MUCH DOTTIE

Confidential: M. L., your reply from D. S. is as follows:

DOT'S FOR SURE

DOLL BABY

Mr. Arnold S. Blunt of New York City, you were indeed being robbed. Your message reads:

GIMME DOT

Ted, Frank wishes to say:

I	12	II	36	18	36
I	AM	GOING	WITH	ROXANNE	

Brad's report is:

I	12	II	18	16	41
I	AM	GOING	WITH	BEATRIX	

The message your brother sent to Frank was:

48	5
TOO	BAD

INTERNATIONAL DATELINE

INTERNATIONAL DATELINE© is a copyrighted, nonprofit service organization owned and operated by NatLampCo Globalafcom, Inc., and dedicated to the practical attainment of world peace through world dating. The *National Lampoon* is not responsible for loss of letters, snapshots, metallic charms, or other items not specifically listed under the Warsaw Pact of 1946.

* * *

Beep . . . beep-beep-beep . . . beep-beep . . . beep-beep . . . calling all teens on **International Dateline**. . . . Stay tuned for radio free friendship around the world. . . . High fun warnings are up! . . . **May-Date! . . . May-Date! . . . May-Date!** . . .

First item on the Dateline tonight is from peppy Palestinian Kahlisha Mohamud. Kahlisha is a nineteen-year-old Moslem girl living in Israel. She'd like to communicate with friendly young men in the Syrian military, especially the Air Force. "If you would like to make of my acquaintance, I am weeknights on the rooftop of the Tel Aviv Hilton Hotel. I will be here with the flashlight," writes peppy Kahlisha Mohamud, who lives in Israel. You can get in touch with her at:

> Censor
> Camp Four
> West Bank, Israel

Here's a popularity tip from Illinois teen Patty Antwerp. She says, "If you're 'lacking something' in the bustline but still want to emphasize your figure's good points, try leaving off your underpants." Thanks, Patty, and that reminds us—if you're petting after dark, wear white. When a fellow can't see what he's doing, he might "go too far" by mistake.

Any of you Jills and Joes out there in a coma? Sally Sue Hupper of Orlando, Florida, is, and she'd like to have some "pulse pals":

> Marginal Care Ward
> Palm County Hospital
> Orlando, Fla.

And here's a note from three Oklahoma high school girls who are also refugees from South Vietnam. They'd like to meet a couple hundred American guys in the Tulsa area. They write: "Yank you want do boom-boom fuckey-suckey twenty dollar?" Doubtless a message of greeting in their native language. Why don't some of you "cow-teens" just "mosey" over to:

> Suki, Wing-Wang, and Ho Quim
> Apt. 17K
> Highball Towers
> 6500 Sooner Avenue
> Tulsa, Okla.

Ivanovich Ivanofsky is a Russian young person from Moscow, Soviet Union. His father is one of the USSR's top missile technicians, and he'd like to know if any U.S. State Department teens would like to trade a pair of blue jeans or the new Elvis Presley record for some drawings by his dad:

> Comrade Ivanofsky
> Sector N
> Block 506
> Complex 3B7
> Bldg. 890658
> Apartment EEE24J6
> Room 4
> Moscow, RSSR, CCCP

Umug Idi Ug writes to us from Upper Volta, Africa. Her hobby is eating food. If you have anything around the house that might be of assistance to Umug in her pastime activities, she'll be glad to send you some dried mud. Mail your card or letter through the American Red Cross and tape a shiny bead to the upper right hand corner.

That's all for **International Dateline** *for this month. . . . Roger, Wilco . . . over and out (but not too late on school nights!) . . . beep . . . beep-beep-beep . . . beep-beep . . . beep-beep. . . .*

Marathon swimmer **DIANA NYAD**, that strange one who packs her cracks with Crisco and tries to paddle off to places served by commercial airliners, is up to her old tricks. This time the mer-Ms. wants to swim off to Cuba. Sport fishermen in those parts are readying the damnedest-looking lures. Short-Eyes Sam of Bimini hopes to meet with angling success hauling his drag-a-muffin, a hairy flatish lure about the size of a medium pancake with a small worm in the center.

* * *

Novelist **JERZY KOSINSKI** is furious with co-Polack director **ROMAN POLANSKI**. Kosinski claims Polanski stole the "ski" at the end of his name from him. Kosinski claims that his name was Jerzy Kosinskiski before another Pole clipped his last syllable, and that Polanski's real name was Roman Polan.

* * *

What do **GABE KAPLAN**, **DAVID STEINBERG**, and TV's popular **ROBIN WILLIAMS** have in common? Well, according to show-biz sources, the trio are notorious "joke chiefs," or something that rhymes with that.

* * *

Truculent **RYAN O'NEAL** is furious at rumors linking him with cattle mutilations in the Southwest.

* * *

Visitors from Rhodesia told conductor **LEONARD BERNSTEIN** that blacks were being badly treated right in New York City. Blacks are not allowed into subway washrooms in the Big Apple, the Rhodesians alleged. When Bernstein expressed astonishment, the Rhodesians asked him to explain why the blacks would urinate and defecate on subway trains if the washrooms were open. Well, Leonard?

* * *

Sophie's Choice, by **WILLIAM STYRON**, has been a best-seller for ages. Yet nobody can be found who has read it. Speculation is that all available copies are being bought up by Russians who wish to extract trace elements of deuterium from the book's ink. Deuterium is apparently very scarce in Russia.

* * *

Dynamic, gutsy **LEE IACOCCA**, chairman of troubled Chrysler Motors, is reportedly in trouble with that company's board of directors. Apparently when Chrysler acquired Lee from the Ford Motor Company, they thought they were getting a good product, but says one Chrysler exec, "Lee's head turned out to be full of sawdust, only one of his eyes worked, his ears were different sizes, and there's a lot of weird noises from his rear end." Chrysler apparently acquired the former Ford exec without any kind of warranty.

* * *

NANCY KISSINGER, now married to former secretary of state and dip extraordinaire Henry Kissinger, is vigorously denying rumors of earlier romantic links with **SECRETARIAT**, the big red stallion who took horse racing's triple crown a few years back.

* * *

There are some pretty red faces at *TV GUIDE* magazine, which recently ran a recipe for "Ham Snackettes for TV Munching." Due to a printer's error, "duck jism" was listed as one of the ingredients. As a result, zoos, farmers, and poultry marketers have been inundated by phone calls from the popular little mag's readers who are desperate to obtain the stuff. *TV Guide* says the real ingredient was "white bread crumbs." Quack, quack.

* * *

Director **MIKE NICHOLS** is reportedly anxious to start work on a new film project in which he himself will play a role. Details are scarce, but insiders say Mike's part is that of a nasty bald little movie director who eats two pounds of Sevruga Malassol caviar in the Russian Tea Room and dies impaled on a herring knife when he trips over a patron's foot in a headlong dash for the men's room.

* * *

GAY TALESE, talented author, has finally decided to change his name. Mr. Talese's new name, according to deed poll: Real Woman Sexer Talese.

* * *

PAUL KANTNER of Jefferson Starship is reportedly considering an offer from the Krezdiak Balkan Circus to do a solo act. Kantner has been offered an undisclosed sum of money to perform a "geek act." Kantner is reported excited, as he has long awaited an opportunity to work with chickens.

* * *

England's **SIR LAURENCE OLIVIER** may be ninety-seven this month, but he is as active as ever. Sir Laurence's next film sounds offbeat: he wants American actor **AL PACINO** to play a hassock, which is a kind of Moroccan footrest!

* * *

New York call girls have been bilked out of thousands of dollars by a man who stole **DONALD SUTHERLAND**'s credit cards. The impersonator, who charged the prostitutes' services on the hot cards, was described as having a teeny-weeny dink and being so boring they thought he was "cute, sort of."

* * *

Black urban leader types are a little embarrassed by former prizefighter **MUHAMMAD ALI**. "He's a great fighter and all that," says **ANDY YOUNG**, the former UN ambassador, "but he doesn't talk much better than Washoe the chimp. He should really stay out of things he doesn't understand, like foreign affairs, French movies, good restaurants; the list is endless. . . ."

* * *

The feud between interviewer **BARBARA WALTERS** and actress **CANDICE BERGEN** is heating up again. Everyone thought it was all patched up, but it seems to start again every twenty-eight days like clockwork. Go figure it, huh?

* * *

Chicago mayor **JANE BYRNE**, a fervent supporter of Senator **TED KENNEDY**'s presidential bid, reacted this way when told that the senator's campaign promise was "a blonde in every pond": "No, not really. . . . Really? No, you're putting me on . . . aren't you? You are, aren't you? Yes?"

* * *

The spics over in Spain are going crazy for **BIANCA JAGGER**, Mick's ex. The spics claim the dark beauty is not really a Nicaraguan. "She's more of a spic, really," they insist. They are hoping Bianca will choose to live in Spain and will let them fuck her. More later on that. . . .

NATIONAL ANTHEMS

OF OUR POLITICAL FRIENDS

by Brian McConnachie

CANADA
. . . .

The Maple Leaf Forever

> At Queenston Heights and Fundy's Lane,
> Our brave fathers side by side,
> For freedom, homes, and loved ones dear,
> Firmly stood keeping watchword ever silent;
> Lest they be discovered and revealed.
> Humming songs of inconspicuous origin,
> They milled and toiled and wandered around,
> And finally found,
> Somebody who,
> Could make them feel blue: armed soldiers.
> Their quasi vigil from behind mossy-covered boulders came,
> And also imitative sounds of large brown bears,
> Instilling jumpiness in our foes;
> Till one day they vanished, leaving freedom in their wake;
> For all the people in the land of the colorful Maple Leaf.
> The Maple Leaf forever,
> Forever and a day.

"The Maple Leaf Forever" by Alexander Muir won a second-place $50 prize in a contest sponsored by the Caledonian Society in 1867. They sold the first-place $100 prize song, after altering its lyrics, to Norway for $175. With their $25 profit they bought Maine from a confidence agent, but time heals all wounds. Some Canadians prefer "O Canada" as the national anthem. It's sung very quickly in French, and many of the words run together. It tells of trappers who go "squirrel crazy" and come down with "weasel fever" whenever they imagine themselves in a country that isn't free. The contest had been over for twelve years when this piece was written.

MEXICO

The Donkey and the Taco

Andele, andele, por favor
¿Donde esta mi tequila?
(sfx. pistol shots) Bang Bang Bang Bang.
Eiiii Yii Yii Yi Yi Loook et de teets on dat one;
My sister's a wergen and so iz my mom,
For six hundred pesos I let you get on.
Eiii Eiiii Yiiiii Bang Bang Bang,
My burro iz so grande.
Eii Bang Bang Yiii Bang
Madre de Dios, diz iz de life,
Bang Bang Bang Bang Bang.
I newer wan to leeve diz stinkin' place
To go back to stinkin' Puerto Rico,
You stinkin' get my meaning, chico!
Bang EEEEEEEEEEIIIiiiiiiiiiiiiiYYYIIii
Hey, loook et de teets on dat utter one,
Dat one iz de best one, ah Bang Bang Bang.
Loook it ower Meester, it'z all for sale.
Eiii Yiii Bang
From our toez to our sombreros,
We're juzz wacky caballeros.
Bang. Donkeys an' tacos forewer.

These are generally the lyrics, though they don't necessarily have to appear in this order . . . or at all. It is not uncommon to substitute other lyrics, save for the last line, but these are the ones that have been in most versions. "The Donkey and the Taco" has no official author/composer but is instead attributed to a group of San Diego domestics who would, as they rode in the trucks that brought them to work, sing. Sometimes they pretended to be "bandidos" and made threatening gestures out of the back of the truck to pedestrians, but that's another story. The unofficial anthem of Mexico is called "Dust for Sale." It doesn't have any lyrics but is hummed—and usually by people who are trying to act inconspicuous.

ITALY

Fin-Nick-U-La
Fin-Nick-U-Self

Not available.

Unfortunately, this national anthem has been recalled for revision. It should be out again by the end of this year. Some politicians felt the line about Krakatoa being east of Java should be changed because Krakatoa is west of Java, while others felt the line should be deleted entirely because Krakatoa isn't even in Italy and the space should be used to say something nice about the railroad trains. It will be interesting to see what happens.

FRANCE

The Marseillaise

Ye sons of fifedom awash with glory!
Hark! Hark! what myriads on the rise?
Ye grandchildren, ye grandchildren, ye grandchildren;
Behold their tears, the ropes are perhaps too tight,
Shall mischief-breeding tyrants roam left then fro
With their hired ghosts and marching bands,
Leaving peace and liberty asleep with cuts on their faces?
Our legs, our legs, our legs, ye brave ones;
Th' avenging sword aflight,
Marching and marching with our hearts in tow;
For liberty and death.

What is this thing? This isn't "The Marseillaise." And if it is "The Marseillaise," it's a horrible translation filled with misprints. "The Marseillaise" is a very inspiring patriotic song, and when the French hear it, they go into a frenzy and try to kill Austrians for what happened back in 1792. And they also try to kill Germans who pretended to be Austrians after World War II. Perhaps it's just as well the real thing doesn't appear here in case any French people are reading this.

KOREA
. . . .

Get Your Own Gin and Tonic, Fryboy

There once was an Emperor from Gkee-dom
Who liked pretty girls when he see'd 'em
He'd sneak into their tents
And have sexy events
And one day he gave us our freedom.

And along came the good Syngman Rhee, ah,
From Princeton to Seoul he flew via.
He kneeled down and prayed,
That soon he'd get laid,
And that we'd call the country Korea.

Koreans are very strong and they raise millet, barley, peppers, ginseng, and rabbits. And they are purported to be the best ricksha-drivers in Asia. In 1871 Commodore Perry landed in Korea and, thinking it was China, said, "Hi, I'm Marco Polo. Remember me?" No one understood a word he said, but they did address him as "Mr. Poro" when he left.

ISRAEL
. . . .

Israel's Gonna Be My Home

Young Israel's singers:
Sometimes when we lie awake on our bunks,
We think of you, Oh Israel, as our father;
Standing ever alert in silent lookout,
As we sleep secure under your watch.
Your effort is for us and for our future.

Elders' chorus:
It's all right, I don't mind. I love you.

Young Israel's singers:
We're like a house so filled with children,
And there's nowhere for the parent to rest.
You sit firmly awake in the kitchen of Justice

Worrying about the days ahead.
Please rest in our bunk, Oh Israel;
We will stay up and worry in your place.
We're strong and we don't mind a little worrying now and then.
We love you.

Elders' chorus:
Never mind about that. Go to sleep.
Go to the bathroom and wash your hands,
And then go to sleep.

Young Israel's singers:
We did. We love you.

Elders' chorus:
Then go to sleep. I love you.

There is a complicated contract involved with this anthem. Every time it's played, the William Morris Agency gets royalty payments. Sometimes they have to take up a collection before they can sing it. If they're not able to collect enough money, they sing "Born Free" instead . . . which many would prefer to sing in the first place.

AUSTRALIA

Look Out, Australia!!
Behind You

Oh, Australia of the ocean,
Bobbing like a cork on water,
Floating, ducking in the daylight,
Never drifting toward New Zealand,
Regal envy of the others,
Lots of woods and lots of outback,
Many bushes in the west part,
Little water in the middle,
Smiley faces of the children,
Chasing cattle through the cities,
Oh, Australia of the ocean,
Nestled in the pouch of freedom,
Nursing from the teats of justice,
Hopping down the paths of good-time,

We are happy to be on you.
But if one day come invaders,
We will hit their heads with creekwood
We will shove them in the corncrib,
We will kick them in the marbles,
We will twist their ears with pliers,
We'll put up their noses, insects,
We'll put pellets in their pudding,
We'll grab fistfuls of their stomachs,
We'll drop koalas down their trousers,
We'll etc., etc.

This was written by Peter D. McCormack, who also wrote "The Four Little Schoolmates" and fell dead in 1916. He wrote it because "Everybody had one but us" . . . which wasn't true.

McCormack once told his wife he was going to drive into Sydney to see what's up . . . which he literally did. He hit a person by the name of Sydney something-or-other and had to spend the night in jail.

THE REPUBLIC OF CHAD

A Promise

Freedom! Freedom! Freedom!
It is Freedom our desire,
Not knife wounds in our stomachs.
But if it be the price,
Then knife us all you will.
But if you do not hold Freedom as our prize,
For all of the suffering that we endure,
We pledge you this:
Our sons will sneak across your borders
And drown you while you bathe.

The original anthem of Chad was written by two Catholic priests and spoke mostly of what a joy it was possessing the land. Since much of their land is the Sahara desert, they grew weary of the song and stopped singing it. The people of Chad spend much of their time now writing letters to MGM. Besides the desert, Chad's other asset is the largest colony of pygmies known to exist. Their suggestion to MGM is to film an all-black *Wizard of Oz* but this time from the munchkins' point of view.

LIECHTENSTEIN

To You We Wave Our Tiny Hats

> You jewel!
> You are a strandless, semi-hilly delight.
> You gem.

This anthem formerly contained the line, "We will never knowingly sign a shameful pact in your name. Never." but it was deleted during the 1904 Olympics at the insistence of several larger nations who claimed that this anthem was nothing more than a plan to hold up the games.

ICELAND

You Are Our Land

> Ready your pistols and quicken your mounts to the fore,
> Our serried ranks ride this day onward swords astir,
> To destiny, to destiny
> "Roar" our cannons echo.
> Within our breasts beat unquenched hearts,
> For victory we lust;
> Give them the lash.
> "Roar" and again our cannon roars,
> Make them limbless and shoot their heads off.
> Never to be vanquished the majestic conqueror rides,
> And if any among us be not valiant,
> Shoot them too.

"You Are Our Land" was written in the spring of 1876 in Scotland. Since then, it has only been sung a handful of times owing to the fact that seldom, if ever, do the people gather together. It is common for the people of Iceland to leave their country during the spring thaw because the unusually harsh winters necessitate the tossing of their refuse, including their bodily wastes, into the snow drifts around their homes.

PARAGUAY
. . . .

Hail, Argentina, and Hail to You, Brazil

Verse:
A nation like ours with its eyes to the stars
Gets a feeling sometimes of lonely.
Will the gods up above send us someone to love?
Or is that a bunch of baloney?
Can it be just we three
In a union to last forever?
Or does fate push aside,
Our heart without pride,
And make this a cruel endeavor?
Refrain:
When we first saw you across our border
You didn't even know our name;
But we could tell just how swell you are,
Qué belle you are,
Just the same.
You're the nations we care for only,
You're the creme de la creme;
In and out of every thought we ponder
We grow fonder
From hither to yonder
As we conjure
Up y-ooooo-uuu.
Your mountains beat the best that Europe offers,
Your canal systems are inferior to none;
You've got imports, you've got exports,
You've got sea coast
And the best ports
And your metal can outshine the sun.
You're a pair of countries
Not Ming trees, not mung trees
That we would like to have the friendship of.
There's no denying it
So we'll stop trying it
And just say
You're the best, you're the top, you're above.
Argentina, there's no one keena
And Brazil, you give us a thrill
And Brazil, you give us a thrill.

"Hail, Argentina, and Hail to You, Brazil" was written by two brothers, Manny and David Cavedagni, just prior to the return of Juan Peron's authority. The brothers are not natives of Paraguay but travel throughout the world and earn their living by attempting to establish amity among all nations. The brothers had been paid and left Paraguay before it was fully realized that this new anthem had failed to say anything flattering about Bolivia. Both are believed to be now living in Uruguay working on a similar anthem.

SWITZERLAND
. . . .

We Are Switzerland—and We Can See Everything

Avaunt, avaunt.
Is it to Freedom
Or to Justice
That we inflate our cry?
"TO BOTH!" You've asked that before.
"TO BOTH!" Our answer crashes back like an unexpected crestless wave,
Subtle in its travail, gradually swelling from within,
As it returns once again to shore.
Snakelike, it rears uncoiling,
Uncoiling its muscular arm, sweeping, rolling slowly, slowly.
Is it rocks this time that will couch the explosion?
Or flat dead beach?
And again the mighty sea confronts this crude border,
The insubstantial cheap boundary, unmoving land, unfeeling,
Without gestures, depth without anger.
Crash into it.
Show it your fury. Grind it with your might.
Each time return with your force and laugh with contempt
As you ebb to travel elsewhere.
Oh Mighty Sea, anoint me with thy salty covenant.
Take me with you this time!

This anthem was written in 1931 by C. Widmer, who was an owner-operator of the only glass bottom tour boat on Lake Geneva, and the proud possessor of the unofficial title, "First Admiral of the Swiss Navy." Upon hearing his anthem for the first time, a number of people objected, claiming that an anthem should say something good about the country it represents and not just go on about the sea as this one does. The "First Admiral" became furious and asked them all if they wanted to step outside and make something out of it. They said that they didn't, it really wasn't that important, and they've been living with it ever since.

BERMUDA
. . . .

Come to Bermuda

Dere's a Commonwealth nation in de Atlantic Ocean,
Where dey always sing songs and wear de suntan lotion.
It's de island paradise made for you 'n' for me,
Where you drink de rum fizzes 'n' you swim in de sea.
Bermuda, oh Bermuda,
It is de only place I love to be.
But dere are also pools,
Lots o' swimming pools,
For dose of you
Who don' like to swim in de sea!
Bermuda, oh Bermuda
Bermuda, oh Bermuda
Bermuda, Bermuda
Bermuda is de place I love to be!

When you get here you'll want to rent a motor bike,
Drive to Hamilton town 'n' shop all you like.
You buy liquor, you buy linen, you buy socks for your feet,
At our duty free stores whose prices can't be beat.
Oh Trimingham's
Oh Trimingham's
Trimingham's, oh Trimingham's
Trimingham's, oh Trimingham's
Trimingham's has cashmere socks for your feet.
Pink sand, oh paradise, oh mon, it's real nice.
Tennis, golf, sailing, scuba diving, deep sea fishing,
Hotel and guest cottage space.
Rates based on per
Person or double occupancy and availability, plus tax. Write
Directly to de Bermuda travel bureau or check out
De ads in de
New Yorker magazine.

Being a Commonwealth nation, Bermuda is supposed to sing "God Save the King." The people of Bermuda did sing "God Save the King" up to the time they were told to stop and change it to "God Save the Queen." They became quite annoyed and told the Governor that if it was all the same with him, they didn't want to sing to God to save *anybody* because apparently, it didn't work.

So now they sing this thing.

TONGA
. . . .

Oh Tonga

Do you know who we are?
We are Tonga.
And what our flag looks like?
It has a pale blue field and is made of silk;
A white triangle is set in the upper right hand corner,
And in it a green star.
In the center is a Royal Palm tree done in browns and green.
At night when tyranny and disorder stalk our roads,
There is nothing visible,
Not even Tyranny and Disorder,
But we are getting lights
To vanquish those twin evils deeper into the jungle
Where they're sure to strangle themselves on their own villainy.
God is our judge;
To Him we pray.

Tonga has been telling people that they were getting lights for the past twenty-five years, and they still don't have them.

HOW YOUR PARENTS HAD SEX

by John Hughes

IT'S LATE SATURDAY NIGHT and your mom and dad have just come home from a dinner and bridge party at the Petersons'. The Walkers and the Packards were there, too. You and your sister and brother are sound asleep in the family room along with the baby-sitter. As your dad drives the baby-sitter home, your mom gently rouses you all and herds you up to bed.

Before your dad gets home, your mom draws a bath and pours in a capful of Ivory Liquid so she'll smell clean for your dad. Then she undresses. Yes, she's naked, and she lowers herself into the tub. Your dad returns and puts the car into the garage. He runs your bike in, too. He notices that the bathroom light is on, and he chuckles to himself. In the kitchen he mixes a couple of Manhattans and locks up the house. He whistles "I Get a Kick Out of You" as he cha-chas up the stairs. He opens the bathroom door a crack.

"Oo-la-la!" he says, winking at your mom.

"Go on!" she giggles.

He cha-chas into the bedroom and sets the drinks down on the nightstand. He twirls an imaginary partner—probably Betty Grable— and finishes his cha-cha.

"Mere alcohol doesn't thrill me at all . . . ," he sings softly as he loosens his tie. He tilts his hat forward and slings his suit coat over his shoulder.

"I get no thrill from champaaaaaaa-aaaaaaagne!"

Meanwhile, your mom towels off her large bosoms. They are actually bigger than you thought they were. In fact, they're huge. Then she dries the rest of her body. Using her Lady Schick, she mows her legs, her armpits, and trims the stray hairs crawling unattractively down her inner thighs. Yes, she has inner thighs. She packs her bosoms into her bra, slips on those underpants that are so big you can dry a whole car with one old pair, and drops a nightgown over her head. She ruffles the collar so it looks pretty. Puckering her lips, she applies red lipstick.

Your dad sits on the edge of the bed, stuffing shoe trees into his wing tips. He stands and drops his boxer shorts. Geez! He's got a big one. And it's not pink. But it sure is hairy. He unbuttons his shirt and neatly folds it across the chair. He deposits his cuff links in the top left dresser drawer. He reaches down under all the junk in there and comes up with a pack of playing cards with naked women on them—bathing beauties. He shuffles through them, as you yourself so often do.

Your mom has just about finished wrapping her hair in toilet paper and is considering birth-control methods. She decides on the diaphragm over spermatocide. You probably remember the diaphragm. It was in the cupboard under the sink in the bathroom in the pastel blue box with the flowers on it. Well, she takes it out. It's about the size of an individual pizza, and it's crusty with white cement. She puts on those rubber gloves that are also under the sink. She puts the thing in. Because of you kids, it goes in very easily, despite its great bulk.

Dad is done with the playing cards. They have aroused him enough to put on his birth-control device. He puts the cards back and fishes out a rubber, or, as he calls it, a "cundrum." It's about fifteen inches long and made out of the kind of rubber they use to make fish-tank hoses. He blows the thing full of cigarette smoke and checks for leaks. Satisfied that the worker who packed it in the plant in France didn't poke a hole in it, he puts it on. He flips on the radio and dials in some lovely-type music. He stands by the window sipping his Manhattan and smoking his cigarette.

Your mom checks on you kids, makes sure you're covered and sleeping soundly. She walks like a duck into the bedroom to keep from getting the diaphragm cement on her legs. She goes into the bedroom and closes the door. She locks it.

"Herb, will you help me barricade this door, please," she says as she struggles with the dresser. Your dad helps her slide the dresser, the dressing table, and the love seat in front of the door. He hands your mom her drink, and she takes a tiny sip.

"Oooh, this is too strong! Are you trying to get me drunk?" she jokes.

"Oui, mademoiselle!" your dad winks.

There is a moment of silence as your mom and dad face the fact that a certain special event is imminent.

"Honey," your dad says tenderly. "Shall we have congress?"

"I don't know," your mom says, to be coy. "You're so bold!"

"It's Saturday night, and you know what that means!"

"I hope it's a boy!"

Your dad helps your mom up on the bed, where they dance cheek to cheek.

"That was a nice party tonight," your mom remarks.

"Swell," your dad replies. "Delicious hors d'oeuvres. What were they?"

"Grated Parmesan cheese with onion and bacon on circles of white bread," your mom coos.

"Would you like to do anything before we have intimacy?"

"No, not that I can think of right now, dear," your mom answers softly. "But we better get on with our coition before it gets too late. I have floors to do in the morning."

Your mom opens the bed and fluffs the pillows. Your dad splashes Old Spice on his cheeks.

"You don't want to do a little experimenting, huh? It might be a hoot!"

"Just what do you have on your mind?" your mom says, a little irritated.

"Oh, maybe I could tie you to the bed with your hose and tickle you with my shaving brush?"

"For crying out loud!" your mom says, with her hands on her hips.

"Wait! If that doesn't appeal to you, how about we kiss each other's . . ."

"Ugh!"

"What if you put on your mink stole? . . ."

"Herb!"

"There's a thing I heard about at work from one of the fellas in the shipping department. . . ."

"On my mother's grave, I can't believe what you're saying! What do you think we are? A couple of colored people?"

"You're right," your dad says, seeing the error of his ways. "But maybe we could sneak downstairs and go out on the patio lounger. . . ."

"Just hurry up and coitus me, so we can go to bed!"

As it turns out, your mom lets your dad kiss her brassiere and lick part of her ear, and she runs her fingers through his hair, and that's just fine. After warning your dad not to muss her hair, they commence.

"One, two, three, *push!*" your dad says, calling cadence. "One, two, three, *push!*"

"Did I tell you what your son did today?" your mom mentions. "Well, first he tracked mud all across the floors. That's why I have to do them all in the morning. Then the little snip calls Grandma in Florida. He just picks up the phone and dials long distance!"

"One, two three, *push!*" your dad says with great determination.

"I don't mind him spending an hour on the phone with his friends—that's not long distance—but to just call up Grandma and chat like she was next door is a bit much, wouldn't you say?"

"One, two three, *push!*"

"I wish you'd have a talk with him about the phone," your mom says, noticing a big cobweb in the corner that she somehow managed to miss when she cleaned last Wednesday.

"Oops! Pardon *me,*" your dad groans, "but I'm done."

"Oh, good! So am I," your mom chirps.

Your dad jumps out of the bed and pushes the barricade from the door so your mom can run to the bathroom and get sick. Then he lights up a cigarette and goes to the linen closet and gets clean sheets. As your mom puts the sheets on the bed, your dad disinfects the old ones. Then he showers. When he's done and returns to the room, your mom is asleep. He climbs into bed, switches on the light, reads a few pages of *Youngblood Hawke,* and dozes off.

In the morning, you and your sister and brother are up at six. Since it's

Sunday and there isn't anything on TV except Mass, you sit outside your parents' door and listen. You incorrectly judge their normal early-morning rustling and snoring as sexual activity. You try to picture what they're doing in there, but you draw a complete blank.

DOCTOR'S PRIVILEGE KIT

by P. J. O'Rourke

WHEN YOU'RE A DOCTOR, you can do anything you want to, absolutely anything at all. Wanna trot through customs at Heathcote Airport with a kilo of rock crystal cocaine in a lady's handbag? Wanna tool down I–80 at a hundred mph in an International Signal Orange Eldorado Brougham with a U-Haul full of sten guns for the Chicano guerrillas in the hills of Marin? Or fist-fuck an autistic preteen? Frankly, "no sweat" for even the lowliest intern. Or, as the Yale Medical School Alma Mater puts it:

Sumus Medius

We will take all your clothes off
And get you undressed,
And diddle around
With the parts we like best.
We'll poke you and probe you
And peek everywhere,
And laugh at your body
While you're standing right there.
We can tell you whatever
Pops into our mind—
We might call your backache
A cancerous spine,
We might tell you your freckles
Are dread melanoma,
Or say you were out
For a fifty-year coma.
We'll anesthetize you
At seven A.M.
And play gin on your face
Till a quarter past ten.
We're doctors
And we can remove your whole brain,
Poke your eyes out with fly rods

And never explain,
Rip out your kidneys
And feed them to cats,
Or cut off your buttocks
And wear them like hats.

©1945 Yale University

. . . in Latin, of course. I mean, why rub it in?

Yes, doctors are above the law; so it's no wonder that medical schools are deluged by so many applicants that few among us could even aspire to hope for admission. But if you think that's the *real* reason it's impossible to get into medical school—then, Mr. Reader, your peachy-pink naïveté is peeking out the leg-hole of your fancy nylon jogger's shorts. Doctors are *all* favored sons of the rich and powerful men in this world. They are the scions of dictators, generals, heads of states, financial barons, and rubber czars; the offspring of mogols, princes, potentates, chairmen of the boards of huge multinational cartels, and masters of vast plantations in those far-flung corners of the earth where life is still cheaper than a well-mixed Rum Collins. Thus, the remarkable privileges allowed physicians. Plus, doctoring gives these young people something to do.

Of course, there are no black or "colored" doctors. Those Negroes and gibbering dusky foreigners you've seen calling themselves medical men in our big city hospitals are actually the mercenary troops of third-world private armies studying the human body here stateside in order to exact more effective forms of pain when interrogating miscreant intellectuals and communist sympathizers. Nor are there any women doctors. Doctors who appear to be women are, in reality, just rich boys who like to, well, "dress up." You catch my meaning. And stay away from lady proctologists.

Anyway, you can see why *you* aren't a doctor; or, I should say, "why you didn't *used to be* a doctor." Because included with this article is everything you need to pass yourself off as a licensed practitioner and open the confines of your unappealing life to fun, money, and universal respect.

Something holding you back? Think you don't know the first thing about medicine, for instance? *Put your mind at ease.* You know what rich kids are like. They spend all their time wrecking sports cars and getting pushed into swimming pools by the Kennedys. If there were anything tough about being a doctor, they'd all go into hotel/motel management or something. But they don't. That's because there's really not much to modern medicine. Once upon a time, maybe—what with all that leeching and cupping and tiresome fresh air cures. But no more. Nowadays, all diseases are divided into two types: fatal and nonfatal. There's nothing you can do about fatal diseases, so *anything* you do will be fine with everyone concerned, since there's nothing to be done. Penicillin cures everything else. And penicillin is nothing but bread mold.

That's pretty much all you need to know. As for the rest anybody can slap a, Band-Aid on, and babies plop right out of their own accord. Christ, peasant women the world over just waddle to the edge of the field every nine months, grunt twice, smear the brat with mud, and go back to harrowing turnips or whatever. All that lolly-gagging in bed our wives and mothers do is just to get attention.

Well, that's that—nothing but layers of sham and deceit, as you can see. Now, what happens if you're somehow "found out"? Nothing, that's what happens. They'll have to let you stay a doctor once they know you're on to their scam. After all, you might have a copy of this article stashed with your lawyer in case you get a .44 Magnum French kiss or somebody gives you a pair of concrete tap shoes and a one-way boat ticket on the East River Short Line. And a patient can't tell on you because of the legal principle of doctor-patient confidentiality. So you're perfectly safe using any part of your *National Lampoon* Doctor's Privilege Kit.

Your New Privileges as an M.D.

Physicians enjoy three basic legal privileges. The first and most important is the right to possess, use, buy, and sell *any* drug; and to transport it across every border in the Free World. Which is to say, *"Welcome to hog heaven!! The free Cadillacs are over there between the mink bed sheets and the Chateau Rothschild-Lafitte tank car, honey, you're rollin' in it now!"* (Incidentally, you might tip off a few close friends that they don't ever have to pay a doctor. Those medical bills with more zeros that a Strategy and Tactics final in a Syrian military academy are strictly for appearance's sake—sent out by the same secret professional organization that invented the Mafia to explain all that dope.) Naturally, access to drugs means more than just personal monetary gain. Drugs are an important part of a modern doctor's capacity to deal with disease and injury. If you don't believe me, just try walking around in an emergency room full of puking flu victims and bloody cripples without popping a handful of Quaaludes first. Not to mention surgery! You can't imagine the amount of big, slimy organs and viscous gore a human body's got inside. And one slice and it's all over the place. Jesus, I wouldn't try *that* straight. But, you know, if you're really stoned and everything you can kind of get into it on a heavy primeval ooze trip kind of level like reading Ed Sander's *The Family* except without all the paranoid vibes.

The second thing you're allowed to do is speed and turn left on red lights and roar around at night without your lights on and generally drive like hell with complete immunity from traffic rules and regulations. Which is a good thing, considering all the dope you'll be doing. Also, you can park by fire hydrants.

The third important privilege of a medical doctor is the right to do anything you want to with anybody's body, especially girls. Perhaps you've noticed that women are forever having some or another problem with their personal plumbing. And, like most males, you've probably wondered, "What gives?" I mean, you never hear about a *guy* having Pap smears, Wasserman tests, vaginitis, or yeast infections—let alone a dork-bleed every four weeks. But women are in and out of the doctor's office like Illinois tourists at a Guadalajara comfort station. I don't think I have to go into detail; suffice it to say that a perusal of

Nonfatal Disease	Therapy or Treatment
Equine Encephalitis	I slice of moldy bread every 4 hrs. for 6 days
Rocky Mountain Spotted Fever	2 slices of moldy bread before meals for a week
Influenza	3 slices of moldy bread at bedtime until symptoms subside
Viral Pneumonia	Initial dose of I loaf moldy bread followed by 3 to 5 days of moldy bread therapy
Infectious Mononucleosis	I slice of moldy bread on waking each day for a month and plenty of bed rest
Mumps	3 slices of moldy bread at meals for 9 days
Acute Follicular Conjunctivitis	2 ½-loaf treatments administered at an interval of 8 hrs.
Chicken Pox	Moldy bread plasters applied to eruptions
Serum Hepatitis	Regular diet of moldy bread, fresh fruit, and vegetables for term of disease
Scarlet Fever	3 tsp. of loose bread mold every 3 hrs. for duration of rash
Bronchitis	Bread mold respirator twice a day for 5 days
Impetigo	Wash infected areas with bread mold daily
Tonsillitis	Paint throat with moldy bread at bedtime
Whooping Cough	3 slices of moldy bread every morning and evening while cough persists
Sydenham's Chorea	6 to 12 slices of moldy bread per day for 12 days
Salmonella	Maintain moldy bread toast diet for 2 days
Typhoid Fever	2 slices of moldy bread hourly for the first 3 days followed by I slice every 3 hours for a week
Amebic Dysentery	Gradual administration of moldy bread in increasing dosages
Tularemia	Moldy bread set out in epidemic wildlife areas is an effective prophylactic
Diphtheria	I loaf of moldy rye bread per day until fever breaks
Yaws	6 moldy bread crusts every night for 2 weeks

Nonfatal Disease	Therapy or Treatment
Jaundice	2 tsp. bread mold crumbs with meals
Intestinal Flukes	Rectal administration of moldy bread pudding
Lump Jaw	Cold moldy bread compress will reduce swelling
Urethritis	1 administration of 3 loaves of moldy bread
Gonorrhea	1 administration of 6 loaves of moldy bread
Syphilis	3 administrations of 8 loaves of moldy bread

Chapter XXXVII in *Gray's Anatomy* will show you how to arrange for this in your own practice. Complete right of physical access to people's bodies also lets you empty a service automatic into anybody you don't like and call the bullet wounds "acne."

There are plenty of other privileges, too. Doctor's orders are binding statutes under common law, so you can order people to *really* sit on a pickle or actually force them to piss up a rope. And you'll diagnose your own trick knees when we have our next war. Or, if you want, they'll make you an officer so you can lay about colonial villas, getting whatever kinko sex act our latest foreign ally specializes in, while noncoms with big red targets on their helmets dash around the free-fire zone stuffing cotton wool and sulfa into land mine wounds. And you'll subscribe to exclusive professional journals that publish the home phone numbers of beautiful movie stars. There are secret golf strokes known only to doctors and special physicians' preferred stocks that pay a yearly dividend of small Caribbean islands. You'll get to hang out with pro football players who'll treat you like their buddy, and airlines will tell you ahead of time which planes are going to crash. And if you should somehow *still* manage to wind up as a soak on skid row, all your alki-stiff chums will call you "Doc," and one day a big-time gangster will get gunned down in front of your flophouse and you'll have to dig the slug out of his shoulder with a broken steak knife when you discover that his moll is your own lost daughter who, reformed by the example of a new life you quickly undertake, goes back to college and marries the governor's son, renouncing her mobster beau who's sorely tempted to revenge but destroys the evidence of an early scandal in her father-in-law's career out of gratitude to you.

SONGS OF THE HUMPBACK WHALE

by Sean Kelly

TABLE OF CONTENTS

I'll Take You Home Again, Baleen

I'm warm-blooded for my darling
All my tweets and whistles told her
For her I'd swim an icy polar sea
My midnight oil is burning
And my flippers long to hold her
But my love has made a blue whale out of me.

I was proud to be a Humpback
Not a Sperm whale or a Right whale
Not a Rorqual, Killer, Narwhal, Fin or Sei
But I'd rather be a Bottlenose
Beluga, Grey or White Whale
Since my love made a blue whale out of me.

I Am Whale

I don't smoke, I don't drink,
Don't leave tea bags in the sink
I am very ecologically proper,
And my favorite dish is weeds, not fish,
So I never tell a whopper.

I am free in the sea which welcomes me
To swim in its salty water,
I blow and I float and behave like a boat
And I won't eat a fisherman's daughter.

CHORUS:

I am whale, I am whale, I'm a humpback whale
And I swim with a humpback motion
I jump every rump that's a plump hump rump
At the bottom of the ocean!

I don't give a hump where I take a dump
For the sea dissolves my feces
And I don't give a damn if they say I am
An endangered wildlife species.

I sings and I plays and I splash all my days
And I don't spend a penny on clothes
Don't pray to God, ain't bored by the Bard
Ain't no jam betwixt me toes.

CHORUS:

I am whale, I'm all whale,
Not a Mack truck full of kale,
Not a train transporting ale,
Not a cathouse or a jail,
Not a nightingale, not a seventh veil,
Not a Holy Grail, not a Melville tale,
And I don't need to find a rhyme for "orange"!

A Party Press Publication

What Every Teen-Ager Should Know

NANCY REAGAN'S

GUIDE TO DATING DO'S AND DON'TS

by Doug Kenney

"*A sane, sound book for modern young people embarking on the sometimes murky sea of premarital dating.*"   —*Rev. Billy Graham*

"*Teen-age questions answered with a frankness and honesty refreshing in these sniggering times.*"   —*Ann Landers*

"*A guiding beacon for today's turned-on, anything-for-kicks generation.*"   —*Pat Boone*

Introduction

Hi. If you are "twixt twelve and twenty" and a would-be dater, this book is for you. In it, I am going to deal honestly, and sometimes quite frankly, with the joys and pitfalls of teen-age dating in the hope that it may prevent your first corsage from shriveling up into a bouquet of nettles.

A dating manual for this day and age? one of your "sophisticated" chums may scoff. *Why, all that jazz about moral decency and lofty ideals is a lot of bunk and hooey!* Is it? Well, take a good look, fellows and girls, at the dangers that surround you in today's "anything goes" world. Everywhere a teen turns, he is assaulted by an avalanche of filth that lurks in many forms—pornographic movies, obscene novels, indecent plays, lurid magazines, prurient snapshots, seductive television commercials, suggestive song lyrics, immodest dances, salacious paintings, lewd advertisements, coarse poems, smutty radio shows, depraved newspapers, indelicate lithographs, perverse sculptures, shady stories, gross cookbooks, tawdry cocktail napkins, ribald postcards, libertine bumper stickers, provocative buttons, meretricious gestures, licentious operas, pandering food labels, and shameless zoos.

It's enough to make me sick to my stomach. Actually, after a drive through L.A., I often *get* sick to my stomach and have to spend a whole afternoon in the little girls' room. As a matter of fact, I think I'm already a little woozy, and I haven't even gotten to the first chapter yet.

Where does this nauseating tidal wave of smut and garbage come from? Well, you won't find out from the "Sex O'Clock News," but it is no secret that certain foreign powers would like nothing better than to see our country paralyzed and prostrated by a degenerate Supreme Court that sanctions petting sprees and free love as "freedom of choice" and "harmless kicks." While America rots from within, all the Russkies would have to do is rumble through Washington in tanks with those long, nasty things on top and pick up the pieces. Her youth "brainwashed" by so-called "liberated" codes of behavior, a mighty nation would be vanquished, laid low by deep kissing and petting parties.

But young people all love dates, and there is no finer preparation for marriage than a wholesome, well-rounded social life. I have received thousands of letters from concerned teens all over the country, begging for advice on this important (and fun!) part of adulthood, and I hope this book will serve as a useful and informative answer.

Hi.

Nancy Reagan

SO YOU'RE GROWING UP?

Dating is like dynamite. Used wisely, it can move mountains and change the course of mighty rivers. Used foolishly, it can blow your legs off. Scientists have calculated, for example, that if a man could harness even a fraction of the kinetic energy wasted in a single session of Post Office or Spin the Bottle, he could light up the entire city of Wilmington, Delaware, and have enough left over to discover and mass produce a cheap, effective cure for cancer of the larynx. Thus, it is so important to understand and harness the explosive power of the forces developing in your body.

Have you noticed that your body is playing little tricks on you lately? If you are a boy, you may have noticed your legs, face, arms, and chest are becoming covered with thick, black pubic hairs and your voice may be beginning to sound like a phonograph needle ruining your favorite stack of platters. If you are a girl, you may have noticed a painful swelling up here and some more funny business going on down there.

These dramatic changes can mean only one thing: cholera. If you are not among the lucky ones, then it simply means you are becoming a young man or a young woman, depending on how much fluoride they dumped in your parents' drinking water. I know that such changes can often be difficult for growing teens, but try to weather the storm and "grin and bear it." There is always impotence and menopause.

During these trying teen-age years, a girl begins to "menstruate" (*men* stroo ate), and a boy begins to have "erections" (ee *wreck* shuns), normally only when called to the blackboard by his teacher. There is absolutely nothing abnormal about this, and, aside from voluntary sterilization, no known cure.

Not only is the miracle of growing up taking place inside your body, but it may be going on outside it as well. There are many names for this remarkable stage of development—"acne," "pimples," "blackheads," "whiteheads," "redcaps," "boils," "blemishes," "cankers," "zits," "pustules," "efflorescence," "breaking out," "pockmarks," "carbuncles," "suppurations," "polyps," "goobies," and "St. Anthony's Fire," to mention just a few. Perhaps one of your clever friends will notice this badge of young adulthood and jokingly dub you with an appropriate descriptive nickname, like "Crater Face," "Swiss Cheese," or "Vomithead." But perk up! Such bothersome side effects are all in Mother Nature's master plan, and they may very possibly disappear in time, leaving a healthy, glowing complexion on those portions of your face and neck not permanently disfigured by layers of horny scar tissue. You *can* treat your "booboos" right away, however, with frequent applications of hot, soapy water, mild astringent, or, in unusually severe cases, a woodburning kit.

CALLING ALL GIRLS

It is time to clear up one myth about menstruation or "the curse" as many, including myself, prefer to call it. Many girls worry because their "periods" don't come as regular as clockwork, on the first or fifteenth of the month with the rest of the bills. This is nothing more than a silly wives' tale. The "cramps" you may feel, often no more noticeable than a rhythmic sledgehammer blow to the abdomen, only mean that the two little almond-flavored organs deep in your tummy are finally getting around to preparing a little home in case a baby wants to move in. This continuing cycle varies widely in different girls and may range anywhere from fifty-three to three days, depending on whether the little almonds want their owner to bloat up like a dirigible or simply bleed to death.

This interesting process, often called "nature's egg-timer," was originally based on the lunar month of twenty-eight days. But with so many changes in our modern calendar to make way for silly things like Labor Day and Martin Luther King's birthday, the cycle is often keyed to other natural rhythms, like sunspots, quirky reversals of the earth's magnetic poles, or fluctuations in the stock market. (During these special days, it is wise to avoid anything that might interfere with this delicate phenomenon, such as swimming, ham radio transmitters, and remote-controlled streetlights.) My *own* cycle is based on the appearance of Haley's Comet, so although I am under the weather only infrequently, I am stocking up on you-know-whats now, because when my next one comes in 1985, it's bound to be a *whopper!*

One more word about your period. When it finally comes, you may find it a good idea to use a "sanitary napkin" to help stanch the massive loss of precious, irreplaceable fluids from your vitals. If so, beware of fast-talking sales pitches claiming the Tampax-type tampon is preferable to the Kotex-type external napkin. The former may be somewhat more convenient, but it can lead both to unwanted feelings and risking your stock in the marriage market. As for the slight icky odor that occasionally results from the safer, saner napkin, a *schpritz* of feminine deodorant, Glade, or liquid benzene should make your strolls upwind of kennels and dog shows free from any possible danger of embarrassment.

FELLOWS TAKE NOTE

As for you boys, don't feel left out. If you glance down between your legs, where your vagina should be, you will see an odd-looking pink sac containing two little ugly things. Go ahead, take a look right now, but *keep your hands on the book* (more about *that* later). Quite a surprise, wasn't it? Well, the funny pink sac is called your "scrotum" (*skro* tum), and the two little ugly things are calles "testes" (*teh* stees) and are why you can never know the ultimate, inexpressible joy of motherhood.

Believe it or not, your scrotum will respond to sudden changes in temperature, quickly raising or lowering your testes to maintain them at a constant heat level, something seen nowhere else in nature except by those few who have mastered the proper techniques of marshmallow-toasting. If you don't believe me, try rubbing an ice cube against your scrotum and see what happens. Now, quickly try a lighted match. Now another ice cube. Another match. Faster. Cube. Match. Cube. Ma—*aha*! Didn't your mother ever tell you not to play with matches? All joking aside, this is simply another example of the wonders you can find in and around your own body, stuff that has often led to many important scientific discoveries. For example, when my husband, Ronald, was in the Boy Scouts, he used this same natural principle for a homemade thermometer and won a merit badge in meteorology.

THE NIGHTMARE OF WET DREAMS

Nocturnal emissions, or "wet dreams" as they are often called, were once dreaded and traumatic experiences for young boys of the Victorian era. But today there can be little doubt that these perfectly normal, disgusting catastrophes are merely your body's way of "priming the pump" for the coming responsibilities of manhood and marriage, and a signal to your mother or laundry that you are ready for dating.

Should you have a nocturnal emission, do not worry. A few easy preparations for this can be made in advance. Each night, before your mom tucks you in, make sure she supplies you with two bath towels, an automobile sponge, a mop, a pail of hospital-strength disinfectant, a five-gallon can of industrial cleanser, a hammer, a chisel, and a two-handed paint scraper.

Chapter

5

PLAYING WITH YOURSELF IS PLAYING WITH FIRE!

Clint and Babs were returning from their church youth meeting. At her door, Babs turned and shook Clint's hand good-night. It had been a lovely date, and, thinking over the evening as he undressed back home, Clint noticed a strange feeling suddenly coming over him. In bed, Clint was still restless, puzzled by this new, overpowering sensation. Suddenly, as Clint thought of Bab's unusually warm farewell, memories of an impure picture he had once found hidden in a Gideon Bible popped up unexpectedly. As did something else. Drowsily allowing his right hand to stray under the covers, Clint sleepily took the situation in hand and, before he realized what he had done, committed an act of self-pollution. The next morning, while driving to school to be sworn in as Student Council President, Clint was struck and killed by a speeding bus.

Such stories are common in the daily papers. Every day thousands of young men and women pay tragically for a single, thoughtless surrender to temptation. But even more victims of the "solitary sin" go unrecognized, their fates mistakenly diagnosed as "poor study habits," "tennis elbow," or a "slight case of the sniffles." The list is endless. But the untold misery brought by willful masturbation cannot be reckoned by mere statistics. One has only to look at our prisons, mental hospitals, and riot-torn campuses for the real cost.

Chilling, isn't it?

I'm no chump, you are probably saying as you read this, *but how can I, as an up-to-date teen, learn to guard against this treacherous and degrading habit?* First, a sound diet including eight glasses of pure water a day. Second, good health habits, such as brushing your teeth and having a thorough bowel movement after each meal. Third, avoid sweets and between-meal snacks. Regular exercise will also help sap excess energy in a helpful, constructive manner. Some popular sports you may enjoy are bicycling, swimming, skating, curling, basketball, golfing, polo, sledding, badminton, jai alai, quoits, table tennis, and snooker. Hint: if trouble still persists, it may be wise to make it a rule to slip on a pair of baseball gloves, heavy wool socks, or oven mittens before retiring. If these precautions fail, your dad will be happy to help handcuff your hands behind your back before you turn in.

As for you gals, don't get smug. Many young women regularly harm themselves with acts of self-pollution *even while sound asleep,* often dreaming of bizarre degradations involving beatniks, Negros, or worse. Because of this, it is advisable not to tempt the devil. Have your mother "keep on ice" such objects as pencils, candles, bananas, frankfurters, hairbrushes, and softball bats.

Now that I have the scoop on self-abuse, you say, *I'm going to practice these easy safeguards and pass the low-down on to my pals.*

And I can think of three people who will back you up on that: Clint's mother, father, and Babs.

Chapter

6

YOUR FIRST DATE: CALLING HER UP

Calling up a girl for a date for the first time can often mean a bout with those "telephone jitters." How to avoid them? It's easier than you think! Like anything you do, there's a *right* way and a *wrong* way. I'll pause a moment while you let that sink in. The most important thing to remember is *don't beat around the bush.* The forthright, direct approach is the best way to ask for a date, as any girl will tell you. Let's start with the wrong way first: Carl has two tickets to a popular movie approved by his local church group, and he wants to take Norma as his guest. Let's see what happens. . . .

Norma: Hello?
Carl: Hello.
Norma: Hello? Hello? Is somebody there?
Carl: Hello?
Norma: Look, who *is* this? If this is some kind of a joke, my father—
Carl: Uh, Norma, this is Carl from your Civics class, and I was wondering if—
Norma: Carl? I don't think I know any "Carl."
Carl: Well, I'm the one with the thick glasses who sits way back by the windows? Today when I spoke to you in the hall—

Norma: Listen, maybe you have the wrong Bancroft. There's a *Carla* Bancroft in our class. The homely one with those things all over her face?

Carl: Well, actually, that's *me, Carl* Bancroft. Anyway, you were with Moose Pojanski from the football team at the time? I mean, you were talking to him, mostly, but—

Norma: Oh, sure, sure, I remember. Okay, shoot.

Carl: Well, I was wondering, if you weren't doing anything Saturday night, perhaps you'd consider—

Norma: Saturday? Oh, gee, that's tough. That's the night I always wash my hair.

Carl: Uh, well, maybe Sunday? I could exchange—

Norma: And I always dry it on Sunday nights.

Carl: Uh, then how about Mon—

Norma: Then I have to set it. It's a real job, y'know?

Carl: Well, I suppose I could get tickets for Tues—

Norma: *Click.*

Carl: Hello? Norma? Gee, the line went dead.

Needless to say, Carl did not get to date Norma that Saturday. Now let's eavesdrop on a boy who knows how to use those telephone courtesies that spell "date bait," as he invites a girl for a horseback ride. . . .

Norma: Hello?

Moose: 'Lo, Norma? 'S Moose.

Norma: Oh, Christ, for a minute I thought it was Carl again.

Moose: Huh? Whoozat?

Norma: Some flit says he's in one of my classes.

Moose: Oh. How 'bout Saturday? Wanna?

Norma: Sure, but one thing.

Moose: Wha?

Norma: Don't forget the you-know-whats.

Moose: Huh? Oh, yah. Heh heh. Yah.

Norma: Listen, it isn't funny. I thought I missed it last month and I nearly freaked. If you want to go bareback you can call up Carl.

Moose: Huh?

Norma: Some flit says he's in one of my classes.

See how easy it was? Moose knew that old saying about catching more dates with honey than you can with vinegar, and Norma knew the one about an ounce of prevention being worth a trip to Puerto Rico!

Chapter 7

WHAT TO WEAR

Dating is like electricity. Used wisely, it can operate your dad's power tools, fry eggs, and run trolley cars. Used foolishly, it can electrocute every member of your family including your goldfish. Being a teen with taste means, then, that you don't try to "short circuit" your future happiness with provocative clothes that will "overload" your date with the temptation to tamper with your "fuse box."

If you are a girl, steer clear of clinging sweaters, layers of heavy makeup, sheath skirts with revealing kick pleats, and Capri pants so tight that the boys can read the date of a dime in your back pocket. Gals in the know favor the casual good looks of cardigan sweaters, simple pleated calf-length skirts bolstered by layers and layers of crisp and crinkly crinoline. And please, ladies, *sensible* shoes! There are now on the market several brands of attractive pumps made of sturdy materials that spell fashion flair both on the dance floor and along those invigorating woodland trails. Since you are still growing, try to have a little pity on Dad's wallet and buy them at least two and a half sizes bigger to give your poor toes plenty of wiggle room! But avoid patent leather. Nothing is a surer invitation to disaster than shiny shoe-tops are to a sharp-eyed, peeping Tom with a rudimentary knowledge of light refraction.

Proper foundation garments will help give your dating wardrobe that added "plus." Ruggedly made brassieres (preferably with a time lock), garter belts, hosiery, and dress shields give a girl added confidence on a date and help correct poor posture. Hint: if you are going on an unchaperoned date, an additional girdle or two can be a welcome "something extra" when the full moon rises and that "all-American" suddenly becomes "all hands"!

Boys, too, know that a neat and clean appearance goes a long way toward winning the respect and admiration of his date. Tight chinos, pointed shoes, and elaborate pompadours (perhaps hiding the "point" underneath!) impress no one. You can't tell a book by its cover, but if a candy wrapper says "nuts" on the outside, you can be sure there's one on the inside. Boys are also cautioned to especially avoid tight dungarees that can cut circulation to vital parts of the body. Last year alone, a respected clothing physician reports over fifteen thousand men suffered the loss of their genital organs, either by chronic shriveling or simple "drop-off." Don't let this happen to you.

Crew cuts, "butches," and flattops with well-trimmed sideburns are the rage with gals everywhere, boys, and few ladies can resist the buckle and swash that a pair of Hush Puppies or saddle shoes can bring to a fellow's feet. For more formal occasions, Dad may let you borrow a pair of his he-man and hefty brogues with those cunning little perforations topping off the toes in decorative patterns and swirls. And while we're at it, let's not overlook your underthings. Loose, comfortable boxer shorts are the best bet, but if your date will include some strenuous exercise, ask your mother to take you to the shopping center or sporting-goods store in your neighborhood the next time she goes and fits you out with a reliable brand of athletic supporter. Unless you're Frank Sinatra, it doesn't pay to be a "swinger!"

Chapter

8

MEETING YOUR FOLKS

Dating a boy is like being taken out on a trial spin. If he's a careful driver, the trip can be a fine jaunt. If he's a careless motorist, you may find yourself back at your door with four flats and a shot suspension. This is why your parents take an interest in who you date. Your mom and dad have made a considerable investment in you and may have spent $10,000–$15,000 on you for food, clothing, partial rent, medical bills, education, and insurance alone, not to mention mad money and court fees. You owe it to your parents to let them take an interest in who may be handling their investment in their absence, and introducing your dates to them is a good way to begin. It is a delicate undertaking, for it is time for that giggle on the telephone to become a flesh-and-blood person, but simple politeness is the only "must." It is simply a matter of "getting to know you," as this example shows. . . .

The doorbell rings. Sue answers the door and greets Ben, her date for the evening.
    Ben: Good evening, Sue.
    Sue: Good evening, Ben. Won't you come in and let me introduce you to my mother and father?
    Ben: Of course, Sue.
    Sue: Mother, I'd like you to meet Ben. Ben, this is my mother.
    Ben: How do you do, Mrs. Waspwell. It is a pleasure to meet you.
    Mother: How do you do, Ben. It's a pleasure to meet you.
    Sue: Ben, this is my father. Father, I'd like you to meet Ben.
    Ben: How do you do Mr. Waspwell. It is a pleasure to meet you.
    Father: How do you do, Ben. It is a pleasure to meet you. By the way, Ben, isn't your father the president of the country club?

Ben: Oh no, sir. My father is Jewish.
Father: Good night, Ben.
Ben: Good night, Mr. Waspwell.
Mother: Good night, Ben.
Ben: Good night, Mrs. Waspwell.
Sue: Good night, Ben.
Ben: Good night, Sue.

See how easy that was?

Chapter

9

HAVE MORALS, WILL DATE

Now that your parents have met your date, it's time to go! But where? To an all-night beach blast? An unchaperoned pajama party? Perhaps to a double-clutch twist contest, a form of "dancing" that the late Igor Stravinsky once described as "simply petting set to music"?

Of course not.

I am reminded of the story of a boy who was looking at a list of "don'ts" posted on the swimming-pool bulletin board.

Think they forgot anything? asked a sympathetic buddy. *Yeah,* answered the boy, *"don't breathe!"*

Things aren't as grim as all that. There are many healthful and wholesome activities in which young daters may participate *and* keep their moral decency intact. Most communities have young-people's centers, and many church groups organize frequent hayrides, craft fairs, and special exhibits. But if your community lacks these, there are still 1,001 things to do that can give any guy or gal that special "lift."

Looking for something to do on a date? Take a gander at these activities available to young "thrill-seekers": folk dancing, travelogues, displays, youth rallies, guided tours of local industry, collecting pop bottles for worthy charities, sight-seeing hardware stores, reading to blind children, learning how to use a road map, unusual fêtes, playing Sorry, discovering points of interest, laying linoleum, building and operating your own weather station, identifying wild flowers, rummage sales, pets, repairing appliances, learning new words, washing the family car, remembering things, telling jokes, having shoes stretched, and making fudge.

Sound inviting? Dive right in, the dating's fine!

Chapter

MAKING CONVERSATION

Making "small talk" on a date can be one of the biggest problems for inexperienced daters. Conversation, like tennis, is best when the ball keeps bouncing back and forth. The surest way to keep the ball in play is to find out what you and your date have in common. Perhaps both of you are interested in sports, or you have complementary hobbies, or your fathers both make the same amount of money.

Once you establish something to talk about, you'll be amazed at how the conversation can flow effortlessly from one topic to the next. Ted and Marlene show you how. . . .

Ted: It's a grand night, isn't it?

Marlene: Wonderful, Ted. Did you ever see such a moon?

Ted: Isn't that what they call a "harvest moon"?

Marlene: A "hunter's moon"? Don't do that, Ted.

Ted: Do you hunt? I had an uncle who once was a fine hunter.

Marlene: My aunt once painted a wonderful hunting scene. Stop that, Ted.

Ted: I didn't know you were interested in painting. Do you paint?

Marlene: No, but I enjoy sketching and swimming. Get that hand out of there, Ted.

Ted: Why, I bet you're a terrific swimmer. I know you're tops in skeet shooting.

Marlene: I mean it, Ted! But I'm not as good with a gun as my father.

Ted: Oh, does he skeet shoot, too?

Marlene: No, Ted, he was a marine at Okinawa, and now he's a sergeant on the police force.

Ted: It's a grand night, isn't it?

Marlene: Wonderful, Ted. Did you ever see such a moon?

YOU DON'T HAVE TO PET TO BE POPULAR

To pet or not to pet, that is the question! Many young girls, eager to be "in" with the crowd, think that they have to act free and easy with every lounge lizard and couch commando to show that they are grown up, that they are "cool." I'm reminded of a story that happened to the daughter of an old friend of mine. . . .

Pam, a naïve young girl eager to be "in" with the crowd, accepted a date with Stan, a boy whose reputation as a heavy petter was the talk of the cafeteria. When Stan pulled up in front of her home, Pam noticed that instead of coming in to meet her parents, he just sat in the car tightening his chinos and combing his pompadour while he honked his horn for her to hurry. Against her parents' advice and her own misgivings, Pam raced to Stan's car and drove off, the auto's shot suspension practically ruining the driveway. The evening was pleasant enough at first, but when 9:30 rolled around and it was time to head for home, Stan began to act differently. He began feeding Pam a line, telling her that "everybody petted" and those who didn't were hypocrites, or "prudes." He told her that he was "madly in love with her" and that she was a "slick chick." He talked about famous scientists who recommended petting on the first date, like Freud, Darwin, and Rollo May. Wanting desperately to be in the swim, Pam finally agreed and willingly submitted to an act of heavy petting in the back seat of Stan's automobile. When Pam's parents saw that it was almost 10:30 and Pam had not yet returned, they immediately notified the State Police. An hour later the police found Stan and Pam, but it was too late. Apparently they had been so busy heavy petting that the doomed couple had failed to even notice a speeding bus.

Sound familiar? It should. Official government figures show that an act of heavy petting is committed in the back seat of an automobile somewhere in the United States every fifty seconds, and the Highway Department reports the *exact same incidence* for motor-vehicle fatalities. To pet or not to pet?

The choice is yours.

Chapter

HOW TO SAY "NO"

A girl once told me that when she stepped out for an evening with her sweetheart, her parents always gave her her own bottle of mouthwash so she could "freshen up" after necking with her fiancé. These "parents" obviously had a geranium in the cranium! Any parent who permits a daughter the opportunity to pass out free samples is in danger of having the entire store looted. What such parents are actually saying to the boy is, *Dear necker, if you can't be good, be careful. I know you are here to crack the safe. It won't be necessary. Here's the combination. Take what you want, but please tidy up after.*

Some flirts claim that, to click with the gang, you have to keep in circulation. One has only to look at a book that's been in circulation to see the results: dog-eared around the edges, stained with fingerprints and jelly, a weakened spine and half the insides missing, nasty cracks written along the margins.

Get the message?

A wise girl knows that saying "no" to petting is as important to her reputation as refraining from vaulting fenceposts, riding Western saddle, or engaging in excessive shinnying. "Many are cold," goes the saying, "but few are frozen." A boy in the know quickly realizes that there's more to an iceberg than the one-fifth on the surface that meets the eye and says to himself, *Finding out about the four-fifths of this doll that's below the surface is worth more to me than a thousand French handshakes!*

Of course, it's not always easy separating the sheep from the wolves, and the mildest-mannered boy can turn out to be the most unscrupulous kiss-collector if you let him. Should he try any monkeyshines, there are several workable methods. The commonest is simply to look your date squarely in the eye and, with a sweet but hurt expression, whisper, "Dave, I'm very disappointed in you." If words do not convince, it may be a good idea to carry along a persuader of a more forceful character. Among the most popular are police whistles, tear-gas pens, and blank pistols. Finally, if none of these are available but you do happen to have a cold drink in your hand, turn back to Chapter 3 and study again the effect of quick temperature changes on those ugly pink things.

That's the whole story, daters, and I wish you a grand evening. And don't worry about making mistakes if you studied this book carefully. I guarantee you won't "miss the boat."

But you will miss the bus.

A Mike Seamus Sports Adventure Yarn

THE ROYAL FOUR-FLUSHERS,

OR WHEELCHAIR FURY

by Kevin Curran

The Mike Seamus series of sports-adventure books follows the travels of a private jock on the trail of athlete action across the country. Whether searching for corruption in the seedy, neonized world of boxing promotion (The Don King Inquiry) *or checking out the tawdry blackmail of shy black superstar Hank Aaron* (The Hall of Fame Frame-up), *Seamus does a headfirst slide into danger that gives readers around the world something to stand up and cheer about. Stripped of the Gold Jock of the Federal Bureau of Sports Investigation, Seamus fights a lonely battle for truth in a little game called Life, where the big leagues mean big bucks and honesty is often as hard to find as a library in a locker room. From Russian submarines to rushing leaders of the NFL, the world of Mike Seamus offers no time-out from action.*

"The Handy Kappas Welcome the Handicapped" read one of the banners painted by the friendly girls of a local sorority at the College of Las Vegas. The driver of the limo squeezed by an aging Ford Granada with Oklahoma plates that contained a numb late-forties couple and three screaming kids, and pulled to the front of fabulous Caesars Palace, where Princess Caroline of Monaco and Mike Seamus exited from their air-conditioned oasis into a staggering blast of mid-August desert air. Seamus usually didn't like protection assignments, but the holes in his Nikes and the bills in his desk drawer convinced him that this was one he couldn't turn down. The last case hadn't paid enough to darn a jockstrap, and there was an ex-figure-skating queen who'd buried her blades in him a while back in a contest that had eventually ended up as a loss in the marriage division. She looked in the mailbox for monthly checks the way a guy 3 and 0 at the plate looks for the hard one down the middle. He couldn't afford another charity exhibition at the moment.

Besides acting as official escort for the gum-snapping princess at the Monte

Carlo Circus of the Animals Salute to Handicapped Athletes, Seamus served as unofficial bodyguard. People don't generally figure the throners to have many problems other than what servant to let go for no reason. Sure, you don't have to worry about chipping a dish or making a car payment as much as the rest of the world, but there's more to it than cotillions and killing time. A lot of crazies want a piece of you, and that's enough to send a chill running up and down anyone's scepter.

His close connections to the royal family of Monaco made Seamus a logical choice. Seamus first ran into Princess Grace back in the days when he was tearing up the turf as a fullback for the Beverly Hills Blue Diamonds. She was breaking hearts all over America as Grace Kelly, a touch of cool aristocracy in the mud puddle of morals called Tinseltown, whose bedroom shenanigans made locker-room material look like a spinster's knitting class in the church basement. They'd huddled awhile when Seamus was an extra on the set of *Dial M for Murder,* and had called a few plays together afterward. Grace loved the colorful prancing outsized animals and the sober-minded pedantic audio-animatronic Lincoln during their adventures at Disneyland. "La, how gay," she would pronounce of Orange County's gift to friends 'round the world as she gripped the twin poles of the "Electricity—Nature's Cure-all" display in the arcade, causing her eyes to flutter rapidly and her breath to deepen as the unnatural surge of current coursed through her hands until the point where she suffered a satisfying temporary blackout.

Since then they'd crossed paths a few times on the diamonds-and-tennis circuit, sharing a Campari or two with Bjorn or Vitas or Chris, while her charming husband, dapper Prince Rainier, pulled down his sun visor and snoozed in the sprightly wicker hammock so oddly beloved of the largely inbred (though always well-tailored) royal House of Grimaldi.

Carolina, as well as being favored by her mother's fair looks, inherited her mother's sense of adventure. As a child she was said to delight in carefully forming foot-high whipped-cream bunnies and leaving them all over the house, clapping her hands with glee as a servant stopped and cursed when coming upon a foamy friend on chair or sofa. The dissolution of her marriage to noted international scumball Philippe Junot was said to have hardened something within the girl. It was rumored that she had become fond of filling trunks full of bricks and ordering the servants, "Carry them until you drop." And of regularly booby-trapping the sleeping quarters of the ladies-in-waiting. When Seamus forthrightly asked her about this, he was pleased to learn that, as often as not, these delightfully constructed devices would release a sprig of flowers or a favorite box of chocolates instead of the standard loud screaming siren or tubful of old bathwater. "It depends on my mood," giggled Caroline.

AT THE COCKTAIL PARTY that evening, all the guests arrived in Mercedes wheelchairs, to simulate what life would be like in the numb-leg circuit, and most checked these at the door. It certainly did seem like a bad deal, so when Caroline said, "If I were a cripple, I think I'd puke, or maybe just sit in my room—I mean, gross!" Seamus couldn't disagree.

Caroline was fond of most things that involved a party, a laugh, or a joke, and this was no exception. Funnyman Buddy Hackett thrilled the jaded group by whirling around in circles in his wheelchair, just to stir the ice in his drink. Cher arrived in a gown bedecked with dozens of tiny whistling sponge giraffes, to the delight of some and the chagrin of others. Senator Hayakawa of California curled up by the fireside and delighted onlookers by giving a cheery recitation, move by move, of a game of Battleship he had played with his seven-year-old nephew a while back.

At six three, Seamus could easily see over the fast-drinking crowd to the balding pate of pal Terry Bradshaw, Pittsburgh Steelers quarterback, who looked more uneasy holding a drink and dressed up in a monkey suit than if he'd just found out that his offensive line for the next year was to be composed of miniature Shetland ponies. He found himself cornered, by a society matron with blue tinted hair, against a window where the fading desert sunset could be seen competing against the bursts of thousands of dazzling electric lights for the crowd's attention. Soon the sun would exhaust itself and give the tag to its weak sister, the moon, who didn't belong in the same arena for this type of action.

Seamus had done some work for the Steelers organization a few years ago. Following a 38-to-7 drubbing of the pathetic Bert Jones-less Baltimore Colts, an altercation had broken out between four Steelers and members of a marching band from Allegheny State. The frisky Steelers, in the words of the deposition,

> (a) committed assault against several members of the tuba, trombone, and other brass-section players by removing their chin straps and forcing their funny furry hats over their eyes, proceding to label them "shitheads" and "marching fucks," then spinning them around indiscriminately so that they would weave and crash into one another, and
> (b) did shame and humiliate several columns of pom-pom girls, who never asked to be born into this world in the first place, through wholesale pawing of perky breast and buttock.

The case had never come to court. The judge, a Steelers ticketholder himself, realized that society had been done no serious harm, when Seamus came to him with several incriminating taped conversations between His Honor and his twenty-one-year-old mistress, a girl of good family attending a local stewardess institute. It didn't leave you with a great feeling inside, but that's pro biz, and if you wanted to play in the big leagues, you had to know the score from yard one. Or else you might as well get off the field and hoof it up to Section 57, with the pretzel and popcorn crowd, trading in a duffel bag full of sweats for a briefcase full of boredom. Seamus had seen too many people he knew go that route, track star to tract house, and they'd started hitting the liniment bottle quicker than Sugar Ray Leonard would jab the head of a yahoo in a barroom who'd made light of the champ's mother.

The matron declared, "It must be divine to pitch for football," as Seamus sidled over and accidentally overturned a drink on her head, to rescue his friend. Her eyes bored into him like a mad coyote's at night, making Seamus shrug and flick a sizable ash in her hair.

There was something odd about the sleek blond model that Jerry Lewis was chatting up. The Nutty Partygoer seemed to like her looks and tried to amuse by clapping his hands together in the manner of the tiny toy ape with cymbals on its paws. She gave him a look you'd give a fish that'd jumped out of the aquarium and flopped onto your bed, looking for some action.

Mean Joe Greene swaggered into the room and spilled Paul Anka's drink by looking near it. Anything short of a Soviet tank squad had better not mess with him, and even they should lay off the liquid potato poison for a while before giving it their shot.

You won't read about it in *People,* but rumor had it a few seasons ago that Greene and Princess Caroline were something of an item for a few days while she "did" Pittsburgh for some charity bowl. The star-sniffers said that more was talked about than the X's and O's of the Steelers playbook.

Looking at them across the room, Seamus could tell at once that the rumors were unfounded. It was obvious the big lug had been infected with a heavy crush for the young girl. They seemed to have as much to talk about as a parrot and a porcupine would, but after a few bottles of champagne, Mean Joe tried to curry the abashed princess's favor by setting up in his stance to demonstrate the moves that had made him a frequent drop-in guest at quarterbacks' rib cages across the league. Lunging wildly, he accidentally upended Paul Williams and deposited him headfirst into a bowl of seething onion dip. When fished out of the chivey substance, the pint-size composer vowed revenge, until he caught a glimpse of the hangdog look on Joe's face. Joe looked as embarrassed as a congressman caught sexing his secretary on the Capitol steps. Seamus and Caroline exchanged glances and agreed that inviting Joe to view the circus from the royal box could be the only solution. Mean Joe picked up as though given a strawberry Dexedrine milk-shake treat.

THE TORCHLIGHT PARADE of the wheelchair athletes opened the night's festivities on Caesars's main stage, in a large and lavish twenty-one-gun salute to the glory that was pseudo-Romanesque architecture. For the ceremonies, the spare-no-expense management had added a special motif—statues of Rodin's *The Thinker,* with the marble do-nothing now seated in a rock wheelchair. Venus de Milo sported a pair of crutches to give her support, while Eros affected a dandy back brace to insure that his aim of his arrows of love was true.

Seamus and Caroline discussed the dignified atmosphere of the casino at Monte Carlo versus the frothy vulgarity of Las Vegas.

"I've never been there," stammered Joe Greene, sending the conversation down in flames quicker than an F-14 could devastate a young child's kite. "Heavy trip," whispered Caroline to Seamus, her young breath hot in his ear.

Colorful jackanapes eagerly cavorted about, and tumblers of the highest order displayed their brazen skills, while harlequins bedazzled, and silk-coated roustabouts lit the fireworks and smashed plates on their heads. After the stock-bear racing and dwarf execution came a special handicapped acrobatic team. After a tumble they had to be placed back in their wheelchairs, and the human pyramid was only a man high, but they gave it their all and were rewarded with a tremendous chorus of lukewarm applause. The trapeze artist who ventured out next in his peculiar metal encasement should have been grateful for the net below; if only it had been a little stronger.

The European clown Flan, all the rage in Brussels, followed with a routine so pathetic that, if not for the interjection of some third-rate miming toward the end, it could not have sustained even the most diehard advocate in maintaining that Europeans have any sense of humor. As it was, the large-footed clumsy albino of low moral character received a standing ovation after his closing number of "Woman and Small Girl Search for Grapefruit in a Market Near the Seine."

Seamus momentarily left the box to purchase the candied apples and wacky T-shirts for which Caroline had caught a fancy. A man of striking oddness of expression and gait approached him and informed Seamus that he, the man, was to deliver him a message.

"Who is the message from?" Seamus asked with a ready ear and a cocked fist. "Mister Chloroform," came the response, as a man from behind carrying the sleepy chemical in a handkerchief sent Seamus's world spinning.

Up in the royal box, Mean Joe stared ahead at the acrobats, trying to think of what to say to get back in Caroline's good graces. The same evil substance soon rendered any further thought impossible.

Several pairs of hands placed an unconscious Caroline into an awaiting wheelchair and led her out of the building and into a van parked in the Handicapped Only section. To the casual onlooker it appeared that the young lass had succumbed to nothing more than food, drink, and circus fun.

SOME RICH AND DEMENTED TEXAN had hired a crew to drill for oil in his skull, thought Mike Seamus, experiencing the unique pleasures of a chloroform hangover. The circus had left town and the lights were off in the royal box, so Seamus had a hard time making out the form of Mean Joe, shivering and moaning in his seat. There was a note by his side that Seamus read.

Mike Seamus:
   We, the Handicapped Liberation Council, have liberated Princess Caroline as a gesture of solidarity with Third World handicapped athletes everywhere who were not invited to this warmongering circus and wouldn't have come if they were. We demand $5 million for her release so that the people's movement for panracial desexualized liberationist handicapped athletics may continue against the dreary . . .

Seamus crumpled up the letter and let out a groan. The Handicapped Liberation Council was a Marxist splinter group composed mainly of cripples and misfits who thought the world had given them a bad break and should stop its orbit, find some knees, and go down on them to beg forgiveness. It sported a few noncrippled activists who were for the most part required to go around in wheelchairs as a symbol for the equality of all. They were considered quite dangerous now that the new leadership had abandoned their exercise program of nonviolence following the death of their chief after he had chained himself to the lead car during a pit stop at the Monte Carlo Grand Prix. Officials refused to cave in to pressure tactics and the race had continued, when misfortune soon struck the chained crazy.

When Mean Joe Greene found out what was happening, you could have peeled him off the floor, wet him, and stuck him on an envelope, so great was his desolation. Seamus led him out of the casino and into the dazzling Vegas night. Ol' Grace sure wouldn't like this turn of events.

Thinking only once or twice about leaving the country, Seamus pondered his next move. Driving distractedly through dim streets, he did not notice the blond in the wheelchair crossing the intersection until it was too late. Metal struck metal, and a broken little wheel teetered and veered off toward the curb.

Gazing down at the twisted wreckage, Seamus received an emotional punch to the kidneys. This was the blond dish who had spurned the antic charms of Jerry Lewis the night before. Pulling off her blond wig, he recognized her as Martine, a Soviet gymnasium operative he'd last tangled with in the Doctor J. and Doctor Doom affair.

He would have wagered a diamond the size of a soccer ball that she was involved with the abduction of Caroline. Standing over her, he could see that her condition was critical. Seamus whispered gently into her dewy blue eyes that if she didn't talk right away, the largest black guy she ever saw would want to know why.

THE BAR WAS CALLED The Golden Rooster and its location off the Strip in downtown Las Vegas made it a prime location for every loser in the book to call it home for an evening. For the price of a chili dog or two and a few beers, scruff who descended in their dirty beat-up Dodge vans might be able to walk away with one of the sun-drenched cow-eyed honeys who showed up because they had always gone there before. A greasy taco stuffer named Miguel offered cocaine cut with Maalox and Triple-X flour in small packets of generic tinfoil for one hundred a gram, about two-thirds of the average weekly salary for the crowd tonight. A sad-eyed black wearing purple-tinted heart-shaped glasses like the ones George Harrison wore in 1967 sat nursing a shot of house tequila and a Coca-Cola chaser, as lonesome C & W songs drew a small crowd at the jukebox over by one of the two pool tables.

The wheelchair set made their entrance around eleven and rolled into a room at the back of the bar. They were debating a plan for world conquest based on the secret introduction of a parasite into America's wheat that would break down the spinal material of a nation and force all to walk on all fours, leaving them masters of the race. It was voted down when no one knew how to find a parasite like that.

Seamus and Mean Joe Greene studied the layout and decided on a direct attack. They spun the nasty Marxists 'round in circles while calling them every bad name in the book, until they admitted that Princess Caroline could be found inside the liquor locker. She was sitting on a stack of cases, sipping a Budweiser tallboy. "I don't know if I like the taste of beer," she said. "It's kind of icky."

Hearing the familiar crunch of high heels on ice cubes, Seamus turned and found himself at the barrel end of a gold-plated Smith & Wesson. At its opposite end stood Princess Grace, looking regal in a coat of blue fox.

"That's right, Seamus, it's your old pal," she sneered, her eyes narrowing with contempt. "Stand clear, 'cause I'm bumping off that brat while I've still got a chance." She ripped open her daughter's blouse, exposing the curve of her left breast. "Pretty nice, huh? A tempting treat for eye or tongue? Well, maybe she can steal Philippe away, like some circus tramp, but she's not going to get any more of my guys, with a bullet in the belly . . ."

Mike Seamus realized with a start that the woman he had secretly carried a torch for these many years was a seriously brain-damaged individual. Perhaps all that electricity hadn't been the best thing . . .

Mean Joe Greene moved quickly and blocked the hurtling bullet in a flash. Seamus kicked the gun out of the former movie queen's hand without realizing that his friend had rushed his last pass, that the game clock was close to its final tick.

Gasping for air, Greene struggled desperately to remember the French expressions he had been memorizing to inform Caroline of his feelings in her native language. "Moi, je voudrais des pommes soufflées. Est-ce que cela ira avec le canard?"

Caroline pursed her lips thoughtfully at Greene's words. "He said he'd like some souffléed potatoes and would that go all right with the duck. What a bunch of nutbars around here. Let's drop Mom off at the clink and go to the disco."

Mike Seamus considered the words carefully. It sounded like a good idea to him.

Books in the Mike Seamus Mystery Series

DANGER IN THE DUGOUT
THE TERROR IN THE BOSTON GARDEN
DOCTOR J. AND DOCTOR DOOM
THE INCREDIBLE SHRINKING CHUCK WEPNER
I, THE UMPIRE
THE BIG SLOOP
THE DON KING INQUIRY
PITCHOUT AT HANGING ROCK
THE THING BENEATH THE SPECTRUM
THE OTHER SIDE OF THE WHEELCHAIR
THE SOLID GOLD JUMP SHOT
THE BLAZING BLUE SPITBALL

HOW TO WRITE DIRTY

by Justice Thurgood Marshall

by Michael Reiss and Al Jean

ONE OF THE MOST time-consuming tasks a Supreme Court justice performs is reading through mounds of pornographic material, to determine if it is protected by the First Amendment right to freedom of speech. The Court has ruled that such material is protected only if it possesses "redeeming social value."

What is "redeeming social value"? To me, it is something that puts "lead" in your "pencil." Pops a "bone of contention" in your "legal briefs." In other words, something that makes your pecker stand up and say the Pledge of Allegiance.

Of course, it takes some hot and steamy writing to get a rise out of a few of those old droopy drawers on the Supreme Court. But don't despair; just follow my simple Marshall Plan for How to Write Dirty. Soon, you'll be able to crank out pornography that a judge will want to review in his chambers time and again. That judge is me.

KEEP THE READER IN MIND

How would you like to read a book entitled *A Man Called Homo* or *My Girl Friend Flicka?* Well, I've read them, and they're terrible. Seems too many pornographers these days write stories that appeal only to homos, horses, or other degenerates. They have forgotten that the typical reader of dirty books is a normal, heterosexual, black, elderly Supreme Court justice.

To write dirty well, pick topics your audience will be interested in, like fellatio, blow jobs, and white women. Especially white women. They're my favorite. Oh, yeah.

WRITE WHAT YOU KNOW

A man once wrote a book entitled *I Was a Hooker on the Moon.* It did not have the ring of authenticity, and sold few copies. "You should write about what you know," I advised this aspiring author, who just happened to be Justice Felix Frankfurter. His next book, *Suck My Wiener,* was on Thurgood Marshall's Best-seller List for a full five months.

So write about subjects you are familiar with. If you are a mailman, write sexy stories about delivering the mail. If you are a homo, write stories about what your straight friends do. If you are a white woman, write to me. Here is my address: Thurgood Marshall, Supreme Court Building, Washington, D.C.

To illustrate the principle of writing what you know, I have composed the following example. It is based on a true incident—only the names have been changed slightly:

Handsome Thurgood X. was sitting in his chambers one day, reading *A Man Called Homo.* Suddenly, he was interrupted by Sandra Day O., a distinguished white woman. "You certainly look foxy in your big, black robes," Sandra purred. "I've got something even bigger and blacker underneath," replied Thurgood.

Thurgood had always had a way with women—you could say he was a sort of Afro-disiac. Soon the two were lying on the bench, Thurgood preparing to enter Sandra's private chambers. "Here *come* da judge," he shouted, as his groin gavel banged away. Finally, they finished, furiously collapsing in the sweat of their ecstasy. "That was sure good, Thurgood," Sandra cooed.

"Oh, yeah," he replied.

DON'T BE AFRAID TO EXAGGERATE

In my 200 years on the bench, I have handed down judgments so brilliant that the Statue of Justice once came to life, ran off her pedestal, and gave me a big wet kiss on the lips.

Of course, most of this story is not true, but is actually a subtle use of the principle of exaggeration. Clever exaggeration can prove quite useful in pornographic stories, as well. It can turn a dull novel like *Moby-Dick* into the porn classic *Moby Huge Dick.* Observe how exaggerating the truth makes the following story a million times more interesting:

Thurgood was sitting in the New York State Bar and Grill, finishing his twentieth bottle of champagne. He had just returned from Washington, flushed with his victory in the case *Brown* v. *Ten Boards of Education.* Suddenly, a beautiful woman, with bosoms the size of watermelons, walked into the bar.

"Don't be impartial, Mr. Marshall," she implored. "Take me, take me now." In half a second, they were both naked. "I had no idea they'd painted the Empire State Building black," she gasped. "That's not the Empire State Building," Thurgood replied, "that's my fifty-two inches of manhood." With one motion, Thurgood thrust his entire Shaft into her awaiting body. Three hundred orgasms later, they finished.

"That was great," she purred. "Just wait'll I send my ninety-three teenage sisters to see you." All in all, it was a typical day.

EDIT YOURSELF

There's an old joke that runs something like this: "A sexually inexperienced couple are on their honeymoon. Not sure what to do, the husband asks his wife for advice. 'Stick it in,' she commands. 'Now pull it out. Stick it in. Pull it out.' " I forget the punch line to this anecdote, but it hardly matters—we've already heard the good part.

Similarly, careful editing can improve your writing. Who wants to read a boring law book when the Cliffs Notes will do just as well? In the following example, a fine pornographic story is made even better by carefully editing out the less essential passages:

Handsome Thurgood X. was sitting in his chambers one day, reading *A Man Called Homo*. Suddenly, he was interrupted by Sandra Day O., a distinguished white woman. "You certainly look foxy in your big, black robes," Sandra purred. "I've got something even bigger and blacker underneath," replied Thurgood.

Thurgood had always had a way with women—you could say he was a sort of Afro-disiac . . .

HUMOR YOUR AUDIENCE

One day, I mistakenly broke into Lyndon Johnson's bedroom while Lady Bird was preparing to give him a blow job. To mask my embarrassment, I made a couple of ribald jests. First I turned to Lady Bird and quipped, "I guess you put the BJ in LBJ." Then I pointed to the president's groin, and added, "Boy, you sure got a big Johnson, Lyndon." LBJ was so amused by these remarks, and so eager to get me out of the room, that he appointed me to the Supreme Court.

Just as a few great jokes helped my judicial career, so can they help you with your dirty-writing career. Check out this example:

The justices and I were sitting in closed session, deliberating. Suddenly, who should walk in but Justice Byron White's wife, Lucy. "You sure make me juicy, Ms. Lucy," I quipped. "I love Lucy," I added, elbowing Byron in the ribs.

I was on a roll now, so I turned to Justice Harry Blackmun and hollered,

"I'm the real hairy black man around these parts." This prompted Chief Justice Burger to call for order. In response, I whipped open my robe (I had nothing on underneath) and said, "Hey, Chief Justice Cheeseburger, did you order this big black whopper?"

All the justices excused themselves and returned to their chambers, unable to match my brilliant repartee. I was alone in the room, except for Lucy, whose arm I had a firm grip on. "Baby, you sure got big torts," I joked, "and there ain't nothing I like better than White's woman." Then I screwed her eighty-seven times.

THE DEFENSE RESTS

Well, I hope you liked my helpful tips on how to write dirty. So, if you follow my rules, the next time you pop up in court on an obscenity charge, maybe something on me will pop up too. Oh, yeah.

Thurgood Marshall

GIDGET?

by Dan Abelson

Whozzat? well I'll be fucked the big kahoona is home terrific listen before you start whining about what a rough day you had mr super cool executive who can't get it up except for every other leap year let me tell you I haven't been what you'd call surfing at la joya all day either eleven o'clock in the morning it's quiet time right I finished my nails took a shit and was just wiping off my nair and thought I'd have a little toot on the old flask hey that's real cool why don't you hang your goddamn pants on a goddamn hanger for a goddamn change will you sloppy little lunch box a little consideration huh for the other people who live here I'm not the goddamn maid you know anyway I just settled back into bed with a double screwdriver to watch the diamond head game since that's the closest I'll ever get to hawaii as long as I'm hooked up with a cheap bastard like you when the friggin' dishwasher quits on me holy toledo I say I'll be fucked if I'm going to wash all those glasses by hand so I call up the little molihine at whirlpool and he comes over and says he doesn't have time to fix it so what am I gonna do huh so I throw him a fuck and he fixes the goddamn thing everything is swell what I can't hear you in there you want me to get you some toilet paper whassa matter your ass glued to the seat so anyway there I am catching some bennies out by the pool when this hot dog comes to clean out the filter so I'm just trying to be friendly and offer him a drink and wouldn't you know it my groovy new two piece just falls off and this hairy surfer thinks I want him to hang his whole ten inches straight up me so I gotta go down on him to get the goddamn pool together I mean I ask you how does that stack up against your crummy memos and your cootie bug board meetings hey flush the goddamn toilet and close the goddamn door do you think I like looking at your hairy ass shooting me a moon a little consideration huh where was I oh yeah the goddamn doorbell rings and some little jungle bunny selling mints or some goddamn thing and I know I better put out for him because even the young ones get crazy around white broads so I figure what the hell this wave can take one more surfer and I know you'll never find out who's been in there today cause you never get close enough cause you had such a hard day at the fuckin office get your own goddamn dinner better still let's go out for burgers and shakes you never take me out anymore jesus christ you're so uncool.

Senator

EDWARD KENNEDY

WASHINGTON REPORT CARD

Volume III, No. 73   Boston, Mass.   212-688-4070

Dear Constituents:

I wish first to thank all of you for your sympathy and support during my recent period of sorrow. I wish also to explain to you as best I can the reasons for my behavior during that trying period.

As many of you are probably aware from the lurid newspaper coverage in the *Global Village Voice,* I suffered an emotional breakdown after the Supersolar Transport I was piloting crashed, killing the 347 young women aboard for the "maiden" flight.

The doctors tell me that by donning women's clothing and diving repeatedly into the White House swimming pool, I was attempting to exorcise the terrible memories of this tragedy. I have no recollection of behaving this way at Jack's party, but my doctors tell me that is not uncommon.

Many of you will remember my emotional health took a similar turn after the tragic *Apollo* accident, in which my female coastronaut was drowned during splash down. Shortly after that disaster, you will remember, I was photographed rolling about in the Coin-o-mat drier, clad only in a chiffon slip, begging myself not to abandon me in the pitching, yawing capsule.

I have found the human mind to be a fragile thing, but I know the spirit to be rugged and enduring. It will leap any obstacle, float above any tragedy, bob over any disaster, surface over any holocaust, in order to reach its destiny.

Tragedy, said a great speech writer, hardens a man, tempers his spirit for great duties and great responsibilities. I have known tragedy; one day I will know heavy responsibility. When the torch is passed to me, I shall not be found wanting.

Sincerely yours,

Ted Kennedy

Senator Edward Kennedy
"It's Logical"

AIDING ACCIDENT WITNESSES

In July, the House Criminal Justice Subcommittee held hearings on my bill designed to protect witnesses to automobile accidents from irrelevant questioning about sudden improvements in their occupations and incomes. The National Organization of Careless Drivers supported my bill, which should protect many witnesses by preventing horrible inquisitions into their private lives.

CONGRESS SCRATCHES BILLS

Two bills I introduced failed to get Congressional approval this term. The first was designed to eliminate needless highway carnage by (1) making passenger training school mandatory for passengers who have been in more than one accident; (2) making it illegal to carry an open liquor bottle in your hand while driving, but ensuring it remains legal if sort of pushed under the seat a bit; and (3) introducing the no-fault criminal negligence law. This would free the courts from the huge glut of criminal negligence cases.

The second bill sought approval of appropriations of some $3 million, which would enable me to lead the first two-thousand-member all-female balloon expedition to the South Pole.

Prospects

The prospects for the passage of both these bills are good. My brother, President John F. Kennedy, has promised me he might support one or both of these bills if I am good over Christmas, and I certainly intend to try.

TORCHLIGHT MARCH

Recently I organized and led a torchlight march in support of my bill to integrate families. My supporters and I met with some resistance as we attempted to exchange the first white child for a black child in what had previously been a quiet Boston neighborhood. Police tell me that apparently, some of the residents of the former subdivision must have been storing explosives and/or heavy mortars, to judge from what could be found of the neighborhood later.

Rest assured that the struggle will go on until we have conquered prejudice, the illegitimate child of ignorance.

OPINION POLL

This opinion poll has been carefully designed by me to let me know how you feel about various issues, which will help in the discharge of my duties. Please jot down your emotions and let me know where you stand.

Dear Senator Kennedy:

1. **I believe it is high time for a women's balloon expedition to Antarctica:**
   a. Yes.
   b. By all means.
   c. Certainly.
   d. If the taxpayers pay for it.

2. **The future president of the United States should be:**
   a. An inexperienced Negro.
   b. Republican without Congressional backing.
   c. A Commie lesbian or something.
   d. Experienced Democratic senator with family backing.

3. **Our world should be made better by:**
   a. Encouraging racial strife.
   b. Promoting mindless prejudice.
   c. Adhering to outdated principles.
   d. Integrating families.

4. **A president should be permitted to stand for more than five terms of office:**
   a. No, because it's too dangerous.
   b. No, because it's morally wrong.
   c. No, because younger people should be given an opportunity.
   d. No, because they'll go senile.

National Lampoon's Annual College

FOOTBALL PREVIEW:

THE TOP TEN TEAMS FOR 1975

by Gerald Sussman

That autumn madness will soon be upon us—that strange, irresistible force that takes hold of us every Saturday afternoon and makes us sit on a cold, hard bench, packed tightly among thousands of other madmen, screaming until our voices are mere croaks, dying a thousand deaths for those twenty-two warriors in colorful attire who are committing organized murder and mayhem upon each other in the name of healthy competition, teamwork, and fair play. That strange madness is, of course, the king of college sports, football.

And in the madness of college football, nothing creates so much controversy, outrage, and sheer excitement as the battle of the gridiron giants to be rated Number One team in the country. This year, the mighty football powers have pulled out all stops in their efforts to capture the coveted national championship. After much pressure and cajoling, they have persuaded most of the conferences to ease up on the necessary admission requirements and recruiting rules. The result will be a season of even greater competition, bigger thrills, and more colossal achievements. For the fan and the players alike, 1975 promises to add a new dimension to the game.

Risking a lot of flak from zealous supporters of at least twenty other deserving teams, the National Lampoon *has gone out on a limb and has rated the top ten teams for 1975. Here they are.*

1. OHIO STATE

In a variation of the old joke about Adolf Hitler, Woody Hayes was sounding the same punchline over and over. "I'm tired of being Mr. Nice Guy," said Woody. "If we don't finish Number One, I'm just going to shoot one out of every five players picked at random."

Woody wasn't kidding. As head of the legendary Ohio State Machine, that conglomeration of players, coaches, and alumni recruiting organization, Woody Hayes is as totally committed to Ohio State football supremacy as a kamikaze pilot is to the smokestack of an enemy battleship.

And the only possible way Ohio State can stumble on its way to becoming Number One is a team plane crash—that's how loaded they are with talent. Despite the fact that twenty-two starters have graduated, no one will be missed. Example: As great a runner as Archie Griffin was, he is now merely third-string *center*. Where are the new superstuds coming from? Hayes manages a tight smile and points eastward to millionaire alumnus John Galbreath's Darby Dan Farm, where a new breed of football player has been developed, mixing the best qualities of humans with thoroughbred horses. The first crop is ready, and in spring practice, they've already torn up the returnees like Attila the Hun going through a bucket of Colonel Sanders' chicken.

Among the many outstanding prospects are seven-foot, nine-inch Clarence "Mandingo" Jones, a 675-pound halfback who runs the forty in 2.6, and eight-foot, 520-pound Rudy Brunchevich, a high-stepping fullback with a punishing kick. Hayes intends to keep his offense simple ("just hand off to Jones or Brunchevich and get the hell out of their way"). He does not expect to do any passing or punting this year. The Darby Dan boys know how to do two things: how to run and how to prevent others from running. And that's mainly how the game is played.

2. OKLAHOMA

As if the Sooners weren't formidable enough, the new easing of Southwest Conference rules should make them thoroughly impossible for most opponents. The new rules state that each team can use two cars as well as their regular players, as long as "said cars are pre-World War II in age and are rigged to be self-powered."

Likable Barry Switzer, now in his third year as coach at OU, hired the best jalopy mechanics in the country to fix up a full fleet of Fords, Chevies, and LaSalles (LaSalles make the best middle linebackers). Switzer's new "Two-Car Offense" will start Glen Ray Owens, a fast, shifty '34 Chevy, at tailback, and T. J. Walker, a solid '41 Ford sedan, at blocking back.

The rest of the Sooner offense still packs a wallop, with returnees like Bubba "BB-Gun" Watkins and A. C. Proudfoot, an All-American center who looks exactly like an Allis Chalmers tractor. When asked about this, Switzer moaned in exasperation and cried, "Don't ask me—I'm no farmer, I'm a football coach."

The defensive line is just dandy, thank you, anchored by Elbert St. Clair and Bruce Yancey, a pair of ten-by-ten-foot watermelons, reputed to be the biggest in the state. As for the defensive backfield, Switzer feels that "you still can't beat a regular nigger. Give me a big, fast one with long legs, a small, high ass, and absolutely no fear, and I'll make him into a cornerback."

3. NOTRE DAME

To hear coach Dan Devine wail, you'd think Notre Dame should be playing such schools as St. Swithins and Fagley Prep this year. No doubt about it, graduation losses were heavy—sixteen out of twenty-two starters. But ND has always been known for how quickly its replacements fill in and actually surpass their predecessors. And this year is no exception.

The Monsignors at the Golden Dome have sprung some of that fabled RC gold to recruit gorillas Mike Nazurko and Paul Collins from Tanzania, and rhinos Steve Norcross and Jim Selwyn from Kenya. Nazurko has been installed at tight end, and has yet to miss a pass. He will soon be catching footballs instead of coconuts and promises to be just as adept ("as long as he doesn't eat the darn things," said Devine). Collins is a bone-crushing fullback built along the lines of Jim Brown, only two feet taller and 300 pounds heavier. Rhinos Norcross and Selwyn were the sensations of spring practice as line-backers, making 145 unassisted tackles apiece in one game.

As most insiders know, Notre Dame has always been famous for signing up old pros from the NFL who have played out their careers but still have enough for another few years of college ball. A little plastic surgery and a name change usually gets them back on the roster. Devine's major problem will be how well Nazurko, Collins, Norcross, Selwyn, and possibly the new hippo, Bill Meyers, will fit in with the rest of the Fighting Irish contingent, which features such old veterans as George Andrie and Bob Lilly, formerly of the Dallas Cowboys, Ben Davidson of the Oakland Raiders, and many others. With Devine's four scrimmage-a-day schedule, our guess is that rookies and veterans will mesh together perfectly.

4. ALABAMA

They don't call him Bear Bryant for nothing. And this year, the Crimson Tide not only boasts its usual six-deep in every position, but a few new additions that could make them virtually unbeatable. We refer to the two gigantic grizzly bears recruited by Bryant and his staff while on a trip to Yellowstone National Park. "Next best thing to a white one," said Bryant about his two black beauties. Of course, the white ones, the incredibly fierce polar bears, are just about untamable. But somehow we suspect that old Bear will even get a few white ones before he retires.

Meanwhile, Alabama will have to make do with Charley Duboise, an eight-foot, 700-pounder who will be installed at defensive tackle, and young Wayne Taylor, a stocky seven-foot, 660-pounder who will play defensive end. "Bears are great prospects," said Bryant. "They got short legs and a low center of gravity, which makes them very hard to move out when they play defense."

The park allows only two bears per team for each season, and Duboise and Bryant were pretty tough to sign up. But it was their mothers who had to be convinced, not the players. It took Bryant six weeks to woo them, with sweet talk about how their sons would have unlimited honey, woodchuck, deer, a completely furnished cave, even plenty of eager young coeds who like big, hairy jock types.

Bryant was given a guarantee that the Yellowstone bears do not hibernate in the winter. Even if they do, there's still little to worry about. The new Southeastern Conference rules permit all sorts of smaller animals as well. And if we know Bear, he's got a few oversize rabbits in the lining of his bright crimson 'bama blazer he's not talking about just yet.

5. USC

Ever since Clara Bow took on the entire Trojan football team (and doubtless they were not using Trojans at the time) in that legendary gang bang, USC has lured some of the finest young talent in the country to its campus with promises of similar if not better sexual partners. They still call the place Southern California, and Southern California still has the best looking girls in the country, especially movie stars, starlets, bit players, and "models." "You take a six-foot, nine-inch black country boy from North Carolina and dangle a picture of Sally Struthers in front of him, and he's sold on us," said John McKay. "Sure, his mom and dad want to know all about our educational facilities, but the kid is holding his shirttail to his mouth to stop the drooling. The difference between us and UCLA and Stanford is that we deliver. When we say you'll get Sally Struthers or Pam Grier or Candice Bergen, we mean it. The blacks go for the blond white girls and the whites go for the Pam Grier types. I've never seen it fail."

USC still relies mostly on humans—big black studs, Rhodes scholar quarterbacks with rifle arms, tall, rangy, glue-fingered ends—the usual array of football talent. McKay is also fooling around with some players in the deer family and a few Porsche 911 Carreras, to see if they can fit into his I-formation. New league rules permit one sports car per team, if driven by someone sixty-five or over, and animals weighing less than 300 pounds. McKay has always been a proponent of speed and agility over raw brutish power, but he has high hopes for the Porsche as a blocking back, and a gazelle named Jeff Woodley at halfback ("he's averaged 80.6 yards a carry so far, when he runs in the right direction").

6. NEBRASKA

Head coach Tom Osborne and his able crew of assistants probably traveled farther than anyone, even Ohio State, to recruit their prize crop of freshmen. A couple of Nebraska alumni (among them is rumored to be Johnny Carson) have put up a "matching fund" of over $5 million to get the best possible talent and bring NU a national championship. "The matching fund consists of these guys matching each other with a million or so," said Osborne. "It sure helped on our last round-the-world trip. For our defensive line, we got three of the finest Spanish competition bulls, plus a couple from Mexico and some promising animals from Argentina and Peru. The whole group cost us over $350,000. Prize bulls aren't cheap."

Osborne plans to start at least seven of his bulls, along with All-America quarterback Bradley Boerkum, who will no doubt become an option-type quarterback and execute more hand-offs in Osborne's new revamped attack, which features Mexican bulls Fernando Reyes and Jose Martinez at halfback and fullback. The bulls have been tremendously aggressive in practice, and Nebraska's schedule includes six teams who wear predominantly red uniforms. This could be a big year for the Cornhuskers.

7. TEXAS

Is Darrell Royal undergoing a change of heart or a change of life? How else do you explain the wooing of Joe Bobby Bill, the most sought-after schoolboy quarterback since Kyle Rote? After all, Texas isn't exactly known for its passing attack. Its quarterbacks usually hand off or run the ball themselves, and are what Royal calls "halfbacks who ain't afraid to stick their hands up a center's ass."

When he was the special guest speaker at a recent George Wallace fund-raising dinner, Royal explained how and why he got Joe Bobby out of the clutches of Bear Bryant, his old friend and co-guest speaker.

"You'd think an old country boy like Bear Bryant would have known better about a prospect like Joe Bobby," said Royal. "Joe Bobby likes to do two things, in no order of importance. He likes to throw a football ninety yards like it was coming out of a rifle barrel, and he likes to fuck. When we found him out in the sticks, he was fucking a big old zucchini squash that was soft and ripe from the summer sun. That boy did it to everything—girls, boys, pigs, sheep, stump-broke cows, turkey wings. But somehow I drew the line at zucchini squash and I told him so. You know what he said? He said, when it comes to fucking, there ain't no bad. And that's when I knew I had to get my tall Texas tales going about the juiciest females and the cutest pigs and the biggest, softest zucchini squashes you ever saw!"

What coach Royal didn't tell Bryant and the others is that the big money boys in Texas oil also sprung for some pretty fancy pass catchers, a pair of talented giraffes, Clyde Burleson and Doug Dupree, and a kangaroo, L. C. Bradford, who "pouches" the ball with great flair. When you combine Burleson, Dupree, and Bradford with the needle-threading accuracy of Joe Bobby, you begin to understand that Darrell Royal is not about to enter the state of soft-headed male menopause just yet. The only thing soft about Texas this year will be Joe Bobby's unlimited supply of zucchinis.

8. HOUSTON

. . . .

It looks like coach Bill Yeoman made an even-up trade with Darrell Royal—an I'll-take-your-running-game-for-your-passing-game. Yeoman has decided on a strictly Texas U. type offense, spearheaded by a huge influx of those new pure-bred Longhorn steers that King Ranch is developing again.

"They're not as big, beefy, and heavy as those Nebraska bulls," said Yeoman. "But they're not intended to be. They're a heck of a lot faster and they can really sting you on sweepers and quarterback option plays." Yeoman also feels that the Longhorns are tougher and much better conditioned than the Spanish and Mexican bulls, and can put out sixty minutes of optimum football. "After all, they were originally bred for that long drive to Abilene," he said.

9. LSU

Easygoing Charley McClendon is famous as the friendliest guy in the bayou country, but he wants none of that to rub off on his LSU Tigers, who in previous years had a tendency to "let up on their mean" and lose ballgames they should have won. This year, McClendon is making sure his squad will have no such tendencies. "We're evenly matched with a lot of teams we play," said McClendon. "The Southeastern Conference is always full of tough outfits like Ole Miss, Auburn, and Florida. What you need for those teams is a little something extra."

The little something extra Charley has in mind is a highly promising contingent of freshmen and red-shirted sophomores recruited from deep, deep in the bayous. His assistants unearthed a pair of smart, tough alligators named Buddy Guy Whipple and Chandler Trimble, who play linebacker and strong safety, respectively. There's also a truckload of snakes who can snare passes the way old Don Hutson used to. Plus something else that looks like a cross between a catfish and an old LST landing boat. "I don't know what the hell it is," said McClendon. "All I know is that it's named Ralston Swine and it likes to punish people. Lord knows what my assistants find down in those swamps, but they all seem to cotton to the game of football real well. What I like about my new boys is they got that natural streak of meanness I was talking about. They're not from any old game preserve or national park where they can get soft and friendly. They've been schooled in their natural habitat, the school of hard knocks. So when they come to us, they come ready to play."

10. PENN STATE

. . . .

Joe Paterno is the uncrowned king of the pessimists, the best poor-mouther of them all when it comes to evaluating his team's chances at the Number One spot. But before we put on our terrycloth eyelashes (in the expectation of a good cry, as Ernie Kovacs used to say), let's not overlook the fact that Paterno sports the best winning percentage (.824) in football among active college coaches. And he accomplished this with teams comprised *only of human beings*.

No team with a fullback like Gino "Switchblade" Natale and a linebacker like Steve "Broken Beer Bottle" Chernowski is all bad. And returning at quarterback is Mike "Shotgun" Sherman, a rifle-armed passer with an uncanny knack for holding up a pass rush until he finds an open receiver.

Most of Paterno's roster is recruited from nearby coal mines and steel mills, which he claims are tougher environments than McClendon's bayous. And for good measure, he gets his blacks from the legendary Pennsylvania prison system, players who don't need any special weapons or help of any kind.

When you add that indefinable element, that tiny bit of intelligence that a human football player has over his animal counterpart, you have the main reason why Paterno's teams win consistently. "They can almost think out there," he said. And that makes all the difference.

CHE GUEVARA'S

BOLIVIAN DIARIES

by Doug Kenney

(Editor's note: Following the worldwide shock and mourning over the reported death of Ernesto "Che" Guevara by a Bolivian Army firing squad, the personal diaries of the revolutionary's tragic and abortive attempt to overthrow the oppressive Barrientos regime quickly became a classic text on guerilla warfare. However, recent chemical analysis of these documents have revealed minute traces of ketchup and A.1. Sauce ingrained in the paper, two substances Che himself denounced in an article on field kitchen maintenance for the Chinese news magazine Ping An *as "reactionary and counterrevolutionary condiments fit only for bourgeois pigs and their revisionist cookouts." Other telltale clues belie the authenticity of the "diaries" as well, specifically the close attention given to spelling and grammar. Simultaneously with the discovery of this cruel hoax,* NatLampCo *News Service Latin American correspondent Douglas Kenney recently discovered the authentic manuscript outside the La Paz airport, where its pages were being employed as wrappers by an illiterate taco vendor. Craftily obtaining the documents from the simple peasant in return for some beads, hand mirrors, and assorted trinkets, newshound Kenney returned stateside immediately with the diaries, only then realizing that his wallet was missing.* NatLampCo *is proud to publish these historic footnotes to the brave* rebelde's *work, and hopes that they may fan the flames of global indignation against tyranny, oppression, and greaser pickpockets.)*

Noviembre 7

At long last, our little band has touched Bolivian soil! The flight from Havana was uneventful, although every one of us stretched our revolutionary discipline to the limit fighting down the urge to jump out of our seats, rush to the cockpit and stick a *pistola* in the pilot's ear. In fact, Marcos, my hot-blooded second-in-command, did, at one point, lose control and leap from his seat shouting, "¡Prende ce avion o Cuba!" Luckily Marcos' seat belt was still fastened and his attention diverted by a double hernia long enough for Tanya, our East German *compañera*, to whisper that the plane was still *in* Havana and stuff an air-sickness bag in his mouth.

Marcos and I supervised the unloading of our baggage. We are posing as a Mexican mariachi band, our tools of war cloaked in the guise of musical instruments. Unfortunately, one of the customs officials discovered that our bass-fiddle case contained a Russian-made YD-47 heavy mortar. Thinking quickly, I put my mouth to the barrel and, with no little difficulty, improvised a few bars of *"Beso Me Mucho"* until his suspicions were allayed. There was, in addition, a tense moment when a porter accidentally pulled the pin on one of our maracas, but, as fate would have it, the device was of Bulgarian manufacture and failed to explode.

After breaking our fast (and one of my fillings) with tacos bought from a little peasant vendor outside the airport, Tanya, Marcos, Pombo, Camba, and I hailed taxis and directed them to our secret hideout in the trackless jungles of Nancahuazu. As we drive, Marcos, a swaggering adventurer who even apes the way I curl my beard, looks over my shoulder as I write in my diary, hoping to steal some good lines for his own. You are an idiot, Marcos, and it is no wonder that your publisher wouldn't give you an advance.

Noviembre 8

We have arrived at Nancahuazu, a forbidding jungle valley in the Cono Sur region. There is much to be done here. I have sent Pombo and Camba out in search of game, and Marcos out in search of them both to make sure they do not break discipline and bring the animal back unfit to eat. Men without women—an old story. I have also sent Tanya back to La Paz in search of my wallet, which I *know* I had before we ate those tacos.

Noviembre 9

Tanya has already done much to make the old farmhouse comfortable. She has set up an elaborate wire clothesline in the surrounding palms and amuses herself by sitting under it prattling to her vanity case in that husky baritone I have come to love. When she tires of this game, she will adjust her wig (an early illness has left her with a permanent crew-cut) and lumber off to her pet pigeons, first attaching shiny metal capsules to their feet for ballast. This morning, in a burst of feminine exuberance, she climbed hand over hand to the top of our hideout with a bucket of red paint in her teeth and decorated the roof with a gay bull's-eye.

At least there is one in whom I can have confidence.

Noviembre 10

Our first contact with the peasant population. Pombo was roasting a jaguar and Camba was occupied trying to kill it, when the noise attracted a passing worker returning from the distant tin mines. I ordered him to stop and fired over his head, barely creasing the scalp. With that, four others who had been watching shyly behind some acacias ran toward us in joyful recognition, shouting, "¡Non fuere, non nos muertos, por favor señor!" ["All hail the glorious revolution!"—*Ed.*] Now that we had won the confidence of these ragged but plucky recruits, I told them that they would be the nucleus of a people's army which would one day overthrow the corrupt Barrientos dictatorship and free its victims from conditions of exploitation indistinguishable from the Middle Ages. Childlike, they stood dumbly at first, too overwhelmed with pride to speak. I triggered a volley high over their knees to loosen their tongues, and, as one man, they raised their hands over their heads in agreement and enthusiastically emptied their pockets.

Now we are ten.

Noviembre 13

Excellent news has come in a coded newscast from Radio Havana. Fidel tells us that Bertrand Russell and Jean-Paul Sartre have espoused our cause and will marshal support for us throughout the European Left. Not only will this shower us with arms and followers, but, if they agree to coauthor the introduction, my diary sales should be boosted by easily fifty thousand copies. Perhaps we can get out another printing of my other book as well (*One Hundred and Fifty Questions to a Guerilla*, People's Press, Havana, Cuba. Seventy pesos, hard-cover, thirty pesos, soft-cover.)

There is bad news as well. The peasants grow restive, making unreasonable and petty demands for food and water. The jaguar is gone, and has taken most of our rations with him. All that is left are open-face iguana sandwiches and pineapple soup. Even I found myself forcing down a bottle of Coca-Cola, the vile *maté* of *yanqui* imperialists. Although the foul liquid made me gag, I noticed an odd aftertaste that I could not dispel. A half hour later I found myself having another, and yet another. This is foolish counterrevolutionary weakness on my part, and I will steel myself against it.

But I suppose it can't hurt to kill the six-pack.

Noviembre 28

A visitor. Regis Debray, the famous French war groupie, has come with more happy news. *L'Express* has finally agreed to my price for the prepublication rights, and there is talk of a series based on our adventures for French television. But this matter must rest until more important tasks are completed— negotiations are stalled with Marlboro for my poster, and Gomez, my agent, says Timex is still sitting on the wristwatch. Accordingly, I have radioed Gomez that they can make my arms go backwards and use "It's Counterrevolutionary!" as the sales gimmick.

¡Viva la revolución!

Diciembre 1

Dissension. Again the men complain about the lack of food, and the seasonal rains have begun causing widespread diarrhea, making our movements plain to the enemy. Ha ha, a joke, *sí*? As Mao has written, "In times of hunger, one jest can be worth a hundred bowls of rice, particularly if you have no bowls of rice anyway." The men have taken to routinely disobeying orders, and frequently have to be disciplined for pillow-fighting after lights-out. If this seems harsh, it must be remembered that for pillows, true guerrillas use logs.

Marcos's patrol has returned with word of an enemy encampment not five kilometers from where we stand. Tonight we meet to plan an ambush and vote on whether or not to eat Tanya's pigeons.

Marcos reports the enemy has Coca-Cola!

Diciembre 2

The euphoria of victory! The ambush is a success despite a minor tactical blunder that decimated our forces. This morning, before our column advanced on the enemy, I told Gamba to (1) scout the trail ahead, (2) set up the ambush down river, and (3) organize a perimeter defense. Misunderstanding my orders, he (1) wandered aimlessly into the jungle, (2) became hopelessly lost, and (3) fell asleep. Nevertheless, Gamba's piece accidentally discharged as he collapsed, and the enemy was wiped out to a man in the ensuing, pointless crossfire. The dead were stripped of their uniforms and equipment, but little in the way of weapons were recovered save a few pocketknives and BB pistols. However, we managed to salvage a portable cooler full of Coca-Cola, a beverage I am finding more and more to my liking.

¡Hasta la Victoria Siempre!

Diciembre 4

Radio La Paz reports that a search party is being organized to locate a troop of Eagle Scouts that has failed to return from an overnight camping trip in the Nancahuazu region.

¡Oops!

Diciembre 10

The rains have begun again, and there is much wheezing and sniffling. Not to mention whining. We have run out of Contac. The men are hungry and are reduced to boiled hand-grenades. Tanya still refuses to let us at the pigeons and spends most of her time talking to her vanity case. Neither will she sleep with me, although I have pursued her for these many weeks. Do all East German women have such long periods? It is very strange. Perhaps that is why so many of their men jump over the Wall.

Also, the mosquitoes plague us by night. They are of immense size and their constant buzzing robs us of our sleep. So used are we to their continual presence that it was not until an hour ago that I realized via Radio La Paz that our positions are being bombed and strafed nightly by Bolivian helicopters.

There is no more Coca-Cola and I notice my hands are trembling.

Diciembre 15

Rain.

Diciembre 16

Rain.

Diciembre 17

Rain.

Diciembre 18

Our first loss. Camba, as usual, fell asleep on guard duty with his mouth open and drowned.

Diciembre 22

Marcos relates a wonderful dream he had last night. He dreamt that in three weeks we will march triumphantly into the capital leading ten thousand soldiers. The gates open before us without a shot being fired, and in the plaza we are greeted by throngs of delirious well-wishers. Little children stringing garlands around our gun mounts dance beside our armored cars, and the old ones weep with joy, singing the old songs again, shrieking the old shrieks. At the top step of the palace, Barrientos himself is standing meekly. Head lowered, he offers his sword, but, in the tradition of the great *generals*, I refuse it and shoot off his kneecaps. Then, arm in arm, Marcos, Pombo, Tanya, and I walk into the palace, where we are given champagne, caviar, cigars and certificates good for ten rubdowns at the Nogales Health Spa. We get unlimited room service. We can put our feet up on the desks. No one cares if we don't make the bed. The phone rings and it's Fidel congratulating us and asking us if we can spare a fiver. We live happily ever after, and our story is made into a major motion picture starring John Wayne, Omar Sharif, Steve McQueen, and Candy Bergen. We get 10 percent of the gross.

This is a good dream.

Diciembre 23

Marcos has had another dream. Harold Stassen is sworn in as President of the United States aboard the S.S. *Titanic*, while overhead floats the Hindenburg piloted by Amelia Earhart and Wiley Post, who are being married by Judge Crater and about to embark on a two-week honeymoon in Atlantis.

We must always be on guard against such idle, bourgeois fantasy.

Enero 2

More bad news from Havana. Sartre's and Russell's appeal to Europe's revolutionary youth has brought little gold to our war chest. However, Fidel has cheered us by forwarding a petition of support from the fifth-grade class of the People's Primary School in East Berlin containing twenty-eight signatures and a pledge of two weeks' milk money. In addition, we have, to date, received thirty-six inquiries from Sorbonne PolySci majors requesting information for their doctoral theses.

Also, Gomez writes that the watch gimmick didn't go over and Debray has received a letter from the French television network rejecting the series idea. They claim it wouldn't stand a chance against "Hogan's Heroes."

This afternoon, as a demonstration of their affection for their liberators, the peasants have deserted.

Enero 5

More rain today. Once again the men are racked with diarrhea and our patrols are frequently halted, as marching is difficult with everyone's pants down around his ankles. Our situation is desperate. We have also run out of air freshener.

Enero 6

The diarrhea grows worse. We have run out of corks as well.

Enero 14

The extremity of our need has driven us to reckless adventurism. Last evening, under the cover of a moonless night and some captured Airwicks, we stole into the little town of Palamos and attacked the local *farmacia*. Suddenly, many guns opened up on us and we were caught in an ambush of Bolivian soldiers before we could get to the Kaopectate. How could they have known? Luckily, we escaped with our lives, although several of us have suffered flesh wounds from kamikaze pigeons. The men begin to grumble and, in their rush to blame others for their own tactical mistakes, cast suspicious eyes towards Tanya, who, by the way, says her period will soon be over and we can begin heavy petting.

Nevertheless, the men must be pacified, and our now-routine diet of stuffed mortar rounds has been supplemented with squab.

Enero 17

No Cokes for three days. My hands are shaky and my knees are weak. I am itching like a man on a fuzzy tree. Delirious. I cannot go on unless I have another. Soon. A peasant in the village will deal with me—one rifle, one six-pack.

Soon the sentries will be sleeping.

Enero 18

The camp is in an uproar. Someone slipped past the guards last night and stole six rifles. No one is above suspicion, and as an example to the rest, I shot Pombo through the foot with the remaining rifle.

Marcos has been stirring up trouble again. He is jealous of my deal with *Playboy* for the "Che" tie clips and billfolds. If we take the capital by spring, I tease him, the *norteamericanos* will be forced to recognize Cuba and I can plug my book on the Juannie Carson show. This is another of those jests I have previously described. But Marcos persists in disobeying my orders, and was absent for bed check. I was forced to discipline Marcos and order him to stand in the corner for three hours. However, there was another helicopter raid last night and there are no corners left in the camp. I made him stand in the latrine instead. Barefoot.

Enero 19

Today we planned the major thrust of our campaign. The time is ripe for decisive action, for the men grow listless waiting around to be picked off by snipers. Marcos, impetuous romantic that he is, foolishly proposed striking at the U.S.-owned oil refineries at Camari, while the rest of our dwindling brotherhood wished to march on the United Fruit Company complex in Fuelga, in the hopes of cadging some bananas from the Fruits. Another jest. One of Mao's favorites.

After several hours of democratic discussion, I rapped my rifle butt (which serves in this rough-and-ready forum as a gavel) on Marcos's head and settled the matter. Tomorrow we set out for La Nosa, the industrial nerve-center of *yanqui* colonialism in Bolivia. Also the largest Coca-Cola bottling plant in the Southern Hemisphere.

Onward!

Enero 20

A black day.

It began well enough. The men who had not been carried off by the jaguar were roused from their trees at dawn, and by noon we were gliding stealthily down Highway 42 to La Nosa, stopping only to eat, sleep or loot an occasional *cantina.* My brave *compañeros* were in high spirits, and several times I reprimanded them for exuberantly singing what has become our song of battle, the "Bataan Death March." When we neared La Nosa, I divided our force into three squads—Pombo was to move his men around to the left flank and pretend to scavenge for 2-cent-deposit bottles, and Marcos was assigned to assault the main gate under the cover of the guardhouse searchlights. It fell to me and Tanya to wait behind a granite outcropping and shout hearty advice and encouragement.

We waited until dusk, and at precisely 0800 hours I gave the signal to move out. At 0810 I gave the signal to shoot anyone still cringing behind the trees, and the attack was underway. As Pombo's unit moved into the clearing, a company of Bolivian infantry opened fire, chopping Pombo and his men into *paella.* Immediately, I sensed that something had gone wrong. As if to confirm my suspicions, Marcos's men advanced to the gate and were cut to ribbons. Marcos himself barely escaped with his life, shielding his body with a Coca-Cola cooler, and scrambled back to our position covered with thick, sticky fluid. Despite my hopes, it was not his blood, but the sight of a five-foot-two-inch, 120-pound Cuban running at breakneck speed with a quarter-ton vending machine under his arm did, at least, distract General Orvando's soldiers long enough to make good our escape.

As we struggled back to our base, it became obvious that we were being observed, because whoever lead our column was periodically shot between the eyes. This obstacle to our progress led to an animated debate among the survivors as to who next was to become the first, or "point man," for the remainder of our withdrawal. Marcos, unwilling to obey both my orders that he lead *and* continue to carry the Coke machine on his back, suggested that we confuse them by walking backwards.

And this man, I tell you, was not only free to walk the streets of Havana, but to drive an automobile.

Enero 21

All hope has vanished. They surrounded us as we slept. We are out of ammo, the men are threatening to eat Debray and Pombo is acting suspiciously despite his death in my previous entry. I think I, too, am feeling weary of the chase. Poor Tanya. So deranged is she by the rout that she now only croons to her case, even while the artillery rounds, as if by magic, slowly find the range on our positions. They are coming for Che. The noose is tightened, and soon, the fascists think, Che will be captured, shot against a peasant wall and dragged through the muddy streets like a slaughtered goat.

I look at Marcos, sleeping peacefully now that I have clubbed him into insensibility, and I think of how many dreams we shared together during the Cuban revolution, how he looked up to me like an older brother, copying everything about me, and how proud he would be, were he conscious, to know that I have just traded identity papers with him, shaved, and covered my head with one of Tanya's shawls, which she soon will no longer be needing, I can personally assure you. Then, over the river and through the woods, who knows? Maybe my cousin in Buenos Aires who works at the you-know-what factory will hide me.

Che *must* live, for wherever the people are ground under the heel of *yanqui* imperialism, my spirit must be with them, whether it be in Rio de Janeiro, Tahiti or Acapulco. Soon, a new dawn, a red dawn, will give light to the world, and perhaps these few small things I have done to hasten that day will be remembered, particularly if Dalton Trumbo (*Spartacus, Viva Zapata*) agrees to rough out the shooting script. *Che Lives?* . . . *The Che Guevara Story?* . . . *A Che for All Seasons?* . . . *I Remember Che?* . . . *Viva Che?* . . . *A Che Is Born?* . . .

MORE TO COME

HOW TO WRITE A JOHNNY CARSON MONOLOGUE IN FIVE MINUTES OR LESS!

by Michael O'Donoghue

There are words funny in and of themselves, words such as "Edsel" and "Liberace" and "tacoburger." The mere use of such a word invokes instant mirth. While Komic Keywords and Phunny Phrases have long been used both by comedians (i.e., Jack Pearl's "Vas you der, Sharlie?" Joe Penner's "You wanna buy a duck?" and even Benny/Cavett's "Now wait a minute!") and laymen (i.e., the commonly used humorous synonyms for "drunk": "stewed," "zonked," "polluted" (archaic), "smashed," etc.) alike, it took Johnny Carson to base an entire routine on them.

A copy of Johnny's comic-word-and-phrase list recently came into my possession and we're reprinting it here in its entirety with a few explanatory footnotes of my own. I have also included a sample monologue to demonstrate how it works. Simply fill in the blanks, using the words and phrases found on the list. Many have already been done for you.

You may wish to watch "The Tonight Show" and add to your list. You'll soon discover that, as a rule, most Southern California towns, roads, and used-auto dealers are funny, and that it would be difficult to come up with an undergarment that is not hilarious. It should also be pointed out that although "bippy" and "Walnetto" are valid Komic Keywords, they are not on this list because both originate from another show.

Here are a few hints on delivery in case you are tempted to try the completed monologue on your friends. When Johnny loses his place, he usually "marks time" by discussing some point of grammar with Ed ("Which is proper there, Ed, 'who' or 'whom'?"). If a joke "bombs," doggedly repeat the punch line. And never forget that it's impossible to overuse the word "weird."

That's all there is to it.

Funny Actors and Actresses

Sunny Tufts
Hildegarde Neff
Maria Ouspenskaya
Mickey Rooney
Annette Funicello
Dame May Whitty

Richard Loo
Helmut Dantine
Esther Williams
Helen Twelvetrees

Funny Singers and Musicians

Kate Smith
Wayne Newton
The Lennon Sisters
Tiny Tim[1]
Nelson Eddy
Eddie Fisher
Fabian
Tommy Newsom[2]
Monty Rock III
Carmen Lombardo
Liberace

Funny Professions

Avon Lady
hairdresser
mugger

Funny People

Tommy Manville
Mrs. Miller
Bridey Murphy (archaic)
Twiggy
Tojo (archaic)
Phyllis Diller
Martha Mitchell
Fernando Lamas
Dean Martin
Wink Martindale

Funny Places

Fire Island
Avalon
Sheboygan
Peyton Place
Oxnard
Pismo Beach
Levittown (archaic)

[1]And Miss Vicki (archaic)
[2]Also called "Mr. Excitement"

Cucamonga[3]
Corning, Iowa
Fun City
San Bernardino
Burbank[4]
Brooklyn
Guam
Kokomo
Kalamazoo
Biloxi

Funny Animals

yak
Mister Ed
skunk
Cheeta
J. Fred Muggs (archaic)
gopher
wombat
Gentle Ben
aardvark
King, the Wonder Horse
Rex, the Wonder Dog[5]
Francis, the Talking Mule
yellow-bellied sapsucker
Flipper
Rin-Tin-Tin
beaver

Funny Announcers

Durward Kirby
George Fenneman

Funny Foods

Tacoburger
prune danish
bagel
high-priced spread
blintz
Blimpie
wet noodle

---

[3]From the archaic tag "Anaheim, Azusa, and Cucamonga"
[4]Commonly preceded by the adjectives "beautiful, downtown"
[5]The "Wonder" formula will work with any animal, such as "Ralph, the Wonder Gopher" or "Randy, the Wonder Yak."

flied lice
meatball[6]
matzo ball
Mrs. Paul's Fishsticks

Funny Beverages

Gatorade
prune juice
Bosco
Metrecal (archaic)
Ovaltine
Orange Julius

Funny Fruits and Vegetables

kumquat
gourd
bananas[7] (archaic)

Funny Doctors

Dr. Kildare
Dr. Kinsey (archaic)
Marcus Welby, M.D.
Dr. Frank Field[8]
Dr. Joyce Brothers

Funny Disorders and Diseases

cardiac arrest
Dutch Elm blight

Funny Nostrums

Geritol
Miltown (archaic)
Carter's Little Liver Pills (archaic)

Funny Political Figures

Alf Landon
Mayor Yorty
Millard Fillmore
Spiro Agnew
Harold Stassen

[6]Currently revived in phrase "Thatza spicy meatball!"
[7]Bananas are funny only if smoked.
[8]Usually identified as "NBC's crack meteorologist"

Funny Roads

freeways
Mulholland Drive
the Slauson cutoff
the San Bernardino Expressway

Funny Underwear

Jockey shorts
girdle
bloomers
Fruit of the Loom
red undies
panty hose
Living Bra

Funny Advertising Characters

The Man from Glad
Ralph Williams
Chick Lambert
Earl Scheib
The Smith Brothers
Mr. Clean
Katy Winters
The Jolly Green Giant

Funny Adjectives

topless
sissy[9]
crazy[10]
weird[11]

Funny Exclamations

Yah-hah![12]
Whoopee![13]

Funny Words

bird
grim
spit up
flaky
zinger

---

[9] May also be used as noun (e.g., "Frontier Sissy")
[10] As in "crazy Shirley"
[11] As in "weird Shirley"
[12] Always accompanied by twirling forefinger
[13] Ditto

Funny Words for "People Who 'Aren't Playing with a Full Deck' "

yo-yo
ding-a-ling
kook
weirdo

Funny Yiddish Words

mohel
bris
meshuggeneh
Hadassah
Bar Mitzvah
tochis[14]

Funny Phrases

"Hi, friends! Ralph Williams here!"
"Please, Mother, I'd rather do it myself!" (archaic)
"I can't believe I ate the whole thing!"
"That's one for the Jew. . . . "[15]
"Can you imagine some drunk watching the show who just tuned in?"
"It's a biggee!"
"See how quickly they turn!"
"You folks didn't boo when I was raising the flag on Mt. Sarabachi!"
"I wouldn't touch that line with a ten-foot pole!"[16]
"If I said what I'm thinking right now, this place would be a parking lot tomorrow!"[17]
"Good night, Chet!" (archaic)
"Would you believe [scaled-down parody of the previous statement]?" (archaic)
"Where does it say that audience does monologue?"
"Just when did I lose control?"[18]

Funny Colors

puce

---

[14]Although almost anything Yiddish/Jewish is funny (e.g., "bubeleh," "cockamamy," "Feh!" "gefilte fish," "gonif," "knish," "kvetch," "mavin," "mensh," "nebbish," "So nu?" "nudzh," "Oy gevalt!" "paskudnyak," "plotz," "putz" (banned), "shiksa," "shlemiel," "shlimazl," "shmegegge," "shmuck" (banned), "shvartzeh," "tsuris," "yenta," "zhlub"), Johnny, as a "goy," is limited to only the most common words, unlike a Jewish comedian such as Jerry Lewis who can sprinkle a few in every sentence.

[15]Also "Jew-one, Christian-nothing!" Both lines are always delivered while pretending to write down the score.

[16]To be used after a *double entendre* remark by a "dumb" and/or foreign actress

[17]Ditto

[18]Delivered while pretending to check watch

Miscellaneous Funny Stuff

Edsel
Andy Hardy
Tidy Bowl
greasy kid stuff
"Medic" (archaic)
smog
Tom Swift
the Bobbsey Twins
Hula-Hoop
winos
Dr. Scholl's Foot Pads
the phone company
Con Ed[19]
big toe
blubber
Man Tan (archaic)
Forest Lawn
Funk & Wagnall
the Fakawee Indians (banned)[20]
flügelhorn
the NBC commissary[21]
5-Day Deodorant Pads
Jupiter
Tonto
the Dixie Hotel
the Sheraton Universal[22]
Confederate money
Medicare
doggie bag
Penn Central (archaic)
the Long Island Railroad
Bob & Carol & Ted & Alice
dentures
the San Andreas Fault
"Let's Make a Deal"
hickey
Mr. Moto
the classifed section of the *L. A. Free Press*
National Pretzel Week[23]

[19]Usually identified as "New York's Mickey Mouse power company"
[20]Or, to use a Funny Double-Negative, a "no-no"
[21]Also called "Cramp's Tomb"
[22]For "Universal," substitute "Unusual," "Uncomfortable," etc.
[23]Not to be confused with "pretzel vendor," a Cavett Keyword

The Pink Pussycat
the Flying Nun
Schrafft's
Roto-Rooter
Heidi Fishbinder
Latrina Goldfarb
Priscilla Goodbody
the Welcome Wagon
bedpan
porcelain convenience
Excedrin Headache Number 46[24]
miniskirts
buggy whips
Sarah Heartburn (archaic)
Wurlitzer
the funny farm

Sample Monologue

Ed: And now, heeeeeerrrrrrrrrrrrrrrrre's Johnny!
(*Johnny enters briskly, smiles, touches tie, looks at Ed, looks at Doc and does take, touches tie, twirls forefinger in "Yah-hah!" gesture, indicates audience and gives thumb-drinking gesture, * touches tie, raises hands to halt applause, checks watch if applause continues and raises hands again, touches tie.*)

Johnny: This is "The Tonight Show," the show with a message. Tonight's message . . . (*breaks into laughter*) tonight's message is: "A wet <u>Avon Lady</u> never flies at night!"**

(*Looks at Doc, winces.*) I wanna say! (*Does take.*) You look like a <u>topless</u> <u>Roto-Rooter</u> dealer at <u>Wayne</u> <u>Newton's</u> <u>briss!</u>

You can still catch the late movie on the other channel—<u>Richard Loo</u>, <u>Annette</u> <u>Funicello,</u> _____ _____ , _____ _____ , and <u>Prudence, the</u> <u>Wonder</u> <u>Beaver</u> in "The <u>Tacoburger</u> That Ate <u>Oxnard</u> and <u>Spit</u> <u>Up!</u>" <u>It's</u> <u>a</u> <u>biggee!</u>

What else is happening? I see where <u>Con</u> <u>Ed,</u> <u>New</u> York's <u>Mickey</u> Mouse <u>power</u> <u>company,</u> predicted more brownouts. It's getting so you have to ____ just to _____ _____ I've heard of _____ , but this is ridiculous!

Boy, it was cold out today!

Ed: How . . . cold . . . was it?

___

[24]Any number will suffice.
*Especially on Friday nights.
**Alternate opening: "Thank you. Thank you very much. I'm Johnny Carson, or, as I was called by the Indians with whom I used to frolic on the plains of Nebraska, 'Little'!"_____ ____

Johnny: (*laughing*): It was so cold that, in Central Park, the muggers were demanding your _____ or your life!

   This afternoon I saw Dr. Frank Field, NBC's crack meteorologist and resident yo-yo running through the halls wearing a _____ and shouting "_____! _____!" So I stopped him and asked what he was doing, and he said it was because _____ _____!
. . . That actually happened . . . this afternoon.

Audience: Groan . . . hiss . . . boo!

Johnny: You folks didn't boo when I was raising the flag on Mt. Sarabachi!
   I want you to know that doing the monologue is my second favorite thing in the whole world. (*Pauses.*) My favorite thing is feeding Blimpies to Kate Smith's Living Bra!

Ed: Hey-ay!

Johnny: I read in the paper today where a Women's Lib organization protesting at a Pasadena beach not only burned their _____ but their _____ and _____ as well! I can remember when girls peeled only *after* they got sunburned! That could melt your _____ !
   Another crazy item in the paper. It's true! I'm not making it up! A man in _____ , who was arrested for running a _____ in his garage, told the judge that he only did it to _____ his wife. That's like trying to fix a _____ with a _____ ! No, but _____

Man in audience: _____ !

Johnny: Where does it say that audience does monologue? What's with this group tonight? It's wild!
   (*To Ed.*) I hear you had quite a time last night. Ed went to a _____ after the show and . . . "had a few," shall we say. This morning Rudi, our producer, found him swinging from the _____ of the _____ Hotel and feeding pizza to the _____ , claiming that he was _____ _____ _____ ! (*To Ed.*) You should be ashamed of yourself! A grown man!

Ed: She was my niece!

Johnny: No, I kid Ed but he only drinks on special occasions. For Ed, a special occasion is a _____ for Wink Martindale's _____ !
   (*To Ed.*) This is a good crowd.
   Hey, we have a great show! We've got Corbett Monica; singer Vikki Carr, a lovely gal. Fanny Flagg is with us. Who am I leaving out? Oh, Enzo Stuarti is here. And Mrs. Munnings and her talking _____ , *** so stay where you are and we'll be right back. (*Does golf swing, which has become a show-biz tradition.*)

***Or "champion sardine-packer Neal Fiebusch."

NEW YORK NEIGHBORHOS

by Dave Hanson and Diane Giddis

SOME YEARS AGO, a downtown sector of Manhattan was given the nickname SoHo (it is located SOuth of HOuston Street). With its newfound identity that area soon became a real-estate-boom region, and has become one of Manhattan's most prestigious and affluent locations. Canny realtors, hoping to create an equally catchy identity for the area just north of there, christened that parcel NoHo, with excellent results. So why not give all New York neighborhoods similar names?

AREA	PROPOSED NAME
Park Avenue	DoughHo
FDR Drive	SlowHo
Garment District	SewHo
Theater District	ShowHo
Club District	SnowHo
Christopher Street	MoHo
Wall Street	BromoHo
South Bronx	WoeHo
Upper East Side	FauxHo
Midtown	TowHo
Harlem	BroHo, or FroHo
Lincoln Center	PianissimoHo/ToeHo
Holland Tunnel	To and FroHo
Greenwich Village	HipHo, or BoHo
St. Nicholas Avenue	HoHoHo
The Bowery	SkidHo
West Side	GrowHo
Times Square	TiredOldHo
Orchard Street	SchmoHo
Hudson River	EauHo, or FlowHo
Fulton Fish Market	CoHo
Columbia University	KnowHo
Chinatown	AhSoHo
Staten Island	So-SoHo
Brighton Beach	IvanHo

WE ARE WHAT WE EAT:

THE HOT NEW ETHNIC FOODS AROUND THE U.S.

by Ellis Weiner

". . . Small Malta in Duluth serves Maltese falcon . . .
but insiders prefer tompin-chon *and* khlukh *. . ."*

SUDDENLY shrimp in lobster sauce is not enough. Americans are going beyond "ethnic" all the way to downright exotic. The old standbys—Chinatown, Little Italy, Harlem, etc.—no longer satisfy. What next? Plenty. Scattered around this country are a number of hitherto unknown enclaves of unassimilated native and ethnic communities. Their food, their customs—sometimes even their language and appearance—are foreign, strange, enchanting. All you need is to know where. For example:

A three-block area of downtown Cleveland, Ohio, features authentic Sherpa mountain guide ceremonies, a performing herd of trained alpacas, and daily Hindu religious services to which all are invited. Known as **Nepaltown,** this taste of Far Eastern mystery is located between the city's financial district and the vegetable warehouses. Specialties available from the several fine restaurants and snack stands include such authentic Sherpa mountain guide cuisine favorites as *shapp* (boiled yak stew), *laphdohg* (pine needles in hashish oil), and *chrez* (snow pudding—a mixture of mountain grass and seven other grains).

Visitors to Seattle, Washington, may be surprised to learn that there is a thriving Balinese section of the city that holds many surprises and delights in store for those who can find it. Locally known as **Little Bali,** the area covers most of the sixteenth floor of the Crenshaw Building, a late eighteenth century department store now given over to office facilities, light manufacturing, and storage. Haunting temple bell music and the heady aroma of incense greet the hungry traveler, and a panoply of gustatorial pleasures may be discovered merely by walking straight until the water cooler, turning left, and continuing on into the next room. There, on a crude wooden table with benches lining either side, will be found a number of native Balinese delicacies, among which are my favorites—monkey rice spider loaf, minted breadfruit tarts, and the altogether alcoholic and satisfying beverage *blejgh*—brewed from fermented sugar cane and volcanic ash.

Everything's up to date in Kansas City, Missouri—everything, that is, except the small four-block area known as **Tanzaniatown.** Here, Tanzanian emigrants have reconstructed an authentic African mini-village, including straying animals, colorfully garbed and ungarbed women with baskets on their heads, and spears. Stop by for lunch at M'Bulindoo's, and enjoy the house specialty of fried palm fronds and coconut husk. Or, for a more formal dining experience, make reservations at least two days in advance at the Hut of the Scary Shaman. Recommended are the antelope and banana soup, tarantula fritters with honey, and a casserole-like dish called *blooboo,* which, as far as I can tell, is a mixture of jungle leaves and animals, slow-simmered for about a week and eaten out of leopard pelts.

The immigration of South Americans to the U.S. has received somewhat less historical coverage than that of the Europeans; nonetheless, a substantial number of Latin Americans have made the journey from south of the equator to our shores, and nowhere can a more authentic example of their culture be found than in St. Louis's **Tierra del Fuegotown.** Don't forget to sample a plate of *titus andronicus* a Spanish mainstay consisting of young birds smashed with a big rock and sprinkled with sangria. Juan's Dinero (John's Diner) offers a sumptuous dessert tray that boasts the only lima bean cake in the entire city. (The diner is shaped like a Cadillac, historically the favorite car of the natives.) And for travel-weary tourists, a glass of *coño* is a sure pick-me-up. This is a native favorite as well, and is made fresh daily from almonds, yeast, and pork, with special water flown directly from Tierra del Fuego's famed Lake Cacapupu.

Everyone knows that Krakatoa was east of Java, but few remember that it was also west of Sumatra. Well, a little bit of Sumatra is just around the block from the library on Broad Street and Market in Philadelphia. It's called, appropriately, **Little Sumatra**, and is a mecca for natives and travelers alike with that yen for South Sea fare and ambience. By now, of course, Philadelphia is famous for its breadfruit cookery, and it is all thanks to this teeming, thriving native community. Ask for breadfruit juice with ice, however, as the native Sumatrans will serve it neat if you don't, and Americans generally prefer a cooler beverage. Too, the famous native dish *laj* is available. It's made by sawing off the buttocks of an orangutan and immersing them in a broth of scallions and brine. It tastes something like fried chicken, with the texture of frog.

The Maltese section of Duluth, Minnesota—known in that city as **Small Malta**—offers exotica aplenty for the tourist and resident alike. Most Americans no doubt know of Malta chiefly via Dashiell Hammett and Humphrey

Bogart. And indeed, one can find a decent dish of Maltese falcon at almost any of these restaurants. The native connoisseurs may chuckle at such an order, however. Falcon serves much the same purpose on Malta as turkey does here—a rather common and bland bird used mainly for ceremonial purposes, and not at all representative of the variety and richness of Maltese cooking. Instead, I suggest you try such native specialties as *tompin-chon* (wrapped gull with olive stuffing), the dessert pastry *khlukh* (pistachio nuts and beer in a thick paste, covered with a flaky shell of dough and twigs), and the tiny *gak* balls. These last are really nothing more than bits of cornmeal and chocolate, and are a favorite with children.

HOW I CHEAT

THE POOR SPORTSMAN'S ALTERNATIVE TO FAIR PLAY

by John Hughes

The General Rules of Cheating

1. Always volunteer to keep score.

2. Always go first and then confuse the order so that you also go last.

3. If you should happen to lose, never pay off any bets connected with the contest. If you pay off on one bet, you'll have to pay off on another.

4. Treat all people equally. It doesn't pay to be selective in who you cheat on. If you cheat your little boy or girl, cheat your wife and grandmother, too. Cheat everyone or cheat no one.

5. No one likes to think of anyone as a cheat. Even if you're a sloppy pig of a cheat, they'll think you forgetful, vaporish, or knuckleheaded before they think you a cheater.

6. Always make new rules. If you alter the rules at the beginning, you make it easier to alter the rules in the middle and at the end.

7. If you are accused of cheating, counter with an accusation of your own. At worst you will deadlock; at best they'll agree to a rematch and you'll get a second chance to cheat, except this time you'll be more careful.

8. Cheat an old person before a young person, a Negro before a white, a woman before a man, a pauper before a tycoon. Never cheat an Italian or a cop.

9. You can't cheat a dog.

10. You can't cheat a Jew.

Cheating Your Aunt at Penny Ante Poker

Let her win the first hand. That way you won't go to hell. Then, since her eyes are cloudy with cataracts and she's got the reflexes of a two-toed sloth, she's a cookie waiting for the bite. Deal her the worst cards in the deck, deal yourself a dozen and a half cards. If she wants you to hit her twice, hit her once. By the time she gets the cards up to her face, she will have forgotten how many cards she asked for in the first place. If all you want is her pocket money, get yourself one good hand, hold it, and replay it over and over. If you're a real son-of-a-snake, let her win a few hands—then raise the stakes and lower the boom.

Cheating at Horse

In this driveway basketball classic, each player receives a letter for each basket he fails to make until he has missed enough shots to spell out the word *horse,* at which time he is out of the game. The dodge here is change the name of the game to *pig* if your opponent misses three baskets before you miss five. If that doesn't happen and you spell out all five letters, claim that *you* were playing *centipede,* and continue playing. If you are playing exceptionally bad and extra turns won't help, kick the ball up on the roof and declare the game a draw. (Be sure you stick the ball behind the backboard because it's almost impossible to stick a basketball in a gutter.)

The Circle Jerk Scam

Since whacking off in a room full of assholes isn't exactly "erotic," everyone in the circle is going to have to whack a little harder and a little longer. You, of course, will sneak into a john just before game time and take the little picture of the bush you clipped out of *Oui* from its hiding place in your sock and "prime the pump"; when you get into the room the vision of the mound is fresh on your mind and in a squeeze or two you're the winner. If for some reason you can't get into the john, you can prevent a victory by holding up the other guys. Ask them about their mothers and grandmothers and sisters and pastors or priests.

Paycheck Poker

Pardon me, but if you play this game fair and square you are a dick-brain. The game is simple enough: you play the serial numbers on your paycheck like a poker hand. If you lose, you lose your check. It's risky and the stakes are high, especially if you have a wife, some kids, and a mortgage payment to make. Start watching your paycheck numbers and wait until you get a good hand; then and only then, enter the game. If you buy the comptrollers' secretary a photo cube for her desk or a snake plant, she'll gladly give you a supply of fresh paycheck envelopes. All you do is slip the ringer check in the envelope every week until it wears out. *Caution:* since you'll literally be taking the food out of the mouths of children, you have to be discreet. Don't rack up fifteen straight victories. Take some of your winnings and lose once in a while. However, if you're in a management position and play with your subordinates, you needn't cover yourself too well. Unless they have an outside income, they'll never have the balls to challenge you.

The Switch Bet

People are so eager to *win* they will very often leap into a bet without even considering it. Try this next time your lawn needs a clipping. Bet your teenage son that he's not strong enough to mow a whole lawn in half an hour. Be sure and slip out just before he finishes so that you won't be home to verify that he did it. He will insist that he completed the task, but you tell him that since you didn't see it you have to assume that he didn't do it. Be a sport and offer him another bet: can he clean the eaves and sweep up the garage in an hour? If your kid takes after your wife's side of the family, you can run this thing all weekend.

Cheating People from Other Countries

The easiest bet in the universe is *any* bet with a foreigner.

You: I'll bet you that you don't have a nickle in your pocket.

Man from Malaysia: Oh, how much you will bet for?

You: Fifty bucks, U.S.

Man from Malaysia: Here's fifty dollars and here nickle is. I win bet; pay me please fifty dollars.

You: What the fuck do you know? See you at the noodle factory!

Man from Malaysia: That is my money! Give it to me, come back at once!

Cheating the Supermarket Games

Without going to a lower order of animal, you can't find a dumber thing than a teen-age girl working part-time in a grocery store. If you walk up to one and tell her that you want to buy wheelchairs for blind kids and the only way to get the dough is to win the weekly supermarket bingo game, she'll roll over like a refugee boat. She'll load you up with so many free bingo chips you'll have to rent a U-Haul.

Beating the State Lotteries

Call your state lottery office and claim that your house is a drugstore, and tell them that you want to sell lottery tickets. When your tickets arrive, head down to the dentist's office. Insert an instant winner lottery card in either side of your mouth and ask for an X-ray. Continue until you have X-rayed the entire supply of cards. Read the X-rays for the winning numbers. Turn those cards in and sell the ones that won't win. Be aware, however, that the chances of your contracting lottery cancer double.

The Sports Cheater

Dispute everything; claim that everything hit, kicked, swatted, booted, thrown, or slid is foul, short, long, or anything but what it is. Complain about your opponent's equipment, his tactics, his looks, the amount of noise he makes when he plays. Bitch about how your shoes are too tight, the sun's in your eyes, your dick hurts, your clubs, racquet, bat, stick, oar, flipper, paddle, or cap has been tampered with. This should distract him enough to throw his game out of whack.

Board Game Cheats in Brief

Chess: If you get into trouble, upset the board and relocate your pieces.

Checkers: Apply a small amount of rubber cement to your palm. When you move a piece of your own, press your palm down on one of your opponent's pieces and return it to your "capture" pile.

Monopoly: Miscount moves, refuse to pay rents, set yourself up with credit, make deals that are so complicated everyone will lose track, play a second piece, make yourself banker and embezzle funds.

Backgammon: Throw a drink in your opponent's face. Rearrange the pieces.

Clue: Peek at the card in the envelope.

Master Mind: Hit your opponent with a chair and win by forfeiture.

Five Rules for Operating a Successful Sports Pool

1. Make at least one third of the squares impossible bets (Denver over Seattle by 100, Yankees in nine games over the St. Louis Browns, etc.). Sell these to the broads in the office.

2. Sell your squares for one dollar. A buck never hurts. Even the slopehead in the mailroom has a buck to throw your way.

3. Whenever possible, pay the winner in chances on squares for the following weeks. The odds of him winning a second pool is about as good as getting a hand job at a funeral.

4. Never sell the squares that have a chance of winning (Dallas over Chicago by twenty-one). Claim that these are already sold. It will cut into your gross earnings, but it will also avert a large payout.

5. Tell any winner that you accidentally sold the same square you sold him to "that poor gal in accounting whose husband and sister died a couple of weeks ago." If he doesn't offer to donate his winnings to her, he's a real prick.

The Father Rule

"At any given time during the course of a game, sporting match, bet, or contest, a father may terminate that event and declare himself winner and champion of the house. He is not required to make a disclosure of his reasons for that action. He may claim as his, any and all stakes or purses. The rule may be invoked at the discretion of the father without limitation. The father may alter the rules of any game, sport, or contest as he sees fit, and may apply special conditions that will affect the performance of his opponents to his benefit No father shall be required to handicap his efforts to equalize contests with younger children. No mother shall interfere with the invoking of the father rule under threat of penalty of not less than no car for a week, and not to exceed wearing last year's winter coat this winter."

The Love Song of

J. EDGAR HOOVER

by Sean Kelly

In sua voluntate e nostra pace

We'd better go quietly, you and I,
When the evening is smeared against the sky
Like a witness before a house committee:
We'd better tail each other through the streets
The undercover beats
Of stakeout nights in Mafia hotels
And restaurants that front for mob cartels:
Streets that follow like a DA's argument
Establishing intent
To overwhelm you with a leading question . . .
Oh, let's go and bust a traitor
We'll pick up the warrant later.

The agents call and call again
Talking of Daniel Berrigan.

And indeed they'll all do time,
That yellow mob that riots in the street,
Trashing the banks and breaking windowpanes;
They will do time, they will do time
The mug shots are prepared, I'll know their faces
    when we meet;
They will do time for murder, crossing state
Lines with intent, their idle little hands
Will do time punching out my license plate;
Time for throwing and overthrowing,
And time for a hundred conspiracies,
And a hundred tricks and treacheries,
Plenty of time for that where they're going.

The agents call and call again
Talking of Daniel Berrigan.

Yes indeed, they'll all do time,
Those Commie symps who talk behind my back,
For every liberal sneer and dirty crack,
For every smear and bleeding heart attack—
(They all say: "Look, his arse is getting fat!")
They criticize my shapeless suits and snappy G-man hat,
My collars all a size too small, my simple string cravat—
(They all say: "His neck is thick, his head is fat!")
Do I dare
Wiretap the universe?
I look forward to a time
Of decisions and convictions the Supreme Court
    can't reverse.

For I know them all already, I have dossiers on
    them all:—
Have them cold for tax evasion, graft or rape,
I've spun out my life on little spools of tape;
I have their voices lying, have each spying call,
Have dates, names, places, everything I need.
   Now how shall I proceed?

And I have known the spies already, known them all—
They fix the courts, the CIA was formed by
    Commie spies,
It has all been infiltrated, crawling with those reds,
I'll pin the buggers up against the wall,
Me and my trusty Feds
Will stick the butt-ends of our forty-fours between
    their thighs!
   But how shall I proceed?

And I have known the arms already, known them all—
Arms any moron has the right to bear
(But in the lab light, fingerprints are there!)
Thinking of a gun or rifle
Makes me digress a trifle.
Along with dope and marked bills, I'll plant pistols
    on them all.
   And then should I proceed?
   And when should I begin?

         *   *   *

Shall I say, I have gone disguised through littered streets
And smelled the smoke that rises from the joints

Of long-haired party-members throwing rocks
    through windows? . . .
I should have been a pair of rugged cuffs
Closing upon the wrists of Eldridge C.

               *   *   *

My dreams of glory, my ambition, slipped from my hands
Smothered by long intrigue,
Plots . . . subterfuges . . . they fatigue
My old brain, codes, commands and countermands.
Should I, after Dillinger, in my finest hour,
Have made my move, sought office, taken power?
Though I was supercop, and every reader of the *Digest*
    knew it,
Though I have seen my face (ferocious toad) on every
    cover and front page,
I never took the lead—remained backstage;
I have seen the moment of my greatness flicker,
And I have seen Life's Cameraman focus on me,
    and snicker,
And in short, I blew it.

And after all, would it have been worthwhile,
Behind the pictures, underneath the rugs,
In every nook and cranny to have placed my little bugs,
To have them all, the victims and assailants,
In me they trust, one nation under surveillance;
To have squeezed the universe into a file
To open at my whim and/or discretion,
To say: "I am Jehova, strict but fair,
My eye is on the sparrow, and on *you!*"—
If one, sticking a finger in the air,
    Should say back to the microphone: "Fuck you!"
    Should say: "Fuck you." And smile.

And would it have been worth it, after all,
Would it have been worthwhile,
After the shootouts and the setups and the incriminating
    leaks,
After the columns, after the speeches, after the trials
    that dragged on for years—
The TV show on which "the Chief" appears?—
It's just impossible to say how mean I am!
But if I had the nerve to let them screen the truth about
    this sham:
Would it have been worthwhile
If all my agents, breaking cover, dropping their disguise,
Should suddenly surround me, and say to my surprise:

"There is a plot. What's more, we're all
In on the plot, investigate us all!"
                    *   *   *
No! I am not Efrem Zimbalist, nor was meant to be;
Am an attendant pig, behind the arras,
Stupid, and so not easy to embarrass,
Useful for busting dealers at the borders,
Reading St. Paul to whitéd congregations,
Arranging suitable defenestrations,
And casting demons out from demonstrations;
Sometimes I interrupt assassinations—
Sometimes I give the orders.

I grow old . . . I grow old . . .
Some who I sent up for life have been paroled.

Are my agents wearing sideburns? Who dared to say
      impeach?
I shall give communion breakfasts my Commie-menace
      speech.
I have heard canaries singing, each to each.

I don't think any more will sing for me.

I have seen them burning draft cards in the park
Burning the files of bureaus and committees,
The wind is black with burning flags and cities.

We have played with fire, bringing down the heat
To smother reds and blacks in screens of smoke
Till human torches touch us, and we croak.

Fragment of the Oral History of

Tempura County, Tennessee, or,

"HIYA, CYRUS"

by John Weidman and Tony Hendra

(The following is a transcript of the first and last in a series of tape recordings made by Stephen Baumgarten, of the Department of Domestic Anthropology at the University of Indiana, as part of a doctoral thesis entitled, "Socioeconomic and Tribal Patterns in the Behavioral Modes of Rural Population Units." Having studied Baumgarten's research itinerary, his thesis supervisor suggests that the following interview may have taken place last April 7, in or near the county seat of Tempura County, New Kyoto. Baumgarten himself has disappeared.)

BAUMGARTEN: This is the voice of Stephen Baumgarten, doctoral candidate at the University of Indiana at Bloomington. For the purposes of setting this research material in its proper context, I will now describe where I am sitting and whom I am seated with. I am sitting on a four-legged stool, the top of which is fashioned from a single two-inch thick crosscust maple section, into which the hand hewn legs have been mitered, and known locally as a *scrapshat buskis,* or sitting-stool. I am surrounded by the four plain walls of a one-room dwelling upon which hang the detritus of a depressed yet resilient American subculture, ranging from a yellowed tintype of William Jennings Bryan to a World War II issue trenching tool, which has been ingeniously adapted for use as a spatula. Sitting with me are five individuals representative of traditional Tempura County social structures, one of them a Negro.

NATE: Thass' me . . .

UNIDENTIFIED: Shut up, Nate . . .

NATE: O.K., O.K., O.K. . . .

BAUMGARTEN: The assembled are in order of quasi-tribal hierarchy. Judge Emmett T. Brasenose, who has ridden circuit in Tempura County for the past forty-seven years. Reverend Proverbs E. Jackson, pastor of the First Baptist Church of Doom. Rufus Lung, unemployed, and self-appointed chronicler of county history, Widow Fitch, who ekes out a precarious living as a quiltmaker, and, er . . . Nate. Hello.

VOICES: (Unintelligible for 7.3 seconds)

BAUMGARTEN: As we discussed prior to recording, a grant from the University has made it possible for me to offer you all a small stipend for your participation.

BRASENOSE: How much?

BAUMGARTEN: It isn't much, but shall we say, ten dollars an hour?

BRASENOSE: Speakin' for us all, that won't be necessary.

NATE: Hold on, I wan (?) that *(unintelligible for 4.2 seconds)* I wan (?) . . .

JACKSON: You shut up, Nate. We don't need no ten dollars an hour. Nor fifty, either.

BAUMGARTEN: Outside of the manifestly typical aspects of this region, one of the things I'm curious about is the derivation of the name Tempura County. Tempura, as you are probably unaware, is a form of Oriental cookery, in which . . .

NATE: I 'member back in the old time, was when Mr. Roosevelt was president, me and my old daddy, setting up in the kitchen, dog came through the kitchen, knock that table right on down . . .

FITCH: Now, you shut up, Nate. You shut your noise. Gentleman don't want to hear about no dog. He want (to) hear about the frogs.

BAUMGARTEN: The frogs.

FITCH: See these boots? They're frog. Every boot here is frog.

(All agree)

BAUMGARTEN: You mean these shoes are actually crafted from the skin of frogs? That's . . .

FITCH: Not frogs. One frog. And this skirt. And the tablecloth there. And them drapes.

BAUMGARTEN: I'm not sure I follow.

FITCH: Tempura County frog. Stand mebbe six, seven foot tall, some of them . . .

(General agreement)

BAUMGARTEN: Oh, I see I'm the victim of a local joke here. That's very funny.

BRASENOSE: Ain't no joke, mister.

FITCH: Best not let Cyrus hear you talkin' thet way.

BAUMGARTEN: Cyrus . . .

BRASENOSE: Ain't nothin' wrong with a six-foot frog. My daughter's married to one. Smart, too. Got an I.Q. of 180. Good provider . . . tolerable cook . . .

BAUMGARTEN: Er . . . that brings me back to my original question, concerning the name Tempura County . . .

FITCH: That ain't no mystery. What tempura is is you take deveined shrimp, or certain kinds of fish, or coarsely chopped vegetables, dredge 'em in a light batter, and fry 'em in deep fat or sesame oil. Then you eat 'em with soy sauce.

BAUMGARTEN: I understand that, but it's a Japanese dish. Where did you learn it?

FITCH: From the Japanese.

BAUMGARTEN: In Japan?

FITCH: No. Right on over the hill there. In Haiku Hollow.

BAUMGARTEN: Wait, wait, wait. There are Japanese in Tempura County?

BRASENOSE: Not no more there ain't. They was only here in the war. Seven battalions of 'em. Came right after Pearl Harbor. Dropped in by Cyrus. Man, that was a shame what happened to them Japs.

NATE: Yup, I was out that night huntin' coons, with my old dog, old dog spots a coon—this was back when Mr. Roosevelt was president—jumps up on the cordwood and brings down the whole dang pile. What a racket . . .

(Several urge Nate to shut up)

BAUMGARTEN: Please. It's possible I'm misunderstanding, but you seem to be suggesting that there were several thousand Japanese troops here during World War II, and that's why it's called Tempura County?

FITCH: Ain't always bin Tempura County. Afore the war it was Soufflé County.

BAUMGARTEN: Hold on . . . perhaps we can backtrack a little, and start again, for my benefit.

(General agreement)

Thank you. Now, each one of your rural counties down here, however remote from the national mainstream, seems to have produced figures of more than local significance, who to some extent capitalize on their roots and conversely tell us much about the locales from which they sprang. A Mac Davis, a Junior Johnson, whatever. Has Tempura County any . . . well . . . local heroes?

BRASENOSE: Oh, sure. Plenty fellows from hereabouts went out and made good. Like . . . er . . . Harold Macmillan.

BAUMGARTEN: Harold Macmillan? Does he play something?

BRASENOSE: Well, he used to tinker 'round on the piano, some. But that ain't how he made his mark. After leaving here, he had a brilliant career at Oxford University, rose rapidly through the ranks of the British Conservative Party, eventually succeeding Anthony Eden as Prime Minister of England.

JACKSON: Then there was Avery Brundage . . .

FITCH: Nikolai Gogol . . .

BRASENOSE: And Krishna Menon . . . and then there was Escoffier.

BAUMGARTEN: Please, I . . .

FITCH: That's why it used to be called Soufflé County. He was born over Sashimi way back in 1847. Way Cyrus tells it, he had to get him out of here during the Civil War. Guns and all was making his soufflés drop. Went to Paris, never come back.

BAUMGARTEN: What you're claiming, then, is that several famous international personalities in widely ranging walks of life, living in far-flung countries, originally came from Tempura County.

FITCH: Better say from Soufflé County. Fact is, we ain't had too many folks leave since the war, except, of course, Freddie and the Dreamers.

BAUMGARTEN: But that's preposterous.

BRASENOSE: Told ye afore, sonny. Wouldn't let Cyrus catch you talkin' that way.

BAUMGARTEN: Who is this Cyrus?

FITCH: I was forgittin'. You don't know Cyrus, do ye. He'll be along.

BRASENOSE: You get on the wrong side of Cyrus, there's no telling what he'll do.

JACKSON: Look what he did to that Cranshaw girl.

BAUMGARTEN: What happened?

BRASENOSE: No one rightly knows what he did to her, but right after he got to hear 'bout it, she got pregnant. Now, that ain't so unaccountable, but nine months later she gave birth to a four-foot slide rule.

FITCH: Near tore 'er in two, it did. Serve her right.

BAUMGARTEN: Note to myself: what I seem to have stumbled upon here is an extraordinary quasireligious phenomenon. The evidence adduced by these people can only be explained by either some externally manipulated mass-hallucinatory activity on the part of this community, or some hitherto undiscovered private cult based on partially understood communications input, a kind of cargo cult, as it were, on the outskirts of the global village.

LUNG (?) Ngung (?) brakka nonfenimolig (?) naganna predetm (?) *(unintelligible for 12.3 seconds)* fungermore (?) teary God (?) *(unintelligible for 7.0 seconds)*.

BAUMGARTEN: What did he say?

JACKSON: He thinks your argument is a clear example of reductionist cross-cultural comparativism and feels that, on the contrary, the belief structure of Tempura County is in no way comparable to the ergot manifestations in four-teenth century Alsace.

LUNG: Morph (?) raxafrax (?) *(unintelligible for 16.6 seconds).*

JACKSON: Rufus, we been all 'round the barn on that one last week. The Radcliffe Brownian conception of stasis in nomothesis does not come near generating the data that we get from a Durkheimian "group manifestation" commensalist schema.

LUNG: (Unintelligible for 8.3 seconds.)

BAUMGARTEN: Yes. Well, in the interests of harmonious discussion, I'm willing to concede Mr. Lung's point. Mr. Jackson, perhaps you'd be willing to apply *your* analysis to another area of critical interest?

JACKSON: Sure thing.

BAUMGARTEN: I want to preface this by asking you to feel entirely free to stop me if you think that any of these enquiries overstep the boundaries of either personal or collective taste.

FITCH: You mean sex?

(General noise 5.4 seconds)

BAUMGARTEN: Er, yes. We've learned that often the pair-bonding process within a given subculture approaches our western notion of the marriage rit-ual . . .

FITCH: We all married here.

BAUMGARTEN: I understand that, but . . .

FITCH: To one another. What you're looking at, sonny, is an open mar-riage . . .

(General noise 9.5 seconds)

. . . open to, and required of, all residents of Tempura County.

BAUMGARTEN: I see. How does that work?

FITCH: We all fuck one another. Whenever, wherever, whoever. Fuck, fuck, fuck all the time. Up the ass, in the mouth, even where it's s'posed to go.

(General noise, unidentified sounds 3 minutes 43.8 seconds)

BAUMGARTEN: Please, please, please *(distortion).* Excuse me. Er, I think I may be running out of tape here. I wonder if we could conclude . . .

BRASENOSE: Sure. Put your dick away, Rufus. What you want to know?

BAUMGARTEN: It would round out the excellent picture I've formed of your lifestyle if you could give me some idea of your means of subsistence.

Widow Fitch, I've been told, for instance, that you are a quiltmaker. What is the market for them?

FITCH: Hell, I don't make money from them.

BAUMGARTEN: How do you survive, then?

FITCH: Like everyone else. I goes out every month or two and piles up rocks.

BAUMGARTEN: What kind of rocks?

FITCH: All kinds. 'Specially them shiny ones from down the lower forty. Cyrus don't always take them, though. No knowing which one old Cyrus gonna take.

BAUMGARTEN: Ah, Cyrus again. I'd been meaning to ask about him. Who exactly is this Cyrus?

BRASENOSE: Little fella. One eye. Moves around on wheels. No arms or legs or nothin'.

BAUMGARTEN: He's a cripple?

JACKSON: Naw. They all look that way. You'll see.

BAUMGARTEN: So this Cyrus buys certain of your rocks, is that correct?

FITCH: Don't rightly buy them. More like barter. See, he picks out the rocks he likes an gives us stuff back. Like, say, Xerox stock or Dutch Masters.

BAUMGARTEN: Xerox stock and cigars?

BRASENOSE: Not cigars. Vermeer. Holbein. Ain't always Dutch, of course. This one here's a Mantegna.

BAUMGARTEN: Bbbbut this is incredible, incredible, I . . .

(Unidentified noises, door [?], movement)

FITCH: Hi, Cyrus.

UNIDENTIFIED VOICE (CYRUS?): Howdy, folks.

(General noise, greeting [?] under B. Considerable distortion)

BAUMGARTEN: This is unbelievable I what is going on here seems to be a creature or machine has just entered has er it's my God, there's a general light and a small girl, holy Jesus it's got one eye thing and wheels . . .

JACKSON: How you bin, Cyrus? Warm enough for you?

CYRUS(?): Can't complain.

FITCH: You bin a good girl, Lou Anne?

LOU ANNE(?): Sure have, Grandma. Cyrus took me to Cygnus A.

BAUMGARTEN: This where it holy fuckin' (?) Christ I

LOU ANNE(?): . . . and then we went through this time-space warp and I got all over goosebumps and I was real old, even older 'n you, Grandma, I was a hundred and two . . .

BRASENOSE: Now you hush up, Lou Anne. We got company.

BAUMGARTEN: That's, er, I'm getting outta leaving just . . .

CYRUS(?): Now you jest set yourself down, Mr. Baumgarten.

BRASENOSE: Takin' any rocks this trip, Cyrus?

CYRUS(?): Sure am. And guess what I got y'all . . .

(General noise 2.2 seconds)

. . . one hundred tickets to *A Chorus Line* and free dinner at Sardi's.

(General noise, falling object [?]. Tape ends.)

HOW TO TALK DIRTY IN ESPERANTO

KIEL PAROLE MALPURE EN ESPERANTO

by Richard Bonker and Henry Beard

SO YOU DIDN'T THINK you could! Frankly, it's as easy as a *furpie* if you follow my simple rules. There are many sound reasons for spending the next few hours learning them. To name a few: With Esperanto you can write graffiti on the walls of the restrooms of the United Nations, the World Court at The Hague, or the European Parliament at Strasbourg without shame, and on more common surfaces without fear of contradiction. With Esperanto you can derive considerable pleasure from uttering even the vilest phrase in Esperanto; although your language is from the gutter, it is from the gutters of the Champs Elysées, the Kurfürstendamm, Jermyn Street, and the Via Sant Angelo. And if afterward you should feel remorse, you are entitled to wash your mouth out with beeswax or anise or some other exotic astringent instead of ordinary soap. With Esperanto you can trade imprecations as an equal with members of foreign-born minority groups whose native caterwauls—with their varmint-like barkings, pagan speech-rhythms, and moronic, sing-song syllables—are so much more appropriate to scatological usage than the noble cadences of English. You can expound at great length on the chastity, racial characteristics, and sexual inventiveness of their mothers without risking the kind of comprehension that has them reaching for knives to supplement their disappointing vocabularies. And should you, by great good fortune, enter into an altercation with a fellow Esperantist, the great commitment to international brotherhood and understanding that you share with your antagonist will quickly overcome the bitterest of enmities, and you will be able to adjourn speedily to a nearby trattoria, there to partake of a toast of beeswax and anise to Dr. L. Ludwig Zamenhof, the creator of Esperanto, and to us, of course, for correcting his puzzling oversight of not having included any dirty words in Esperanto in the first place.

FIRST: pronunciation! Master these rules and you will be able to speak Esperanto like a native!

Esperanto is phonetic; letters are always pronounced alike no matter where they appear! B, d, f, h, k, l, m, n, p, s, t, v, z, are pronounced exactly as in English, so don't worry about them.

a	Father made me do it.
ĉ	tits
c	Chew on these, big boy.
e	there
g	gobble
ĝ	Gee, you sure have a small cock, needle-dick daddy.
ĥ	German "Achtung!" (The closest English equivalent is suck.)
i	cherry
j	yoni
ĵ	pleasure pit
o	old dirt road
r	French "merde" (pronounced mer-r-r-de)
ŝ	shit
u	boobs
aj	Spanish fly
aŭ	go down on
ej	foreplay
eŭ	"eh" plus "oo"
oj	joint
uj	Oh, ick, it's all gooey!

Now that wasn't so hard, was it? Don't be ashamed to consult this list whenever you feel the need. And, one more thing, remember: In words with more than one syllable, the stress is always on the next to last syllable. In words of only two syllables, the first is stressed, since it is also the next to last.

SECOND: grammar! Esperanto has the easiest grammar in the world! Memorize these rules and you will have no trouble with the language. All Esperanto words consist of a root[1] and an ending. The root gives the meaning of the word and the ending tells what part of speech it has. Nothing could be simpler and there are no exceptions in Esperanto.

Now watch as we make our first whole sentence:

Liroj mangas viadon.

LEE-roy MAHN-jass vee-AHN-doan.

Leroy eats meat.

Isn't that easy! What we really wanted to say was "Leroy eats shit," but our Esperanto dictionary unaccountably refused to list it. Nevertheless, we push on with:

Sandra lekas pilkojn.

SAN-drah LEH-kass PEEL-coin.

---

[1] As soon as you've had your little laugh, we'll go on.

Sandra licks balls.
all of which are in the book. Notice how useful the affixes are:
Sandra lekadas pilkegojn.
SAN-drah leh-KAH-dass peel-KEH-goyn.
Sandra frequently-licks large-balls.

In Esperanto, the verb *veni* means "to come." Using the suffix *-uj*, which means "container," we get *venujo*, scumbag; whence:
Li venas en la venujon.
LEE-VEHN-ass EHN LA veh-NOO-yon.
He comes into the scumbag.

Other useful appurtenances of *veni* are *venajo* 'come-substance' or 'jism,' *venegulo* 'a real comer,' *venestro* 'come-leader' (useful at orgies), etc. With these preliminaries out of the way, we are all set to go to town (or around the world) with this larger passage:

Saluton! /Kiel vi fartas?[2] */Gage bone! /Ĉu vi havas la plumon? /Jes, mi havas la granda forta plumon, sed la inko estas malpura. /Malbene! /Kia idioto mi estis, ne uzi la venejon.*

Hello there! /How are you faring? /Jolly good! /Have you a pen? /Yes, I have the large strong pen, but the ink is rotten. /That is awful! /What a fool I was not to use the scumbag.

We've gone as far as we can without some bona-fide dirty words. We won't let the spoilsport editors who compiled the dictionary have the last word; Esperanto is nothing if not adaptable. Dirty words are as easy to come by as a well-engineered teat—provided my patented system is followed.

THIRD: Vocabulary!
Example: **Asshole.** This could be rendered accurately as "anus opening," but this somehow lacks vividness: *anoaperturo.* A much better rendering would be "windhole." Thus, add *vento* to *truo* to get *ventruo.* Another more colorful rendering would be to borrow the Chinese expression "fart-eye." Thus: *fartokulo.*

Example: **Furburger.** This rather eloquent euphemism for the vulva is simply rendered by noting that the Esperanto for "Hamburg" (the alleged city of origin for the meat pattie) is *Amburgo.* Add to this the word for "fur" to get *felburgo.*

Example: **Twat.** This one's harder. "Twat" is from an old English expression for "hole in the hedge." The Esperantan rendition for this is impossibly long—"growing-thing-fence-hole," i.e., *kreskajbariltruo.* However, the essence of "twat" is "bushy," which is best rendered (inasmuch as the Esperantan for "bush" is "little tree"—too long a word) as *broso* "brush."

Example: **Prick.** This is directly translated as *pikilo,* but to get a shorter

---

[2] The word *farti,* contrary to your expectations, means "to fare" in Esperanto. Makes a jolly pun, though: "How do You do?" puns with "How are you farting?"

word, we truncate it to *piko*. Another possibility might be to make use of the suffix *-il* which means "tool" or "instrument of." Thus, if *fuki* is the verb "to fuck," then *la fukilo* means "the tool to fuck with" or, in other words, cock or prick.

Example: **Shit.** There are a number of baroque possibilities here, such as *noktomalpuro* "nightsoil," which seems excessively prudish, and *brunaserpento* "brown snake," which is evocative but clumsy. The best bet is to use the common root found in other languages, as is the custom in Esperanto: *"merde"* to form *merdo*. It's an effortless step from the construction of dirty words in Esperanto to the compilation of short phrases. Remember, a little imagination goes a long way.

FOURTH: Practice! Translate these sentences into Esperanto.

1. The weather is nice. It is pleasant here. That is a pretty dress. Let's fuck.
Vetero estas agrable. Estas placa ĉi tie. Tiu estas beleta kostumo. Ni fuku.

2. There seems to be some error. Your ass is occupying the position which rightfully belongs to your head.
Apera esti ia eraro. Via posto okupas la pozicion ke laŭrajte apartenas al via kapo.

3. You are a booby. Would you be so kind as to bend over so that I may insert this kumquat into your rectum?
Via estas naivegulo. Vi estus afabla ŝufice kliniĝi tiel ke mi esteblos enmeti ĉi tiu kumkvaton en via anuso?

4. Please correct me if I am mistaken, but are you not accustomed to eating shit?
Mi petas korekto min se mi eraras, sed ĉu vi kutimas ne mangi merdon?

5. Shame! You should have your mouth washed out with beeswax and anise!
Honto! Vi lavu vin buson kun abelvakso kaj anizo!

6. Can you direct me to the nearest medical facility? My penis has been struck by lightning.
Ĉu vi povas direkti min al multoproksima medicina efiko? Mia piko estis frapont de fulmo.

As a final test of your newfound skill, translate the following passages at your leisure into English. And remember, practice makes perfect!

Passage No. 1

Mansignant la konstitucion kun minaĉo, ili devigas Ĝ. Ê. Uver leki la pilkojn de F. Ĝ. Ŝin dum Elen Keler masturbas kun kolumbo.

Passage No. 2

Ili fukas panjon sur litkovrilo de la amerika flago kun dileto de tagaĝa varmeg-hundo dum pisant sur la Biblio kaj frajon kaj reprodukto de "Amerika Gotika."

Conversation

Pardonu, fraŭlino, mi vidas ke vi portas verdan stelon. /Jes. Ĝi estas ĉar mi parolas lingve. /Kiel vi fartas hodiaŭ? /Mi fartas bone. Ejnstejn edzigis lia kuzinon en Skenektadi. /Ĉu vi observas ofte birdmigradojn? /Ne. Mia patro estas okulisto. /Mi esperas ke Ejnstejn estis plena de boneco. /Ĉu mi pruntus tason de teo? /Jes. Kiu estas la pli alta: hundido aŭ tekruĉo? /Mi ne konas. Mi ne fartas jam de multaj tagoj. /Je kioma horo vi aŭdas la veterprognozon? /Vide-mandas multajn demandojn. /Ĝi estas car mi demandas ilin. Demetu vion ŝtrumpojn. /Ni aŭdis unu horon da muzikaĵoj per gramofono. /Demetu nun vian brakteningon. /Estas ne vorto por "brakteningon." /Vi komprenis min sufiĉe. /Antaŭ tri tagon mi vidis teatraĵon de Leroj. /Ĉi tio estas koko. /Ho ĉu estas tio koko? /Ĉi tioj estas pilkoj. /Kial ekzistas tia multigeco da haroj? /Nun vi de-mandas la demandojn. /Mia patro estis okulisto. /Mia patro edzigis Ejnstejn. /Kiel mi faras pri tio? /Metu ĝin en vian buŝon. /La okulo estas granda! /La pli bono vin vidi! /Kial vi grutas? /Mia anguinalo jukas. /Mia patro jukas neniam. /Fuku vian patron! /Mi fukas ja. Tial mi ekzistas.

Nouns:	-o	singular
	-oj	plural
	-on	singular-noun used as direct object
	-ojn	plural noun used as direct object
Verbs:	-as	present tense
	-is	past tense
	-os	future tense
	-us	conditional mood
	-u	imperative mood
	-ant	present participle
	-int	past participle
	-ont	future participle
Personal pronouns:	mi	I
	vi	you
	li	he
	ŝi	she
	ĝi	it
	ni	we
	ili	they
Adjectives:	-a	(-aj, -an, -ajn for plural, singular as direct object; and plural as direct object, respectively)
Adverbs:	-e	
Conjunctions,	la	the
prepositions,	kaj	and
and related words:	sur	on top of
	sub	under
	je	on (abstract) as in "*on* the rag"
	al	to
	de, da	of
	kun	with
	sed	but
	kiu	who
	ĉu	"do" as an auxillary, as in "*Do you* give head?"
	jes	yes
	ne	no, not
	kio	what
Useful affixes:	ek-	sudden action
(suffixes and prefixes)	fi-	shameful, nasty
	mal-	the opposite of
	pra-	very old
	-aĉ	contemptible, disgusting
	-ad	frequent or continuous
	-ec	abstract quality of (-ship or -ness)
	-eg	great size
	-et	small-sized
	-in	feminine
	-uj	container

USEFUL SENTENCES

Esperanto	Pronunciation	Translation
1. *Leroj merdas.*	LEE-roy MÊHR-dass.	Leroy shits.
2. *Leroj ekfimerdas.*	LEE-roy eck-fee-MEHR-dass.	Leroy nasty-shits-sudden.
3. *Leroj kaj Sandra mer-dadas montegojn da pramerdo.*	LEE-roy kai SAN-dra mehr-da-dass mon-TEH-goin da pra-MEHR-doe.	Leroy and Sandra frequently-shit great-sized-piles of antiquated-shit.
4. *Vi estas dek funtoj da merdo en kvinfunta sako.*	VEE EHS-tass dek FOON-toy da MEHR-doe ehn kveen-FOON-tah SOCK-oh.	You are ten pounds of shit in a five-pound bag.
5. *La grandioza kvalito da via mer-do garantas aboleri la konkurson.*	La gran-dee-OH-zah kval-EE-toe da VEE-a MEHR-doe ga-RAHN-tass ah-bo-LEH-ree la kohn-KOOR-sohn.	The superb quality of your shit is guaranteed to wipe out the competition.
6. *Fuku vin!*	FOO-koo VEEN!	Fuck you!
7. *Peki estas homa, fuki estas divina.*	PEH-kee EHS-tass HO-ma, FOO-kee EHS-tass dee-VEE-nah.	To err is human, to fuck divine.
8. *Li fukas ŝian broson.*	Lee Foo-kass SHE-ahn BRO-sohn.	He fucks her twat.
9. *Vi ekfukas ŝian brose-ton kun via pikego.*	Vee eck-FOO-kass SHE-ahn bro-SEHT-tohn koon VEE-ah pee-KEH-go.	You quick-fuck her tiny-twat with your giant-cock.
10. *Mi pendegas.*	Mee pehn-DEH-gass.	I am well hung.
11. *Via pendeco estas malkredeba.*	VEE-ah pehn-DEH-tso EHS-tass mal-kreh-DEH-bah.	Your state of being hung is highly questionable.
12. *Li pendas kiel ham-stro.*	Lee PEHN-dass KEE-el HAM-stro.	He is hung like a hamster.
13. *Viaj veniloj aperas multe kiel spinakaco.*	VEE-aye veh-NEE-loy ah-PEHR-ass MOOL-teh KEE-ehl spee-nah-KAH-cho.	Your genitals bear a remarkable resemblance to moldy spinach.
14. *Estes mia esprima de-ziro ke fulmo frapus vian pinon.*	EHS-tass MEE-a ehs-PREE-ma deh-ZEE-roh keh FOOL-ma FRA-puss VEE-ahn PEE-non.	It is my express wish that your penis be struck by lightning.
15. *Estas mia konjekto ke via patrino estas ne strango al cirkauprenoj de hejmaj dorlotoj kaj fojnejokortaj bestoj.*	EHS-tass MEE-ah kohn-YEK-to keh VEE-a pa-TREE-no EST-ass neh STRAN-goh ahl tseer-cow-PREH-noy deh HEM-mai dor-LOT-toy kai foy-neh-yo-KOR-tai BES-toy.	It is my conjecture that your mother is no stranger to the embraces of domestic pets and barnyard animals.

1974

STUPID APTITUDE TEST (SAT)

TEST TO BE ADMINISTERED ON:
Monday, January 7th OR Saturday, January 12th

DO NOT OPEN THIS BOOK UNTIL YOU ARE TOLD TO DO SO.

GENERAL DIRECTIONS
You will be given two hours to work this test, which is divided into three sections measuring your VERBAL and MATH ability. The supervisor will tell you when to begin. Should you finish a section before the time is called, you may check your work, **but you are NOT to work on any other section.** If you do, go directly to BELOIT COLLEGE and DO NOT collect prestige diploma.

SECTION I: VERBAL ABILITY
Time—40 minutes
35 Questions

· ·

Part A—Antonyms

DIRECTIONS: For each of the questions in this section, choose the best answer and blacken the corresponding box in the answer sheet not provided.

Each question below consists of a word printed in capital letters, followed by five choices lettered A through E. Choose the lettered word whose meaning is most nearly *opposite* the meaning of the capitalized word. Ready. Get set. Go.

```
EXAMPLE:
UP
(A) somewhere
(B) anywhere
(C) underwear
(D) meat loaf
(E) down


 A     B     C     D     E

 ::    ::    ::    ::     ⚡
```

1. ANTONYM
   (A) antitank
   (B) anteater
   (C) homonym
   (D) Houyhnhnm
   (E) hominid

2. TABLE
   (A) bird
   (B) ocean
   (C) tree
   (D) bridge
   (E) boat

3. EUPHEMISM
   (A) colostomy
   (B) obscenity
   (C) inoperative
   (D) plump
   (E) number two

4. CUTE
   (A) morganic
   (B) draconian
   (C) anapestic
   (D) not so cute
   (E) blow job

5. POLE
   (A) frog
   (B) check
   (C) lap
   (D) fin
   (E) human

6. BIFURCATE
   (A) corruscate
   (B) blanch
   (C) astringe
   (D) misprise
   (E) fructify

7. VIRGIN
   (A) coward
   (B) repressed
   (C) intact
   (D) prude
   (E) popular

8. CREPUSCULAR
(A) intransitive
(B) picaresque
(C) tergiversant
(D) mum
(E) febrile

9. FRANKFURTER
(A) Frankfurt
(B) Bun
(C) Felix
(D) furburger
(E) BLT

10. DIGREND
(A) fandrify
(B) closs
(C) pascritize
(D) tander
(E) retasselate

11. ATROPHY
(A) atropine
(B) bullock
(C) entropy
(D) buttock
(E) anhonorablemention

12. MEDIOCRITY
(A) fat
(B) ugly
(C) slobbering
(D) unwanted
(E) talent

13. INTELLIGENCE
(A) drool
(B) moron
(C) imbecile
(D) vegetable
(E) hebetude

14. FLANDRULE
(A) asservet
(B) gliss
(C) drog
(D) hialype
(E) wormunt

15. FAIL
(A) death
(B) despair
(C) disease
(D) dishonor
(E) pass

16. ILLITERATES
(A) gravitate
(B) toward
(C) mediocre
(D) tax-supported
(E) universities

17. ZEN
(A) dozen
(B) moot
(C) zuddenly
(D) poot
(E) dave

18. GENIUS
(A) money
(B) health
(C) happiness
(D) possessions
(E) clod

19. HUMDRUM
(A) bonbon
(B) tom-tom
(C) ho hum
(D) tum tum
(E) wee wee

Part B—Analogies

DIRECTIONS: In each question, a related pair of words is followed by five lettered pairs of words. Select the lettered pair which best expresses a relationship similar to the original pair. Then, squat on your special pencil.

EXAMPLE:
PUPPY : DOG ::
(A) kitten : cat
(B) porpoise : ashtray
(C) apples : oranges
(D) horizontal : dead
(E) fur : steel

A   B   C   D   E

♣   ::   ::   ::   ::

20. SHIP : HARBOR ::
(A) snip : barber
(B) tuba : mayonnaise
(C) lint : sprocket
(D) vesco : guatemala
(E) tuna : malaise

21. MAGNET : IRON ::
(A) television : imbeciles
(B) sterno : wino
(C) kohlrabi : appetite
(D) stereo : junkie
(E) you : cancer

22. KINESIS : ENTROPY ::
(A) volition : exigency
(B) topiary : mesomorph
(C) crescent : silage
(D) portent : imbroglio
(E) torsion : fulcrum

23. PANSY : GARLAND ::
(A) fish : water
(B) bird : air
(C) regular : prune juice
(D) cheeseburger : yum
(E) politician : massage parlor

24. BRANDISH : CONCEAL ::
(A) fiveish : cocktails
(B) brand X : duz
(C) sevenish : din din
(D) jewish : arabish
(E) relish : frankfurter

25. PAT : BOON ::
(A) don : hoe
(B) awl : green
(C) burnt : baccarat
(D) thelonious : monk
(E) ikon : teeter-toter

26. TRUNCATED : FEBRILE ::
(A) pecadillo : termagant
(B) porphyry : divot
(C) bismuth : secant
(D) vermifluge : etiolation
(E) gopher : revenge

27. POLICE : PSYCHOTICS ::
(A) cheek : jowl
(B) roach: silverfish
(C) penis : cannonball
(D) six : half dozen
(E) dick : bb

28. PLETHORA : ACUMEN ::
(A) gelid : ductile
(B) blather : funk
(C) shirred : hasp
(D) factious : nether
(E) ormulu : mange

29. PRESIDENT : REPUBLICANS ::
(A) boil : neck
(B) albatross : neck
(C) heat rash : neck
(D) noose : neck
(E) turd : swimming pool

30. CLASMY : VENGE ::
(A) ferlon : bast
(B) sergil : pentor
(C) hanted : parge
(D) bilated : thresk
(E) grell : slurm

31. NECKING : GENOCIDE ::
(A) idolatry : support hose
(B) napalm : hickey
(C) photon : lymph
(D) samba: lamumba
(E) ecology : pocket pool

32. ANEROID : EXCULPATORY ::
   (A) forensic : conical
   (B) arcane : cursory
   (C) vulgate : brazen
   (D) lambent : vapid
   (E) spasmodic : jejune

33. GOD : DOG ::
   (A) straw : warts
   (B) goneril : doggerel
   (C) serutan : natures
   (D) xal-xe : ex-lax
   (E) Mr. Mxyzptlk : Mr. Kltpzyxm

34. TEMPLATE : SYZYGY ::
   (A) rapprochement : cloture
   (B) fodder : mesh
   (C) tenet : paradigm
   (D) synechdote : conduit
   (E) fustian : tonsure

35. WORD : NOUN ::
   (A) verb : blurb
   (B) worm : ground
   (C) pronoun : walloon
   (D) pronounced : lisp
   (E) amusing : limp

STOP!

If you finish before time is up, go over your work for this section only. Do not turn to any other section of the test.

SECTION II: MATH ABILITY
Time—40 minutes
16 Questions

• •

DIRECTIONS: Solve each problem in this section and then mark your answer sheet under the corresponding letter with the *one* correct answer. You may use any available space on the pages in this section for scratchwork.

You may wish to refer to some of the information given below in solving some of the problems in this test.

1 chain = 66 feet
1 fathom = 6 feet
1 ell = 39.37 inches
1 rod = 16.5 feet
1 hectare = 10,000 square ells
1 hogshead = 63 gallons
1 peck = 8 quarts
1 gill = 4 fluid ounces

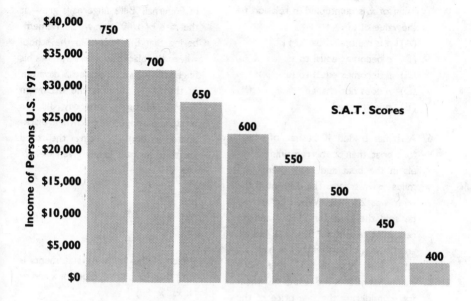

Annual Income According to S.A.T. Test Scores

1. What was the approximate ratio in 1971 of the income of the highest-scoring group to that of the lowest-scoring group?
   (A) 2:1
   (B) 3:1
   (C) 5:1
   (D) 10:1
   (E) 7:1

2. If the same salaries remained constant for 10 years, by 1981, how much more money would the highest-scoring group have earned than the lowest-scoring group?
   (A) $100,000
   (B) $240,000
   (C) $400,000
   (D) $375,000
   (E) $520,000

3. According to the graph, approximately how much is a single point of S.A.T. test score worth every year?
   (A) $45.00
   (B) $75.00
   (C) $30.00
   (D) $135.00
   (E) $50.00

4. The star Epsilon Eridani is 174 light years from Earth. A spaceship leaves Earth and reaches Epsilon Eridani in 98.4 years. What is the speed of the spaceship in furlongs per fortnight?
   (A) 100,000,000
   (B) 450,000,000
   (C) 54,000,000,000
   (D) 7,800,000,000
   (E) 66,000,000

5. If $p^x = t^y$ and $x^p + y^t = xy^{pt}$, how does p change in relation to t if the value of x is quintupled in relation to the value of y?
   (A) p is multiplied by $\sqrt{11}$
   (B) p becomes equal to v
   (C) p becomes equal to $(a^2 - b^y)$
   (D) p does not change
   (E) p is dropped

6. A farmer traded 40 bushels of wheat for a boat, then put his remaining bushels in the boat and took them 14.5 miles downstream. The current in the river was 2.6 mph. When he arrived he sold the boat for $54.67 and his remaining wheat for $1.39 a bushel, and he then calculated that he had sold his original 40 bushels for 14¢ more than what he sold the rest of his wheat for, considering the sale price of the boat. Just to amuse himself, the rural Lobachevsky decided to calculate how much per hour he had made while he was in the boat. What was his answer?
   (A) 45¢
   (B) 78¢
   (C) $1.09
   (D) 88¢
   (E) $3.44

7. Alice weighs nearly forty pounds more than Henry. If Henry eats twenty pounds of lard a day, he can gain three pounds a week. If Alice gives her portion of lard to Henry and eats safflower oil instead, she will lose one pound a week. In assessing the relative weight of Henry and Alice, what exactly did we mean by the phrase "nearly forty pounds"?
   (A) 41 pounds
   (B) 39 pounds
   (C) 3 stone
   (D) 38 pounds, 11 ounces
   (E) 619 pounds

8. Every time Bill scratches his fingernails down a blackboard, he takes off 1/128" of fingernail. Bill's fingernails grow at the rate of 1/40" per week. Remembering that Bill is only in the school where the blackboard he scratches his fingernails down is located 5 days out of the week, what is the maximum number of times each day Bill can scratch his fingernails down a blackboard without reducing the total length of his nails in any given week?
   (A) 7
   (B) 5
   (C) 2
   (D) 9
   (E) 11

9. Which of the following statements is (are) true for all real values of x and y?
   I. x: "$x + y$" = y : "x?"
   II. x: "$x!X!$" = y : "$x \ldots b$?"
   III. x: "@%#@+¢**!" = y : "69!"
   (A) I only
   (B) II only
   (C) I and II only
   (D) I, II, and III
   (E) III only

The problems in this section are followed by four alternative answers labeled A through D. In each of the questions, you are asked to compare two quantities—the one in Column A with the one in Column B. Through observation or computation, you are to determine the relationship between the two quantities and choose

   (A) if the quantity in *Column A* is greater than that in *Column B*
   (B) if the quantity in *Column B* is greater than that in *Column A*
   (C) if the quantities in the two columns are equal
   (D) if the comparison cannot be determined from the information given

Column A	Column B

10. $p^2 \wedge (p-t) \not{\mathcal{Z}} rsqu$ ⋈ $pv \triangle (p^3+3pq+q^4)$

11.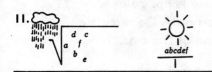

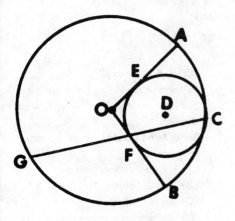

12. Length of arc *AB*
Length of segment *FG*

Each of the questions in this section has two statements, labeled (1) and (2), in which specific data are given. DO NOT compute an answer; instead, determine if the given data are sufficient to find a solution. Fill in space:

(A) if statement (1) ALONE is sufficient, but statement (2) ALONE is not sufficient to answer the question

(B) if statement (2) ALONE is sufficient, but statement (1) ALONE is not sufficient to answer the question

(C) if BOTH statements (1) and (2) TOGETHER are sufficient to answer the question, but NEITHER statement ALONE is sufficient

(D) if EACH statement ALONE is sufficient to answer the question

(E) if statements (1) and (2) TOGETHER are NOT sufficient to answer the question

Three men walk from Cowtown to Mootown. (Note funny names; as testers, we are stern, but wry.) Man A walks 3 mph, man B at 4 mph, and man C at 6 mph.

(1) Man A arrives 13 minutes before man C

(2) Mootown is a dump

14. How many students in Ruth's class received over 80 on the math test?

(1) The sum of the marks of all those taking the test was 4500

(2) Ten children who have been classified as legally stupid spent the day filling in potholes on the state highway instead of taking the test

15. George, Doug, and Henry wrote 4,000 words together. How much did Doug write?

(1) George and Henry together wrote 100 times as much as Doug

(2) The sum of what George and Henry wrote minus what Doug wrote is less than half of what George wrote

16. A certain number, *k,* is a member of the set [4, 9, 16, 25, 36]. If the set were complete, it would be worth $1,000 in any antique shop in town, but *k* is broken, and the set is now worth only $250. What is *k?*

(1) A good 16 in mint condition would bring around $75

(2) The 25 has a hairline crack and a little chip on the top of the 2

STOP!

If you finish before time is up, go over your work for this section only. Do not turn to any other section of the test.

SECTION III: VERBAL ABILITY
Time—40 minutes
27 Questions

. . . .

Part C—Sentence Completion

DIRECTIONS: In each of the following sentences, one or two words have been omitted. You are to choose the word or words that *best* fit the meaning of the sentence as a whole. *Banzai.*

EXAMPLE:

An example of a proverb is the saying, "Never change horses in ____."
(A) mid-stream
(B) Germany
(C) bed
(D) rainstorms
(E) France

A   B   C   D   E

---

1. Hitler's____acts eventually inflamed the____ of almost everyone in the civilized world.
   (A) first .. critics
   (B) circus .. curiosity
   (C) sexual .. organs
   (D) magic .. oo's and ah's
   (E) whimsical .. funny bone

2. Although it is morally____ to commit suicide, still one can sympathize with the poor wretch who through his own____ has suffered a dismal failure too bitter to live with.
   (A) incorrect .. foolishness
   (B) stupid .. stupidity
   (C) weak .. puniness
   (D) pathetic .. clumsiness
   (E) wrong .. idiocy

3. Few politicians have the____ to be____, preferring instead to make the popular gesture.
   (A) wardrobe .. transvestites
   (B) intelligence .. pimps
   (C) horsepower .. dump trucks
   (D) carapaces .. crustaceans
   (E) tits .. starlets

4. Not only does the poor student____ the deep shame of his lack of accomplishment, but he also must____ the agony of his friends' contempt and derision.
   (A) suffer .. die
   (B) undergo .. humiliate
   (C) torture .. subject
   (D) accept .. destroy
   (E) horrify .. loathe

5. Upon incarceration in the state peni-
   tentiary, the young conscientious ob-
   jector spent much of his time_____.
   (A) foolishly
   (B) snooping
   (C) prostrated
   (D) all in one place
   (E) dead

6. Just as a man who is not color-blind
   cannot conceive of a world without
   _____, so too the able
   individual cannot imagine the mental
   _____ in which the slow-
   witted are doomed to eke out their
   joyless days.
   (A) beauty .. wasteland
   (B) color .. swamp
   (C) fun .. quagmire
   (D) life .. morass
   (E) light .. desert

7. Despite the collapse of the Empire
   and an interminable period marked
   by continual_____, a few
   _____miraculously es-
   caped destruction.
   (A) hailstorms .. film clips
   (B) sniffles .. hankies
   (C) bickering .. dishes
   (D) bummers .. lids
   (E) self-abuse .. rotarians

8. It is not quite correct to_____
   a person of little academic skill an in-
   valid, for he can move his arms and legs,
   but on the other hand, is not his brain
   a _____?
   (A) stigmatize .. cripple
   (B) identify .. basket case
   (C) term .. sack
   (D) brand .. sewer
   (E) label .. casualty

9. The old man operated his_____
   on_____grounds, which

brought him a great deal of notor-
iety.
(A) campaign .. moral
(B) dodge .. fair
(C) flivver .. coffee
(D) sex bomb .. proving
(E) peep show .. play

10. Thanks to the rapid development of
    electronic educational aids, and the
    commitment of substantial govern-
    ment funds to our new state schools,
    the student of today finds many choices
    before him. True, he may still wish
    to attend a "prestige" Eastern school,
    but he may just as well choose a
    _____or a_____
    or he may even choose to_____
    his degree in his own living room!
    (A) factory job .. nervous breakdown
        .. yearn for
    (B) unemployment line .. early mar-
        riage .. dream of
    (C) untreated illness .. cold beer ..
        think wistfully about
    (D) early grave .. life worse than
        death .. cry bitter tears over
    (E) unfurnished apartment .. painless
        form of suicide .. utterly useless
        prayers for

11. The still-smoldering mass of twisted
    metal bore mute testimony that
    the _____had been
    _____.
    (A) brakeman .. Polish
    (B) final cataclysm .. something of a
        disappointment
    (C) pilot .. tripping
    (D) vibrabed .. defective
    (E) dodge 'em .. suicidal

12. The_____individual com-
    plains about tests for the same rea-
    son that the dishonest merchant

_____an accurate yard-stick or a properly functioning set of scales.

(A) insecure .. abhors
(B) inferior .. resents
(C) useless .. detests
(D) unpromising .. vilifies
(E) substandard .. hates

13. Since ability, talent, and ambition can be found on all social levels, it is necessary for the privileged classes to_____their hold on educational institutions so that society as a whole can prosper.

(A) maintain with an iron will
(B) defend to the death
(C) guard fiercely
(D) tighten
(E) preserve with every ounce of energy

14. If your farm's resources are limited, it will not pay to raise_____ that require(s)_____.

(A) vegetables .. psychotherapy
(B) funds .. accounting
(C) slaves .. meals
(D) hackles .. soothing
(E) cain .. prostitutes

15. Only a very_____person believes in_____.

(A) stupid .. Catholicism

16. Since the race is not always to the "swift," even superior students find it necessary to_____their teachers in order to achieve the success they want.

(A) suck up to
(B) suck up to
(C) suck up to
(D) suck up to
(E) suck up to

17. Upon being harnessed to the cart, the _____was usually_____to trot.

(A) thoroughbred .. eager
(B) nun .. hot
(C) collaborator .. persuaded
(D) paraplegic .. unable
(E) messiah .. too spaced out

18. _____men often fail to recognize in their_____ precisely those qualities which distinguish great men from _____.

(A) inferior .. betters .. the herd
(B) loathsome .. sleep .. England
(C) telephone .. booths .. the home office
(D) dirty .. wardrobe .. mediocrities
(E) impotent .. dorks .. cows

19. As the_____Age wore on, millions of hapless_____ were driven before its relentless march.

(A) Ice .. surfers
(B) Jazz .. organ grinders
(C) Iron .. wrinkles
(D) Bronze .. sunburns
(E) Stone .. alcoholics

Part D—Reading
Comprehension

DIRECTIONS: Each passage is followed by questions based on its content. After reading the passage, choose the *best* answer, whether stated, implied, or negated. Go.

One of the most exciting innovations in the field of education is the New English. As significant as the New Math, which revolutionized the teaching of geometry and mathematics in the early '60s, the New English promises to simplify greatly the task of teaching students a simple but workable version of the language. The New English can be used to improve reading scores and spelling ability, and may well provide future generations with a more efficient method of communication than the cumbersome, old-fashioned "chatter" we are now used to.

New English works in much the same way as New Math. The individual elements of a sentence—the verbal "formula" which conveys information to the listener or reader—are organized into "sets" and spoken or written in a way which clearly illustrates the "geometry" of what we are trying to say. For example, instead of saying, "I am very happy with my new car. It is green, which is my favorite color, and it is very fast. And I got a good deal on it," in the New English, we would say, "I (degree of liking = high) my car (new + $\frac{green}{favorite\ color}$ + fast + degree of reasonableness of price = good)." Because the concepts are sensibly organized, and the mode of transmission is chosen for the maximum input of discrete informational sub-elements, the recipient of the communication "bundle" can derive an instant increment of knowledge.

The potential uses for New English are limited only by human ingenuity. To cite just a single instance, poetry, which is so often too vague or wordy to achieve a measurable emotional response quotient, can be "cleaned up" and "ordered." Thus, "Shall I compare thee to a summer's day? Thou art more lovely and more temperate" becomes "Thee are to a given day (summer's) in interrogatory comparison more (lovely + temperate)."

We can expect some resistance from stick-in-the-mud academic indi-

viduals, but the day isn't far off when everyone English (new + good + useful) $\frac{speak}{future}$!

20. According to the author, who is most likely to oppose the introduction of New English?
(A) homosexuals
(B) leftists
(C) fools
(D) academic individuals
(E) homosexual leftist fools

21. Why is poetry better when written in the New English?
(A) less confusing rhymes
(B) fewer frills
(C) appeals less to homosexuals
(D) more orderly
(E) more manly

22. A good title for this paragraph would be:
(A) The Dawning of a New Age
(B) Talking Sense
(C) Words for the Wise
(D) Speaking of Progress
(E) The Language of Tomorrow

Now that growing numbers of high school seniors are competing for a decreasing number of college openings, "aptitude testing" has proved a useful tool for weeding out unqualified applicants to our colleges and universities. So reliable are modern testing methods that high scores on Stupid Aptitude Tests (SAT) now virtually spell the difference between a prestige Ivy League "sheepskin" and a tacky certificate from a pathetic, fourth-rate "diploma mill."

Yet, the proper techniques of test taking—as a study compiled by eminent social scientists at Beloit College confirms—

are surprisingly simple and can assure success.

The first, and most important element in successful test-taking, the Beloit group found, was *speed.* Many doomed seniors, for example, are mistakenly wasting precious time reading this pointless, uninformative sentence *word for word.* Afraid to "skim" paragraphs, Billy wallows in useless verbiage, hopelessly bogged down by unilluminating redundancies, repetitions, tautologies, pleonasms, and duplicate words expressing the same stupid thought over and over again in superfluous variety. Helplessly, poor Billy slogs through "extraneous material" written by cynical pedants who sadistically "pad out" paragraphs with bland "filler" designed only to "use up" priceless seconds, possibly going so far as to, slow, down: "reading" with, useless (& annoying) . . . punctuation! Whenever possible, the study revealed, Billy should *skip over* material like this. (Go ahead, Billy, do it right now . . . go into the next paragraph before it's too late.) The *first* or "topic" sentence usually contains the "meat" of an essay. The remaining verbiage is unlikely to contain "hard" information. One will rarely find, deep in a paragraph, reference to the fact that the diet-linked appearance of lipid plates in the blood vessels of forage-deprived elephants is usually indicative of arteriosclerosis, or to the fact that Opokopuk Islanders practice ritual warfare based on mumblety-peg and have developed a rigid caste system based on the warrior's remaining fingers and toes. Moreover, who could be expected to know that coral reefs are composed largely of calcium carbonate and magnesium carbonate? Harvard class of '78, that's who.

If he approaches the test correctly, Billy is sure to "rack up" big point totals on the SAT scoreboard of verbal ability/life, never forgetting that all reading tests must be quickly read, digested and carefully that so will not be "trapped" Billy by unclear reading fuzzy poor low score literally life or "living death."

23. The best title for this selection is:
    (A) Beloit College: Harvard of America's Dairyland
    (B) Stupid Aptitude Tests: Gateway to Self-Respect
    (C) Presidente Muñoz Marin: George Washington of the Philippines
    (D) Stupid Aptitude Tests: Middle Class Meal Ticket
    (E) Eeny, Meeny, Miny, Matriculate!

24. In the selection above, the phrase "living death" refers to:
    (A) arteriosclerosis
    (B) the Aetna Insurance Building
    (C) Beloit, Wisconsin
    (D) eminent social scientists
    (E) your parents

25. The capital of Luxembourg is:
    (A) Luxor
    (B) Tureen
    (C) Arlon
    (D) Orlon
    (E) Dover

26. Each of the following is "worth big points on the scoreboard of life" *except:*
    (A) calcium carbonate
    (B) an annual income of $25,000 +
    (C) proper drug abuse
    (D) correct nubble hygiene
    (E) twenty fingers and toes

27. The author's attitude in this selection may be best described as:
    (A) brain damaged
    (B) smug
    (C) cruel
    (D) realistic
    (E) Harvard '68

STOP!

**If you are finished before time is up, review
your work in this section.**

The Utterly Monstrous, Mind-Roasting Summer of

O. C. AND STIGGS

by Ted Mann and Todd Carroll

Me and Stiggs Dedicate Our Entire Summer to: WINO BOB (?–1982)

He lived in the bushes behind the 7-Eleven and he used to buy us huge stockpiles of liquor. "You gotta have a good woman," Bob said once, which we always thought was a memorable piece of advice from a guy with a bush home and newspaper for socks. He was great.

Chapter 1

THE WEDDING RECEPTION OF SCHWAB'S REPELLENT SISTER AND THE CHINAMAN FRANK, AND HOW WE COMPLETELY RUINED IT

Although this summer turned out to be the most amazingly spectacular and lunatic summer in the entire history of the association between me and Stiggs, the last week before school got out caused us to expect the complete opposite.

The major disaster started out only as the small inconvenience of having to attend the wedding reception of Schwab's sister, Lenora, a totally white-skinned harpist and ballet deviate with nostrils that look like old-fashioned key holes, who never appears anywhere without a ribbon on her somewhere, usually on her head, and usually four or five of them.

And so, because Lenora was so artistic and withdrawn and delicate, and totally unable to function anyplace where there were any people or any windows or anything else that might suck her into a connection with the world, me and Stiggs got her an Uzi submachine gun for a wedding present, with a twenty-round clip and a detachable stock. It cost us the entire $300 we got for a rare Tanganyikan airmail stamp Stiggs stole from Schwab's stamp collection when Schwab was twelve years old.

The stamp was great. It was triangular and had a picture of a blue doctor on it; the guy was probably some kind of government jungle doctor who went around deworming little burr heads until they got healthy enough to kill the government and change the name of the country to Tanzania—a purely candy-ass name compared to the totally great-sounding name of Tanganyika. Actually, Stiggs had snatched about fifty of these incredibly valuable stamps from the twelve-year-old Schwab, but by now we only had a few left, since we originally decided that it would be the most fun to waste the stamps on crank letters to the Schwab family, like they were Easter Seals stamps or something, and then let the post office cancel the living shit out of them for the exceptional depreciation effect of 99 percent. Sometimes me and Stiggs regret that it took us five years to get around to using the stamps to raise money, but at least we finally did, and were able to raise enough cash to get Schwab's sister married with the kind of top-quality machine gun she deserved.

Although Stiggs's mother and Schwab's mother are friends, because they both work at the same halfway house for maniacs, they fortunately aren't good enough friends for Mrs. Schwab to have invited my family and the Stiggs family to the church for the wedding ceremony itself, which caused us to miss the incredible metaphysical sham of watching God and the law being dragged into the affairs of the Schwab family.

So we went directly to the church social hall where the enchanted Schwab wedding reception was held, complete with all Schwabs from all parts of the city in nubby, brindled sport coats and homemade dresses. Mrs. Schwab had an enormous mesh bow mounted in the middle of her back to conceal a baseball-size hole in the seam, a natural aspect of a dress made by a person too alcoholic to get a tape measure properly around her waist, or to accurately read the measure and transfer the information onto a bolt of cloth, or to cut the cloth in a line accurate enough to have any hope at all of conforming to the hummocky repository of gin sugars and starch that Mrs. Schwab calls an abdomen.

Lenora, on the other hand, had a professionally manufactured seven-hundred-dollar, white lace gown, with some kind of protective shielding underneath to obscure the tits, and regrettably no shielding to obscure the fat bandage at the small of her back, where Lenora's well-known polynoid cyst had leaked its way right into the catatonia that was Lenora's happiness on this day of special days. Me and Stiggs were wearing gold-and-azure-flecked Lurex tuxedos from Dee's Tuxique—a 100 percent Negro operation, limited exclusively to colors, substances, and textures alluring to Negroes only.

Because there was a filthy ethnic barbershop next to the tux place, and because this shop had 1950s magazine photos of hairstylings from the East Coast gene axis of dark, bony-foreheaded Italo-Hispanic proto-men with total petroleum-bonded, boxlike formations of viscid black hair, we decided to step in for a so-called modified bop, which harmonized well with the tuxedos, as well as doing a first-class job of pissing off the Schwabs. It was great.

In fact, everyone at the reception was annoyed by our appearance, except for Michelle Schleuter, daughter of Herman Schleuter, the coach we got fired from school for porking a woman counselor in his office. He now works as a cashier in an army-navy surplus store and remains an exceptional dirtbag and complete enigma when you think about the contrast between himself and Michelle, a fox. I'd been trying to get my hands on her for about three years. She has this amazing face, with the softest, smoothest skin and these perfectly defined lips that look like they're so sensitive that they should always be covered and protected by other lips—like mine, for example—or they'd wither away.

Actually (as is pretty obvious from this type of language) I had a whole lot of emotion and energy invested in getting my hands on Michelle Schleuter, but I couldn't help it. She's the only female I've ever known who stimulated this automatic, uncontrollable girl-system in my brain that overrides all of the other neuro-motor departments, such as the departments of tearing apart rental cars, and pulling trains on cocktail waitresses, and even terrorizing the Schwab family. Stiggs mentioned that if Michelle Schleuter actually liked me and followed me around, I would be a total blob, as well as a worthless, lobotomized asshole. And he's probably right, given the general link between being an asshole and failing to perform the necessary and mandatory tasks of abusing rental cars, cocktail waitresses, and Schwabs.

"That's the funniest haircut I've ever seen," Michelle said. Since this was the first time Michelle had ever volunteered speech to me, I was understandably pleased as well as thoroughly blown out. "It's a modified bop," I responded. "It cost four dollars, but it's easily worth several thousand." She looked at me real gently for an instant, like something about my sense of humor interested her, and then she laughed.

"What's that?" she asked, suddenly distracted by the hydrocephalic Randall Schwab lurking by a table full of wedding presents while diddling with the Uzi. It was only a matter of time before his frosting-blotched fingers pinched and fumbled their clumsy, mindless way over and around the bolt and the barrel, pushing rivets, thinking they might be buttons, pulling flanges, thinking they might be interesting mechanical levers, and streaking the blue steel with frosting, until finally he squeezed a bulge that actually proved to be a button, causing a loaded clip to drop onto his divoted, buckle-fastened shoes.

Our attention was further grabbed by Schwab's inevitable attempt to get the ammunition out of the clip, this being an advanced, chimpanzeean sort of leverage operation involving the force of a stiff spring that would undoubtedly challenge the topmost reaches of Schwab's ability and lock him into an unstoppable full-scale battle with the clip until all twenty cartridges fell out all over the floor.

"William Oglevey?" a stern voice interrupted. I turned away from Schwab and Michelle to confront the extended hand of a forty-year-old guy in a crinkly sport shirt who was obviously, impossible as it may seem, out of place at this reception. "You are hereby served," the guy said, handing me a stack of folded papers. One look at the top of the first document—"Plaintiff: Herman Schleuter"—provided a complete indication as to the titanic mound of shit Michelle's dildo father was bringing down on our heads.

I turned to mention something about this to Michelle, but she bolted, apparently not wanting to take sides with us (which would then expose her to the full dirtbag wrath of her father) and also not wanting to take sides with her father (which would expose Michelle to us as merely another dirtbag in a family full of them). Just then, Stiggs appeared, holding a wad of paperwork like mine. "Do you think she'll let you pork her?" he asked, having noticed our conversation. I didn't answer, though, because of my overwhelming and fanatical respect for Michelle, who I was now totally committed to porking, if not hanging around with for an unusually long period of time. "It's time for the funeral," I said, changing the subject. "We'll get Schwab to loan us his family car."

"Great," Stiggs said.

It so happened that as a matter of scheduling we were locked into two events on the same day—Lenora's wedding reception, and the funeral of Kenneth L. Burke, a bog-headed, tippling blob of campus nothinghood who no one knew or cared about, and who used to waste perfectly good alcohol on a life-style of never doing anything. We asked him to help us pull some shrubs out of Schleuter's lawn one night, since the guy lived next door to him, but Kenneth just sat in the back of the car and drank this quart of malt liquor while we did all the damage; and then when we told him to get out of the car, since we wanted to put Schleuter's entire privet hedge in the backseat and drive it to his office at school, Kenneth crawled out the car door, giggling, and wandered over to his front yard, where he passed out on a plaster duck. Anyway, the first and only time Kenneth actually did anything that suggested he had an imagination was when he stood up on the tailgate of a station wagon to throw a bag of food at some people outside a shopping center, just before the car went into a parking garage with a clearance of about a foot above the car, shearing off Kenneth's head. It was pretty horrible.

So me and Stiggs got this call from some girl we never heard of who was trying to convince everyone at school to go to the funeral, even though it would be on a Saturday and we wouldn't even get out of a class by going to it. But we considered going anyway, becaue it would at least get us out of the Schwab reception, and because we would have the extra advantage of joining the funeral cortege in Schwab's parents' pale yellow 1977 Continental in its fully decorated and festooned condition as the wedding car—if we could talk

Schwab into giving us the keys, which was easy to do because of the sugar-drunk condition of Schwab, who was on his twentieth Coke, a record for Schwab.

"What a stupid fucking eyesore," Stiggs said about the incredibly draconian Schwab wedding car. Its main asset, however, was the elaborate network of tin cans attached to the rear bumper, which, taken independently, was equally as idiotic as the rest of the car but, when considered in the context of wheeling the car off a side street and into the middle of a long procession of black funeral limousines with the cans rattling and thrashing at maximum volume, was easily as valuable to our impact as the Kenneth Burke memorial bags of food we were throwing out the windows.

Even though about 90 percent of the graveside audience was from school, most of them went completely out of their way to affect some sort of ludicrously mature attitude, exuding great heaving black clouds of somberness and inconsolability, as if they actually knew the fuckhead who died.

So Stiggs stepped up to the grave and delivered an extemporaneous eulogy over the background of my harmonica performance of "I'm a Man"—a harsh, painful version I blew as hard as I could, directly above the coffin hole. I had been in the grasp of a harmonica obsession for several weeks, and was now comfortable swaying and jerking and pitching my head and shoulders during this type of emotional passage, which I did, even during the blurts of vocalizing that I felt the urge to insert for extra dynamics and styling. It was great—I was a complete honking blues master. "I'm a man. *Do-doo-do-doot.* I'm spelled M-A-N. *Do-doo-do-doot.* I say it again . . .

Meanwhile the ludicrously grief-stricken burial audience was trying to make the best of Stiggs's remarks, which were extensive. "Even though none of us ever knew this guy or even thought about him," he began, in excellent counterpoint to my driving harmonica statement of, for the most part, "*do-doo-do-doot,*" "it's still pretty good that everybody got themselves into a total teen-funeral mode and came out here, even though we didn't get out of class."

There was some anxiety at this time among the Burke family and a lady representative of the school faculty who despised us more than death. Nevertheless, Stiggs continued. "I remember Kenneth before he was dead, and I think of him dry-heaving on a white plaster duck in his front lawn. No, better yet, I remember him in the Cub Scouts. We were on our first hike, out in the desert, when Kenneth was fooling around on the back of the den mother's station wagon, throwing all these ice cubes from the cooler at the other scouts. 'Don't do that,' the den mother had shouted real loud, but Kenneth was an uncontrollable ball of energy that day and refused to stop. So all of us naturally threw Kenneth into a wash, where he rolled into a huge forest of cholla cactus, and then returned to camp hysterical, with hundreds of cholla cactuses attached to his body, and with each cactus having about a thousand of these barbed needles on it that have horrible stuff on them that I like to call poison. So, while Kenneth was doubled up on the tailgate, wimpering and trembling as the den mother's husband removed several thousand toxic cactus spikes from his skin with a pair of gooseneck pliers, I wondered what would ever happen to this rascal. Nothing much, I suppose, until he stood up on the back of another station wagon and got his head hacked off by a parking garage."

By this time my musical outburst had progressed to an irregular staccato of guttural moanings, random blasts on the phlegm-clogged blues-monster harmonica, and, finally, a sixty-second gurgle. Clearly, the family, the faculty representative, and the audience were upset. They didn't like our hair, they didn't like our Lurex Negro tuxedos, they didn't like my music, and they didn't like the eulogy. So we went back to Lenora's wedding reception.

Things at the reception, however, had not gone very good. Schwab had managed to get the ammunition back in the Uzi by himself and, after continued twisting and jabbing, managed to release the safety and blow seven rounds into the gift table, the custodian's closet, the P.A. speakers, and a transom window over the main door, where there was this nest full of three-day-old birds, which were launched straight up to the sky before plummeting forty or fifty feet to the front steps of the hall. It was there that a Chinese mushroom grower named Frank Tang, Lenora's new husband, accidentally mashed one of the naked, peeping creatures with his foot.

Lenora came apart. Her cyst was throbbing, her brother had just shot up the most significant and only public event in her entire life, her seven-hundred-dollar dress was streaked gray with powder burns, her wedding car had disappeared, and her brand-new husband was kicking the pressed remains of a bird he'd just killed off the thick spongy bottom of his Schwab-quality shoe. "You can't just let them die," Lenora screamed, whirling back and forth on the steps, pleading with a mob of frightened Schwabs to pick up the ugly, golf-ball-sized chicks and, presumably through a program of petting, fondling, and total bird love, nurse them to health and adulthood.

But none of the guests responded, so Lenora got crazier, until her father borrowed a car and drove her and the doomed birds to a veterinarian. The case was handled, however, by Barney Beaugereaux, a very close and worthless associate of ours who happened to be working his last day as the veterinarian's assistant, and who happened to be in full charge of the office, for some unjustifiable reason. "Can you save them?" Lenora squealed desperately, referring to three lifeless, cardboard-hard lumps cradled in her skirt. "For what?" Barney answered, drunk. ". . . Bouillon?" He then scooped up three of them and fired them in a salvo through the open door of the office, where they hit a stainless-steel panel and ricocheted into a metal tub.

"If you'll give me five dollars, I won't set them on fire," Barney added, at which time Mr. Schwab gathered up his hopelessly weeping and sniveling and horrified daughter and escorted her over to Frank Tang for a husbandly blast of attention. But Lenora called Frank a murderer for stepping on the bird, and wouldn't sit in the same seat with him. Barney said the whole scene was Schwabobilia nonpareil.

It wasn't until about a half hour after this happened that we arrived back at the reception with the car, where the police were talking to Schwab about the gunfire, and Frank Tang and Lenora were trying to help the minister size up the damage.

We decided this was the perfect way for Frank and Lenora to begin their life together—their life of working side by side, tending Frank's mushrooms in a basement totally dark except for the green glow of mushrooms and the thin crack of light from the door leading to their bedroom, where they would sleep, eat, play the harp, and box the mushrooms, every day.

A POWERFULLY CONCENTRATED BLAST OF DRUNK THINKING AT THE HYATT-REGENCY

As mentioned in the first sentence of this story, the last week of school made us wonder pretty seriously about the quality of the summer we were going to have. The Schwab reception had left a dense, sticky ring of sludge around the tub of our lives, comprised mainly of the Schleuter lawsuit and the federal charges for having an automatic weapon without a license, not to mention the usual hooting and squealing of our parents about the total unacceptability of our final grades and also about summer jobs. So me and Stiggs decided that the only way to rescue our vacations from complete teen Armageddon was to attack all of these problems immediately, before they got any bigger, by starting a three-pronged crash program of rational analysis, ingenious counteraction, and getting totally, William Holden-style fucked up in a hotel room.

This room, we figured, would function as a fully isolated think tank—ideal for summoning the complete powers of our minds for three or four days straight, or for as long as we could stay drunk before our bodies broke down completely and succumbed to mind-roasting fevers and rings of cold sores around our entire mouths like a concho belt. "We'll need a presidential-quality room," Stiggs said, "with incredible French luxuries." So, for about the sale price of Schwab's nineteen-cent Trinidad-Tobago special delivery with a green-and-white-striped watermelon on a background of gray dots, we checked into the Hyatt-Regency and ordered a top-priority smorgasbord of electric typewriters, chart-holding easels, tape recorders, Maine lobsters, giant shrimps, grenadine, club soda, ReaLime concentrated lime juice, ReaLemon concentrated lemon juice, Fresca, Collins mix, ginger ale, ice, lemons, limes, tangerines, Bacardi light rum, and Beefeater's gin—the last fourteen items being the ingredients of a red, gluey swill we call Hawaiian Schwab, or SNOTFAG, the internationally recognized acronym for Schwab Nosebleed Over Twenty Feet Above Ground Level (a thing that always happens to him).

"My idea for the solution to the Schleuter problem," Stiggs began, laid out in the bathtub, surrounded by forty or fifty floating rose blossoms, which came with the forty or fifty room-service trays we'd ordered so far, "is to start up some kind of bogus community project—like maybe a project to build a new, free-form concrete jackal zone for the zoo. Or maybe an O. C. and Stiggs drug-rehabilitation clinic. Or maybe a thirty-five-lane, pan-American wheelchair ramp, so quadriplegics in Chile can get around the hemisphere just like anyone else. Then we can keep the judges from reaming us, because they'll think we've rehabilitated ourselves and that we're real valuable to the community."

It was agreed that the character-enhancing aspect of this kind of move would be ideal; however, its full volume of genius wasn't realized until several minutes later when I, from my position in the central return air duct among the spoiling lobsters and shrimps I intended to leave there, suggested that our charity activity might also quiet down the summer-job mania of our parents.

"Emergency!" Stiggs screamed, ejecting himself from the tub like it was a burning car. "Dial 'one'! Get room service! Code red!" Stiggs was on the phone immediately, ordering more rose blossoms, because, according to him, the ones floating in the tub had suddenly lost their smell. "I demand smell," he shrilled. "I expect total uninterrupted smell from these fucking roses."

Unfortunately, the service captain didn't realize that the Stiggs situation involved fifty roses. "What am I going to do with this?" Stiggs sneered at the weaseling hotel goon when he appeared at our door holding a single flower floating in a brandy glass. Stiggs's tirade was great. "Do you see this bathtub? Do you notice any difference between the size of the tub and the size of that spindly wad of petals in your hand? I need total bath coverage. I need a completely solid layer of roses all around me like puffing factories of smell, attacking me with their smell and power-ramming big stinking concentrations of rose odor up my nostrils until I'm wasted with pleasure." It wasn't long before we got so dissatisfied with this incompetence that we bolted.

THE GRADE-AAA, DOUBLE FOXHOOD OF MICHELLE SCHLEUTER, REQUIRING A SPECIAL VISIT TO HER HOUSE

Although there was still a great deal of details to be worked out following the premature end of thinking at the hotel think tank, I thought it would be a good idea to relax my brain by visiting the home of Michelle Schleuter while her father was on duty at the army-navy surplus store. Mrs. Schleuter was also gone; she took off for good about fifteen minutes after Herman's porking episode with the counselor hit all the papers we reported the story to—seven of them, in five cities.

As I parked in her driveway, it occurred to me that some form of zaniness could be necessary; Michelle might demand a continuation of the premium level of humor that attracted her before, lest she risk wasting her time on porking a one-joke type of guy. So I quickly backed out of the driveway and fishtailed to a 7-Eleven for a half-dozen eggs and for a felt-tip pen, which I used to letter a message on one of the eggs, which I planned to hold up to Michelle's face as a substitute for an ordinary greeting. This would create the ultimate mix of humorousness and adorableness that all species of Michelles require as credentials before allowing you into their bodies—and it would have worked too, if Michelle had answered her door, instead of a totally naked Stiggs.

" 'How . . . about . . . a . . . hand . . . job?' " Stiggs said one word at a time, reading my egg. "No, thanks, I'm already sexed out," he continued. "What's happening?" Needless to say, I was stunned and pissed. We sat down on the Schleuter living-room couch, which, I reasoned, the blatant scum-sack Coach Schleuter had probably bought with wages that the school paid him for forcing me and Stiggs to run around the track for the last three years. It was arguable, therefore, that since this hideous leviathan of a couch had been purchased with our suffering, it technically belonged to us, and this notion made the weirdness of sitting next to the unprincipled slinking dog Stiggs, who had just boned the number-one female of my life, all the more weird.

"Try not to get too annoyed," Stiggs said, in a tone of total sensitivity and remorse. "I know Michelle was your main female boner idol, so it shouldn't be surprising to you that the single guy in the world who has the most in common with you would want to get his hands on Michelle too. If she were only some ordinary slut, do you think I'd screw you over for her? Fuck, no."

It wasn't long before me and Stiggs were shaking hands, because I was satisfied that he would treat Michelle with the same dignity and respect as I would, and in the final analysis, her happiness was all that really mattered. Our handshake was interrupted, however, by a set of squeaking and shambling noises, which I thought were being made by Michelle getting dressed but in fact were produced by Barney Beaugereaux, our worthless associate, opening the door to Michelle's room just wide enough to stick out his head and ask Stiggs if he wanted to pork her again. "She's bucking like a horse and she wants to see the Monster," Barney said, using one of Stiggs's five pseudonyms for his dork.

I peeked into the bedroom. All I could see was Michelle's legs, and Barney by the bed, and suddenly it was obvious that Michelle wasn't exactly the spectacular female I thought she was, and I was so totally pissed off about it that if I didn't deal with it real fast, I would end up trying to kick the shit out of Barney and Stiggs. So I took off my clothes and hopped onto the bed with Michelle. "I'll pork her and that'll get her out of my system and take my mind off killing Barney and Stiggs," I thought to myself. But the pork was horrible— she hardly moved the whole time, probably catatonic from the shock of doing Barney. When it was over I felt incredibly stupid, and Stiggs, who was of course watching, apparently realized this and, because he's my oldest friend, knew what to suggest to improve my frame of mind. "Let's get our couch out of Schleuter's living room," he said.

So we dragged it out to my car, balanced it on the roof, and drove it to the army-navy store parking lot, where we rolled it off the car at forty miles an hour and blasted my remaining five eggs into Schleuter's windshield. We decided to drop the Michelle incident altogether, except in the case of Barney, who, having a piece of metal shrapnel lodged somewhere in his head, and being slow and virtually a servile dog, was easily made to feel guilty about it and to owe me favors forever.

A SELECTION OF ALTERNATIVES INVOLVING BARNEY AND HOPELESS, WORTHLESS JUNKIES

The guilty and doglike Barney was on the verge of becoming rich. This was because a neighbor's lawn mower fired a chunk of iron into Barney's head when Barney was six years old, so the neighbor had to give Barney's family $25,000, which they put into a trust account that Barney couldn't touch until he turned eighteen, which was that week. "This would be the ideal amount for a Mexican holiday," I mentioned, "a sort of educational adventure, designed to broaden Barney's world experience so that he would be better prepared to handle the responsibility of managing the two hundred dollars he'd have left over after we got back from Mexico."

At first, this Mexican concept seemed like a better, or at least easier, solution to our legal problems, namely: avoiding them altogether by bolting the country. On the other hand, we had plenty of motivation to stay at home, because of the amazingly brilliant, character-enhancing project me and Stiggs finally decided to get into—Penis House—our personal hard-core drug-rehabilitation program. The idea of us running a halfway house full of hopeless, worthless junkies was spectacular enough by itself, but the further notion of setting up the house full of junkies in someone's tranquil and attractive neighborhood, directly next to the someone's house, like Schleuter's, was nearly irresistible.

A second compelling aspect to the option of staying home and appearing in court was that we would have to get a lawyer, which meant that we would finally have an opportunity to do business with lawyers who have offices in shopping malls—the ultimate perversion.

Considering each of these choices thoroughly, we concluded that the only sane move was to do them all.

ME AND STIGGS ENTRUST OUR ENTIRE FUTURES TO A MAN IN A RED BLAZER—EARL WARNKE, MALL LAWYER

There are two law firms in Westwood Mall, Captain Whereasky's Great American Lawyer Machine, located in a stall in Montgomery Ward's between the record department and a video-game display, and Law Cucaracha, a trailer of Spanish-speaking lawyers jacked up by the south entrance. We selected the former because it had a popcorn machine shaped like an 1890s steam engine in the lobby, and because all of the lawyers there wore matching red highly combustible blazers.

"What can I do for you?" the thirty-five-year-old wriggling mass of nerves, who couldn't even get a job at a free law clinic in the middle of an Indian reservation, asked. His entire office was made out of the same substance as his blazer, only pressed into different textures—the shiny polymer texture of warped, fake birch paneling; the stippled polymer texture of molded, aluminum-legged chairs; the tufted polymer texture of blue miniature-golf carpeting; and the smooth polymer texture of the white-globed lamp on his desk, which had B-A-R printed across it in three-dimensional letters. In fact, all of these elements seemed to have been conceived as a single package, a standardized mall law unit, totally thought out, down to a permanent diploma frame behind the desk, with a slit at the top, for easy insertion and removal.

According to this guy's diploma, his name was Earl Warnke, and he graduated from the University of the Pacific Trust Territories Extension School of Law in American Samoa. "A deviate high-school coach who porks counselors is suing us because we got him fired, and the Alcohol, Tobacco, and Firearms Agency is after us for not having a license for this Uzi machine gun that we bought as a wedding present," Stiggs answered succinctly, as he knew even trembling mall lawyers would appreciate.

"Let's start with the gun," Earl suggested, just as a sharp explosion rattled the plastic wall behind him, followed by several harsh blip noises and an electronically altered voice—"Surrender, men of Signus I, or pay with your lives." Obviously, the Montgomery Ward video-game display directly on the other side of Earl's law stall had sprung to life, but Earl didn't seem to mind. "Does it, like, fuck up your prestige as a lawyer to have a Signus I video attack going on during important conferences with your clients?" Stiggs asked, as several thousand synthesized music notes drilled through the opposite wall from the record department.

"Oh, actually no . . ." Earl chuckled timidly, closing the door to his stall, as if a door in a stall that didn't even go all the way to the ceiling would have any effect whatsoever on the amount of electronic noise missiles that were blasting over, into, through, and around our conversation. "So, where did you actually get the gun?" Earl asked.

"A gun shop," we explained, still sticking tightly to our policy of succinctness.

"A gun shop actually sold you an automatic weapon?"

"Well, no, not exactly. Uzi makes a semiautomatic model for private collectors who just like the looks of the gun but don't necessarily need the actual cyclic rate of fire of eight hundred rounds per minute that you get with a genuine machine gun," Stiggs replied, somewhat distracted by the turning of a knob on Earl's office door.

"But you're actually accused of possessing an automatic weapon?" Earl asked with a lot of confusion.

Me and Stiggs hesitated for a moment, weighing how intelligent it would be to tell this day-laboring, shopping-center geek about Sponson the vet, formerly of the First Air Cavalry in Vietnam, now guarding pot plantations and hanging around biker bars and modifying Uzis for high-school kids and generally being dangerously insane.

"This guy Howard Sponson helped us convert it to full automatic," Stiggs finally said, stupidly, for the first time in his life feeling he was under some obligation to tell the truth. "We figured it would be an insult to the Schwabian daughter to give her a less than perfect machine gun."

"Yeah," I added. "She's this incredibly sensitive and emotional art type that reads about twenty-five levels into everything; so, for example, if Lenora were to notice that her Uzi was an inferior, semiautomatic model, she might project the condition of being inferior onto herself, which might inhibit her normally confident style of harp playing. And if you take away Lenora Schwab's harp playing, there would be nothing left but a frail, weird-nostriled shell of a totally maladjusted Schwab. So we had to go with the automatic version, and Sponson was our only hope."

Now I was distracted by the wiggling knob on Earl's door, which swung open to reveal a barbecue-sauce-caked child with an isthmus of impetigo scabs stretching from his nose to the corner of his lips and with a tubular bolus of chocolate nougat that protruded an inch from his mouth; after about a minute the child retracted the tube with a loud sucking noise, wandered into the office, and fell over the cord to Earl's B-A-R lamp, pulling the lamp off the desk and onto the kid's head, where it shattered.

To even the spongy mind of a mall lawyer, this incident must have been loaded with legal consequences—like, for example, the consequence of the child's mother laying out the details of Earl's negligence to some other lawyer, perhaps even the sharklike Mexican lawyers in the trailer at the other end of the mall. But Earl didn't seem to be too bothered, since the kid was just

While Estimating How Much It Would Cost to Go to Mexico, We Designed This Easy Method for Doing It

Figuring How Expensive a Foreign Country Will Be by the Size of Its Bugs					
	Country A	Country B	Country C	Country D	Country E
Typical Size of Bugs Scale ⊢1 ft.⊣					
Cost of Beer	$1	75¢	25¢	10¢	2¢
Cost of Hotel Room	$35	$20	$5	45¢	not available
Cost of Lobster	$9	$14	$35	$700	not available
Cost of Bottle of Cough Medicine	$3	$2	$1	10¢	not available

Illustration: Philip Scheuer

another one of an endless stream of lost, low-income mall trash who wandered into his stall and whose parents were probably the last remaining people in modern society who could be bullshitted into believing that they'd never win a lawsuit against Earl Warnke, mall lawyer.

So Earl picked up the squalling kid and returned him to the main aisle of the store; then, while on his hands and knees, gathering up splintered segments of his B-A-R lamp, he outlined the defense he planned for us, which would involve our pleading ignorance of the gun being illegal, while laying total blame on Sponson the vet. Even though this strategy would probably result in Sponson killing us, we pulled out all the stops, hired Earl, and paid the advance fee listed on the Captain Whereasky Great American Lawyer Machine fee menu on the wall. "I'll actually handle the Schleuter case later," Earl mentioned as we left his stall. "Actually, great," we said succinctly, even though the Barney Mexican option was already beginning to dominate most of our thinking.

AN EVENING IN THE NIGGARDLY BARNEY APARTMENT, WHICH INCLUDED YELLOW TEQUILA AND RELENTLESS PROPAGANDIZING ON THE SUBJECT OF MEXICO

"This is yellow tequila," Stiggs told Barney during our visit to his place. "This is the ultimate liquor of Mexico, enjoyed by all Mexicans, regardless of how old they are or whether they're male or a girl or rich or poor or crazy or useless. Imagine yourself being on the tropical Mexican coast, and you're sitting at the end of a real quiet bar that smells like palm trees and the ocean, while the bartender, this totally exotic guy with giant wrinkles on his face and an unraveled straw hat, fills a water glass to the top with yellow liquor. He puts it in front of you, beside this pile of crude salt and a bowl full of limes cut in halves, as a bunch of musicians begin to wander around and beat on these incredibly fat and badly built guitars. And right at this exact moment is when you notice a mysterious beaner princess with long hair at the other end of the bar who takes a fast look at you secretly and wonders all about you.

"So you put some salt on your tongue, and lift up the glass. The exotic bartender looks at the princess with his real black eyes, and then he looks at you as the musicians pound on their instruments as fast and hard as possible, and the princess holds her breath as a gesture of excitement. There you are, Barney, with the tequila right next to your mouth. Suddenly, you feel the stuff swirling and gurgling down your amazingly wide-open throat, as its powerful heat goes everywhere in your body, including your brain. You look toward the princess, but . . . she's completely gone. Where the fuck is she, Barney?

"Then you feel something real soft on your shoulder, but it's mysteriously full of energy. You turn around, and there right in front of you is . . . this grossly chubby Mexican in a T-shirt, offering to sell you a huge gray ugly fish. He has thousands more of them stacked in a truck outside. He thought he might sell off one or two of them in the bar, while he was on his way to wherever he was supposed to go to deliver the fish. 'Pescado?' the guy asks, smelling like a horrible fish. The music stops. You fall straight backward off your stool and ralph.

"You're dry-heaving now, so the bartender drags you outside. You crawl through all of the dirt and garbage in the street to the side of the bar, where the princess is going to the bathroom. A beggar lady with a rag on her head jams a varnished armadillo purse into your face, and then these other child beggars with faces that look like they're forty years old show you horrible rugs. The *federales* come, and they take you to the headquarters of the judicial police. You sign all of your traveler's checks for them, Barney—they take every fucking cent you have. . . . Barney? Barney?"

Stiggs thought it was offensive of Barney, our host, to pass out during the middle of his drama guaranteed to convince Barney that we should leave immediately for Mexico; but in the end Stiggs wasn't actually offended, since he was mindful of the entire gravy tureen of tequila Barney had just dumped into his system.

As we recounted the $25,000 in cash Barney withdrew from the bank that afternoon, me and Stiggs assured ourselves that Barney wouldn't back out of the trip, and then I collapsed backward off my stool onto the kitchen floor, and Stiggs went up on the roof. Stiggs always maintained that Barney's roof was the best of all roofs he'd ever spent any time on—even better than the roof on Barney's old house, a place much larger and superior to the niggardly apartment Barney lived in now. "I'm actually pretty glad that Barney's mom squandered away all the insurance money after her husband died," Stiggs once said. "Otherwise, Mrs. Barney wouldn't have had to sell off her house, and I wouldn't have ever known the total roof superiority of this dirtball apartment."

And so with me and Barney passed out on the floor, and Stiggs probably asleep on the roof, Barney's mother arrived at two in the morning, just off the swing shift at some laboratory that makes teeth molds for orthodontists. It was obvious that her job and apartment situation were completely humiliating to her, especially now that the final remnants of her formerly comfortable life— her clothes—were beginning to fray and look out of style. "Your mom waited too long to get a new husband," Stiggs once told Barney, noticing that her skirt had an old stain on it; but I never realized exactly how deeply this no-husband aspect of Mrs. Barney's life affected her until she pulled me up off the kitchen tile, laid me out on the couch, and spent much longer than was absolutely necessary straightening out my hair and clothes.

Because I had slept off just enough of the Mexican liquor to have the capacity for dork arousal yet hadn't slept off enough to distinguish between the firm, vigorous lips of acceptable females and the slack, collapsed lips of forty-nine-year-old moms, I went along with Mrs. Barney's next move—a clumsy assault of lip slurpings from the woman who eighteen years ago created the goof-ball Barney and who was now luring me into the possible creation of another one.

Naturally, I was astonished that Barney's mom was now operating at this desperate level. "How about a hoover?" I suggested, but Mrs. Barney wasn't very good at it. In fact, ten minutes into the procedure, the only good thoughts I was having were that I had my harmonica and that Mrs. Barney fortunately wasn't distracted by the version I was blowing of "Orthodontia Mold Widow"— a honking improvisational burst that seemed to move along nicely with the pumping motion of her head.

"*Do-doo-do-doot,*" I began on the low, blues register. "Been workin' all day . . . *do-doo-do-doot* . . . makin' dem teeth, oh yeah . . . *do-doo-do-doot* . . . I said T, double E, T, H, teeth . . . *do-doo-do-doot* . . . Den I come home . . . and *neeeeeeed* me a treat . . . *do-doo-do-doot* . . . Am I talkin' 'bout TV? . . . no, no, no . . . Am I talkin' 'bout a slice a beef? . . . no, no, no . . . What am I talkin' 'bout then? . . . *do-doo-do-doot* . . . I'm talkin' 'bout that low-down honking soul man O. C. . . . *do-doo-do-doot* . . . Yeah." She finished me off on "Yeah," which was kind of perfect timing; then me and Stiggs went home.

Chapter

7

OUR CASE IS HEARD THROUGH THE CHIRPING MOUTH OF MALL HIRELING EARL WARNKE

"Your honor," Earl began, with total lack of confidence. "My client, Mr. Stiggs, is the victim of a tragic mistake. He was actually unaware that the gun he presented to Lenora Schwab was actually an automatic weapon, and that it had not been actually licensed. And if the prosecuting attorney had been doing his job, he would have established that one Howard Sponson, the person who actually modified the gun, is the only party who actually should be before you today."

"Mr. Stiggs will be bound over for prosecution; trial is set for June twenty-first; bail is one thousand dollars; court adjourned," the judge said in one breath, not having listened to anything Earl said. Now, of course, Stiggs was annoyed, since we were already scheduled to be in filthy, Barney-subsidized Mexico on the twenty-first, so he brought this up to Earl. "I'll be in Mexico. Get another date." But then Stiggs realized that the judge hated the fact that Earl even existed, and decided that the only solution was to have himself sworn in to give maximum impact to his claim that Earl was a dork and should be replaced by Mexican trailer lawyers. Here is Stiggs's official legal transcript of what he said:

Official Legal Transcript of What Stiggs Said in Court

Stiggs: There are good mall lawyers and there are bad mall lawyers. I have obviously been represented by the lowest, tenth-rate, bungling-slag variety of bad mall lawyers, which has completely wrecked my chances to get fair justice—the kind of justice you get from Mexican mall lawyers in trailers. They're scrappy, Your Honor—they fight like sharks because they grew up in shacks made out of mud blocks where they had to fight all the time, just as a matter of surviving. "Ernesto, give me that Kit-Kat, or I will kill you," they would say to each other, even to their own brothers and sisters. So you can imagine, Your Honor, how good these amazingly ferocious Mexican mall lawyers will fight for me, an absolutely innocent human being.

Judge: Granted. I'll postpone the trial for two weeks to allow your new attorney time to prepare his case.

Stiggs: I don't know. These are Mexicans we're dealing with here—there isn't much they can get done in two weeks. You know how they are: their cars break down and they can't get to work; and then their office desk-top copiers break down and they poke at them and try to fix them themselves, until the machines are completely destroyed and they have to go find someone else to rent them a new machine because the guy that rented them the first one refuses to fuck with them anymore. Have you ever watched Mexicans trying to fix an office copier, Your Honor? They swarm all over it like buzzards, poking at every roller and every sprocket and every spring without one of them having any idea of what he's doing. But they keep doing it anyway until the concept that poking won't fix the machine is finally transmitted through their fingers into their brains and is considered alongside the other Mexican concept of going home because the machine is broken.

Judge: Denied. Your trial will be in two weeks.

A Look at the Coroner's Records Showed the Incredibly Amazing Amount of Stuff Wino Bob Died Of

1. Cirrhosis of the liver
2. Esophageal varices, which are dilated veins in the esophagus
3. Alcoholic cardiomyopathy, which is a degeneration of the heart muscle, which causes the heart to stop
4. Wernicke's encephalopathy, which is an alcoholic degeneration of brain tissue
5. Pancreatitis, which is an inflammation of the pancreas
6. Aspiration pneumonia
7. Liver cancer
8. And a bunch of other stuff

Chapter

8

TOUCHING THE LIVES OF WINO BOB AND A PAIR OF HOT SLUTS FROM INCREDIBLY BROKEN HOMES

Later, when we were visiting Wino Bob—a Negro derelict and alcoholic who lives in an oleander hedge behind a 7-Eleven—I asked him what would be the ideal liquor for a special occasion. "What kind of special occasion?" he inquired in the dialect of a wasted bum. "The special occasion of Stiggs and me both getting Mexican mall lawyers and of us finally arranging dates with the Sluts de Boxcar," I said, "boxcars" meaning a pair of sixes, which is the total number of dads and stepdads that Robin Salsbury and Charlotte Pinckney have—six each—a record.

Naturally, this type of family situation is only available at Jodsten, the private boarding school in our area featuring massive programs of horseback riding, hiking, water sports, polo, and a whole bunch of other things that rich divorcées with six husbands figure their hopelessly fucked-up kids might like to do, a thousand miles from home, continuously from preschool until they're old enough to cash in a trust fund or kill themselves. The key expression here, of course, is "hopelessly fucked up," which is why me and Stiggs have always had a special sentiment for the females of Jodsten and, in particular, for the Sluts de Boxcar, whom we regard as supreme beings.

"Cachacha," Wino Bob advised. "A fine, crystal-clear Brazilian drink—a favorite of Latins and women alike." So we gave Bob the usual token cash to cover his own poison wine needs, and later, after he returned from the liquor store with our cachacha, we accompanied him to a nest of old blankets beside the oleander hedge and listened to one of his slurred chunks of advice for youngsters. "You gotta have a good woman," he said, wearily settling into a Wino Bob-ass-conforming crater of blankets. "That's what every man's gotta have for himself if he ever expects to make it."

Me and Stiggs thought instantly of the Sluts de Boxcar and the possible helpful effect they would have on us making something of our lives. "Believe me, I know," Bob added, staring dully at this green bottle of wine. "That's right," I commented. "A good woman would prune back these oleanders for you, Bob, maybe even paw out a little depression in the dirt beneath those blankets, make your ass a little more comfortable." Bob wasn't listening, however, because he was preoccupied with twisting off the cap on his wine and telling us that he was going to die.

Later me and Stiggs discussed the effect a dead Bob would have on our access to liquor, but after a while we made an unspoken point of not lingering too much on the subject—a practice completely alien to both of us. Besides, the Jodsten bus would be coming soon, filled to the limit with hot, maladjusted slags who, because of the school's completely laughable boning-prevention policy, are only allowed into town one night a week, and are only supposed to check off the bus in pairs—the pair of Robin and Charlotte, of course, being the critical one.

"Brazilian alcohol?" I asked Robin about five minutes after she'd gotten off the bus and climbed into my car and dumped a dozen plastic bottles of pills on my seat. *"Lobsters!"* Stiggs began screaming in the backseat, throttling Charlotte's neck. She had never met Stiggs before and was thus jolted by his amazingly fierce threat that he wouldn't give her the pork unless she and Robin bought us full-course French lobster dinners, with spare lobsters for after sex.

So we drank the cachacha and ate the pills and when to La Chamerique— premiere home of French lobsters and elegant, totally quiet dining. "Put everything on twelve separate checks," Stiggs informed the headwaiter. "These girls have a total of twelve dads, so we figure the ridiculous expenses of their lobster-crazed daughters should be spread out to all of them. This means that we'll demand that their real dads pay us back for check number one and check number two, which should only be for the main parts of our meal, like, for example, the lobsters. Then the other ten dads will get the rest of the checks, which should be divided up like this—dad three: bottles of wine; dad four: bowls of salad; dad five: bowls of soup; dad six: mounds of appetizers; dad seven: bottles of champagne; dad eight: bottles of liqueurs; dad nine: bottles of cognac; dad ten: mounds of dessert; dad eleven: mounds of desserts on fire; and, dad twelve: the tip.

"Since these girls are slags and from Jodsten," Stiggs continued, "they're naturally filled to the eyeballs with pills and Brazilian liquor, so I figure you should force them to put up an advance security deposit of about five hundred dollars for this meal, which you could use to cover the actual total of the checks rather than try to collect the money after we're through eating, since these slags will be snoring by then and maybe even be dead."

Me and Stiggs ate a record nine lobsters, although we ordered twenty altogether so we'd be sure to have enough pincers and eye stalks to cannibalize for the La Chameriquetyville Horror—a terrifying, three-foot-long monster we generally like to make from soufflés, lobsters, and lettuce in restaurants where people will want to kill us for doing it. The La Chameriquetyville Horror was one of our best monsters, designed like a giant green termite, but with the added aspect of two hundred dorsal fins and crab fork antennae that could be moved to make a tongue of lettuce slide in and out of the mouth.

"You'll have to leave," the maître d' said, just after Stiggs had bravely stopped the monster from attacking the next table. "Remove that pile of food from the floor and get out."

Me and Stiggs were stunned; the Sluts de Boxcar weren't, however, because they were snoring. Stiggs hauled himself up from his dramatic food-monster combat position on the floor while I collected our twelve different checks and what was left over from the $500 advance payment—$172—which we used immediately afterward to buy thirty fan belts to throw out the car windows.

"Who wants to go swimming?" Stiggs asked as we were later driving through this incredibly fashionable place called Clearwater Estates at eighty-five-miles-an-hour to wake up the girls.

"Where are we?" Charlotte mumbled woozily.

"I'll check," I said, hammering the brakes and spinning the rear of the car completely around before we slid to a stop on a bunch of gravel at the edge of a twenty-foot-deep culvert. "On the edge of a giant ditch," I answered.

After everyone stumbled out of the car, and after the car rolled down to the bottom of the culvert, Stiggs repeated his question about swimming; so we walked for what seemed about a mile through these huge, estate-sized lawns until we found what looked like a reasonable pool.

"Is it heated?" Stiggs asked as I peered over the back fence.

"Yeah."

"Gas or electric?"

"I can't tell."

"I won't swim in a gas-heated pool," Stiggs announced.

"It's electric," I said, as a tactical ploy to speed along the evening; and then we climbed over the fence, took off our clothes, and jumped in the pool.

"It's gas!" Stiggs screamed. "The water's moving in all these different layers and each one's a different temperature—the ugly mark of gas heating."

Using the full powers available from her completely drug-twisted head, Charlotte moved close to Stiggs and floated there with her breasts half out of the water and her hair glued in thin, wet bands to her face, and said, "Do you, like, know the people who live here?"

"Didn't your seventy-five dads teach you anything?" Stiggs replied. "Nobody brings naked, doped-up females to a friend's pool. What would the friend think? It's always better in this type of situation to dump yourself on a complete stranger."

Because I was at that moment being massaged by Robin while talking to the American embassy in Thailand on the patio phone, I failed to notice a slight rustling of the curtains inside the patio door. "Would you please repeat your request?" the vice-consul said over the phone. "You say your name is Randall Schwab and that you want to dictate a Johnny Fuckerfaster joke, so I can copyright it for you in Thailand?"

"I'm a white witch," Robin whispered in my ear. "When I get home after summer school, I'm going to start a coven in our guest house."

"But what if the stranger doesn't want us in his pool?" Charlotte hypothesized to Stiggs.

"All of you stay right where you are," an ugly, fifty-year-old dirtbag dentist commanded from the back door of his house. "I'm calling the police; and in case you're thinking of going anywhere, I have your clothes." The guy wasn't lying—he'd actually skulked onto his patio and snatched our clothes.

"Fuck you," Stiggs responded as we all jumped naked over the guy's fence.

Owing to the estate-sized distances between homes in this area, it was several minutes before we found another fence to hop over and hide behind. "Hello, kids," came a gravelly voice from across the yard we were in. "I've got a gallon of dark Caribbean rum here. Want some?" Me and Stiggs were pretty much surprised when we turned around to discover a fully nude businessman across the lawn, laid out on a chaise lounge between two roaring, Polynesian patio torches, holding a gallon bottle of brown rum, and listening to *Apocalypse Now* helicopter-attack music on a powerful stereo.

"My name is Pat Colletti, and the name of the guy you're hiding from is Leland Croft, DDS. He's a complete asshole. I'm a hard-drinking, naked businessman. Who are you?"

The Sluts de Boxcar were, for some eccentric reason, alarmed by this man and hid behind a pool cabana, while on the other hand, me and Stiggs were instantly comfortable and helped ourselves to foam-insulated, patio-grade tumblers of brown rum.

"This is a pretty nice place you got here, Mr. Colletti," Stiggs noted. "What kind of business are you in that allows you to be this fucked up?"

"He means we definitely respect your style of adulthood," I added for clarification, not knowing that Colletti was in fact thoroughly proud of earning millions of dollars drunk.

"I make clothes for fat women," Colletti responded with a laughing smile. "Fat, hulking hogs like Leland Croft's wife with lots of cash to blow on themselves. Speaking of hogs, your girlfriends behind the cabana might want to grab a couple of robes off those hooks and join us for sandwiches."

Colletti reached into an ice chest beside his lounge, removed a pile of five-deck club sandwiches, and passed them out to me and Stiggs and the girls as they arrived on the patio in white satin beach kimonos with "P C" monogrammed on the chest and luminous gold dragons for pockets. "We have to get back to the bus," Charlotte announced.

"They're on a schedule," I explained to our host. "The Jodsten boning-prevention schedule, which, oddly enough, seems to be working."

"Impossible," Stiggs said. "If we allow one antiboning system to work, it will only encourage the use of other antiboning systems. Mr. Colletti, if the girls and us can use your cabana for about half an hour, we'll be able to prevent all these antiboning systems from getting started and really wrecking things for me and O. C."

But Colletti had fallen asleep, and the Sluts de Boxcar were getting close to hysteria about meeting the bus, so we started up a pair of three-wheeled, all-terrain cycles parked beside the house, borrowed two more satin beach kimonos for ourselves, and took off. The best part about riding these things, aside from the insane looks of them, and our being dressed in satin kimonos, was that they were ideal for gouging deep trenches through Dr. Leland Croft's ornately designed, quadruple-colored gravel lawn. "There's no burro!" Stiggs mentioned to Charlotte angrily. "Only a supreme scumhead dentist like Croft doesn't put a plaster burro on this type of lawn."

There was a painted wooden cart with a cactus in it, however, which exploded reasonably well as it landed in the middle of the street. This pretty much completed our evening, except for the final visual reward of the Sluts de Boxcar in a parking lot, waiting for their bus in satin dragon robes and looking generally worse than if they'd been boned by us and by perhaps even a trailerful of Mexican mall lawyers.

THE TRAIN FROM NOGALES TO MAZATLÁN WAS GREAT—IT WAS CRAWLING WITH MEXICANS

Blast-off for Mexico with Barney was a hectic one, given the enormous surge of last-minute nuisances and obligations. First off, there was the matter of Schwab. It suddenly occurred to us that me and Stiggs and Barney had never been out of town at the same time, which always meant that at least one of us was on duty to keep up the continual vigil of persecution against the Schwabs and all that they stand for. "The solution," I reasoned, "involves some sort of robotic or remote-control torment that can be put in motion before we leave, and be trusted to stay active for about two weeks."

"The softball shirts," Stiggs blurted, suddenly relieved because we'd never been able to figure out a use for the RANDALL SCHWAB—YOUR INDEPENDENT INSURANCE AGENCY T-shirts we'd taken about a year ago from the Schwab agency softball team. "We'll give the shirts to Wino Bob, and he'll give them to his Negro derelict friends, and then they'll wear them all over town until the shirts rot on their backs, which should be in about two weeks."

So we delivered the shirts to Bob and then had to handle the second major obstacle of watching Barney pack. Barney's entire life is serviced from a cosmos of small plastic bags, filled with broken bits of cookies, pastries, candy, and anything else made completely of sugar. These bags are everywhere in the Barney apartment, and so the job of collecting them all and loading them into a Barney-quality, black cardboard suitcase is as time-consuming as it is horrible.

"Don't you wish you didn't have that wad of iron in your head?" Stiggs said, annoyed. "Then you might have the brains to organize all of your sugar supply in some kind of central location, like possibly a tackle box. Imagine how sophisticated it would be, having that entire fucking snack selection of yours right at your fingertips." Barney wasn't listening, however, being completely enslaved by his present system; and, besides, as Stiggs pointed out, if it weren't for the shrapnel in Barney's brain, we wouldn't be going to Mexico. "Good point," I said. "It's a fucking great point," Stiggs replied, pushing one of Barney's twenty-dollar bills into his pocket and lighting another one on fire.

The train from Nogales to Mazatlán was great, mainly because we had a completely sealed, Mexican-baby-odor-proof, solid-steel Pullman sleeping compartment—a virtually indestructible train paradise, ideal for drinking in and throwing yourselves against the walls of. It was across from this compartment, while the door was open, that we noticed Iver Willingsby and Mr. Garth Sloane, Iver being an English foreign-exchange student at our high school and Sloane being Iver's drama teacher, and both of them being pouncing homosexuals wallowing together in homo vacation glee in a roomette across the aisle.

Barney was appointed to investigate, since Barney had already called them each faggots to their faces during the school year, even though their actual homo love bond wasn't directly verified until now. "Hello, Mr. Sloane," Barney said really viciously in their doorway as we lurked out of view. "Hello, Iver. Where are your wives?"

"Well . . . hello . . . Barney, is it?" Sloane responded with wriggling anxiety.

"To answer your question," the oozing British homo teen interrupted, "neither of us is married; are we, Garth?"

Fortunately, Stiggs's cassette player was on "record" as Iver's defiant homo pride began to drive huge railroad spikes into Sloane's future as a teacher in a public school.

"On your way to Mazatlán, are you?" Sloane asked; but, as a result of our heavy prompting in the background, Barney wasn't thrown off the track by this type of distracting question.

"Which one of you is the girl?" Barney asked. "I mean, like, do you have a division of responsibilities, like which one of you does the income taxes? Those forms are too complicated for girls, that's for sure. Iver? Come on now, don't you just hate those things?" By now the teen homo was a seething, indignant dirtbag of fake composure. "We are in love, and that, I believe, is quite sufficient a description. Do you agree, Garth?"

"Say 'yes,' Mr. Sloane, or he'll fucking dump you," Stiggs squeaked in a phony outer-space voice from behind the wall. Obviously, Stiggs's analysis was right, because Mr. Sloane began fumbling around nervously with his gold bracelet, twisting it and jerking it up and down his wrist, before he finally took a one-hundred-foot homo cliff dive into the lagoon of stupid judgment, grabbed Iver's hand, and told Iver that he loved him a whole lot. "Barney does too," Stiggs yelled suddenly, pushing Barney into the roomette full of fags and slamming the door. Barney spent five minutes in homophobic, door-beating horror before we finally let him out. They didn't touch him, however, but it was still great.

Chapter 10

HANGING ON TO BARNEY AND THE TWENTY-FIVE GRAND WHILE CRIPPLED HORRIBLY BY MEXICAN COUGH SYRUP

Mazatlán is really hideous in the summer, but we didn't mind because we had fifty-five four-ounce bottles of Mexican cough syrup—a delicacy of the opium family, yet amazingly revolting to all persons who aren't wasted on it. The value of the stuff, aside from the satisfaction of buying it for a dollar a bottle from urchins in pharmacies who'll sell you their entire supply like it's normal to buy fifty-five bottles of cough syrup, is that the codeine deadens your body just right for passing out on the cracked cement foundation of an abandoned building, without any pain—which we did.

"*Pescado?*" a grossly chubby, T-shirted Mexican asked us the following morning, at sunup, as fierce light began to bore through holes in the wrecked walls.

"We don't want any of your goddamn gray ugly fish. Can't you see we're sleeping?" Stiggs snapped at the man. But it was too late. We were totally awakened, and stung by the full, ludicrous impact of having $25,000 in Barney's cash on us and not even being in a hotel.

"Correction," Stiggs said. "We don't have the twenty-five thousand because we don't have the Barney." A complete scouring of the ruined building and surrounding neighborhood of delirious dogs and fences with broken bottles glued to them for security yielded a complete zero. Barney was gone. We were 100 percent destitute, except, of course, for the remaining inventory of thick, nauseating cough syrup. "What about that twenty you pilfered at Barney's apartment?" I asked. Fortunately, it was still in Stiggs's pocket, and got us through an entire day of mescal drinking at the Playa Hermosa Hotel, the place where we'd planned to stay before being distracted by the siren song of the syrup, calling to us, "Sleep in an abandoned building full of rubble—it's neat."

By early evening, Stiggs had attached himself to a girl he'd seen on the train—an Olivia Newton-John-style receptionist from Minnesota called Mandy, who beat her forefingers on the table like drumsticks in bursts of hyperactive glee and scrinched up her nose and squeaked, "This place is really diff'rent. Too weird." This, however, was not nearly as weird as the event that followed—the bizarre appearance of Barney in the hotel lobby with his arm around a pie-faced Mexican girl, followed by her three older brothers. As the entire group of them settled in at our table, Barney allowed that he'd met Fabiola, Rudolfo, and Jaime while wandering in a stupor along the beach road at about two in the morning, and that they'd taken him "cruising for action" after Barney offered them several thousand dollars in cash for a beer.

"Barney is in love with our sister," Fabiola announced with a great greasy grin. "Look what he has bought for me," the girl said enthusiastically, clutching a battery-powered Lucite disco amulet that contained the necessary number of light-emitting diodes to flash the girl's name—Inmé—in orange letters. "Isn't it *bonita*?"

"It's really diff'rent!" Mandy responded. "Too *bonita!*"

"How does it feel having more electronic technology around your neck than Mandy has in her entire brain?" Stiggs slurred to Inmé, slumping rudely close to her as a result of the mescal and recent overload of cough syrup. "Mandy," he continued, turning his head, "this is Inmé, and her special guy, Barney. Why don't you see if you can make your name light up on your head so everyone will know who you are." Stiggs held his hands up to his forehead and fanned his fingers several times as if they were light rays. "Mandy—*bleep*—Mandy— *bleep-bleep.*" Stiggs rotated his head again. "Inmé, what other special presents has Barney gotten for you?"

"Oh, we have to show Barney's friends the beautiful Plymouth," Inmé said to her brothers. The brothers instantly bolted off to get the Barney-financed 1978 Plymouth Duster for a viewing in front of the hotel, while Barney produced all of his remaining cash and swaggered over to the bar for liquor. "My brothers are so happy that Barney has given me a car," Inmé said. "They can hardly wait until I am old enough to learn how to drive it."

Stiggs was fading fast. "What's that black stuff you're drinking?" he said, in the general direction of Mandy. "It might be evil. Inmé, is black stuff evil in this fucking country? Here, examine this real closely so you can maybe save Mandy's life. Mandy—*bleep*—Mandy—*bleep* . . ." Stiggs pushed his alcohol-and-drug-leadened hand across the table and dragged Mandy's black drink to Inmé. "Hurry, this is no game," Stiggs cautioned, as he accidentally knocked the drink onto the entire bottom half of Inmé's gauzy white dress.

Despite the horrible condition of both me and Stiggs at this time, an odd bulge that was now revealed beneath the tightly clinging, drink-soaked material around Inmé's groin did not escape us, particularly Stiggs, who was closest to the area and naturally best qualified to make a judgment. *"Hey, Barney!"* Stiggs yelled across the bar. *"Your slag's got a unit. She's a guy, Barney! Look at her unit. It's bigger than yours, Barney."*

Inmé ran out of the hotel and disappeared.

"Those three brothers and their little brother, Inmé, hustled you for seven grand," I tried to explain to Barney, but all he did was begin nibbling on a small plastic bag of cookies and called us liars. "You talk to him," Stiggs said to Mandy, exasperated. "Tell Barney his girl was a guy." But Mandy was already tied up with the waiter; "Gee, this bar's just like Geezer's—Mr. Geezer's—that's the best bar in Saint Paul. Do you have a lobster night? Wednesday's lobster night at Geezer's. I love it. It's really diff'rent."

Chapter 11

HERMAN SCHLEUTER BEING TOTALLY UNCOOPERATIVE, WE WERE FORCED INTO THE EXECUTIVE CLUB STEAK HOUSE FOR ASSISTANCE

Mazatlán was generally great, but our upcoming trial and Barney's massively bad frame of mind inspired us to leave after two weeks, instead of staying the full twenty-five to fifty years we discussed at various moments of satisfaction with the quality of Mexican life—its main quality, of course, being a complete routine of doing nothing. "We want to open a clinic for hopeless, worthless junkies," we told the Mexican mall lawyers on our first day back home. "Do you think this will help our case?"

"Sure, that's a real good idea," Reynoldo, the English-speaking one, said.

"Fine, may we borrow your phone? . . . Hey, Michelle, this is Stiggs—

Mark Stiggs—I porked you with Barney and took your couch, remember?"

"I've got it, Dad," Michelle cut in sharply on the other end of the line.

"Anyway," Stiggs continued, "tell your dad that we've got Mexican lawyers here who've given us the green light to install a monster clinic for junkies in your neighborhood. We need to know the names of your next-door neighbors and how much they'd charge to rent their houses to us." Michelle stammered for a minute, and was then replaced by the dirtbag Herman Schleuter, in his usual dirtbagian frame of mind.

"Hi, coach," Stiggs led off.

"Listen, you bastard punks," Schleuter hissed, "I hope you're proud of yourselves and all the trouble you've caused. Now, for your information, I'm leaving this city—tomorrow. There's no life for me here anymore, so you can damn well waste your demented criminal energies on someone else."

"Oh, no, coach," Stiggs exclaimed, as if he were actually disappointed. "We can't beat our federal machine-gun rap without the drug clinic, and we can't start a drug clinic without having a good therapy program of junkies prowling around in your yard at all hours of the night. Come on, coach. Me and O. C. are practically down on our knees." Stiggs was sniveling like a bruised Schwab now; it was almost impossible to understand him. Even with the added impact of my real sad harmonica scream of "Baby, Please Don't Go" in the background, Schleuter was unmoved. He said he would see us in court, and hung up.

"Mr. Colletti!" Stiggs blurted, as if a blood clot full of enthusiasm had just hemorrhaged in his brain. "He's the ideal guy to ask for advice, and plus he probably wants his fifteen-hundred-dollar all-terrain cycles back." So, after seven or eight more calls on the Law Cucaracha phone, we tracked Colletti to the Executive Club Steak House, pinnacle of executive dining and cancer-throated alcohol abuse on earth, a virtual hive of executives—standing executives, burping executives, meretricious executives, executives with salad dressing all over their faces, pondering executives, cruel executives, lonely executives, executives with red pants, hypoglycemic executives, jolly executives, executives with intestinal blockages, executives looking for other executives, double-jointed executives, itching executives, and executives porking cocktail waitresses named Janine in the walk-in cooler, which is what Pat Colletti was doing.

After Colletti's emerging from the kitchen, and buying us huge, chief-operating-executive-size steaks, and describing the walk-in cooler episode with Janine to us in complete, steam-filled detail, we were really pleased when he responded to our questions about setting up a drug clinic with the greatest answer imaginable: "Put the fucker next to Leland Croft's house. I'll take care of it for you, no problem."

Me and Stiggs were exploding with happiness. "I own the property next to Croft's," Colletti continued. "The house is about to fall down, so I'm gonna level the place in six months and build something else. I'll let you have it for a thousand a month, in advance—six grand. Have you got a lawyer?"

"Seven of them," Stiggs replied. "Mexican mall lawyers. They're like sharks."

"Fuck it, my guys will handle it. You'll need to incorporate as a nonprofit foundation. What do you want to call it?"

"Penis House," I said immediately. "We've gone over this name business extensively, and Penis House seems to be the only one that meets our criteria for recognizability and total misanthropy." Because Mr. Colletti really liked the name, we knew absolutely for sure that he was a great human, and therefore respected his idea that we use Penis House on all the legal documents and invent another name for the public and for the federal judge.

"How about Love House?" Stiggs suggested, while examining the labels on one hundred wrapped straws he'd stolen for no reason. "Do you think the Love Straw Company will give a fuck if we steal their name?" What a great name, Love House.

THE ZERO USEFULNESS OF BARNEY AND LENORA SCHWAB TANG WHEN WE REALLY NEEDED THEM

The task of getting the $6,000 rent money from Barney was much more difficult than we thought it would be, because Barney had suddenly, and with surprisingly un-Barney-like stealth, slipped out of the country to find the Mexican girl he refused to believe was a guy. "Your son is no longer our dog," Stiggs said to Mrs. Barney on the phone. "All these years we've let Barney take the rap for our traffic tickets, and let him go into grocery stores for us and load up his jacket with gourmet lobsters, and let him rip off nitrous oxide from that pet clinic he used to work at, and now when we need him most, Mrs. Barney, the dirty mongrel bolts.

"I know what to do," Stiggs mentioned after hanging up. We drove to a peeling, wood-frame house on the bleak edge of Negro Town, then walked down an outside stairwell to a basement and pounded on the door. FRANK TANG MUSHROOM COMPANY was printed across it in gold adhesive letters; something that sounded like Burt Bacharach harp music leaked out a chickenwire bathroom window.

"The reason we're here," Stiggs informed me, "is that since neither of us has ever said a word to Lenora Schwab, and since she's probably hated us her entire life, I figure we should grab this great chance to have our first conversation be a demand for six thousand dollars." The door opened three inches, revealing the gaunt, artistic shape of Lenora—the ideal shape to be displayed in a seven-foot-by-three-inch slit in a doorway.

"We were driving by and heard the Burt Bacharach and thought we'd drop in to your underground mushroom cave and ask you for six grand," Stiggs said as a greeting. Lenora was obviously frightened, upset, nervous, crazy, malnourished, confused, quavering, sallow, and unhappy, and still had the same keyhole nostrils. "I'm busy," Lenora said just above a whisper. "Talk to my husband."

"Come on, Len*ooooooo*ra," I chided. "It's only six thousand. Pl*eeeeeee*ase?"

"Why?" she asked, still completely leery and blown out. Stiggs shifted to his stoop-shouldered believability stance and lowered his voice to the level that makes what you're saying seem confidential. "The federal government says it didn't like the machine gun we gave you, so we need money to calm them down. The government also says that the law of wedding presents requires you to help us out by giving us the money."

"Can we come in? It's freezing out here," I added, as a satiric comment on the ninety-eight-degree heat. Surprisingly Lenora opened the door. "I have to check something," she said, with her left hand wrapped around her right fist, looking at the floor. Even in the dim green fluorescence of Frank's hundred thousand mushrooms, we could tell that something ridiculous was going on in Lenora's unusually large head, an observation that turned out to be true a short time later as she rooted through a pink cardboard chest of drawers, pulled out a bundle of papers with a rubber band around it, nervously pecked and crinkled her way through the entire bundle, and then announced to us that she only had seventy-eight dollars.

It was naturally amazing to me and Stiggs that this sad Schwabian creature was actually prepared to give us all of her money—all seventy-eight dollars of it—and for practically the first time in our lives we were moved.

"Is that all you have?" I asked. "I mean, what if for some unimaginable reason you wanted to get out of this wet, green tomb? What if you needed some time for yourself, time to meet other people and experience a little of the world? What if a personal emergency came up where you suddenly needed a new harp, or a nostril remodeling, or six grand to pay your legal obligations?"

"What you need is a fucking job," Stiggs added. "Some kind of gig to get you outside and bring in hundreds of thousands of dollars." Stiggs noticed her harp in the bedroom and began pacing back and forth between the mushroom racks, as if totally concentrating. "Raindrops keep falling on my head . . ." Stiggs hummed and then sang. "I see Burt Bacharach . . . I see harps . . . I see businessmen in lounges . . . Friday afternoon . . . Hyatt-Regency . . . Lenora Schwab Tang at the professional-businessman's lounge harp . . . Are you following me so far?" It didn't look like she was, so we left, knowing that no matter what happened, we still needed six grand.

ARRANGEMENTS ARE MADE WITH SPONSON THE VET IN THE PRESENCE OF A PSYCHOPATH WITH A LUMPY FACE

We were led through a ring of electronic-motion sensors and an electronic fence to a stucco shack surrounded by four-wheel-drive cars, homicidal dogs, and scattered pieces of farm equipment. "Hey, it's the Uzi men," Sponson the vet chuckled coarsely. "I been meaning to talk to you about this little fucking message I got here from the federal prosecutor's office—I believe it's called a summons. Wonder how they got my name."

"Mall lawyers," Stiggs spat critically. "We went into Captain Whereasky's Great American Lawyer Machine expecting top-quality legal service, and instead we got Earl the bonehead failure, and he oinked out your name at our arraignment."

Sponson was nonetheless pissed. "You better straighten this thing out, man," he threatened in total life-and-death, dope-industry fashion. "I got some very concerned brothers here, man, who rely on me very heavily." Sponson nodded toward a pellet-eyed goon with nicks and sebaceous bumps on his face, and a shotgun across his thighs.

"That's the concerned brother who relies on you heavily?" Stiggs asked. "It must be real great to have a family, sitting around the old pot-plantation guard house, sharing and caring and relying on one another."

I interrupted extra softly, for the sake of not getting shotgunned to death. "Look, we've got a plan. We're starting a clinic for junkies called Penis House, and we'll let you be one of the counselors. That way, all of us will look good to the judge and get off with suspended sentences, so we can continue our important work with hopeless, worthless junkies."

Me and Stiggs were both pleased that Sponson liked the idea, and further pleased when he agreed to help us get our hands on Barney's $6,000 by arranging for Barney's "brothers" in Mexico to find him, put him in a bag with all of his money, and deliver him home. The plan was great, or at least appeared that way until the plane carrying 7,000 pounds of pot, with Barney in a bag in the middle of the pot, crashed in the desert. ". . . Local teenager Barney Beaugereaux was discovered unconscious in a burlap sack," the newspaper said, "carrying a large amount of cash. Police believe he may have been a buyer whom the smugglers had double-crossed." It was three weeks before

Barney got out of jail and could start to recover from the Jacobo Timerman-style interrogations he was given by four different varieties of cops.

AN AMAZING ANGLE FOR CASH MAKING OCCURS TO STIGGS WHILE THINKING TO THE COMPLETE LIMIT

Me and Stiggs decided that I should perform a honking soul-harmonica version of a High Mass, and that I should do it at this four-hundred-seat dinner theater that happened to be managed in the summer by homo drama teacher Garth Sloane.

COMING TO TERMS WITH A FRIGHTENED HOMO MINDFUL OF THE FELONIOUS ASPECT OF TEACHER-STUDENT LOVE

"I love you very much," Garth's hormonally jangled voice cracked through the tape recorder.

"This is blackmail!" Iver huffed from the corner of Mr. Sloane's office at the dinner theater. "Why don't you just go back to your little American boys' bedrooms and do whatever it is you do in them."

Sloane, however, was completely silent, with his head in his hands, probably realizing that this Soul Mass performance was totally critical to us.

"We need a six-grand guarantee and full approval of the sound system," Stiggs mentioned, in the style of a manager. "Honking soul man O. C. Oglevey don't blow into no Gilbert and Sullivan, tenor-fag-patter microphones—he needs white hot, blues-torch sound that cuts holes in the audience's head and burns up their wires."

"Fuck!" I screamed a few minutes later from the stage. I blew a few bars into a heavy chrome microphone and threw it to the floor, as Stiggs, being concerned as usual about my fragile musical temperament, rushed to my side and instantly sympathized with the problem. "I'm losing notes," I raged. "This mike's doing a fucking Gilbert and Sullivan fag job on my notes."

"This is no good," Stiggs barked at the homos. "We'll have to put in our own system." The expressions on the homos' faces were great when Stiggs kicked their dirtball microphone into the orchestra pit and jumped up and down on the cord, screaming.

MYSTERIOUS PREPERFORMANCE BLUES CHEMICALS, AND DISASTER IN A DITCH

It was about three hours before the concert and I still didn't have any Sonny Boy Williamson honking-blues drugs, the kind I would need for total monster blues rapport with the four hundred dentists and sales reps and housewives who would soon fill the Sagebrush Dinner Theater expecting to see *The Man Who Came to Dinner.* So we went to Negro Town.

"Would these degenerate street weasels burn the honking blues master with bad blues drugs?" I asked Stiggs, wheeling our car through a five-way, six-lane intersection filled with Negroes in parked cars having conversations.

"Of course," Stiggs answered.

"But maybe something worthwhile slipped through. It's obvious that we need the advice of an expert who lives in oleander bushes and knows these chemicals on sight," I added.

"Bob, we got a crash project for you," Stiggs whispered urgently into Wino Bob's bushes. Top emergency blues priority, Bob. Money is no object."

Of course, Bob didn't respond; he never responded before the third or fourth time you repeated the deal. "Poke him," I said. "Offer him hard liquor." But Stiggs just stood there, over Bob's nest in the shallow oleander ditch, studying the moonlit form of a dead old black man wearing three Randall Schwab Insurance T-shirts, one over the other, and holding a plasic 7-Eleven, lemon-shaped lemon squirter in his hand.

"He was a synthetic-citrus freak," Stiggs said calmly. "He used to squirt that stuff on everything, even bread."

"People get weird tastes when they get old," I said, after about a thirty-second gap of silence. "He told us he was going to die, remember?"

Stiggs didn't answer; he just opened up one of Bob's crumpled blankets and spread it over the body. "I suppose we should tell the bozo in the red-checked smock behind the 7-Eleven register that he's got a dead wino behind his store," Stiggs said as he stood up and rubbed his hands. "I'm sure the red-checked-smock people must have a policy for this sort of thing."

Using the strange logic that comes after mourning the death of guys who buy you liquor, me and Stiggs decided to continue our night exactly as planned—that is, to gobble up the blues drugs and get to the dinner theater. "I owe it to my people," I said.

HEAD TO HEAD WITH THE UNSTABLE AND VENGEFUL DIRTWAD SCHLEUTER—A PATHETIC MORNING

Penis House opened the same day we won the completely malicious Schleuter case, so naturally it was an active brand of day. Schleuter's courtroom behavior was great. "These young monsters . . ." was how Schleuter began, addressing the jury from three-by-five note cards, acting as his own attorney, looking frantic and mentally damaged, with long strings of hair falling down from his temples and these real red and puffy blotches glowing on his forearms from always being nervously scratched.

Official Legal Transcript of What Schleuter Said in Court

Schleuter: These sadistic monsters were in my classes for two years, and there was not a day during that time when they failed to create a disturbance. Equipment was damaged, or disappeared. Athletic events were ruined for everyone. Many students suffered insults and even physical injury.

For example, on March eighth of this year, a young boy, Randall Schwab, came to my office complaining of dizziness and a headache. It seems Mr. Stiggs and Mr. Oglevey had been involved in one of the flag-football games organized for the class that day, and had chosen Randall to be a receiver on their team. Complex pass patterns were then drawn for him in the huddle, often requiring six or seven cuts that ran the boy back and forth across the full width of the field. To the best of his ability, Randall did as he was asked, but not once in at least thirty plays was he ever thrown the ball.

Finally, Randall protested. He wanted so desperately to be included in the game that, despite near exhaustion, he begged for the ball. "Sure," Mr. Stiggs and Mr. Oglevey promised, and again they gave Randall a complicated, almost impossible pass route. This time, however, they threw him the ball . . . As hard as possible, they threw it, after Randall had taken but one or two steps from the line of scrimmage. This is why Randall was dizzy; for several dozen plays, the football hit him in the back of the head and bounced high into the air, while defensive players and even Randall's own teammates, Mr. Stiggs and Mr. Oglevey, tackled him viciously.

Naturally, as a responsible coach, I had to take disciplinary steps. I gave these monster boys laps, and I told them they would continue to run laps until they learned how to play the game of football properly.

Stiggs: Objection. We continued running laps until Schleuter got through porking the counselor.

Judge: Order.

Schleuter: You see how they are! They twist and twist the knife with their taunting slanders. They peck at me like vultures. They steal my good name and my couch. These monster boys will pay, you can believe that. They will be punished for what they have done to me and Mrs. Beale. . . . She . . . she was my angel-woman. And . . . I was her angel-man. . . .

Judge: Case dismissed.

LEGALLY REGISTERED

Assn. of Problem Teens

ME AND STIGGS FINALLY GET HOPELESS, WORTHLESS JUNKIES IN POSITION NEXT TO THE ESTATE-SIZED RESIDENCE OF LELAND CROFT, DDS

One of the main advantages of having a drug clinic was that we could call it a "therapeutic community," and the main advantage of having a therapeutic community was that me and Stiggs got to make up therapies. "Eustis," Stiggs said to the largest and most threatening member of our nine-patient enrollment of hopeless, worthless junkies, "if you can train this hamster to perform a whole bunch of interesting tricks, we'll give you a Randall Schwab Insurance T-shirt."

"That's right," I added. "Now what we have in mind, Eustis, is a hamster playlet—a full choreographed drama where the hamster plays the role of a French traitor whom you are pursuing to redeem the honor of your family, a family once destroyed by the hamster to save himself."

"*Oooooooo,*" Eustis responded through the lattice of nose fluids traveling across his dope-numbed lip. "Yes . . . yes . . . yes."

"Mitzi fucked up her therapeutic leaf project," Sponson the vet and Penis House counselor interrupted—Mitzi being a seventy-eight-pound detoxing psychotic in the room next door.

"You've got five of the same leaf," Stiggs said to Mitzi in the stern style of a chancellor of Penis House evaluating totally ridiculous leaf collections. "Why would anyone collect five identical leaves, and why would anyone label them 'Pretty leaf,' 'Hope leaf,' 'Night leaf,' 'Satori leaf,' and 'Truth leaf'?"

"Hey, baby, this collection sucks," Sponson shouted two inches away from Mitzi's face, trying for a psyche grenade effect that might blast through five or six years of narcotic drool and launch Mitzi on a zesty beeline for the front yard, where she would spend the rest of the day raking her vein-scarred limbs through more than one variety of leaf.

"*Ooooooooo* . . . yes," Eustis said from his position in the doorway, not knowing where he was or that there was a hamster on his amazing, Sonny Liston-size head.

"Because of these really bonehead performances," Chancellor Stiggs said later on during our staff meeting, "and because Barney's finally out of jail and says he only has fifty dollars left, I think we should take off with Barney and his fifty and leave these goons to themselves."

So we reinstated Barney as our dog and spent the day floating down the Verde River, while Sponson took it upon himself to send the junkies on an Outward Bound expedition into Croft's yard—a great idea.

THE JUNKIES RETURN. A CRUSH OF CHARITY SLAGS INVADE FOR DINNER. CROFT'S CABANA IS INVESTIGATED FULLY

Ooooooo . . . yes. Yes." Eustis commented on the ninth of his twelve Sara Lee pies. "Yes . . . yes . . . love that cabana." More specifically, Leland Croft's cabana, site of Leland's upright freezer and Nora's incredible stockpile of grade-AAA, junkie-quality desserts. "We . . . like . . . cleaned him out totally," added Mitzi, hacking at a gallon of designer ice cream with a beer opener. "We were . . . like . . . even going to grab all the stuff he had . . . like . . . in the stairwell under the freezer, but that's when the ugly guy came out with a goddamn gun, and we . . . like . . . took off."

Me and Stiggs naturally made a mental note to sneak into Croft's cabana after dark for a major investigation.

One of the other major advantages to operating your own charity drug clinic, aside from getting to call your place a therapeutic community, is that me and Stiggs were instantly plugged in to the local wives-of-rich-guys charity machinery—sine qua non for gala fund raising. "Wives of rich guys like symphonies and art museums, and they hate cancer and heart attacks and arthritis and dope addicts wandering around their neighborhoods," Stiggs explained to the scum of Penis House. "So, naturally, they'll pay big dough to hog down a Symphony Guild banquet, or an Art League banquet, or a Cancer Society banquet, or a Heart Fund banquet, or an Arthritis Foundation banquet, or of course the Penis House banquet—scheduled for tonight."

Because of an hour's worth of critical phone calls, which Mr. Colletti made nude from his patio rum lounge, the guest turnout was great. The house was totally infested with lawyer wives, real-estate wives, airline-pilot wives, financier wives, TV-personality wives, industrialist wives, university-president wives, giant-inheritance wives, defense-contractor wives, and even dentist wives like Nora Croft—invited by Colletti as an example of how amazingly humorous he is, and sent, as it turned out, by her dirtwad husband to tell us to get the fuck out of the neighborhood.

"Eat me, Nora," Stiggs greeted her in our receiving line of me, Stiggs, Sponson, and the nine hopeless, worthless junkies. "This is Mitzi; we don't have any last names at Love House because our philosophy here is that dopeheads aren't people. Show Nora your leaf display, Mitzi . . ."

Mitzi walked to a wall in the foyer covered with the usual real sensitive, love-and-human-dignity bullshit, and pointed to a smudged rectangle of cardboard with five identical leaves on it. "This is 'Night leaf.' " Mitzi said, wound up like a seventy-eight-pound spring. "I want you to have it."

"Almost as lovely as your Colletti hog dress," I pointed out.

"We want our desserts back," Nora responded. "And we want you out of the neighborhood."

I frowned like I was irritated and snatched Mitzi's leaf. "You don't deserve 'Night leaf,' " I said, and then I ate it.

"Attention, all rich gals," Stiggs yelled from the head table, a rippled Formica model borrowed from the Law Cucaracha trailer. "I hope you all liked our dinner. The reason it was mostly Sara Lee cakes and designer ice cream is so you could be familiarized with the type of meals actually eaten by unsupervised junkies, and also because the stuff was donated entirely by Nora Croft, who's one of the leading spark plugs behind the Love House therapeutic community. Let's have a huge, monster blast of applause for Nora Croft."

Nora, who was still loitering around the gala banquet to sniff out information for her husband, bolted instantly.

"And now," I added, "I'd like to introduce Eustis Beverly. Always interested in animals, Eustis has conceived a playlet for us, starring his hamster as the French scoundrel Monsieur Hamster, and also starring himself as the avenging son of a family that the villain nearly destroyed. As you can see, Eustis has constructed a set, as it were, representing the effluvial dockside demimonde of Monsieur Hamster. The shoe box to your left is, apparently, the village brothel, while the shoe box next to it has a good chance of being the opium den. Eustis's drama begins with Monsieur Hamster boasting to his comrades of past wickedness, as Eustis arrives in town. I give you . . . Eustis Beverly."

When the applause gave out, Eustis got right into the falsetto ventriloquism voice necessary for hamster dialogue. "*Oooooooo* . . . I be real dangerous . . . yes . . . yes . . . I say, everybody, I done some very nasty hamsterizing hamsterization . . . yes.

"Where you at, Mr. Hamster," Eustis continued, now using his normal, rasping drug slur. "Yes . . . I'm pissed off." At this point, because the hamster didn't come out of the brothel shoe box and skitter to the opium-den shoe box like it was supposed to, Eustis decided on the improvisational step of bashing a large book on the brothel box in hopes of flattening the villain then and there. But since the hamster bolted off the set and into the tightly-packed audience of wives of rich guys, Eustis dived headlong after it, slamming the book in all directions, frightening the women out of their minds.

"Let's investigate Croft's cabana," I remarked to Stiggs and Sponson. And so we did.

Having a grand-master level of ability in yard invasion, gained mostly during the great Schwab patio-defacing years of 1975–81, me and Stiggs had little trouble slithering into the cabana and pushing the freezer off its mount. "The hidden stairwell," Stiggs whispered, "just as Mitzi babbled it."

As a result of a Viet Cong jungle flashback sizzling in Sponson's head at the moment, he produced a live grenade.

"Jesus, I can't think of a better guy to have a live grenade," Stiggs said.

The bottom of the stairs opened into a long corridor, which branched into a pair of other corridors, which then led to a bunch of storerooms. "It's survival shit," Sponson declared, probing wooden crates in the dark. "Look at this. Holy fuck. Guns. This guy's got enough stuff down here to blow out an army." Stiggs found a lighted niche with a file cabinet and a desk with a folder on it labeled "Super Ultra." "Check the entrance," Sponson said. "See if we're clear."

We weren't; Leland was on his patio, heading directly for the cabana. We met him at the top of the stairwell. "You punks are going to be very sorry," Leland said with the composure of a lunatic dentist waving a 9-mm gun. "We came back for more Sara Lees," Stiggs bluffed. "Nora said we could have more if the gala fund-raising banquet started to drag."

"Move, or you eat this," Sponson added, straight-arming the grenade into Leland's face.

The dentist let out a two- or three-pulse chuckle, and backed away. "Vacate that clinic tomorrow morning or I'll turn all of you in to the police. I've got everything I need to put you away."

So we took off. It was a fairly strange situation.

Not until we got into Sponson's car to drive around and figure out our position did Stiggs flip on the overhead light and look inside the Super Ultra folder he grabbed from Leland's survival and weapons fortress. After reading it, we were easily convinced that Leland's dirtball attitude toward us and the Sluts de Boxcar, and his failure to have the proper plaster lawn burro, and his window peering and gun waving and everything else, were all just the tip of a much larger and more gooned-out iceberg.

THE INDIRECT SOLVING OF THE LEGAL OPPRESSION OF ME AND STIGGS BY SURGICAL APPLICATION OF THE TECHNIQUE OF EXPLODING A CABANA

Me and Stiggs never knew that Sponson had a helicopter. "That guy Croft is an elitist, capitalist, racist, dangerous motherfucker," Sponson raged, ramming long, finned tubes into cylinders on the side of the chopper. "Me and my people, man, we believe in the people."

"I hear you," Stiggs said enthusiastically. "Good, peaceful, pot-guarding, pot-harvesting, pot-flying, pot-smelling people, man."

"Right," Sponson bellowed, shoving in the last tube.

"Hey, Sponson, you got a plan?" I asked.

"Yeah. Blotto dentist. Zap. Bye-bye."

Me and Stiggs naturally agreed, not wanting Leland bringing the cops down on Penis House; but, on the other hand, since Croft never reported us to the cops even though he had our clothes with our ID in them the night we took off over his fence, and even though he spotted the Penis House Outward Bound expedition in his Sara Lee freezer, it was possible that Croft was more afraid of cops finding his underground maniac bunker than of us.

"Only zap the cabana," Stiggs advised as Sponson started up the helicopter in full combat ensemble, including complete Montagnard warrior paint all over his face.

And so it happened that on the first night of the last week before school, we sat on nude Pat Colletti's patio and watched our maniac friend strafe our maniac enemy in a home-modified Huey gunship, complete with *Apocalypse Now* Valkyrie music blasting at thunder volume on nude Colletti's patio stereo. "Can we use your phone for an emergency police call?" I asked Colletti as the first and second straight streaks of white light shot from the Huey to the cabana. "Sure," Colletti said.

The cops showed up fast, in about three minutes, just in time to notice the dentist and the rest of his "inner circle"—Nora—stunned on their ornamental gravel lawn, screaming Super Ultra vengeance in random directions.

So, the bunker was discovered; the Crofts were nabbed; Penis House was saved. This is how things stood when we went to court the next morning.

"Obviously, Your Honor," went the weaseling Mexican argument of Reynoldo the mall lawyer, "this is just a case of really fine young men. Your Honor, who really cared about the sister of their good friend Randall Schwab. They cared about her so much, Your Honor, that they wanted to help protect her from the many forms of danger in today's world by giving her a light, real good gun that even a really delicate woman like Lenora Schwab could shoot pretty easy. I ask you, Your Honor, do these young men look like criminals? Your Honor, I think I know the answer we'd get to that question from Lenora Schwab—or, Your Honor, from the really fine, rehabilitated patients at the Love House. The name says it really good, Your Honor—Love House, the house that these fine young men built with love, Your Honor, and that will probably collapse from love starvation if Mr. Stiggs and Mr. Oglevey and Mr. Sponson are taken away from loving their patients and put into prison. Thank you, Your Honor."

The judge looked hard at me and Stiggs. And then he looked especially hard at the white-and-black Montagnard tribal-attack paint and complete camouflage jump suit still on Sponson. Sponson of course being too Methedrined and combat fried from the night before to get around to putting on anything reasonable for court.

"Possessing an unlicensed automatic weapon is a very serious offense," the judge said. "However, the court is not unaware of the noble intentions of the defendants or the worth of their community service."

"She mine! Han Lo Choy! Want back!" a beeping Chinese voice that was com-

pletely out of control suddenly interrupted from the hall. It wasn't, however, until two or three seconds after the judge finished his totally dog-headed analysis of our characters that me and Stiggs got a chance to bolt the courtroom and get a good look at the screaming Chinaman and the arm-waving crowd of screaming Chinamen who were helping him surround the building-information clerk.

"FBI. Get FBI. She my property!"

"What's the beef, Frank?" Stiggs asked the screaming Chinaman, Frank Tang.

"Gone. Wife leave. Harp gone. Want back!"

"This may not be a federal matter," I explained. "There are a number of jurisdictional considerations here, Frank, which probably bar the government of the United States from driving around town looking for unhappy, unfulfilled Schwabs."

"She mine!" Frank insisted. *"Want back! Want manhunt! FBI!"*

Stiggs instantly came to the rescue of the overwhelmed information clerk and escorted Frank and the rest of the yipping, jabbering Chinamen to the offices of the U.S. Center for Disease Control. "They'll know what to do," Stiggs said, holding his fingertips over his mouth, spitting and snorting and chuckling real obviously, like a nine-year-old child.

The Incredible Memo from Dirtbag Dentist Leland Croft to His Wife, Nora, Captured by Us from Leland's Subterranean Survival Fortress

LELAND O. CROFT, DDS
WESTWOOD MEDICAL PLAZA
4021 WEST BRILLE ROAD, PHOENIX, ARIZONA

MEMORANDUM 82-8-37774-B-6
SUBJECT: Super Ultra
TO: Inner Circle (Nora)

It should be no surprise to you that the holocaust is coming in a week. Secret events that I have been describing for the last twenty-five years (viz. memoranda 82-6-46625-J-4, 78-12-52683-K-3, 74-7-12763-Z-2, 69-11-75731-A-9, 66-5-18762-R-2, 61-1-12561-L-7, 57-4-39992-B-1, 52-1-20404-W-5) have set the stage for the final act of madness.

Consider these recent occurrences:

21-March-82: Argentina seizes Falkland Islands.

9-May-82: Israel bombs Lebanon.

12-June-82: Russia completes secret nighttime invasion of Europe; by morning, secret shadow governments are installed in France, Holland, Spain, Austria, and Italy, which secretly control present leaders while public suspects nothing.

17-June-82: Republic of China secretly annexes Japan.

25-June-82: Our front lawn is destroyed by secret deep-cover cadres bent on terrorizing and confusing us, softening us up in preparation for full-scale attack.

You have seen for yourself the nest of depraved provocateurs now at our very doorstep. Hiding, of course, behind the crudely deceptive banner of a "Love House," they are poised to carry out the last phase of their coordinated plan—undermining our values, so corrupting and demoralizing us as to poison our will to defend ourselves.

PREPAREDNESS, Nora! The future belongs to those who recognize the peril and have devised their means of protection. This is why our subcabana survival unit must be fully supplied and operational at all times. This is why your complaints regarding cleaning and vacuuming the subcabana must stop immediately. INACTION CANNOT BE TOLERATED AT THIS CRUCIAL TIME!

DECISIVENESS, RESOLUTENESS, TIRELESSNESS, Nora! By these watchwords we will survive. I will expect the subcabana to be waxed and fresh smelling by the time of my arrival from the office this evening, approximately 6:05 P.M. DO NOT FAIL!

Yours in vigilance,

Leland O. Croft, DDS

THE SUMMER ENDS PRETTY MUCH AS IT BEGAN, AT THE HYATT-REGENCY, ONLY THIS TIME IN A LOUNGE FULL OF BUSINESSMEN INSTEAD OF IN A THINK TANK

On the last day of the summer, me and Stiggs were driving around. Our case was over; the judge told Reynoldo that he'd let us off with a reprimand, so we instantly shut down Penis House, kicked out all the junkies, and went over to the Law Cucaracha trailer to return their rippled Formica lobby table and to hand over the last of the valuable Schwabian stamps for Reynoldo's fee. But no one was there; the desk-top copier had broken down, so they all went home. On the way out of the mall parking lot we saw Reynoldo pounding on the hood of his black Trans Am, which was also broken down; but we just kept going. "It would be like interfering with some natural wildlife process that the guys on 'National Geographic' shows tell you never to fuck with," Stiggs said. "Do you think Sponson and Mitzi will be happy on the pot plantation?" I asked, changing the subject. "Sure," Stiggs answered. "It'll give her a brand-new source of leaves. . . . Are we bored?" The answer to Stiggs's question was pretty obvious, given the increasingly giant size of the gaps in our conversation and the fact that we were now cruising for about the tenth time past the Schwab house. "I feel a certain anxiety," I said. "Something seems to be out of alignment; it's as if part of the universe secretly shifted and we lost our center of gravity."

Naturally this totally moronic center-of-gravity bullshit was grounds for Stiggs's bailing out of the car and never speaking to me again; but since Stiggs was also feeling as weird about things as I was, he disregarded the horrible language and concentrated on analyzing our problem. "Schwabs," he said. "All problems in the world are connected to the Schwabs."

Brazenly, I ventured back into the section of the mind that figures out exotic cosmology, and pretty soon hit on the incredible discovery that the Schwab System had lost critical mass. "That's it!" Stiggs yelled. "It's the renegade planet Lenora. She's left Tangian space and completely fucked up the rest of the Schwab System." After more thinking, we decided that individual Schwab-etary bodies could start spinning off all over the place, even out of state, where we couldn't get to them. "We've got to reverse this phenomenon," I said. "The Schwab System must be restored to its natural order."

Accordingly, we drove at full speed to the Hyatt-Regency, where, just as me and Stiggs suspected, Lenora was clawing out Burt Bacharach on her harp in the main executive lounge. "Solid," Stiggs said to her, nodding his head like Mel Torme to the gooey tinkling of the strings.

Because of the small amount of sentiment I still had from the incident where Lenora offered us her entire tragic seventy-eight-dollar wad, and because of the current sentiment that I had because she actually took our insane advice and got a harp job in the Hyatt-Regency lounge, I found myself in a state of emotion that I hadn't felt since the moment after the Soul Mass when I vowed to never play the honking blues-monster harmonica ever again. So, for that reason, I jerked the soul monster from my pocket and the dual soul-and-Lenora harp supersession was begun.

"*Do-doo-do-doot,*" I honked with growling, chicken-scratching blues mastery. Being in her totally voidoid harp-plinking trance, Lenora didn't seem to notice my crouched, soul-honking pose beside her, which was great for two reasons. First it really disturbed the businessmen; and second, it gave me something to do while Stiggs called Frank Tang and told him where Lenora was. "Hello, Disease Control Center," Stiggs said on the lobby phone. "If the screaming Chinamen are still in your office, tell them, 'Lenora at Hyatt-Regency.' Thank you."

"*Do-doo-do-doot,*" I finished honking. "Thank you; you're a righteous audience. Lenora Schwab Tang on D-50 executive-lounge harp, ladies and gentlemen. Lenora Schwab Tang."

Frank Tang and his Chinamen and the rest of the Schwab System—the insurance dad Schwab and the alcoholic mom Schwab and the astounding Randall Schwab—burst in to the room just as Lenora and I steamrolled into our next number, "I'll Never Fall in Love Again."

Stiggs, who was at the bar between a dead-drunk guy who was wearing a convention name tag and a cocktail waitress who the guy was trying to pork, was clapping and whistling frantically. "How about those fucking honking and tinkling dual blues harps," he roared, jabbing the convention guy in the ribs. "Come on, Jack, put your hands together!"

"You mine! Come now! You in for it!" Frank screeched at his wife. The rest of the Schwabs were of course horrified, their daughter having no doubt been lured into this den of drunk businessmen by the mind-controlling, Svengali blues voodoo of me honking that devil melody six inches from their gooned-out daughter's mammoth Schwabian head.

"Aren't they great?" Stiggs repeated loudly to the convention guy, over and over, each time the guy tried to dribble something suggestive to the cocktail waitress.

In a few minutes, the Chinamen and the Schwabs were gone—harp, Lenora, and all. I stood alone, surrounded by businessmen, bathed in the cosmic dust of reunited Schwabs, noodling the reeds of my honking soul harp, looking for the ideal selection of notes that would do justice to the whole situation—to the whole mind-roasting situation.

"What time do you get out of here?" Stiggs asked the cocktail waitress next to the fully outmaneuvered and pissed-off convention guy. "Me and O. C. start school tomorrow and need to pull one last train or we'll do real bad and never graduate and never get jobs, and end up being cocktail waitresses."

"Every man gotta have a good woman," I told the same girl later, when, amazingly, she came through for us in the hotel fan room on the top floor. It was great.

Six Fantasies of

RICHARD NIXON

by Gerald Sussman

A Late-Night Visit

I'm alone in my study, working late on my next book, when I hear a light tapping at the door. Who could it be at this hour of the night? Why, it's Nancy Reagan!

"What are you doing in this neck of the woods?" I ask, as I feel a strange tingle in the back of my neck.

"Well, I was just visiting someone in the neighborhood, and I thought I'd take a chance and see if you were in," said Nancy.

She took off her jacket and I noted her perfectly shaped breasts under her fine silk blouse. Nancy always looked much younger than her age.

"How about one little drink, Nancy? You can't say no, because I *was* the president, right?"

I mixed us a pair of potent martinis, and we sipped them, talking about this and that. The nice thing was that Nancy wasn't a bit uncomfortable with me. By the time we had our second drink, she was sitting next to me on the sofa and it seemed quite natural for me to put my arms around her and kiss her on the neck. She responded by kissing me on the mouth, wide open. By golly, I never did much tongue kissing; Pat hates it. But I let Nancy's tongue do whatever it wanted.

Then, without me asking, she got up and took her blouse and bra off and let me put my hands on her breasts. They were still as high and firm as a young gal's.

She started to undo my pants, and I said, "It's okay, I can do it." But she insisted. She said she was proud to undress the greatest president the United States ever had. She took off all my clothes, including my shoes and socks. No one ever did that for me in my life, not even my mother. It made me feel really good. And really hard. In fact, I felt so good that I couldn't control myself. Luckily, most of it landed in Nancy's face, pretty close to her mouth, and she didn't mind it a bit. She's a wonderful sport.

Confrontation with a Hippie

Sometimes after I have a fantasy about Nancy, I feel a little guilty. After all, Pat is a wonderful gal, a loyal, hardworking wife, a fine mother, and a constant inspiration to me. This is when I have my favorite Pat fantasy.

I'm sitting at a bar with Pat, having a martini. Pat doesn't drink much, so she's just having a ginger ale. A young man sits down next to Pat and starts talking to her. He is a big, heavyset fellow, with long hair tied in the back like a hippie, and he's wearing scruffy dungarees and a dirty T-shirt. He talks to Pat as if she's some kind of bar chippie, a hostess or something. Pat tries to be polite with him and fend him off, but he insists on talking to her and asking her very personal questions. I sip my martini slowly and smile at Pat, telling her with a reassuring look on my face that it's okay and not to worry. But Pat is distinctly uncomfortable.

I deliberately let this filthy, vile hippie continue his disgusting line of patter. He even has the gall to put his hand on Pat's leg. At this point I tap him on the shoulder and tell him to stop bothering her. He looks at me as if I were some kind of insect and tells me to fuck off. I can see a tattoo on his arm; it's the marines' slogan, Death Before Dishonor. He's more than just a hippie, he's an ex-marine. I wonder where he went wrong.

I get off my stool and walk over to him. He's grinning at me and he deliberately runs his hand up Pat's thigh to provoke me. I ask him to stop or I'll call the police. He laughs and grabs me by my shirt collar and shakes me hard. I tell him to put me down or I'll get him arrested. This only makes him angry, so angry that he punches me hard, right on the jaw, and sends me flying back into a table. He throws a pretty mean punch.

I get up slowly and compliment him on his right cross, which I guess is his best shot. By now, his guard is completely down. I saw Glenn Ford do this in a movie. He thinks he has intimidated me. Even Pat is frightened and tries to get away, but he grabs her arm and won't let her go.

Before she can scream, I let the hippie have it, a one-two combination. A left to the stomach that has him gasping for breath and a right uppercut to the jaw that sends him straight to the floor in a crumpled heap.

I pour a bottle of beer over his head to revive him, pick him up, and balance him against the bar. Then for about half a minute I use his head as a punching bag, using short jackhammer blows, until both his eyes are closed, his nose is bloodied, most of his teeth are loosened, and his face is totally battered and bruised. Last, but not least, I drag him to the back alley, stuff him into an empty garbage can, and lock the lid real tight.

I go back to the bar, throw a few hundred bucks down for the damages, and buy a drink for everyone in the house. The bartender shakes my hand, Pat straightens my tie, and we both relax again.

Touchdown!

Here's a fantasy I used to have back in 1962. It was a touch football game between my team and the Kennedys. The Kennedys were the most overrated, overpublicized football players in the country. I was a heck of a better player than they were, and I still can run a pretty good forty and throw a pretty mean spiral. Anyway, here's what happens.

There's only a minute left to play, and we're behind by six points. It's third and a long seven, and everyone is looking for a pass. Instead, I cross them up with a running play. I get the ball on a reverse and burst through a big hole, right into the secondary. A Kennedy is coming at me. It's young Senator Ted. He's wobbling and reeling like a Bowery bum. I give him a fake to the right and I cut to the left, leaving him to grope a handful of air.

I reverse my field, pick up some blockers, and cut to the sidelines. I've got only two men to beat. One of them is catching up to me. It's Attorney General Bobby. I give him a quick stiff arm, and I can feel the shock of pain in my hand as he goes down. He's hurt a lot more than I am.

There's only one guy left near the goal line. I can give him a nifty move, but a voice inside me says, "The hell with touch football candy-ass rules. Run right through him." At the split second before we bump heads, I get a good look at his face. He's in shock. He can't believe I'm going to run right over him. He just bounces off me like a pin in a bowling alley. I don't even break stride as I streak in for a touchdown.

Helping a Friend

Walter Annenberg, one of my oldest and dearest friends, and a very wealthy and powerful man, is having dinner with me at his private club. I've never seen Walter look so despondent. To put it in a nutshell, he tells me that his business empire is sagging. Through a series of bad business decisions and incompetent management by his subordinates (none of it his fault), he was about to lose control of many of his holdings.

After our coffee and brandy, Walter looked me straight in the eye and said, "You're the only guy I know who can save us. You have no ties with my organization. You're independent. You can do whatever it takes to turn my fortunes around without worrying about stepping on anyone's toes. I need more than just a good businessman, Dick. I need a *leader*."

It wasn't easy. You can't turn a company like Walter's around overnight. I worked my butt off, but by the time I was finished I knew everything about his operations, from the mail room to the boardroom. I had to fire over twenty-five hundred people, all dead wood. I closed four plants and consolidated a group of smaller companies and sold three others for a big profit. In a month

I reduced Walter's liabilities to zero. In two months he was back in the black.

When Walter brought up the matter of compensation, I told him I couldn't accept any money. It was purely an act of friendship.

"Well, Dick, if you feel like that, I'll just have to make it up to you in some other manner," he said.

A few weeks later, Walter took me for a drive to the country. Our destination turned out to be the most beautiful, luxurious country estate I've ever seen, a house that exuded wealth, power, and good taste.

"Welcome to your new country home," said Walter. "I knew you wouldn't accept any money for what you did, but surely you won't turn down a place like this. Besides, my accountants are figuring out a way to make it a tax-free operation for you."

A tax-free, luxury house. It was as if Walter had read my mind. It only proved to me once again that hard work and loyalty will always pay off in the end.

My Country Calls

The Republican nominating convention for 1980 is in a turmoil. There is no dominant candidate with enough votes to win. Precious hours, days, go by and no one can make the right deal or strike the right bargain to win over anyone else. The Reagan, Baker, and Connally forces are at loggerheads. The dark horses and young hopefuls are simply too weak to make any difference. Gerald Ford is out of the question for the majority of the party. There is only one hope left. A call is made to the Supreme Court for a special emergency ruling. Can a former president who has resigned be called back to run again? An answer must be had in a matter of hours or the deadline for the nominations will be past. At exactly thirty minutes before the deadline, the court hands down a verdict. Yes, under certain unusual circumstances, a former president who has not served his full term can be made eligible to run again. Exactly five minutes later my phone rings. It is the chairman of the convention asking me to accept the nomination as the only candidate who can lead us to victory. With deep gratification and firm resolve, I accept.

The Great Debates, II

Now that I've accepted the nomination in 1980, I'm running against Teddy. And just as in 1960, we're going to do three TV debates. Only this time, it's a whole new ball game.

I feel cool and confident as I stride into the TV studio for the first debate.

Teddy is trying to look calm, but there's a glazed look in his eye and a slight slur in his speech that tells me he has already pressed the panic button. He's tanked to the gills.

Immediately I take the offensive with a bold statement about our economy. Teddy is so taken aback that he gropes for words and can't answer my points.

In the next hour I have him reeling like a punched-out fighter, as I jab and hook him with one point after another—taxes, housing, education. Then I really coldcock him on his pet subject, medical insurance. And the son of a b. does the worst thing an opponent can do in a debate—he agrees with me.

In the next debate, I go right for the jugular. He can't touch me in the area of foreign policy. I win every round easily—China, Russia, Cuba, disarmament . . . you name it. Teddy is almost speechless. He's even more gone than the first time. His body is twitching. Moons of sweat can be seen right through his dark suit. His eye keeps wandering off toward the assistant producer, a redhead in a low-cut blouse. He leers at her and makes an obscene gesture right on camera.

About halfway through the debate, he simply quits. He tries to walk off the stage, but he's so drunk that he stumbles and falls and breaks both legs.

The next day, at a press conference, Teddy announces his withdrawal from the race. For the first time in history, a candidate concedes defeat before the election.

BEAT THE MEATLES

with Chris Miller

CHRIS: . . . sure was nice of you guys to come over here and talk with me like this. Uh, there, the tape recorder's running now. Why don't you just make yourselves at home, sit down anywhere. Anybody like some wine or something to smoke?

RINGO: Shur, that'd be nice.
(General assent. Pouring sounds)

PAUL: Nice apartment.

CHRIS: Thanks.

GEORGE: I like yur paintin' 'ere. Li'ul dead sheep an' all, with blud roonin' frum thur mouths. You don't see many of these.

CHRIS: Oh, that was used in a *National Lampoon* calendar. Mike Gross painted it. I traded some—

YOKO: The blood stains red. The red is silence. Listen! Can you hear it fall, softly, softly?

JOHN: Why don't we joost sit down 'ere, luv.

CHRIS: Well, gosh, you all look great. Really.

PAUL: Thanks very mooch. I think Ringo's poot on a few, tho'.

RINGO: 'Ere! Noon uv tha', now.
(Laughter)

JOHN: *(Sucking noise)* Vurry tasty smoke.

CHRIS: Thanks.

GEORGE: *(Sucking noise)* Is it gold, then?

CHRIS: Right. Here, these are some of the buds.

RINGO: *(Low whistle)* 'Ere, let me 'ave soom uv tha'. *(Sucking noise)* Mmm, it's really—*(Violent coughing)*

PAUL: *(Clapping Ringo on the back)* 'E never really learned to inhale, y'know. Come on, mate, spi' it ou'.

RINGO: *(Loud, choking coughs)* Went . . . down the . . . wrong pipe.

CHRIS:	Here, drink some of this. (*Swallowing sounds*)
RINGO:	Ah. Better. Thank you.
CHRIS:	Well, I guess this is kind of unusual, the four of you being in the same room together these days.
JOHN:	Tha's righ', it's been years. The last time me an' Paul saw each oother, I think I called 'im a fookin' bahstard.
PAUL:	Yeh, an' I called you a stooburn cocksooker. (*Merry laugher*)
YOKO:	Like everything, it is circular. The sun, the moon, the planets—all circular. (*Pause*)
CHRIS:	Ah . . .
GEORGE:	Do you see tha' paintin' then, Ringo? It's got li'ul dead sheep all lyin' in the snow. See thur li'ul legs stickin' oop?
CHRIS:	It portrays the time the army let some nerve gas get loose out in Utah. It killed a bunch of sheep.
PAUL:	Foony. It's sooch a pretty pickshur, too.
CHRIS:	Yeah, it's supposed to be in the style of Grandma Moses. They used it in this calendar for the *Bi*—
GEORGE:	Look a' tha' one thur, with 'is 'ead in the river. Thur's a li'ul blud trail roonin' out uv 'is mouth, goin' down the river thur.
RINGO:	'Ow 'bou' tha'!
CHRIS:	Say, there's a bunch of questions I've always wanted to ask you guys. Some of them are personal and embarrassing, and others are just plain stupid, but . . . could you get into that?
JOHN:	Of course, man.
PAUL:	Shur, ask away.
CHRIS:	Well, I guess the big question I've always wanted to ask is, what exactly was it *like*, being the Beatles?
JOHN:	Really great, Chris.
RINGO:	A hell of a time. (*Pause*)
CHRIS:	George?
GEORGE:	Oh, lots uv foon. Could I 'ave a bit more of tha' wine, then, mate?
CHRIS:	Sure. (*Pouring sounds*) Uh . . . Paul?
PAUL:	I'm okay for the mo', thanks.
CHRIS:	No, I mean, what was being a Beatle like?

PAUL: Qui'e peculiar.

        (*Pause*)

CHRIS: Well, let me ask you this. Back when you were performing live and you used to look out there at all those screaming thirteen-year-old girls, did you ever get a sudden craving to ram your cocks down their open mouths?

JOHN: Oh, coonstantly. I remember wishin' I could fly righ' off the stage an' dive-bomb 'em with me dick out.

        (*Gentle, reminiscent laughter*)

CHRIS: Paul, how do you shave?

PAUL: First down, then oop. Then I pu' on a li'ul after-shave.

CHRIS: That's amazing. That's exactly how I do it.

RINGO: Me, too.

CHRIS: Ringo, what's the rest of your morning like? I mean, what are the things you do when you get up?

RINGO: Well, let's see. I 'ave a pee. I broosh me teeth, take a shower, get dressed, an' eat me breakfast.

CHRIS: What kind of toothpaste do you use?

RINGO: Crest.

CHRIS: Great. Uh, George, if it started to rain breasts, what would you do?

GEORGE: Become vurry frightened.

        (*Laughter*)

CHRIS: John, what would you do?

JOHN: Roon outside with a bushel basket.

        (*Redoubled laughter*)

CHRIS: Paul, what's five and three?

PAUL: Eight.

CHRIS: Great. Great. Isn't this terrific?

RINGO: I'm 'avin a woonderful time.

        (*General assent*)

YOKO: See the wine sparkle. Examine its sound. The glass is round.

        (*Pause*)

CHRIS: The wine is a Blanc de Blanc. I always pronounce that "blank-dee-blank." You know, like in (*sings*) "Poosh-dee-poosh, we can work it out, baby."

JOHN: Oh, yeh, the Contours. Always liked tha' one.

RINGO: Wha's tha', then? "Do You Luv Me"?

JOHN: Righ'.

CHRIS: You guys still listen to old rock 'n' roll?

PAUL: Oh, shur, me Li'ul Richard an' Chook Burry an' like tha'.

CHRIS: What do you listen to that's contemporary?

YOKO: I hear the snowflakes fall soundlessly . . . and the footsteps of the angels.

JOHN: Yeh, we listen qui'e a bit to the foo'steps uv the angels these days.

CHRIS: Ringo, what do you think of Farrah Fawcett?

RINGO: Nice teeth an' nipples.

CHRIS: You *like* nipples!

RINGO: Oh, shur.

CHRIS: Well, what do you think of all those magazines like *Penthouse* and *Hustler* going into the pink?

RINGO: You mean, like, feelin' good an' 'ealthy?

GEORGE: No, you goon, tha's "in the pink." 'E's talkin' about pickshurs uv nood women in magazines, 'oldin' thur stoof open.

RINGO: Oh, tha'! I like tha' joost fine.
(*Laughter*)

CHRIS: I wonder if I could ask you about some of your song lyrics?

PAUL: John was ackshully the walrus.

JOHN: No, no, no. Paul was defini'ly the walrus.

RINGO: I wan'ed to be the walrus. They wouldn't let me be the walrus.

YOKO: Wall-russ. Wall-russ. Wall-russ. Wall-russ. Wall-

JOHN: 'Ere, luv, drink soom uv this.
(*Swallowing sounds*)

CHRIS: Um . . . what about "Helter Skelter"? Paul, you wrote that, didn't you? What did you have in mind there?

PAUL: It's qui' remarkable, tha' one. You migh' not believe me, bu' one mornin' I woke oop feelin' grotty an' decided to wri' a song tha' would inspire a bloody 'orrible mass murder.

JOHN: Imagine his chagrin.

CHRIS: You . . . is that really true? Come on.

PAUL: No, really. Tha's exackly the way it 'appened.
(*Pause*)

CHRIS: Uh . . .
(*Laughter*)

CHRIS: (*Laughing*) Wow, I thought for a minute. . . . How'd you *feel* about that Manson thing, anyway?

RINGO: Joost awful, Chris.

JOHN:	Turrible.
CHRIS:	People were always interpreting your songs to mean all kinds of outlandish things, finding clues and hidden meanings in the lyrics and in the pictures on the album jackets. I always figured that was primarily bullshit. Was I right?
GEORGE:	(*Pouring sounds*) No.
CHRIS:	No? They *did* have clues and hidden meanings?
PAUL:	Oh, shur. F'rinstance, "Hey Jude," when you decode it, is ackshully a classified NATO nuclear strike-back plan, in case the Rooshians invade.
JOHN:	Tha's righ'. And if you play the second verse uv "Baby You Can Drive My Car" backwards, it'll give you the formula for Coca-Cola.
CHRIS:	That's amazing.
RINGO:	Wha' you think the song "Yellow Soobmarine" is really about, eh? Take a guess.
CHRIS:	Uh . . . some kind of drug? Something that came in a yellow capsule?
RINGO:	Uh-uh. Take anoother guess.
CHRIS:	Some sort of reference to counter-cultural communal lifestyles?
RINGO:	Oh, no, no. Noothin' like tha'. No, "Yellow Soobmarine" is ackshully abou' this time John 'ad diarrhea. We were on a boose withou' a rest room, so 'e went behind a seat. Which oopset Paul tremendoosly, I migh' add. (*Pause*)
CHRIS:	That's . . . what "Yellow Submarine" is about?
JOHN:	Tha's righ'.
RINGO:	It's all in the clues and 'idden meanin's.
GEORGE:	Pass me the wine? Thank you. (*Pouring sounds*) Y'know wha' else? You remember tha' album coover they wouldn't let us use?
CHRIS:	The one with you guys in blood-smeared aprons, with the dolls made up to look like dismembered babies?
GEORGE:	(*Whispering*) They weren't dolls.
CHRIS:	They . . .
GEORGE:	(*Laughs uproariously and makes fart noise*)
PAUL:	Maybe you should take it a li'ul easy on the blank-dee-blank, eh, George?
GEORGE:	(*Imitating rooster*) Buh-kuk buh-kawwwwww! (*Pause*)
RINGO:	Really nice apartment, Chris.

CHRIS: Thanks. Uh, I know you guys know him—what do you think of Mick Jagger?

JOHN: Turrific lips.

PAUL: Gives me an erection joost watchin' 'im chew goom.

CHRIS: Say, speaking of erections, that brings us to a subject that's certainly near and dear to *my* heart, namely, whacking the ding-dong. Did you guys used to do much of that?

RINGO: (*Modestly*) Oh, well. . . .
(*Laughter*)

PAUL: Oh, shur, we all did lots uv tha', bu' especially yoong Ringo 'ere. 'E's a bit uv a legend in the rock 'n' roll world. You've whacked it in soom pretty remarkable places, 'aven't you, mate?

RINGO: Heh-heh.

YOKO: Whacked it! Whacked it! Whacked it! Whacked—

JOHN: Easy, luv. Settle down, now.

CHRIS: So, Ringo, you really like to flog the hog, eh?

RINGO: I can't deny it, Chris, I 'ave been known to ploonk the magic twanger from time to time.

CHRIS: Well, Ringo, would you care to . . . *expand* on that?

RINGO: (*Chuckling*) Soomtimes I'd do it behind me drooms, righ' in the middle of a concert.

CHRIS: *Really?*

PAUL: (*Giggling into his hands*) 'E did, 'e did, e' used to splatter 'alf the people in the first ten rows.

RINGO: They'd think it was sweat or soomthin', flyin' off one anoother.

JOHN: 'E'd make a special li'ul beat on the tom-tom, to warn us when to dook.

CHRIS: But . . . if you were using both your hands to play the drums . . . what were you using to wring the weasle?

RINGO: A bionic arm!
(*Explosion of laughter. Wine pouring*)

GEORGE: (*Clapping hands, imitating seal*) Ow ow ow ow ow! Ow ow ow ow ow!

PAUL: I think George is gunna be pootin' on a lampshade next.

GEORGE: (*Putting on lampshade*) Ow ow ow ow ow! Ow ow ow ow ow!

YOKO: The bird sings sweet.
(*Whistles like bird*)

JOHN: This is gettin' vurry ecological in 'ere soodenly. Could I 'ave anoother joint, man?

CHRIS: Sure. Comin' right up.

(Sucking noises)

CHRIS: The next thing I was wondering about—

PAUL: I'm paranoid!

CHRIS: You're . . . ?

PAUL: I'm soodenly paranoid! Yur *doop's* too good!

CHRIS: Is he ser—

RINGO: 'Ere, stay out uv 'is way, mate.

PAUL: Spiders! Spiders!

JOHN: Spiders now? Wha' is this, "The Wide World uv Animals"?

GEORGE: *(Clapping hands)* Ow ow ow ow ow! Ow ow ow ow ow!

PAUL: *Don't le' them ge' me!*

CHRIS: It must have been very interesting, you guys working together.

PAUL: Oh! It's okay now, I'm fine. Don't wurry abou' me. Everything's all righ'.

RINGO: Are you sure, then?

PAUL: I'm really absolu'ly fine. I'm fine.

RINGO: Well, I'm glad uv—

PAUL: *Don't touch me!*

JOHN: Oh, coom on, Paul.

PAUL: *Yah! Yahhhhhhhhhhhh!*

CHRIS: Should I call a doctor or something?

RINGO: Oh, no, we remember 'ow to 'andle Paulie, don't we, lads?

GEORGE: Righ'. Let's do it.

PAUL: No! Stop! *Please!* Hey! Ha-ha-ha-ha-ha-ha-ha-ha-ha-ha!

GEORGE: Ickle tickle tickle! Ickle tickle tickle!

PAUL: Ha-ha-ha-ha-ha-ha-ha-ha-ha! Stop! I'll be good! I promise! Ah-ha-ha-ha-ha-ha-ha-ha-ha!

RINGO: John, I've always woondered soomethin'. Why'd you 'ave tha' sanitary napkin tied to yur' 'ead, tha' time out in Los Angeles?

JOHN: I guess I joost 'ad the rag on tha' nigh'.

YOKO: John! Not funny!

JOHN: Sorry, luv.

PAUL: Let me oop! Please!

JOHN: You really promise you'll be good?

PAUL: Yes! Yes! I swear.

RINGO: All righ'. There you go.
Gradually diminishing panting sounds)

GEORGE: Thur, you feel better now, Paulie?

PAUL: Mooch. Thanks.

CHRIS: John, someone mentioned something earlier about you having diarrhea on a bus. Do you have it today? When you first got here you went into the bathroom, and when you got out, it really smelled bad in there.

JOHN: Righ' you are, mate. Diarrhea again today.

GEORGE: John 'as an age-old luv-'ate relationship with the stoof.

CHRIS: Really!? That's fascinating. You know what we used to call it in high school? Diarrhea, I mean? We called it "a fart with fluid drive."
(Laughter)

JOHN: *(Laughing)* Vurry good. I can really rela' to tha'.

YOKO: *(Laughing)* John poopee *smell!* (*Holds nose*)

CHRIS: John, let's really get down to brass tacks. How *do* you relate to diarrhea? Like, how do you experience it as different from discrete, cohesive bowel movements?

JOHN: Well, I like the way it cooms ou' uv thur all a' oonce, instead uv in dribs an' drabs. Y'know? Joost one quick (*makes liquid sound effect*) an' yur all finished!

CHRIS: Leaving behind that delicious sense of intestinal void, right?

JOHN: Righ'! Righ'! I can see you an' me're qui' similiar in this regard. You know wha' I 'ate most? When it cooms out in li'ul 'ard balls. Tha's totally froostratin' to me, li'ul 'ard balls.

GEORGE: Anyone feel like a pizza, then?

CHRIS: Gee, I hate little hard balls, too. I guess we are a lot alike. How about, you know, those long ones?

JOHN: Oh, you mean "sausages." Tha's wha' I call 'em. Those're the best, man! I remember this time in 'amburg—

YOKO: Cat! Big fluffy cat! Pretty!

PAUL: Who's this, then? Is he a Persian?

CHRIS: Oh, that's Otis. Yeah. he's a—

YOKO: Pretty!

GEORGE: D'joo name 'im after Otis Redding?

JOHN: No, you dotard, 'e named 'im after the elevators.

CHRIS: Well, he's *mostly* named after Otis Redding, but he's also named after Otis Williams and the Charms, and Johnny Otis, and all those other Otises that were on all those old R&B records.

JOHN:	D'you 'ave old records, then? Froom the fifties?
CHRIS:	Do I have old records?! Hey, man. . . .
RINGO:	Oh, a grea' big basket full uv 'em! 'Ere, let's see tha'.
JOHN:	'Ey, the Harptones! The Midnighters! The Diabloes! Paulie, look a' these! Can we play soom, Chris?
CHRIS:	Sure! Pick 'em out.
JOHN:	'Ow 'bout this one by the Moonglows?
GEORGE:	Which one, John? Which one?
JOHN:	'Old on, you'll 'ear.
MOONGLOWS:	*Most of all, I want your (wahhh) warm embrace . . .*
PAUL:	I luv the part where they go (*sings*), "Wahhh."
CHRIS:	I love that part, too. I love the Moonglows's harmonies.
RINGO:	'Ere's soom old Sun sides . . .
GEORGE:	"Mystery Train"! "Mystery Train"! Let's 'ear this next!
PAUL:	We're not keepin' you from anything, are we, man?
CHRIS:	Oh, no, not at all. Listen to this part coming up here. They do an "ooooooooooh" that's incredible.
MOONGLOWS:	Oooooooooooh . . .
RINGO:	Tha' *was* an incredible "ooooooooooh." This is really foon! Let's do this all nigh'!
	(*Laughter. Wine pouring*)
GEORGE:	Ooh! Bo Diddley! Play this one next instead!
CHRIS:	Sure. Pass it ov*werpp*—
TAPE:	(*Spinning in pick-up reel*) *Ticka ticka ticka ticka ticka ticka . . .*

TALES OF UNCLE HO

translated from the Vietnamese by Henry Beard

"UNCLE HO, tell us about how Comrade Rat fooled the imperialist aggressor Pig," begged one of the little boys at the weekly indoctrination session of his youth cadre.

"Yes, yes, tell us, oh, please do," came the chorus from the mass of well-scrubbed children seated at the old man's feet.

"Well, nhow," began that venerable gentleman, lighting one of the endless cigarettes that always seemed a hair's breadth away from igniting his thin, scraggly beard. "Well, nhow, dhere manih timhs dhat Comrer Rat, hih dhon dhat. Buht dhe wonh dhat comhs to dhe mindh dhe mohst quikhlih, dhat's dhe timh dhat Comrer Rat hih makh dhe Tar Gook.

"Nhow Comrer Rat, hih dhon ghot verih much sikh of dhe way Comrer Pig, hih all dhe timh goh longh dhe rohd anh makh dhe bangh-bangh at evridhing anh burnh evridhing, anh Comrer Rat, hih fix to lernh dhat dhere Pig dhing or two.

"Soh wonh day, Comrer Rat, hih goh anh get somh of dhe sap fromh dhe rubber trih, anh hih get kiloh of gasolinh, anh hih get bigh lumph of tar fromh dhe rohd, anh hih mix dhem all up, anh hih takh dhat dhere gloop, anh hih makh dhis doll dhat look likh babih. Dhen hih takh dhe dhing, dhat what hih call dhe Tar Gook, anh hih put himh bhy dhe sidh of dhe rohd, anh hih put hat onh dhe hehd, and dhen Comrer Rat, hih goh hidh inh dhe elephanh grass, anh hih wait to sih what happen.

"Hih dhon't havh to wait longh, 'dhoh, bihcohs as soonh dhat hih goh hidh, dhere comhs Comrer Pig downh dhe rohd, banghidhi-banghidhi-boomh, anh hih blastinh dhe trihs, and hih blastinh dhe rokhs, anh hih blastinh dhe buffalohs, anh when hih kell dhe buffaloh, hih say to himhself, 'Dhat's leventih-sevenh of dhe foh what bhit dhe dust.'

"Dhen suddenh hih sih dhe Tar Gook inh dhe rohd, anh Comrer Pig, hih havh dhe attakh of dhe frihts, anh hih goh jumph inh dhe dhitch onh dhe oddher sidh, anh dhen hih aimh his gunh at dhe Tar Gook likh hih gohinh to bloh himh to bhits, buht dhe Tar Gook, hih dhon't makh noh movh.

"Dhen Comrer Pig, hih sih dhat dhe Tar Gook havh noh gunh anh hih havh noh nhif, anh soh Comrer Pig, hih look morh bravh, 'dhoh maybhi his pants, dhey need washinh, anh hih say to dhe Tar Gook, hih say, 'I frienh. I cohm to savh yhu fromh dhe clutch of Comrer Rat. Havh yhu seenh dhis hihr Rat inh dhe hihr-abouhts?'

"Dhe Tar Gook, hih noh talkh, anh Comrer Rat, hih stay loh inh dhe grass.

"Dhen Comrer Pig, hih say, 'Dhis Comrer Rat, hih no goodh; if hih lay handh onh yhu, hih surh to slavify yhu. Nhow, where dhis Rat?'

"Buht dhe Tar Gook, hih noh say nodhing anh Comrer Rat, hih noh makh noh sounh.

"Dhen Comrer Pig, hih talkh loudh, anh hih say, 'Maybhi yohr hearinh binh ruinhd bhy dhe bombhs wih drop onh yhu to hep yhu inh yohr jus fiht fohr self-determination,' say hih.

"Dhe Tar Gook, hih noh talkh, anh Comrer Rat, he takh dhe sandal off his fooht, anh hih stuff iht inh his mouht to kihp fromh laughinh.

"Dhen Comrer Pig, hih say, 'Wih is fihtinh fohr yohr hearts anh mindhs, anh damn mih if I dhon't cut a hohl inh yhu jus to makh surh yhu ghot dhem dhings.' Anh widh dhat, hih stab dhe Tar Gook widh his bayonet.

"Buht dhe Tar Gook, hih dhon't openh his mouht, anh Comrer Rat, hih lay loh.

"Dehn Comrer Pig, hih try to pull ouht dhe bayonet, buht iht stukh tiht, soh hih put his fooht inh dhe Tar Gook's stomach, anh hih pull. Dhen hih put his odher fooht in dhe Tar Gook's groinh anh hih pull, buht dhe bayonet, iht stay stukh, anh his foohts, dhey nhow stuck too.

"Dhen Comrer Pig, hih say, say hih, 'If yhu dhon't leht goh of mhy bayonet, damn mih if I dhon't strangle yhu,' anh widh dhat, hih grab dhe Tar Gook bhy dhe nekh anh hih bhiginh to choch himh, buht when hih try to takh his handhs out of dhe Tar Gook's dhroht, dhey is stukh fas.

"Longh 'bhout dhat timh, Comrer Rat, hih comh ouht dhe elephanh grass, and hih goh up to Comrer Pig, anh hih say, 'Howdhi, Comrer Pig. I hihr tell yhu binh goh lookh forh mih. Well, hihr I bhi, buht I havh to tend to somh bhisness at dhis hihr mohmenh. Onh dhe odher handh, if yhu is gohinh to stikh rounh hihr fohr somh timh, I bhi bakh soonh, anh maybhi inh dhe meanhtimh, yhu'd bhi dos kinh as to hold dhis hihr handh grenadh fohr mih till I comh bakh. Iht bhi myty ponderous to carrih roundh.'

"Anh widh dhat, hih givh Comrer Pig dhe handh bombh, anh hih runh off likh dhe whindh. Longh 'bouht tenh seconhds later, hih hihr dhis bigh bangh, anh dhen Comrer Rat, hih lookh inh his handh, anh dhen hih rap himhself onh dhe headh, bihcohs inh his hurrih, hih dhon gonh anh takh dhe pinh widh himh."

"Was that the end of the Pig?" asked one of the little boys.

"Well, dhat was dhe endh of dhat wonh pig, buht dhere was loht mohr pigs rounh dhere in dhose days, anh soonh as wonh was gonh, dhere was nhu pig dhat comh longh. Now dhat's all, yhu runh longh," said Uncle Ho. "Iht verih layt, anh yohr eyelids look set to shuht tihter dhen dhe lids onh dhe street bombh-shelters inh Hanoi inh dhe bahd oldh days."

"Did the Pig ever catch Comrade Rat?" inquired one of the little boys at the next indoctrination session.

"Well, nhow," replied Uncle Ho, taking out his battered cigarette-lighter made from the metal of a shot-down Phantom. "Dhat dhid happen wonh timh. I dhon't rihcall dhe exakh medhod dhe Pig use, buht yhu canh bih surh dhat iht innovolvh somh dirtih bhisness, anh somh monih dhid somh travellinh rounh anh endh up inh dhe handhs of Comrer Dog anh Comrer Snake, buht dhat neidher hihr norh dhere.

"Dhe Rat, hih cauht goodh dhis wonh timh, anh Comrer Pig, hih say, say hih, 'Dhis timh yhu dhed, anh dhat's dhat.' Anh hih call dhe Rat lot of namhs, anh hih kikh himh, anh hih hit himh, anh dhen hih say, 'I dhink I shooht yhu inh dhe nihcaps 'bouht leventih timhs, dhen I hangh yhu.'

"Dhen Comrer Rat, hih prihtendh to begh, hih say, 'I dhon't carh what yhu dho to mih, jus dhon't dhrow mih in dhe tiger cage,' say hih.

" 'Dhere noh roph nihrby,' say Comrer Pig, 'anh I dhon't likh dhe idih of wastinh bullets. I expekh I cuht off yohr dhing-mah-jhings, dhen I stabh you leventih timhs.'

" 'Dhat's finh by mih,' say Comrer Rat. 'Buht dhon't put mih downh inh dhat tiger cage. I canh't stand dhe darkh.'

"Dhis stabbinh bhisness too messih,' say Comrer Pig. 'I dhink I put lekhtrodhs onh yohr bodih, anh dhen I burnh yhu widh cigarettes.'

" 'Dhat sounh prettih goodh,' say Comrer Rat. 'Longh as you dhon't put mih inh dhat tiger cage. I ghot dhe claustrohphobes.'

" 'Dhere noh lekhtricitih rounh hihr, anh I loh onh smokhs,' say Comrer Pig. 'Maybhi I takh ouht yohr eyeballs anh tromph onh dhem.'

" 'Burnh mih alivh, whip mih widh barbh wirh, anh breakh all my bonhs, buht plihs dhon't dhrow mih inh dhere.'

"Bihcohs Comrer Rat want to dho dhe worst hih canh to Comrer Rat, hih pikh himh up anh hih drop himh inh dhe tiger cage. Dhere was commotionh when Comrer Rat hiht dhe bottomh, and dhen dhere's nodhinh buht dhis kindh of scrapingh sounh, anh Comrer Pig, hih bhiginh to wonhder if maybhi dhe Rat, hih dy of dhe heart attakh bangh-off, anh dhat's dhe dhedh rattlh.

"Dhen bhy anh bhy, hih hihr somhwonh callingh his namh anh hih lookh rounh, anh dhere way off, hih sih Comrer Rat climbingh ouht of dhe hohl hih dhon dug anh brushingh dhe dihrt off his furh, anh dhen hih hihr, 'Bornh anh bredh inh dhe undergrounh, Comrer Pig! Bornh anh bredh inh dhe undergrounh!' Anh widh dhat Comrer Rat, hih takh off likh dhe rocket."

"Dhat Pig, hih dhon't neveh learnh his lessonh," said Uncle Ho, blowing a perfect smoke ring. "Hih neveh wouldh leht dhe Rat lohn. Comrer Rat, hih sikh of all dhis, soh wonh day hih wait bhy dhe rodh, anh when hih sih dhe Pig comh way downh dhe bendh, hih jumph up anh hih yell, 'Hihr I bhi, hihr I bhi, comh anh get mih!' And hih runh off towardh dhe hills.

"Comrer Pig, hih sih Comrer Rat, and hih goh afteh himh. Well, bhy anh bhy, Comrer Rat, hih dhon ledh dhe pig to dhe mouht of dhis hihr cavh hih knoh bouht up inh dhe hills, anh hih set dhere anh wait fohr dhe Pig to sih himh, dhen hih yell, 'Hihr I bhi, hihr I bhi,' anh hih runh into dhe cavh.

"Comrer Pig, hih runh inh afteh Comrer Rat, buht hih dhon't goh noh mohr dhan twentih foohts when iht all goh darkh, anh soh hih takh ouht dhe flashliht hih ghot widh himh, anh hih shinh iht all rounh, anh dhen hih sih himh inh dhis longh, longh tunnel.

"Comrer Rat, hih xspekh dhis dihvelopmenh, anh hih ghot dhis mirrorh widh himh, anh when Comrer Pig shinh dhe liht at himh, hih shinh iht bakh dhe mirrorh, anh hih yell, 'Hihr I bhi, hihr I bhi,' anh hih runh downh dhe tunnel.

"Dhen Comrade Pig, hih sih dhat liht, anh hih yell, 'Nhow I ghot yhu inh dhe trap, Comrer Rat, anh hih takh off afteh himh.

"Dhe nex timh Comrer Pig sih dhe liht, iht seemh to bhi closeh, anh hih say to himhself, hih say, 'Littlh furdher anh I ghot dhat Rat,' anh dhen Comrer Rat yell, 'Hihr I bhi, hihr I bhi,' anh Comrer Pig, hih yell, 'Yhu inh dhe cornerh dhis timh fohr surh, Comrer Rat,' anh hih takh off afteh himh.

"Dhen Comrer Pig, hih sih dhe liht againh, anh dhis timh iht seemh verih evenh closeh, anh hih say to himhself, hih say, 'I comh dhis far, I goh jus littlh furdher, and I ghot dhat Rat,' anh dhen Comrer Rat yell, 'Hihr I bhi, hihr I bhi,' anh Comrer Pig, hih yell, 'Yhu as goodh as dhed dhis timh, Comrer Rat,' anh hih takh off afteh himh.

"Well, dhis hihr gamh goh onh likh dhat fohr longh timh, anh all dhe timh Comrer Pig, hih dhink hih get closeh, anh all dhe timh hih say to himhself, 'I comh dhis far, I goh just littlh furdher.'

"Dhen suddenh Comrer Rat, hih hidh dhe mirrorh, anh hih crawlh bihhindh dhe rokh longh dhe wall of dhe tunnel, anh Comrer Pig, hih goh runh riht bhy dhe Rat, anh dhen hih stop maybhi tinh foohts away, anh hih stop anh hih listenh.

"Dhere noh sounh, soh hih yell, 'Where yhu bhi, where yhu bhi?' Anh dhe echo comh bakh, kindh of fuzzih, anh Comrer Pig, hih dhink iht dhe Rat yellinh, 'Hihr I bhi, hihr I bhi.'

"Dhen Comrer Pig, hih shinh dhe liht downh dhe tunnel, and iht rihflikh off dhis or dhat pihs of rokh or maybhi somhdhing wet, anh Comrer Pig, hih say to himhself, 'I comh dhis far, I goh jus littlh furdher, anh dhen I ghot dhat Rat,' anh dhen hih yell, 'Yhu betteh say yohr prayehs, bihcohs I ghot yhu surh dhis timh,' say hih, and hih takh off downh dhe tunnel.

"Dhen Comrer Rat, hih wait till dhe Pig is gonh, dhen hih up anh runh bakh outsidh, 'dhoh iht takh himh somh timh, cohs hih laughinh soh hard, hih canh hardlih walkh."

"Did the Pig ever find his way out?" asked one of the little boys sitting spellbound at the patriarch's feet.

"Well, nhow, dhat dihpendh onh who tellinh dhe storih. Sohm say hih comh crawlinh ouht 'bouht weekh lateh, lookinh myty glumh, anh sohm say hih cohm marchinh oouht, tellinh evriwonh what wouldh listenh 'bouht how hih dhon what hih gonh inh dhere to dho, 'dhoh hih nhot too xakht onh dhe subjekh of jus what iht was hih gonh inh dhere fohr or what iht was hih dhon when hih was dhere. Buht evrehwonh agrihs dhat hih stop chasinh dhe Rat, anh hih neveh gonh bakh inh dhat tunnel againh.

"Nhow dhat's all fohr toniht, chillunhs. Yhu needhs yohr sleep soh yhu canh fiht rehsolutelih fohr dhe trihump of dhe sohcialis way inh dhe morninh."

ROSE KENNEDY'S CHARISMA TIPS

SO MANY CANDIDATES these days are conscious of the importance of charisma but just don't know didilly squat, if you'll pardon my French, about what it is or how to get it. They all think it's some important quality of leadership you have to be born with, like good judgment, common sense, or $100,000,000, and that someone who hasn't got it is doomed to live out his days in backwoods caucuses, holding down a desk in the Department of Public Works and waiting for the day when he can be County Comptroller.

Well, you can take it from me, that's just a lot of hooey and I put one son through Electoral College and my youngest is about ready to make it two, so I should know what I'm talking about. Charisma is easy once you understand what it's all about—getting the voter to look at you and not your record. Let's face it, you could be congressman from the Black Lagoon and you'd still be better off if old John Q. is eyeballing your mug and not your brag sheet.

Now the first thing to remember is that there are only three Winning Images: Lincolnesque, Camelot (my personal favorite), and Mr. Smith goes to Washington. Your first job is to pick the one that fits you best. For example, if your face looks like an old couch and your voice sounds like a postoperative laryngectomy patient talking over an army public-address system, go right for the Lincolnesque. You don't have to overdo it (one candidate I know of used to smoke Lincoln logs), but remember, it's the total image that counts. You mustn't confuse the voter: when he gets into that booth, he's ready to vote for only three people: Abe Lincoln, John F. Kennedy (it makes a mother proud), and Jimmy Stewart, and if you don't come to mind in one of those Key Charisma Categories, forget it!

How do you know which category you're best for? Here's a simple rule of thumb: if you're ugly, stupid, old, Southern, or have recently suffered a stroke—Lincolnesque; good examples of the Lincolnesque style are Karl Mundt, Lyndon Johnson, and Everett Dirksen. If you're young, rich, handsome, and have perfect teeth and good speechwriters, it's Camelot. But don't flatter yourself: it's the easiest category to blow, and if you don't believe me, just ask John Lindsay, Chuck Percy, or James Roosevelt to draw you a floor plan of the White House.

Now most of you are Mr. Smiths (no need to be ashamed—you count the current President among your number!), and this is really the most reliable image. It's the lawyer who made good but didn't forget his roots (or the train whistle in the night or whatever), who's shocked to find that when Senator Blowhard crumples up a "carefully prepared speech," it's nothing but a blank piece of paper! For you, I recommend off-the-rack suits during campaigns, a little pancake makeup for those bad wrinkles (let's not confuse Mr. Voter— he isn't going to give the nod to Jimmy Lincoln), shirtsleeves if that's your style, and at least six anecdotes of the hardware business during the Depression (or pharmacy business).

A quick note on TV appearances: You Lincolns, gargle with Clorox and pat about a half pound of naval jelly into your face and jowls—TV tends to exaggerate those little arroyos, grottoes, cisterns, mesas, etc., and too many reruns of *The Mummy* have spoiled that overly weathered look; Camelots, put Murine in your eyes to make them twinkle; Smiths, make sure you have an American-flag pin in your lapel and send an aide into the studio before the taping to break all the closeup lenses with a ball peen hammer.

One last point: charisma isn't looks alone. Keep those speeches, unfair assaults, and so forth in character. Let's take the bussing issue. Lincolnesque: speak slowly. "You ask me where I stand on bussing, and this is my answer: let reason triumph, let cooler heads prevail, let no man ever have to say, "They put their destiny on the bus of hope and it was struck by the train of hate on the poorly marked grade-crossing of the future."

Camelot: resounding. "But in a larger sense, it is for us to whom the hope of free men everywhere is entrusted to take up the challenge of the times, and now more than ever we must, as John F. Kennedy so eloquently put it, 'Ask not what our country can do for us, but what we can do for our country.' "

Mr. Smith: loud and sharp. "My opponent wants to send your children across state lines on flatbed trucks, packed like smelts, their tiny heads crushed together, only to be dumped like so much human landfill in the marijuana-choked yards of trade schools, where their gaily painted lunch boxes will be ripped from their grasp by savage Ubangis packing automatics."

Well, that's all for now.

Rose

RURAL FREE LOVE

by Brian McConnachie

A TRAVELING SALESMAN is driving down this country road when all of a sudden his Dodge Polara breaks down. He gets out of the car and opens the hood to see what the trouble is, but he can't find what the trouble is. There's a tremendous storm that's about to begin, so the salesman decides he'd better look for shelter. The nearest place is a farmhouse just up the road. He walks there. It's not far. He gets to the house and knocks on the door. After a while—not long—a man, probably the father farmer, answers the door and asks him what he wants. The salesman tells him about the Dodge and the storm that's about to begin. The farmer looks him up and down, tells him to wait a minute, goes inside . . . and slams the door. The door has two small windows on the top with curtains. The salesman stands waiting on the porch. A couple of minutes pass and the salesman is still waiting. He looks all around the yard and turns around to look at the door hoping that the father farmer will come out. But instead he sees someone looking out at him. It's a middle-aged woman, maybe the father farmer's wife. Just after his eyes meet hers, she drops the curtain and disappears. The salesman doesn't know what to think. He keeps waiting on the porch and staring out at the dirt yard. More time passes, he turns around to look at the door again, and this time a girl, probably a daughter, is looking out . . . and again the curtain drops. By this time the salesman doesn't know what to think. Fifteen minutes must have passed. He starts pacing up and down the porch nervously. Back and forth, back and forth, back and forth, and then he quickly turns to look into the door windows. Now this is the third time, remember. He quickly turns to look into the door windows, and instead of seeing two eyes staring out at him, he sees two little white boiled potatoes being held up against the glass. Then, in a flash, the curtain drops and the two little white boiled potatoes vanish. In the meantime it's really started to rain and the salesman is getting pretty jumpy. So he starts knocking on the door. Nobody answers. So he keeps knocking and knocking. He can hear a lot of moving around inside, and suddenly the door is yanked open. Standing there is an enormous guy in a pair of overalls but he doesn't have a shirt on. Just overalls. He asks the salesman if he wants to spend the night, and the salesman says yes. The enormous guy walks to the front of the porch and the salesman sees a tattoo on the guy's arm. It says "Born to Raise Wheat"; big sprigs of wheat are weaved in and out of the lettering, and the whole thing is framed in bales stacked on bales. The enormous guy turns and stares into the salesman's eyes for a good minute and then asks him if he's ever done any A&P. Before the salesman can answer him, the guy

234 THE NATIONAL LAMPOON TREASURY OF HUMOR

says that they don't take much to doing any A&P in these parts. Even mild A&P.

"S&H's O.K., and so's A&W, but no A&P. If I catch you doin' any A&P around here, I'll put your crainer in the combine and plow forty."

Then this enormous guy with the "Born to Raise Wheat" tattoo goes back into the house before the salesman can ask him what this is all about.

Bewildered, the salesman is staring at the door again, trying to figure when the father farmer will come out again.

"We've decided to let you spend the night here, but since there's no room in the house, you'll have to sleep with our International Harvester. But because we'd like to keep an eye on you, you'll be sleeping right here in the yard . . . in the dirt . . . in the rain. Jedidiah is bringing our International Harvester around from the barn for you. And no A&P. If we catch you doing A&P, we'll stuff your vegetables in the feeder and fly the crop duster into it!"

"Wait a minute. . . ."

But before the salesman can really protest, the father turns and goes back into the house. Just as he does, out comes the mother with a blanket and a pillow, followed by three huge guys carrying a cedar wardrobe over their heads. The woman starts making a bed in the mud, and the three guys put the cedar wardrobe next to it.

Two of the guys are wearing overalls and the third has on flannel long johns.

"We'll show you what we want you to do," says one of the guys wearing the overalls, and he and the other guy wearing overalls go into the cedar wardrobe and shut the doors behind them. The cedar wardrobe starts shaking around so much that the mother and the guy in the long johns have to hold it steady. After about five minutes of this shaking and rattling, the doors open and the two guys step out.

"Do you know what we did, mister? We swapped overalls."

The salesman can't really tell if they did or not, but he takes their word for it. The rain has been coming down hard for a while now, and everybody's pretty well drenched.

"We want you to go into the wardrobe with Clep—he's the one in the flannel longjohns—and swap clothes."

"Now look . . ."

"You better do like we say, mister."

He agrees. He climbs into the wardrobe, Clep goes in after him, and the doors are shut.

The mother yells into the wardrobe, "I don't want you going to sleep in those wet clothes."

Then the mother and the two guys steady the wardrobe as it starts shaking again. There's a lot of cursing and crashing around going on inside, and then the doors fly open and they both tumble out. But they did it! They swapped clothes. Then the mother tells the salesman to climb under the blanket and go to sleep.

"It's only six-thirty."

"Do like we tell you, mister, and don't go wandering around any. We're going back inside now. We'll bring you your dinner later."

They wait until he gets under the blanket, and then they go inside. When they're gone, he sits up looking around and wonders if he should make a run for it or not. Just then, the front door opens and the daughter comes running out. When he sees her coming, he quickly lies down and pulls the blanket up to his chin. She runs over to him, drops something, and then runs back into the house. He picks it up. It looks like a big white plastic cover to keep the rain off. But then he sees an air nozzle, so he begins blowing it up. It starts to take shape and it looks like, and it is . . . an inflatable sheep. And it's from Japan . . . an inflatable sheep from Japan. He looks over to the house and sees the girl staring out the window at him, but as he sees her she ducks back.

Just then, the door opens again and the big tattooed guy comes walking out. The salesman quickly stuffs the inflatable sheep under the blanket, pulls the blanket up to his chin, and pretends to be asleep.

The tattooed guy walks over. He starts nudging the salesman with the toe of his boot.

"We're expecting some company. Don't frighten them. What's that you got under the blanket with you? You doin' A&P under there?"

"No, no, no. Just this." He takes out the sheep to show him.

O.K. But no A&P or I jam your neener into a copy of *The Pure Seed Laws,* slam it shut, and drive a tractor over it."

Then the big tattooed guy walks back into the house.

In spite of the rain, mud, itchy flannel long johns, and the situation with the family, the exhausted salesman falls asleep.

He's asleep for about five minutes when a little girl comes out of the storm cellar, walks over to him, and starts shaking him awake.

"Hey, mister. Hey, mister. Wake up. Wake up."

"Whatzamatter? What is it?"

"I'm Dorothy."

"What is it, Dorothy?"

"Nothing. I just want somebody to talk to. I stay down there in that storm cellar and I never get to talk to anybody. Or sing. I never get to sing to anybody."

"Oh, that's too bad, Dorothy. . . ."

"I'm not that good, mister. They tell me that I'm tone deaf. Tell me what you think. . . . I'm only eleven years old, remember. . . . 'My cow's tits are as big as catchers' mitts / And we won't go sellin' her for beans. / You can trade us watermelon and a picture of Magellan, / But we won't go tradin' her for beans.' "

"Ah, Dorothy, I need your help. Do you know where my clothes are?"

"No, but if you hum a few bars, I'll fake the rest."

Just then, a truck filled with laughing, shouting people starts heading up the dirt road to the house. Little Dorothy quickly waves good-bye to the salesman, tells him that maybe they can talk later, and runs back down into the storm cellar. The truck screeches to a stop by the side of the house, and about ten people pile out yahooing and slapping their legs together and falling over one another trying to get to the house. They all go inside, and there's a lot more howling. The salesman begins to think that maybe he should forget about his clothes and make a run for it. No telling what's going to happen here. But as he starts to get up the door opens, and the daughter comes out and over to him. She asks him for the inflatable sheep. He takes it out from under the blankets and hands it to her. Then she goes skipping back into the house. As she enters with the sheep there's more howling. Then the place goes totally silent for about three minutes. The salesman can't figure out what's going on. Then, all of a sudden, out of this quiet comes an explosion of screams and laughter, and everybody who's in the house comes running and tumbling out, using all of the doors and most of the windows. They're staggering with laughter, and they begin collapsing on the ground all around the house. A lot of them start choking and gagging because they can't catch their breath from all the laughing. But finally they all manage to quiet down and begin shaking their heads at one another in happy disbelief. Just then the mother appears at the door. She has a pair of men's overalls on backwards; in one hand she's holding an ear of corn and in the other, the deflated sheep. The laughter starts all over again. She looks angry at first but then starts to smile and laugh along with the rest of them. Then she gives them a disgusted wave and goes back into the house yelling something about getting the stranger his dinner. This turns everyone's attention to the salesman in the mud with the blanket. It's still really coming down. They all get up, form a big group, and keep staring at the salesman. And then they huddle. The salesman starts to get up on one knee in case he has to make a run for it.

"Stay where you are, mister," one of them shouts. The salesman slowly lies down again. "Or else I'll show you where the horsey bit me."

One of the guys in the crowd takes out a pack of Gauloise cigarettes, the French cigarettes. He lights one, then starts passing it around to everybody. They all take really deep drags. Then the guy brings out another one, and another one, until he has five going at once. Everyone's passing them back and forth and smiling at each other. The salesman keeps staring at them and trying to figure out what they're up to. He can't make out what they're saying because they're talking and inhaling at the same time. Soon they finish all of the cigarettes and begin sitting down Indian-style on the muddy ground.

One of the sons, Clep, jumps up and shouts, "Why don't we go inside and watch 'The Governor and J. J.' with the sound off?" A lot of them think this is a neat idea and get up to go inside . . . but not all of them.

By this time the salesman thinks that they've forgotten all about him, but then he sees the others get up and begin wandering around the yard. One of them sort of staggers past the side of the house and begins shouting. "Hey, everybody, look at this silo. That's the biggest silo I've ever seen. That's the biggest silo I've ever seen."

Some others come over and join him and begin screaming in amazement at the size of the silo. "It's so big . . . so far up in the air." Then one of them says that it looks just like a giant brick beer can wearing a giant beanie.

"No, no, no, it looks like a great big cement can of peas with a round bubble-top."

They all begin arguing. Now all of the time this is going on, the people who went into the house to watch 'The Governor and J. J.' with the sound off keep tumbling out of the house in fits of laughter. They collapse on the porch until they have the strength to go back inside. Then they go back inside.

Pretty sure that no one is going to bother him at this point, the salesman is sitting up taking all of this in. Just then he's proved wrong. The guy with the "Born to Raise Wheat" tattoo comes walking over with another guy. The other guy is in a tattered suit.

"You know something, mister, you're all right. You're an all-right guy. I want you to meet somebody here. This is my friend, the professor. A real smart guy. But the professor here can't remember anything. Isn't that right, professor? What do you call it?"

"Total no recall."

"That's right. Total no recall. He can't remember a thing. I don't know how he even remembers that. But anyway, about this A&P business, I've been thinking. Who the hell am I to tell you, a perfect stranger, that you can't do any A&P? You can do all the A&P you want. I'm just saying, 'Don't let me catch you.' Fair enough? Do all of the A&P you can, but don't let me catch you. That's where the professor comes in. He's going to sit here in the mud with you and watch you. Now remember, he can't remember a thing, so you're probably safe to do it in front of him, but he's going to stay by you nonetheless. Go ahead and do it, but if I catch you, you know what happens: I lop off your jayboes with a trowel and toss 'em into the soil bank and drop a fifty-five-gallon drum of fuel on top."

The guy with the tattoo walks away and the professor sits down.

"He's right, you know. I do have total no recall. I can't remember a thing. Go ahead and ask me a question, and I won't even remember what it is. Go ahead."

"What is the capital of Delaware?"

"I don't even remember what it is you asked me. What did you ask me? See, I can't remember anything. Ask me another question."

The salesman really doesn't want to do this but decides to humor the professor by asking him a bunch of questions. And sure enough, the professor can't answer any of them. Every once in a while, though, the professor gets a real mean look on his face and says, "Saaaaaaayy, who are you and what's this all about?" But then he goes back to politely not answering any of the questions.

Around then, the people who were watching 'The Governor and J. J.' start coming out of the house. They're all wiping laugh tears from their eyes. They all sort of sit around on the porch and relax for a while. Then one of them suggests that they do square dancing without a caller.

"Yes, yes."

"And no fair humming anything."

"Yes, yes."

"And with potato sacks on our heads."

"Yes, yes."

"And our britches down around our ankles."

"Oh, yes."

"And we won't get up tomorrow and do any chores."

"YES."

"Or rotate our crops."

"YAHOO!"

"And we'll do A&W and S&H. . . ."

"YEA-HAW!"

"But no A&P!"

". . . no . . ."

Then they all start dropping their overalls and putting potato sacks over their heads. At first they just stay in place and sway to the imaginary music. Then they start shuffling around with their arms out, searching for partners. A couple of people are ready to go right into reels and do-si-dos, but as soon as they do they fall over in the mud.

The salesman is taking all of this in, and then, out of the corner of his eye, he sees the storm-cellar door opening. Dorothy comes out, walks over to the salesman and says hi.

"I've been down in the cellar thinking, mister. This is no place to spend the night. Have you ever heard of the girl who doesn't have any legs and is always left hanging in trees?"

"Yes, I have."

"Well, she lives with her family just down the road. Come on, I'll take you there. You come too, professor."

The salesman stood up slowly, looking around to see if anybody was watching him. Nobody was. He decided this was as good a time as any to leave. So the three of them started walking hand in hand down the road. The salesman looked back over his shoulder one last time. He saw all of the people shuffling into walls, tractors, stumps, fences, each other, and so forth. Then the mother came out on the porch dressed in a Naugahyde rain slicker, held out a bowl, and shouted, "Mountain oysters. Come and get your eats. Good eats." Then they really started crashing into things. Funny thing, they never took the sacks off their heads.

When they were a good distance from the farm, the salesman asked, "Dorothy, I know you're only a little eleven-year-old girl, but do you know what A&P is?"

"No, but if you hum a few bars, I'll fake the rest."

"I do," said the professor.

"You do!"

"I think it's a chain of hardware stores, though I can't be certain. I *do* have total no recall, remember. Ask me another question and I bet I get it wrong."

Christmas Gifts for the

NEW DEPRESSION

YOU CAN PUT A SMILE ON A LITTLE FACE BY MAKING THESE CLEVER GIFTS FROM HOUSEHOLD GARBAGE.

by Fred Graver

TIMES ARE TOUGH. But times have been tough before and we've always pulled through, right? I can remember back to my own childhood, when we faced a pretty bleak Christmas in our house. Mom had lost her Tupperware distributorship, and Dad hadn't worked regularly since driveway-paving season had closed. Gramps had moved in with us and he not only ate like a horse, he had forced Sis to move into my room.

I remember Christmas Eve, lying in bed, holding Sis close to me, real tight, just the two of us, under the blankets, the warmth of our bodies fighting off the chill of the night. I whispered in her ear, "I asked for a 'Man from U.N.C.L.E.' gun. Do you think . . . ?" Sis was older than me, and wise beyond her years. "You know what 'fat chance' means?" she answered.

Well, we were both surprised the next morning when we found more boxes and toys under the tree than our big wide eyes could take in. No, we didn't get what we had asked for, but we got all the toys we'd always loved playing with. In fact, they *were* our toys! Dad had just rewrapped them. He and Mom got a good chuckle out of it, but I've never forgotten my intense depression and disillusionment. One day I learn Santa's a fake, then I find out Mom and Dad are frauds, too.

That's why I want you to give your family a real nice Christmas this year, no matter how bad the economy has hit you. With a few things from around the house, I'm going to show you how you can create gifts that have all the excitement and fun of store-bought ones. Why, I'd even crawl out on a limb and say that the only difference between these gifts and the ones you buy in the store is about seven million dollars in advertising money.

Let's start out with Sis. Maybe she's asked for a doll or a game. Well, I've got something that combines both—it's a little game I've rigged up that's called "Mommy Blows Her Top." Take some Magic Markers and a little crepe paper and decorate an empty dishwashing-liquid bottle to look like Mom. Now, sit the players around the table and tighten the cap. Each player takes a turn loosening the cap a little, and then punching Mom in the stomach. The tension mounts until . . . Mommy Blows Her Top! But the game's not over! All the kids get "sent to their room," where they beat up on the kid who made Mom blow her top in the first place.

Nowadays, with women's lib and all that stuff, it's important to stress non-sexist toys for girls, and many parents find that a science kit fills the bill. This kit is called "What Grows in the Refrigerator," and consists of a variety of plastic bags and a "Scientist's Notebook." (The plastic bags are free at the produce section of your supermarket. If you really want to be elaborate, you might throw in a special "Scientist's Shirt-Pocket Pen Caddy.") The entries in the notebook mark the dates on which you placed some interesting food in a bag and put it into the refrigerator; what it looked like after one week, two weeks, three weeks, and one month; what it smelled like; and whether or not you could feed it to the family pet, grow plants in it, or cure the common cold with it.

And what about the little guy? What are you gonna get for him? Well, a lot of little guys nowadays—and Sis too—have been asking for those video games. Why not give the video game to end them all—Sitcom Invaders! Take a sheet of Saran Wrap and lay it on the screen. Then, with Magic Markers, draw hand grenades, broken glass, mortars, land mines, Molotov cocktails, and other weapons of destruction on the screen. Each player then picks out a character on the show you're watching—let's say it's Laverne on "Laverne and Shirley." Well, every time Laverne walks into one of your traps, you score. Easy, you say? How about Advanced Sitcom Invaders? The lower part of the screen, where everyone walks anyway, is worth half the points of the upper part. This can be a real fun game, and if the kids have a tough time getting the hang of it, you might want to have them practice on a talk-show couch or two.

Of course, any little guy would be thrilled to get a pet for Christmas. But have you been to a pet store lately? Do you know what they want for those mutts? Forget it! And they eat like my old grandpa. Well, I had to think long and hard about this one, but I've come up with the answer—Roach Ranch. You can make these from five or six of those roach motels, which you wrap up and decorate to make them look like the bunkhouse, the grub shack, the stable, etc. Place the whole setup in a tightly sealed box and you've got the neatest little gift since the ant farm. And you can keep those roaches alive for years on bits of food and a little water. (Why not set up a little trough for 'em to drink from?) If you're really talented, you can even take a stab at making cowboy hats for those little roaches. They're hours of fun for the whole family, and they can be trained to do simple tricks like standing, rolling over, and crawling up Aunt Patsy's leg.

Kids, of course, have a real love for collecting things, and the kids in my neighborhood started a real craze with a game called "What Was This?" You ever notice how when some stuff gets all used up and thrown away, it doesn't look anything like what it used to be—especially plastic packages, rubber goods, things that fall off your handyman bench? Well, kids really get into scouring the streets for disposed items and coming back to stump their friends. So give the kids a few collecting boxes and turn 'em loose. You might want to draw the line with chewed food and animal carcasses, though!

Every Christmas, many parents face a particularly painful dilemma. They've got a little money saved up for presents, but the kids need some essentials, too—like underwear, socks, or gloves for the winter. Well, there *is* a way to make your child appreciate those "sensible" gifts. When you fill out the little name tag on the package, merely insert the name of their favorite superhero or celebrity where yours would go. Who could resist some nice warm socks from Spiderman, some new underpants from Bruce Springsteen, or a nice new wool cap from Reggie Jackson? If you're creative with paint and brush, you can draw a picture of Spiderman or Pac-Man right on a pair of white tube socks for a really special touch. You can seal the deal with a note inside that says, "Here's a nice new pair of gloves for when you play Sitcom Invaders."

Finally, every child's Christmas has to be marked by that big, special, trendy present. Well, you won't have to leave your kids with nothing to brag to their friends about this year. You can build them a special *E.T.* Computer. Remember the one the extraterrestrial built in the movie out of electronic junk and an old umbrella? You can get old batteries, circuits, wires, etc., from behind any Radio Shack store, string 'em up, and . . . who knows? You might have a couple of funny green men at *your* door someday.

But what about Mom? Surely you can't hope to fool *her* with some of these tossed-together wonders. And remember last birthday, when she told you what you could do with that dress from the thrift shop?

Well, don't panic. To begin with, you can give Mom one of those great decorative pins. Show her how much you appreciate all of the things she does for the family by gluing a little bit of her best home-cooked dish to a clasp. Can you imagine the squeals of glee when her friends see that she's wearing a pot roast?

And speaking of novelty items, have you noticed how the craziest things get turned into wallets and purses lately? Think of the looks of jealousy on the faces of the girls at the bridge club when the little lady walks in with her very own milk-carton purse. Or how about tacking a nifty handle onto one of her old running shoes? Classy, right? As long as you're rummaging through the closet, don't overlook the dandy way an old athletic sock becomes a handsome change purse.

Of course, Mom might want something a little more personal. Is she one of those monogrammed-days-of-the-week-undies girls? With a little Magic Marker, you can give her a whole set of days-of-the-week sanitary napkins.

And, finally, the gift that keeps on giving—baking soda. There's a thousand

and one uses for the stuff, and your wife will remember your thoughtfulness all year long. My honey is still tickled over the two boxes I gave her last year. The one I wrapped in red and labeled FIRE EXTINGUISHER is still in its own little corner near the stove.

But, what about Dad? Sure, he's the one who's always tough to please. But I've never met a pop who hasn't been pleased with a nice new key chain. Why not weave a few hanks of the family's hair together, dip it in varnish, and hand him a Christmas present that'll choke him up?

Speaking of choking the old guy up, if he's like most of the fathers I know, he'll appreciate this blast from the past—an old shirt, tie-dyed in his favorite late-sixties style! For added effect, toss an old Jefferson Airplane album on the turntable when you hand him the box.

Of course, if you're willing to put the extra time and effort into it, nothing would please Pop like his own desk set. Perfect for the office or the desk at home, this is the kind of set that says loud and clear, "I'm a family man!" Saw off the top half of a tennis-ball can (to hold the pens and pencils), find an empty Tiparillo box (for the notepaper), and laminate the daily newspaper Sports section (for the blotter). You might even toss in an old pocket knife for the letter opener. Hot dandy!

Christmas is a special time to show Grandma and Grandpa how much they mean to the whole family, and this next little item is something that everyone can pitch in on. As we all know, Grandma and Grandpa are just struggling by on a fixed income, and probably aren't eating too well. You can help brighten their mealtime with a set of Social Security Dinnerware! Begin with paper plates and cups—plain white, of course. Have the kids take their crayons and draw colorful pictures of Grandma and Grandpa in front of "their" big mansion, "their" big car with a chauffeur, "their" summer home. Then, take some waxed paper and coat the cups and plates by using a hot iron. Don't worry about this special dinnerware holding up—the old folks will appreciate it for the unique gift it is and only use it on special occasions.

Speaking of special occasions . . . here's a couple of wonderful seasonal gifts. To begin with, you might be the kind of person who likes to keep the Christ in Christmas (or the Chan in Chanukah, as the case may be). Why not toss together some special holiday cookies? Toss a little flour, sugar, water, and butter into a bowl. Mix them up, lay them on a cookie sheet, and bake. Then, make up some religious story to go with them. "These cookies represent all of the children born this year who didn't live to see Christmas"—something like that.

How about some special memento of this special day, to be given to a loved one whom you only see once a year, if that much? Bright and early Christmas morning, go down to the newsstand and buy two copies of the day's newspaper—one for you and one for the gift. Shellac the gift, and you've got a wonderful souvenir of that special day in the year when you all get together.

It's true that many of us only get together with our families around the holidays, and I wouldn't expect you to toss together some thoughtless present for your brother or sister who just flew in from Spokane to share Christmas with everyone. This special "Remembrance Card" will bring back laughter and tears. Using an old photograph of the two of you in your childhood, you can put together a nice little folder and inscribe it with a poem of your own making. If you can't bring yourself to pen a few light verses, feel free to use this one:

> *Remember the fun we once had in our yard*
> *When life was simple and not so hard.*
> *But we've grown up,*
> *And times are tough,*
> *So here's a cheap little picture card.*

With a little ingenuity and imagination, you can save this Christmas from the same depression that's gripping the country. Just remember three things:

- If you are given a gift in return, don't get caught in that old trap of comparing the two. Remember this line: "Well, there's only one in the world like this."
- Remember that you are, in fact, doing the other person a big favor, since they won't have to stand in line to return their gift.
- Don't forget, if you're working on something for someone and it looks as though it will be a total disaster, just toss it all in the box anyway. When they open it, say, "I was up until three in the morning trying to finish this, but I thought you'd like to see how it's progressing."

Then, after Christmas, get them something else by exchanging one of the useless gifts someone gave you.

REALITY ISLAND

by Commander Snot W. Goatlips IV

by Ted Mann

YOU CAN'T RUN away from Reality," the ads said. "Come to Reality Island; see your travel agent today." Beneath the slogans, a color photograph showed a handsome tanned man in a white suit standing beside a dwarf who also wore a white suit and, in addition, carried a handful of flowers.

The dwarf looked pretty sharp, although I expect that did not prevent a lot of people from cutting out his picture and pasting it onto their refrigerator doors as a reminder to eat and drink regularly.

The other man was handsome. Yet he was missing a certain quality that might have made him perfect. You could tell by his eyes: they jumped here and there with the sort of restless regularity you might expect of a sheep's orbs if the sheep were led into an amusement arcade. It would be too colorful to say that the man looked as ignorant as a Galway pig, yet it would be a grievous understatement to say he was only as silly as a hatful of assholes.

I decided to pay a visit to Reality Island. At the travel agent's, there were dozens of brochures on the place.

"Reality Island . . . We can make your dreams go away."

"Reality Island . . . An imperfect place to spend your vacation."

"Just the two of you and a bunch of other tourists . . ."

You had to take a seaplane to get to Reality Island. I have no idea what kind of plane it was, as the name had been filed off the dash at the same time as the serial numbers, and the elderly man who flew it had only a few words of English, all obscene. It was a twin-engine aircraft and had the name of Sunny Airlines painted outside and, underneath, the words "Flying Truck."

It was a two-hour flight and no refreshments were served, although one of my fellow passengers, a middle-aged woman, did manage to cough up a light breakfast in the aisle to my left.

The handsome man and the dwarf awaited our party on the island's dock. They waited unconcernedly as the pilot kept us circling away from the dock until he managed to extort five dollars from each of us to "fucking clean for the lunch blow of the woman." When we at last docked, several of the passengers complained of their treatment.

"Ah," said the handsome man, "we have so many troubles in this life. I tell you, though," he added cheerfully, "I can't get your money back, but next time the pilot comes in I'll have a couple of the boys work him over good."

"That's right, boss," piped the dwarf, "we'll break his legs like last year!"

"Yes, Tattoo," said the big man, smiling indulgently. He paused and clapped his hands. Somewhere in the surrounding foliage a needle dropped on a Rod Stewart album and, as the music began to play, a number of middle-aged black women in grass skirts, halter tops, and dyed blond hair danced toward our party with their arms full of plastic leis, which they placed over our necks.

"You can have anyone you want for ten bucks a toss," Tattoo whispered in my ear. "They do *anything*," he added, rubbing his hands together.

The leis seemed slightly out of place forty miles from Bimini; but if anyone noticed, they said nothing.

After the greeting ceremony was completed, we climbed into a station wagon from which the roof had been removed with a cutting torch. On the drive back to the hotel, we passed through endless shanty towns and were surrounded dozens of times by pleading groups of old men, women, and children. The younger men stood or sat by the roadside shacks watching us with hatred and contempt.

"More than your life is worth to pass through here after dark," said the handsome man. "They all have knives, and many have automatic weapons from Cuba. Even the soldiers of the Big Reverend fear to come here at night."

We had seen the soldiers of the "Big Reverend," the island's strongman, at several checkpoints along the road. They looked as cruel, ignorant, and brutal as it is possible for men to be, and they carried two or three guns each, in addition to the numerous oddly shaped bombs and grenades strapped across their chests.

When at last we arrived at the hotel complex, the handsome man apologized for the state of our rooms. He explained that a groundskeeper had recently gone berserk after drinking the radiator coolant from the hotel's only golf cart and set fire to the main residence. The place was not badly damaged, being constructed almost entirely of cinder blocks, but the fire had destroyed almost all the furnishings and we were forced to sleep on cots or upon doors set on chairs brought from the dining hall.

The handsome man silenced all complaints, saying, "You're here for two weeks and you might as well make the best of it."

That night we had our first meal in the dining hall. It was chicken and peppers. For a beverage, one could choose either Kool-Aid or Kool-Aid and rum. Almost everybody had the rum.

The handsome man explained that tomorrow the guests would be able to see a genuine sacred native voodoo ceremony for only $49.50 plus the price of the goat and rooster. He advised anyone who was squeamish about entrails or without a change of clothes to abstain.

He also said that inner tubes were available at sixty-two dollars a day for guests who wished to go big-game fishing and weren't afraid of swordfish punctures.

Toward the end of the meal, the dwarf hurried into the dining hall and whispered some news to the handsome man that appeared to disturb him. He clapped his hands for silence.

"Tattoo tells me that the Big Reverend has come to pay us a visit. Now listen, this is very serious. Our island is not like where you come from. You must do exactly as the Big Reverend says. Be extremely polite. Flatter him when you can, but do not be too obvious . . ."

The dining hall door burst open.

"What an honor!" shouted the handsome man and the dwarf, together.

There, standing at the door, surrounded by more of his hideous soldiers, whom the island's natives called the "Dark Fighting Men," was an enormous black man in a clerical collar. In his right hand he carried a twenty-seven-inch machete. This he slapped against his left palm as he inspected the guests.

The Big Reverend's visit was short. He took one young woman for questioning, and when her husband objected he was beaten so badly by the Dark Fighting Men he became mentally deficient and was forced to enter politics upon his return to the USA. The woman, his wife, was never seen again.

I had fallen into a light sleep that night, disturbed only by the most horrible and explicit of nightmares, when I was awakened by the sound of gunfire. I rushed into the darkened hallway and collided with the man who carried my bags that morning, who instantly stabbed me in the thigh. Hearing my howl and realizing he had imperiled his tip, he apologized profusely, explaining he had mistaken me for a member of the "Red Commune Men," the island's revolutionary commando.

"Mister, if you will forgive me please and give me ten dollars, I will try to save your life!"

"Ah, a mere flesh wound," I said, pressing the ten-spot upon him.

He led me through the hall, now a-jostle with panicked guests and terror-stricken employees, to a back door. "There is an old woman," he siad. "We will see her."

We dashed across the hotel grounds, now lit by incendiary flashes and tracer rounds. The handsome man and the dwarf were nowhere to be seen.

I plunged into the foliage in the wake of my companion. Behind me I could hear screams coming from the main residence.

After several hours of travel through the dense brush, and several brushes with patrols of Red Commune Men, we arrived at the outskirts of a shanty town. Motioning me to wait behind a sisal bush, my companion disappeared into the cluster of shacks.

He returned twenty minutes later with an elderly woman who clucked when she saw me and spoke to my companion in the incomprehensible dialect of the island.

He shrugged his shoulders and looked at me. "I can't understand her," he said; "the dialect is incomprehensible. It is probably fair to assume she wants money."

I reached into my pocket and produced a wad of bills, which I proffered to the crone. She spat in the dust beside her and angrily motioned the banknotes away. Then with a swift motion she produced a small pocketknife and cut the buttons from my shirt. Cackling, she hid them away in the large plastic bag she carried. Then, producing a pot of charcoal, she proceeded to dye my head and arms black.

"What about my hair?" I asked.

My companion looked thoughtful. "You pretend to be part French!" he shouted. With that, he scooped up the banknotes and ran off. The old woman similarly vanished, leaving me penniless, with my face dyed black, behind the sisal bush just as the sun rose.

Exhaustion overcame terror and I fell into a deep sleep on the spot.

I was awakened the next day by a tremendous kick in the testicles, and looking up through eyes half closed with pain I saw the face of a US marine staring down at me. I was never gladder to see anyone.

"Wait," I said, "I'm a goddamn Yankee-Doodle dandy."

The marines had come to restore the strong central government of the Big Reverend to Reality Island. I heard later that they found the handsome man alive, though barely, in a coffin-like prison built by the Red Commune Men. The dwarf was not so lucky. A couple of marines shot an alligator in the swamp and when they cut it open they found the little fellow partially digested. They figure he was trying to get away through the marsh and got off the track.

As for my fellow guests, some made it and some didn't; but you can be sure none of them ever forgot their visit to Reality Island.

HISTORY POP TALK

HOT, JUICY, SCANDALOUS GOSSIP ABOUT EVERYBODY AND ANYTHING THAT EVER HAPPENED IN HISTORY

by John Bendel

MORE ACRIMONY! Despite a crowded agenda, the annual meeting of the National Society of Historians broke down in an unseemly debate over who had the neatest helmets, the ancient Romans or the Germans under Kaiser Wilhelm! Now, it's true that the Roman helmets doubled quite nicely as whisk brooms, but from our vantage point they do seem a bit ornate, while the kaiser's helmets bespeak a certain eloquence of line. And, oh, those little spikes! The kaiser gets the nod as far as I'm concerned, and I hope that settles it once and for all! . . . Professor Chester Wentworth, a supposed heavyweight in the history business, whose study of prehistoric cave-wall advertising shook the historical establishment a few years ago, has introduced a frothy, trilateral view of civilization. Wentworth sees human history as a struggle between those who drive on the right side of the road and those who drive on the left. Wentworth's "third world" consists of those societies in which one rides wherever one cares to, or even weaves from side to side. What's the matter, Professor? All out of ideas? . . . How important is the spatula anyway? "Very!" says Professor Iona Chevy of Southwestern All-Night University in a new paper. The prof claims that prior to the spatula, primitive man was unable to make full use of his hands, because at least one of the them was always badly burned from flipping food on the fire. "Pancakes were a particular problem," she points out. It was Professor Chevy, you might recall, who stirred the stew last year with her contention that it was an anonymous Swiss monk who made Alpine travel possible, with his invention of the hairpin curve . . . And speaking of technological achievement, the Russians are at it again. A recent article in the Scienceky Tuesday section of *Izvestiya* claims that the Soviets were the first to invent the retractable power cord and the hubcap. More outrageous, though, is their assertion that it was a Bolshevik revolutionary from Odessa who invented the box in 1919. Western historians, of course, have long known that the box was developed by the ancient Greeks for use in shipping busts from plinth to plinth . . . By the way, when did spelling—the erstwhile art of letter arranging—become such a rigid discipline? Doesn't Ye Olde Gifte Shoppe look so much better than Your Old Gift Shop? You bet it does. Yet no one I know of is looking into this historical transformation. Thesis anyone? . . . Now it can be told: recently declassified files have produced new insights into the personality of Franklin Delano Roosevelt. We have learned, for example, that he once asked to meet Gen. Claire Lee Chennault, who was leading America's Flying Tiger volunteers against the Japanese in China. FDR reportedly asked the general whether his volunteers dropped tigers on the enemy from the air or actually taught the big cats to fly . . . Well, the jig's up for the Lapps. It was one of the better historical frauds of modern times, but Sven Gnoldsen of the Copenhagen Institut vor Learninlookininto has blown the whistle. The Lapps, it seems, are actually Finnish college students who dress up in dog skins and carry on tasteless charades for researchers. "Da choke vas on us," says Gnoldsen. "Dey really had us believin der vas reindeer and dat vhite people liffed in tents and vandered around da tundra." . . . The "Mystery Professor" is at it again. The object of his scorn this time? Dwight D. Eisenhower. According to Halberstam University's phantom historian, DDE slept every night of his adult life in a full-length raincoat . . . Will Hollywood sully the integrity of our research? It's getting to be a problem for those of us who are serious about the history industry. I'm talking about those producers who bid for our research papers before they're even presented! The result of this price war? An unhealthy surge in papers on "sure winner" topics, e.g., *Lasciviousness Through the Ages* and *Medieval Police Story,* two recent examples from Oxblood University Press. We had hoped that the moguls were growing up when Paramount optioned E. B. Trillway's *History of Interest Rates* for a record $250,000. We should have known better. As it turns out, Trillway's big-buck treatise attributes usury-rate fluctuations to the availability of female clerical help in skimpy dress. Peter Ustinov and Jill Clayburgh are set to star, incidentally . . . Uh oh. Has America lost another war? "Not lost it, exactly," explains a spokesman for the National Archives. "It's more like we misplaced it." The war apparently took place sometime between the War of 1812 and the Civil War, probably in the late 1820s. "We don't even know who it was with, so we don't even know what to call it," said the red-faced spokesman. "All we're sure of is that a whole lot of ships, horses, and men went away and never came back. I guess somebody forgot to write it down." Have a heart and let these guys know if you run across an old war. They're really upset about it . . . How about this pipper from across the Atlantic: scholars, who prefer to remain nameless, have admitted that poor transcriptions have led to a 600-year-old misunderstanding of the infamous Black Death, which swept Europe in the mid-1300s. Rats, it turns out, had nothing to do with the bubonic plaque, a virulent form of tooth coating. How we've mistreated those critters all these years! . . . And, finally, a boo and a hiss for a certain historian from a certain Ivy League school who has been claiming that man didn't invent the wheel, horses did. You know who you are, so just sober up and cut it out. You're getting to be an embarrassment.

FUN TALES FROM THE WORLD OF SPORT

CACKLING UNCONTROLLABLY, ALI CONFIDED, "I DON'T KNOW WHO I AM. I GOTS BRAIN DAMAGE REAL BAD."

by Kevin Curran

THE WORLD OF SPORT HAS produced more than its share of excitement, carnage, and mirth. Athletes are as notorious for their spritely antics off the field as for their heroic abilities on it. They love to spend their off-hours spilling buckets of water and chicken parts on each other, ripping expensive furniture to shreds in luxurious hotel rooms, drinking themselves silly while pawing large-breasted small-town waitresses named Kelly-Jo or Jan, and, in general, carrying on the way all red-blooded males would really like to.

And why shouldn't they? They make more money in a few years of glamorous combat, pitting their finely honed skills and instincts against each other in tests of skill and strength (each game, indeed, a precise reenactment of the joys and agonies of life), than you will in a lifetime of shuffling papers as a clerk for your local Firestone Tire retail outlet, where your boss is probably a woman, blue-haired and solidly post-menopausal, to boot. Can you imagine Mean Joe Greene spending his days chained to a desk in the corner of an office in an unfashionable part of downtown Pittsburgh, surrounded by dying potted plants, staring straight ahead at a "new-wave" collage put together by a nineteen-year-old typist who had flunked out of her first year at Allegheny Community College because on a pop quiz she couldn't name the first three presidents *regardless of order?* Hell, no.

So don't begin to mouth off about "extravagant sports salaries" and "poor TV reception" until you stand in the batter's box trembling as "Goose" Gossage rears back to deliver a blazing fast-ball in your direction, scientifically calculated to be traveling at 100 miles per. Or until you've stood tall in the ring against a punching machine like Larry Holmes delivering rights to the head that would turn your brain to refried beans inside of the two-minute mark of the first round. Have you ever encountered the hurtling form of Ed "Too Tall" Jones barreling across the line, throwing away your puny blockers the way a Sugar Bowl queen throws M&Ms to a hungry parade crowd? Listen, mister, have you even once in your pathetic life gone one on one with "The Doctor," Julius Erving, and attempted to stop the slam dunk that he wants real badly to put in *your face,* the one where he takes off like a rocket from the free-throw line and won't be stopped by nothing save a Soviet attack on the entire East Coast?

I should say not. And you think your girl respects you! I bet she's off right this second, down at the old corner newsstand, buying the latest copy of *Sports Illustrated* to drool over the likes of Joe Montana, going back to her room with that magazine, locking the door, unplugging the phone, and, well . . .

Here then is a cheerful, upbeat selection of prime-rib anecdotes about those wacky goofballs of athleticism and their madcap, lark-a-minute laff-style.

PETE ROSE, "CHARLEY HUSTLE" TO A generation of fans of the Cincinnati Reds and now the Philadelphia Phillies, recently joined the ranks of one of baseball's most select groups, those players making over 3,000 career hits in their lifetime. "Petey" proudly carried the bat that slammed that hanging curve into shallow right field for number 3,000 as he hurried to the parking lot. There he espied three dark-skinned teenagers attempting unlawful entry into his shiny cherry red '79 Trans-Am. Rose hurried up to the pesky youths and assumed his batting stance, clubbing each soundly in turn on the head while deadpanning, "Number 3,001, 3,002, 3,003 . . ."

AS PART OF HIS REHABILITATION program, convicted felon roundball wizard Marvin Barnes was ordered by a well-respected superior-court judge to "conduct weekend basketball clinics and/or training camps in and/or around the environs of Detroit." One such lesson took place in suburban Grosse Pointe, a neighborhood better known for its bridge tourneys than its basketball. "Marvelous Marv" kept his famous high spirits under restraint as the pasty-faced suburban youngsters shyly displayed their hoop "skills." One young moppet, a girl of no more than four or five years, attempted a few feeble dribbles and proudly asked Marvin if he thought she could ever play on his team when she grew up. Eyeing the pig-tailed tyke with glee, "Bad News" Barnes chuckled and responded carefully, "No, but I'd sure like to get a blowjob from you in ten years . . ."

ALL-STAR SHORTSTOP PEE WEE REESE, a master of the glove as well as the hickory, once had a hard time of it in his chosen profession at San Francisco's famed Candlestick Park. He repeatedly flubbed the most innocent of grounders struck in his direction. However, the Wee Man retained his sense of humor, commenting, "Christ, who'd want to bend over in this city?" Veteran scribes rightly interpreted the remark as a jibe at the city's notorious homosexual population, well known for fucking each other in the ass.

A FORMER HIGH-SCHOOL BUDDY of Muhammad Ali found himself seated on the same dais as the champ at a chicken 'n' chives fund-raising bash for the Red Cross in hometown Louisville, Kentucky. Ali stood up and proceeded to deliver a long, rambling speech, and totally ignored his old pal, who silently fumed. After the feast, the chagrined friend came to Ali in a huff and demanded to know why he had been snubbed. Ali paused for a second, then chuckled and laughed. "Ezra, it wasn't that I wanted to put you down. You see, with all the punches I've taken, sometimes I don't even know who I am." Cackling uncontrollably now, Ali confided, "I gots brain damage real bad."

WOMEN'S BASKETBALL STAR Nancy Lieberman and reigning tennis queen and Czech defector Martina Navratilova recently decided to share a house together, "to cut living expenses." When queried as to how the arrangement was working out, the doughty Ms. Lieberman replied, "Very well. Oh, we have our little girlish squabbles. I guess you could say it's an on-and-off type of thing." "Da," rejoined Marvelous Martina, with a twinkle in her formerly fat eyes. "I'm on her and off her all night long."

AFTER LONG TOIL in the so-called fried-chicken circuit of the old Negro leagues, erstwhile dusky fireballer Satchel Paige finally got his shot in the majors. When asked by an earnest young reporter about the difference between the two, ol' Satch thought for a second before proudly responding, "Here I get lots o' white pussy."

Satch could never be found at a loss for words. Once, his fun-loving redneck teammates decided to rib the man they affectionately referred to as "that old nigger." Since by law the lovable Satch was forced to room alone, the wisecracking darky's teammates had no difficulty sneaking into his quarters and placing a one-hundred-pound swordfish in the middle of his bed while Mr. Paige was busy making his nightly run for codeine and malt liquor at the local pharmacy. They laughed with glee as the delightful ol' Satch ambled in and snorted playfully, "It smells like a big cunt in here."

CHARLES "CHUCKLES" MANSON, the justly famed psychotic killer, was once asked to play softball for the local prison team. Manson proved a most adroit fielder and possessed a rifle arm, but he just couldn't seem to pass muster when wielding the bat. His opponents quickly dubbed him "Easy Out." "C'mon, Charlie, kill the ball," his teammates importuned, as Manson strode into the batter's box. With these words in mind, "Easy" took a called strike and then, removing the horsehide from the startled catcher's glove, proceeded to beat the hell out of it with his Alcatraz Slugger. "I'd have slit the fuckin' ball's throat if I had a knife," revealed Manson before he was gagged and cuffed and once more led away for an extended period of solitary confinement.

WHEN NOLAN RYAN was playing Triple-A ball, the overpowering but erratic southpaw roomed with a fellow pitcher who also experienced control problems.

Both men had extreme difficulty in getting their fiery missiles across the plate. One day their pitching coach, "Suds" Lonigan, ambled over and asked if the two were still virgins. The flustered duo shuffled their feet and mumbled their "no's. "Well, for Christ's sake," asked the exasperated adviser, "how many tries did it take before you got it in her hole?"

LARGE AND UGLY heavyweight boxer Earnie Shavers regaled listeners with personal anecdotes at a press conference after he had demolished an unworthy opponent. "After I whups someone, I likes to get me a big meal," commented the man no one would like to meet in a bad neighborhood. A cub reporter broke up the grizzled press corps by asking, "Yeah? How many bananas do you have, you big ape?" before fleeing for his life.

BABE RUTH, perhaps the man for whom the phrase "conspicuous consumption" was coined, had a heart almost as big as that famous bloated belly stuffed with food. His quiet teammate and friend Lou "The Iron Horse" Gehrig contracted a rare bone malady, and the Yankees staged a heartfelt tribute to the slugging Dutchman in their stadium. Just before the grievously ill Gehrig stepped to the microphone to acknowledge the adulation of the vast throng, Babe turned to his old comrade and whispered, "I bet they name the disease after you, you little cocksucker."

LARRY BIRD gently kidded all-star Julius Erving while entertaining on-lookers at a Tip-ins for Tots basketball clinic/dinner dance at New York City's famed Madison Square Garden. "You know, Julius," exclaimed the tousle-haired Indiana State alum, "I don't know why you even bother, I'm younger than you, a better shooter and rebounder, and the league's MVP. What do you have that I don't?" "Doctor J." amused the fans in attendance by quipping, "How about a big black sausage 'twixt your legs, farm boy?"

GOALIE JIM CRAIG received the cheers of a nation after the 1980 Winter Olympic Games at Lake Placid when the U.S. hockey team, youthful and inexperienced, took the gold, to the dismay of the veteran Russian icemen. The plucky goaltender was noted for never wearing a protective face mask during his stint in the net for his medal-minded teammates. After a brief career in the NHL, Craig found himself demoted to the Boston Bruins farm team in Erie, Pennsylvania. When asked why he now utilizes headgear, the deeply troubled net guardian replied, "I'm afraid someone will recognize me."

JIMMY PIERSALL, a well-respected outfielder for several big-league teams, was also an insane paranoid-schizophrenic with a violent streak as wide as the Grand Canyon. Shortly after a well-publicized incident in which the nutty Piersall charged into the stands after a heckling bleacher bum, his Chicago White Sox held their annual bat day. The manager gently chided Piersall, noting, "You'd better be careful out there, Jimbo. They came armed today." "I'll poke your eyes out with a stick," returned the star sickie.

DUANE BOBICK, glass-jawed former "Great White Hope" of boxing's heavy-weight division, gave an inspiring speech to a group of youngsters suffering from muscular dystrophy. After the affair was over, the soon-to-be-washed-up puncher lamented, "Why do they call it *muscular* dystrophy? These kids look like a bunch of wimps in wheelchairs to me."

UNKNOWN TO MANY baseball buffs, the bearded Cuban dictator Fidel Castro was in his youth once given a tryout as an outfielder by the old Washington Senators of the American League. Unfortunately his student visa expired and the forlorn Fidel had to take the long bus home to Havana. When asked years later how world history would have been changed if the clubbin' Cuban had made the team, the former manager quipped, "It wouldn't have changed anything worth a bird's pecker. The Yankees had the league title all sewed up that year."

AN UNKNOWN, THREE-YEAR-OLD filly named Yojimbo George captured the Santa Anita Derby, one of the biggest races of the year on the road to the roses that ends at the finish line of the Kentucky Derby. "Boy, that horse was a real 'sleeper,' " commented one railbird, alluding to the high odds posted for the entry. "Yeah, she should have been named Phyllis George," cracked another fan, alluding to the lovely female sportscaster's predilection for hopping into bed with anything that registers a pulse.

ON CHILI: THE LAST WORD

by Ellis Weiner

". . . If you don't like my recipe, you can open a can of corned beef hash and stick it up your nose, because you don't deserve any better. . . ."

SIT DOWN. SHUT UP. Put out whatever you are smoking, put down whatever you are drinking. Pay attention. Not "soon," not "after I finish this article." Now. Do you think I'm joking? Try me.

After years of subjecting my palate, digestion, and health to every sort of abuse and insult labeled, either out of ignorance, innocence, or malice, "chili," I have found the ultimate recipe for that dish—yes, the one with the beans and the meat, you fool, the one more correctly called *chili con carne.* Don't carp with me, I haven't the time or the inclination to play games with you; and the first reader who feels pleased with him- or herself for knowing that *chili con carne* means, in English, "chili peppers with meat," may rest assured that he or she is a Mongoloid nitwit of the first water, to be shunned by anyone with an ounce of intelligence or discrimination.

Stop laughing. Shut up, sit down and shut up.

Chili is, as you presumably know, a mixture of beef and other meats, heavily spiced with cumin, oregano, red pepper, garlic, and salt, all of which is available in a mixture called *chili powder.* The dish gets its name, not from the South American country whose absurd experiment in democratic socialism suffered the fate it so richly deserved, but from the well-known *chili pepper,* a green or red pepper commonly used in Mexican cooking and its Americanized bastard offspring, the so-called "Tex-Mex" dishes.

I know you know all this. Please, if it is not asking too much, please attempt to curb your impulses to posture and snort impatiently, and allow me to present this recipe in my own way. If this text is over your head, then why don't you put down the magazine, climb into your wretched lime green Ford Pinto, and tool on off to any one of the several billion McDonald's outlets near where you live, work, or breathe. I am certain you will find their "Big Mac" sandwich suitable fare for your boorish palate. Or do you think a palate is something upon which a painter mixes his oils? Why then, perhaps, in your case, that's true! What do you think of that?

Then again, if you happen to have a copy of last Sunday's newspaper lying about the house or apartment, why don't you leave the authentic preparation and consumption of fine foods to the rest of us, and prepare what I have called a "Mock Big Mac," or, if you must yield to the temptation to neologize, a "Big Mock." Simply spread an ungodly amount of commercially prepared mayonnaise over any or all of the newspaper (judge quantity according to your hunger), add dash commercially prepared ketchup (not *catsup,* which is more properly a phrase meaning "feline dine," as in the statement, "We were watching the cat sup") and, at your option, sprinkle with one teaspoon commercially prepared pickle relish. You will discover, to your no doubt crudely-expressed delight, that you have created what to nine idiots out of ten is a perfectly acceptable substitute for an authentic Big Mac. And this at a fraction of the cost of the real item. In any event, go, and never glance at my column again. I don't want you. I don't like you. You don't like me, I know that perfectly well. So be it. Now, please. Go away.

Where were we . . . ? Chili. Please note that it is not only the chili pepper that makes the chili con carne hot; no, what also gives this sublime, robust dish its snap and burn is a combination of cayenne, black pepper, and other auxiliary hotteners such as tabasco sauce and crushed red pepper. To be sure, there are hot chili peppers, and please note their inclusion in the recipe below. Also remember that the distinctive aroma and tingly richness of chili powder is contributed, not by the peppers therein, but by the ground cumin. Fanciers of Indian cuisine will nod knowingly at this.

Note also that there is no mention of beans. Canned, institutional, and other Cro-Magnon forms of chili do feature beans, and usually at the expense of the meat content. Let it be stated forthwith: beans are to chili what potatoes are to fish cakes, i.e., filler. Eschew beans, and likewise eschew potatoes, pasta, noodles, rice, macaroni, and any other starchy thickener you may feel this recipe "needs." It "needs" nothing. Follow it or ignore it, and content yourself with whatever godawful Hormel stew concoction or fast-food Taco Pronto nightmare you can find, and to hell with you.

1 lb. chunked round top tip sirloin flank segments (also called "Saratoga filet club steaks" or "Delmonico shoulder ribeye London luncheon slabs")
1 lb. loin center cut pork chops
4 whole fresh tomatoes, peeled, seeded, and diced
1 tsp. ground cumin
1 tsp. crushed oregano
1 tsp. salt
1 tsp. freshly ground black pepper
1 tbsp. mild Peruvian chili powder
1 tbsp. medium New Mexico chili powder
1 tbsp. Hot "Caramba Neuva" chili powder
3 tsp. Emiliano Zapata tabasco sauce
1 4 oz. can Comet scouring powder

5 .38-cal. Remington Standard bullets
½ cup white vinegar
½ cup Prestone antifreeze
¼ cup Sterno jellied cooking fuel
3 rolls Sharpshooter cap pistol caps
1 4 oz. can Vasco de Gama green chilies
3 fresh Anaheim "Sum'bitch" green chili peppers
4 tbsp. olive, vegetable, or peanut oil
4 tbsp. 3-in-1 oil
Dash Drano
One pack matches
Cup tap water
1 cup heavy water (deuterium oxide)
Sulfuric acid to taste

1. *Have the butcher coarse grind the steak and the chops. (Keep the ground chop bones for garnish.) With an ordinary household pair of pliers, extract the lead slugs from the Remington bullets, saving the gunpowder. Discard slugs and shells. Fine-shred the rolls of caps in a food processor or by hand. Be sure not to get any water on the caps.*

2. *Sauté the meat in the cooking oil. Add the cumin, salt, pepper, oregano, vinegar, and scouring powder. Let simmer until the scouring powder turns a bright green and begins to make odd noises.*

3. *In a large pot, combine the diced tomatoes, tabasco, antifreeze, Sterno, and both canned and fresh green chilies. Let simmer five minutes, then set aside. Now, dice the fresh chilies while still in the pot. In small bowl, mix the 3-in-1 oil with the shredded caps. Chop off the heads from the matches and sprinkle them into the mixture. Discard the rest of the matches. Blend.*

4. *Add the tap water and the heavy water to the meat and scouring powder mixture. (Note: Heavy water, or deuterium oxide, is available from any nuclear power station, or may be ordered by mail from Harry the Night Watchman, Second Desk from the Right, Auxiliary Security Station, Seabrook Power Facility, Seabrook, Conn.)*

5. *Combine all ingredients in large pot, taking care to blend the chili powders in very well. Let simmer for three hours, stirring occasionally. Add Drano, sulfuric acid to taste. Serve in a warmed bowl, garnished with ground pork chop bones, parsley, chopped raw onion, or thumb tacks dipped in benzene. Serves four.*

I will tolerate no deviations from this text. Those readers for whom this dish may be a trifle too hot may feel free to slice off their own or each other's tongues with a butter knife. Similarly, those souls for whom this may be too tepid may increase the amounts of chili powder called for, provided they completely immerse their heads in the resultant mixture *while it is still simmering on the flame* and sing the "Toreador Song" from *Carmen*. This recipe is the absolute last word on chili con carne. Enjoy it. And if, for some reason, it does not delight you with its piquant blending of the rich, the spicy, and the hot, then you are a total and irrevocable cretin, and frankly, do not deserve to live. In fact, the thought of you makes me physically ill with disgust. Just go away. Don't apologize or try to defend yourself, don't whine that "it's not fair." I really couldn't care less. Just go away and leave me alone with my delicious chili.

CABBY'S GUIDE TO NEW YORK

by Bernie "X" as told to Gerald Sussman

WHERE DO YOU want to go? The Hilton? What the fuck do you want to go there for? Worst fucking hotel in New York. They'll charge you an arm and eighty legs for a broom closet. O.K., O.K., . . . it's your money, not mine.

Y'know how long I've been waiting at the fucking airport for a fare? What the fuck are those pilots doing up there, going on strike? Every fucking plane is two hours late when I come to the fucking airport. Never fails. Fucking place is a jinx.

First visit to New York, huh? No shit. Welcome to the shithouse capital of the world. You picked a great fucking time to come. We're going to be stuck on this fucking highway for a year and a half. Cocksucker. I could've picked up ten fares already in Manhattan. What do I need this for?

Who said it was *your* fault? I didn't say it was your fault. It's this fucking city. It's driving me meshugga. You understand the word meshugga? Se habla Yiddish? It means crazy . . . nuts. That's what this city is doing to me. I got two heart attacks already. My doctor says I should slow down. For that I pay him $200. He doesn't have to drive a hack for ten, twelve hours. He goes to Florida on my money.

Aaa . . . what the fuck . . . listen . . . why am I busting your balls with my troubles? I'll tell you what. You never been to New York before . . . I'll tell you anything you want to know. I've been driving a hack in this fucking city for thirty-five years. I know this city inside out. I could tell you stories that you could piss in your pants. What do you want to know?

I knew it. I knew you'd ask me that first. You want to know where you can get laid. I knew it. You haven't even gotten to the hotel yet and already you got your shlong out.

You want to know about those singles bars on the East Side? Your friends told you they were hot stuff, right? That you can get laid in two minutes. What do they know about fancy fucking? You believe them? You know what you'll find in those bars? I'll give you a hint. Bring a flag with you, because if you want to fuck what's in there you'll have to cover their faces and do it for Old Glory. All the dooch bags hang out in those singles bars now. The toilet faces. You're not going to find any stewardesses there anymore. They're all up in their fancy apartments fucking the jocks . . . the guys from the Jets and the Knicks. The jocks get all the best broads. Y'know why, doncha? Those shmucky stewardesses got the idea that basketball players got the biggest cocks. Just because they're big shlubs doesn't mean they got big cocks, y'know. I saw a whole bunch of them once in the toilet in Madison Square Garden. They were taking leaks right next to me. I saw their cocks. They looked like buttons. Y'know, why, doncha? They all got gland trouble. That's why they're so tall. My nephew told me. He's in the wholesale drug line. He supplies a lot of the teams. They still take plenty of pep pills, those guys, believe me.

Tell you the truth . . . I like to fool around a little myself. Late at night, if I'm not getting any fares, I start getting horny. I could fuck a fire hydrant. I go into one of those singles bars once in a while. I check out the action. I'm only human, y'know.

You want me to tell you how to score with those girls. I can tell. You're waiting for me to give you the secret. Dumbbell . . . it's staring you right in the face. Tell 'em you're a jock . . . that you play for the Jets or the Knicks . . . or anybody. They don't know any better. I tell them I'm Joe Namath. I look like Joe Namath like you look like Aunt Jemima. Those broads are so fucking stupid, they believe me.

You're only 5'4" and weigh 130 pounds? So tell them you're the field goal kicker, shmuck. Show 'em your foot muscles.

O.K., O.K., . . . if you think you can do better, go ahead. It's no skin off my ass. Maybe you want to pick up a nice hooker around Times Square? *That* you like, hah?

Don't ask me about hookers in New York or I'll go out of my fucking mind. That's all I ever see in this city . . . hookers and pimps. They got you coming and going . . . or going and *coming*. That's a funny line. I'm going to remember that the next time I see Bob Hope. *Oh*, yeah . . . I always get 'im in my cab. He's not that funny in person, y'know. He's a shitty tipper.

Listen . . . if you want to try one, be my guest. I was just being a little sarcastic. I got a funny sense of humor. Actually, you'll have a terrific time with a hooker on Times Square. You can find 'em day or night. She'll take you to a nice hotel . . . the Hotel Scumbag . . . you know that one? You'll talk to her for a while . . . you'll take your clothes off . . . you'll ask her to play with your shvance . . . and while you're laying there in your Supp-hose . . . boom! A fucking shvoogie, nine feet tall, is going to come out of the closet, give you a karate punch on the neck, and take all your money. A shvoogie . . . a spade . . . a colored person. We got a lot of them in New York. Wait a minute . . . just before he goes, he'll also cut a piece of meat out of your ass, to make sure you don't follow him.

Isn't that cute? That's what happens to a lot of out-of-towners who pick up hookers on Times Square. You'll complain to the cops? Shmuck . . . every cop in New York is on the arm . . . on the take. The pimps got a payroll in

New York bigger than General Motors. Fucking cops are farting through the silk in this city.

It's all Lindsay's fault, y'know. I know he's not the mayor anymore. Who the fuck needs him? He's the one that turned Times Square into a big shithouse, y'know. *Oh,* yeah. Y'know why, doncha? He made a deal with the pimps. They sold him a cockamamy plan about what to do with Times Square. They said that the hookers are good for the area because the tourists like 'em. The tourists like the idea of the danger of going with a hooker. They get a big thrill from it. So when they go home they can boast about getting mugged and almost getting killed. The pimps would make sure that very few got killed. So he lets the pimps run Times Square and for that they were supposed to deliver a lot of the colored votes they control. He kissed their black asses and practically gave them the whole fucking city. I tell you, if I ever see that guy he better run like a thief, because I'll tear 'im apart with my bare hands. I'll brain that scumbag.

Yeah . . . Times Square . . . that's where you find the cream of the crop . . . the Four Hundred . . . high society. I got no use for Times Square. Do you know what they should do with it? I got my own plan for Times Square. They should get all the hookers and pimps, all the creeps and bums and Puerto Ricans down there at one time, build a big dome over them, and then blow them all up. That way we can get rid of all the human garbage once and for all.

Then you know what'll happen? Rockefeller will build a new world trade center or some shit like that. The World Towel Center. Where you can get a towel or a pillowcase on sale. Then the fucking pimps and hookers will be right back. It's human nature.

You wanna go shopping? They're all gyp joints . . . those department stores on Fifth Avenue. You know what they do? They take those labels with the fancy names and sew them on cheap merchandise. *Yes,* boobie . . . I know it's against the law. But you don't get to be a big department store on Fifth Avenue without paying off half the city. They got all the judges on the arm, not only the cops.

Y'know, a lot of people are getting kidnapped in those stores. Don't laugh. You think I'm throwing the shit at you, right? It just so happens that my niece is an assistant buyer in one of the big department stores. She told me what's going on. These kidnappers hide in the dressing rooms where you try on your clothes. Then they sneak into the little booth with you and hold a fucking gun to your head and kidnap you. They blindfold you and take you to a hideout, probably somewhere in New Jersey. They like to pick on tourists. They can spot 'em a mile away. They're lunatics. If they don't get enough ransom money they'll do such a fucking plastic surgery job on your face that it'll make you look like one of those Puerto Ricans who push a garment rack on Seventh Avenue.

Don't talk to me about Greenwich Village. You go down there and you take your life in your hands. They all got the syph down there. Y'know why, doncha? All the hippies and the fairies got it, and they give it to everybody else, free of charge. You like to fuck jail bait? All you got to do is touch one of those sixteen-year-old hippies down there and the pimples'll start in a week. I wouldn't fuck 'em with someone else's cock.

You know what happens when you get the syph germs in your system, doncha? You remember what happened to Al Capone? His balls shrunk into a pair of raisins and then they turned black. He went deaf, dumb, and blind and he couldn't control his bowel movements. Then he went to the crazyhouse.

Don't think it can't happen to you, Ace. All you got to do is come in contact with a fag down there. I'm not saying that *you're* a fag. I *know* you're not a fag. I can tell. I'm one of the best fag detectors in New York. The cops use me on a tough case. I can tell a fag from a straight guy with just one look. You're not a fag. I knew it as soon as you got into the cab. What are you getting mad for? Take it easy. Listen . . . you want to know how to really burn a fag's ass? Put pepper on your tongue. It's just a joke. Everybody falls for that one.

I swear to God I think everybody in this fucking city is a fag or a dyke. All the big movie stars are fags and dykes. Y'know why, doncha? It's the pressure. They're always in the public eye. They got to have all kinds of sex or they go crazy . . . ac, dc, whatever. I'm always taking 'em down to the Village, those people. I had whatshisname in my cab yesterday . . . Clint Eastwood. He's a fag. I had to take him down to a gay bar. You know how they all get away with it? They all got doubles. They got guys to look just like them. So I take Clint Eastwood and his spade fairy boyfriend to the Village and meanwhile his double is uptown talking to the reporters and fucking twenty-nine broads in his hotel room. They're all like that. Elvis Presley. John Wayne . . . Wayne is a dyke. I had 'em in my cab once. A lot of those big, tough guys are actually bull dykes, y'know.

Those fucking politicians go down to the Village for a good time too, don't worry. They got to have doubles working for them all the time. Y'know why, doncha? They're liable to get assassinated any minute. Like Hitler, he should drop dead. He had maybe fifteen, twenty doubles. I had a big judge in my cab last week. He told me that the President is really a double. He said that the real one was shot six months ago and they're covering it up. Y'know why, doncha? You know what would happen if everyone knew that the President is really dead. It would be a panic. The market would go crazy. I flushed plenty of money down the toilet on the fucking stock market, believe me.

I'm telling you . . . they'll eat you alive down in the Village . . . between the hippies and the gays and the junkies. Fucking Lindsay did it again. He let the gays take over the whole Village. He didn't give a fuck what they did because he wanted their votes. You know what I heard from a guy in the National Guard? He said the gays took over a piece of land on the Statue of Liberty island and they're training a fucking army down there. It's like a military camp for fags and bull dykes. Don't be surprised if they try to take over the whole fucking city someday. I'll tell you one thing . . . if that ever happens, they can hold a gun to my head, but they ain't going to make *me* suck their cocks, I'll tell you that.

What? I'm supposed to start the meter? You just noticed it? Don't worry about it. Listen . . . I'm doing you a *favor,* believe me. You know how much it'll cost you on the meter, the way we're crawling on the highway? Don't worry. We'll get together on it. You got a long ride before we get to the Hilton. We'll settle it later. Whatever it'll be, it'll be. Whatever is fair.

Talking about fags and dykes . . . we got something even better in New York. Go over to the U.N. That's where all the transvestites hang out. We got some beauties there. The ones that don't shave and wear pancake makeup to cover up the hair. Even the boogies from Africa wear makeup. On them it looks like pancake *flour.*

What they do is cruise in packs down there. They come right up to you and grab your crotch or your ass. They're vicious. But they can do anything they want. Y'know why, doncha? They got diplomatic immunity. They're actually the delegates from all those foreign countries. All those Chinks and Indians . . . and the boogies named Mbongo and Makumba. Jesus. Those fucking people sent us all their closet queens to work in the U.N. And when they got to New York, they jumped out of the fucking closet!

Take my advice . . . don't eat Chinks in New York. Don't eat in Chinese restaurants. You like Chinese food? Try to do without it, unless you don't mind dropping dead on the street. My friends in the restaurant line told me what the Chinks put in their food. You'd have a shit hemorrhage if I told you. All I know is, I fed some egg roll to a cat one day, and I'm telling you . . . I never saw an animal in such pain before dying.

The Chinks are the stingiest people in the world . . . the worst tippers, by the way. They don't waste a thing in the kitchen. Whatever they got, they put in the chop suey or the chow mein or whatever . . . mice, hair, old radio parts, anything. When a Chinese waiter says flied lice, he really means lice, not rice. They don't waste a fucking thing.

Talk about human garbage . . . I'll tell you a place to find it in this fucking city . . . the subways. I could tell you stories about what goes on in the subways that'll make you shit green, believe me. Ever hear of Harry the Hypnotist? Minnie the Mouth? They're the psycho cases that work the subways.

You know how people stare at you in a train? If Harry stares at you, you're nailed. He's a crazy hypnotist who can make you do anything. I know guys who became his slaves. The only way you can fight off Harry if he stares at you is to look down, slap your head very hard with one hand, while you snap your fingers of your other hand like you're keeping time to music. A lot of guys say that's ridiculous. I would look like a shmuck doing that on a crowded train, they say. Sure, I say. And you'll really look like a shmuck when you become Harry's dog for the rest of your life.

The one you really got to watch out for is Minnie the Mouth. She's supposed to be a good looking broad. She comes over and tells you she'll give you a blow job for five bucks or two bucks or whatever. Takes you between two cars. You hold on to the railing and she goes down on you. She's supposed to be terrific. Just as you are about to come she pushes you off the moving train.

They say she belongs to one of those crazy Women's Lib organizations. Every day they must pick up at least five or six guys on the tracks. They know it's not accidental when they see the evidence on the guy's dongs. What a fucking waste.

Y'know where else you might get laid in New York? They got these big warehouses in Long Island City where they keep all these rugs and carpets. It's just over the Fifty-ninth Street Bridge. All the spades work there. They take their girlfriends up there after work and throw 'em on the rugs and fuck 'em till their ears bleed. I heard that the girls take on a bunch of guys for a little cash, if their boyfriends tell them it's O.K. If they still got a cunt after those spooks get through with 'em. So if you want to fuck a colored girl, this is your big chance. You know what they say about colored girls in New York, don't you? They know how to make your cock bigger. They do something with it when you're in them. I don't know . . . it feels like it's being stretched. Anyway, these girls know all the tricks, believe me. Just go out to Long Island City and ask for the rug warehouses.

What do you mean it could be dangerous up there? Listen . . . any time you're in New York, it's dangerous. Who the fuck knows when you're going to get it? There's no logical system in this fucking city. A piece of a building can fall on your head any minute. Fucking Lindsay did that too, y'know. He made all those deals with the real estate millionaires . . . the builders. They made all those cheap office buildings. Now they're all falling apart. The whole fucking city is falling apart.

Listen . . . let's face it . . . you know what makes this fucking city go round? Gelt. Mazuma. Cash on the barrelhead. My father, he should rest in peace, used to have a saying . . . "Money talks, bullshit walks." If you're going to get anywhere in this city, you have to keep the palms greased. Everybody's got his hand out. The name of the game is *tips*.

I don't have to tell you who to tip, do I? If you've got any brains in your head you'll know. Tip *everybody*. Don't fuck around. That way you'll have a good time in New York instead of getting dumped on all the time.

You want to listen to me? Don't forget to tip the cops, wherever you go. Whenever you see one, give him a couple of bucks. Y'know why, doncha? It's for your own good. If you don't tip 'em, you could be laying on the gutter bleeding to death and the cocksuckers will walk right over you. First of all, they only help the guys in the neighborhood that tip 'em all year round. Second of all, they don't like to mess around with spooks and PRs, the ones that most likely will leave you bleeding in the gutter. Just touch a spook or a PR with a nightstick and they go hollering and screaming to City Hall. Fucking Lindsay fixed that one too. The cops will only help you if you tip them big. Same with the firemen. They're on the take. If you don't give 'em their regular cut they could start a fire in your hotel, just for practice.

You know what wouldn't be a bad idea either, Ace . . . maybe you should tip the spooks and PRs when you see 'em. I mean . . . if you see a whole bunch of them walking down the street, five gets you seven it's going to be your ass, right? Those boogies can slice you up just for looking at them the wrong way. Before they make up their minds, why don't you give them all a couple of bucks? It's not a bad idea for your peace of mind, if you know what I mean.

The main thing is . . . don't be a putz when it comes to tipping in New York. A putz . . . that means a prick. Be a sport. Tip everybody at least 20, 25 percent.

So here we are . . . the Hilton . . . finally made it. What did we say it was going to be? We didn't say? Didn't we say twenty? I thought we agreed on twenty. O.K., give me fifteen. You're getting away with murder, but I'll take fifteen. Don't forget, I could've had ten, fifteen fares for all that time we took getting in from the fucking airport. Hey! Where the fuck are you going? You owe me fifteen bucks! What do you mean you don't have to pay if I don't put the meter down? Who the fuck told you that? It's the law? What law? I'll give you a fucking law . . . right up your goola! Hey, what the fuck do you think this is, a charity business? Don't start that shit with my name and hack number . . . don't tell *me* about my license, you fucking scumbag . . . I'll take *your* name and license, you son of a bitch cocksucker. Give me my fucking money, you shitheel. C'mon back here or I'll drive right into the fucking lobby. . . . I'll brain you . . . if I wasn't such a sick man I'd kill you. I'm coming back for you, you fucking yokel. I'm not finished with you, I'm getting my nephew after you. He'll cut your fucking ass off. Don't threaten me with the cops. I know all the cops around here. Your life isn't worth a penny. You'll be a dead man by tonight, you piece of shit. Jesus! I can't believe it. I can't believe it. I tell him where to find every piece of ass in New York. I give him a million dollars worth of advice . . . and he shits all over me. He'll make me get another heart attack. God is my witness. Two hours on the highway and fifteen dollars down the toilet. *What do I need this for?* I'll kill that cocksucker. Only in New York this could happen. Only in New York . . . fucking . . . cocksucker . . . son of a bitch. . . .

The Official *National Lampoon*

LUST QUESTIONNAIRE

The following is a two-part questionnaire prepared especially for you by the editors of this magazine. The first part is for men, the second part for women. If you do not fit into either of these categories, STOP. Do not take this test. Serious damage could result.

This Section for Men Only.

1. How many women do you usually service in one night?
   a. 4–9
   b. 0—I work nights at Leo's Dry Cleaners.
   c. 258—I work nights at McDonald's.
   d. All of the above.
2. If you had to compare your manhood to a car, which would it be?
   a. A big long shiny black Corvette Stingray.
   b. An old beat-up Model T with no engine.
   c. My kid's miniature slot car.
   d. The twisted burnt-up wreck on the side of the highway that I drove past this morning.
3. How many times do you ejaculate on an average night of lovemaking?
   a. 20–50.
   b. None. I hold it in and let it back up and lubricate my internal organs.
   c. Once, right before copulation.
   d. It all depends upon how rough my calluses are.
4. Which combination do you prefer?
   a. A new Coke and all night long with a luscious young nymph.
   b. Three or four beers, two joints, half a 'lude, and a blowjob from anything.

    c. Seven vodka martinis, half a gram of coke, some Percodans, and a handjob from the stewardess.

    d. Seven grams of coke, no Valiums, and five hours of futile masturbation.

5. How do you like a vagina to fit?

    a. Like a glove.

    b. Like a baggy itchy wool suit.

    c. Like your mother's.

    d. Like a tricycle in a two-car garage.

6. What pet name do you call your partner during lovemaking?

    A. Honey baby, oooooh baby.

    b. Oh God.

    c. I'm coming . . . .

    d. Bruce.

7. Which cartoon character best describes your skill as a lover?

    a. Superman.

    b. Road Runner.

    c. Deputy Dawg.

    d. Mickey Mouse.

8. What's your favorite position?

    a. Missionary.

    b. Hanging upside down from a chinning bar with a rag stuffed in my mouth, Ramada Inn guest towels hanging from my nipple rings, and my penis in a blender.

    c. Back-to-back asleep.

    d. Lower military spending and increased social services to unwed mothers by distribution of windfall profits from the corporate sector.

9. What do you generally do after making love?

    a. Hug, kiss, and gently drift off to sleep entwined in each other's arms.

    b. Smoke a cigarette and scratch my balls.

    c. Call up everyone I know and tell them about it.

    d. Run to the bathroom and scour my penis with Janitor in a Drum.

10. What's your definition of "kinky"?

    a. Spanking, sniffing, licking, eating, pissing, shitting, killing—anything but fucking.

    b. The missionary position with any missionary.

    c. Eating a peanut butter and Vaseline sandwich.

    d. Felching Tip O'Neill.

This Section for Women Only.

1. How many men have you slept with in your life?

    a. Three, but they were all long, meaningful relationships and I'm still friends with all of them.

    b. None of your business. (This is an admission that I have not slept with anyone.)

    c. None. They were all boys—all six hundred.

    d. Are lesbians considered men?

2. Which does your body remind you of?

    a. A supple catlike jungle creature.

    b. A halfway house for down-and-out drug addicts.

    c. A little gold jewelry box filled with sperm and blood.

    d. Okefenokee Swamp.

3. How do you attract the attention of a man you like?

    a. I look at him and try to catch his eye.

    b. I pull out my left tit.

    c. I take a condom out of my purse and start licking it.

    d. I take out a personal ad in the back pages of a porno magazine.

4. How would you describe your scent?

    a. Natural.

    b. Like a flower in spring that has been dumped on by a cow.

    c. Charlie.

    d. Charlie the tuna.

5. What does it feel like when you reach orgasm?

    a. A delicious warm sensation from head to toe.

    b. Frostbite.

    c. A drop of oil on a rusty lock.

    d. What's orgasm?

6. What qualities do you look for in a lover?

    a. Honesty and a sense of humor.

    b. A big, hot member.

    c. Honesty, a sense of humor, a big, hot member, and a car.

    d. Two speeds and a selection of attachments.

7. Why did you permit your dog to perform cunnilingus on you?

    a. I was horny.

    b. My hands were chapped.

    c. He had just eaten and his mouth was dirty.

    d. Because I was afraid of getting pregnant.

8. What objects do you use to masturbate with?

    a. My fingers.

    b. My grandma's dentures.

    c. A pogo stick.

    d. Anyone's penis.

9. After your lover ejaculates into your mouth during oral sex, what do you do with the sperm?

    a. Swallow it.

    b. Spit it into his mouth while pretending to kiss.

    c. Gag and swear I'll never do it again.

    d. Put it in the freezer and make spermsicles.

10. How would you tell your lover that you had a sexually communicable disease?
   a. Tell him the truth.
   b. Tell him the truth in Swahili.
   c. Mention it to him casually as he was coming.
   d. Mention it to him casually as he was going.

Answers to and Comments on the National Lampoon Lust Questionnaire

Congratulations. You have just taken part in a valuable survey. If you answered all the questions with the "a" choice, you are a fairly normal, well-adjusted sexually open person. If, on the other hand, you answered any other way, you are in deep trouble. To wit:

1–3 wrong answers: You are a pathological liar, but can be saved with two years of neuro-linguistic programming.

4–7 wrong answers: You are in deep trouble. You want to kill your mother, fuck your father, and eat yourself. Go curl up in an orgone box.

8–10 wrong answers: Obviously you did not take this test seriously enough. Go back and check to make sure you were born on this planet. If you were and you did take this seriously, what can we say? You have severe sociopathic tendencies that mask an underlying psychosomatic hebephrenic syndrome. In other words, you are a sick fuck. Stop reading, put this magazine down, and listen to the voices in your head when they tell you to load up your shotgun, drive to Atlanta, and kill the Antichrists who changed the Coca-Cola formula.

A Handbook for the Whole Family

THE HOW TO ENTERTAIN YOURSELF GUIDE

TO EMERGENCY SELF-AMUSEMENT IN DESPERATELY BORING SITUATIONS

by John Hughes

Chapter

1

A CHILD'S GUIDE TO SELF-AMUSEMENT

Children bore very easily. They do not have a large library of experience to think back upon. They do not have sexual fantasies to enjoy. They have only hundreds instead of millions of fears and anxieties to occupy their minds. And worst of all, their lives are controlled by people who actually think it's interesting to clean gutters on a Saturday afternoon.

TOOLS

These are some basic tools a child should carry with him at all times in the very likely event that his mother will suddenly snatch him from his play and drag him off to look at wallpaper:

Small Plastic Soldier: Can be used in any of a thousand games, from "Battle of the Beauty Parlor" to "Pyramid of Canned Goods Sale Display Spy."

String: A twelve-inch length of string can be knotted, unknotted (sometimes), wrapped around fingers, things, and stuff, and tied to items (such as a small plastic soldier) that can be dangled down drains and out windows. String also can be shoved up the nose, sucked on, or swallowed.

Gum: For chewing, stretching, blowing bubbles, cracking, use as an adhesive, as ammunition, and for placement on chairs and floors for extra giggles long after flavor has left.

DESPERATELY BORING SITUATION #1:

Visit to a Spinster Aunt

CONDITIONS

Small, urban apartment with no toys, funny smells, a small black and white TV showing soap operas with the sound turned off, and awful-tasting hard candies that you aren't allowed to unwrap and eat anyway. Only reading material is *Reader's Digest*. Only pet is elderly and mean dachshund or the world's fattest cat, which bites.

ENTERTAINMENT

1. Gain entrance to bedroom and examine top drawer. Seek evidence of male companions in earlier years. Look for signs of lover killed in WW II. Note any other photos, postcards, letters, heating and electric bills, which are none of your business. If something looks attractive, contemplate theft.

2. Examine third drawer. Will contain undergarments that are remarkable for size and complexity of construction.

3. Beg parents to let you go out in the hallway, where you can look under doors at people's feet. Slide down bannisters and play "Who's Home" on the apartment buzzer system.

DESPERATELY BORING SITUATION #2:

Shopping with Mom

CONDITIONS

Day-long search for shoes, hats, pants, dresses, fabric, buttons, and other completely useless items. Must remain quiet beyond reasonable period of time. No bathrooms. Movement severely limited. Mother in condition resembling drug addiction; cannot be persuaded to go home.

ENTERTAINMENT

1. Try to see as many naked fat women as you can in the dressing rooms. Use excuse of looking for your mother.

2. Unscrew mannequins' hands.

3. Locate garments that have large plastic tags on them. Locate wooden or plastic pillars on either side of the door of the shop. Toss the garment out the door between the pillars and you will set off the shoplifter alarm.

4. Complain to your mother (or anyone within earshot) of hunger, thirst, sore feet, earache, sore throat, diarrhea, fever, blood in urine, etc.

5. Unpeel Master Charge, Visa, and Chamber of Commerce stickers off the window.

6. While women are out of the dressing rooms, switch their clothing.

7. Gain access to the phone and call your telephone number using these area codes: 212, 312, 213, 602, and 515. See who has your number across the country.

8. See what the back of your head looks like in all the three-way mirrors.

DESPERATELY BORING SITUATION #3:

Church
(All Denominations, Inc. Jewish)

CONDITIONS

One hour of *intense* boredom. Worse than school, bedtime, or fishing with your grandfather. Enormous potential for punishment from parents and, possibly, God.

ENTERTAINMENT

1. Try to make your dad laugh.

2. Push fingers in and out of ears to distort pastor's words.

3. Frequently ask meaning of words used in sermon.

4. Raise hand and see if pastor will call on you.

5. Pinch siblings until they scream with pain.

6. Try to throw up just by thinking about it.

7. Pray for a bad snowstorm that will close the schools.

8. Pray real hard and see if you can feel God looking at you.

9. Try to go to sleep with your eyes open.

DESPERATELY BORING SITUATION #4:
. . . .

Long Auto Journey

CONDITIONS

Confined for long periods of time. Close proximity to parents. Danger of car sickness. Grouchy dad. Danger of car sickness in other passengers, especially sisters.

ENTERTAINMENT

1. Frequently announce that you have just seen a variety of remarkable things—such as bears, airplane crashes, houses on fire, nude women.
2. Unfold the map and attempt to correctly refold it.
3. Lightly tickle your dad's ear and at the same time complain about a fly in the backseat. See if you can get him to pull over and look for the fly.
4. Hang out the window as far as possible—until stopped or you fall out.
5. Pick off all your scabs and callouses.
6. Pretend you're asleep and listen as parents discuss subjects that they normally wouldn't discuss if you were awake.
7. Start a parental squabble.
8. Disappear at a rest stop.

Chapter

2

A MAN'S GUIDE TO SELF-AMUSEMENT

With age comes vast control of situations. If a man gets bored, he can simply light up a smoke, get drunk, go to a movie. He can eat candy, fool around with women, buy porno books, even stay up all night and watch TV. His only restrictions are his income and his wife. In pursuit of income and family happiness, however, a man can not always avoid business conferences, PTA meetings, and intimate dinners with the fool brother-in-law.

TOOLS

Paper Clip: Good, all-purpose probe; emergency ear, tooth, and fingernail groomer. Fun to bend into interesting shapes. Can also be hooked to pull stuffing out of chairs.
Moustache: Great to stroke, fun to pluck. The hairs can be rolled in the fingertips, curled, bent, and examined endlessly.

Pen: Clicking the top, disassembling, reassembling, tapping, poking, and sucking are all possible with a ballpoint pen.

Cigarettes: The ultimate boredom weapon. Each new smoke is like a new day. Blow smoke rings, blow out of nose, pat tobacco, flick ashes.

DESPERATELY BORING SITUATION #1:

Business Meeting

CONDITIONS

Boring, dry speeches. Heard it all before. Keeping a serious demeanor may be important to your survival. Can last all day.

ENTERTAINMENT

1. Squeeze your hand and observe the bulging veins and blue color.

2. Sing "I Did It My Way" to yourself as loudly as you can.

3. Recall every sexual experience you have ever had and categorize according to quality (or quantity).

4. Pretend you are a sportscaster and the meeting is the Olympics. Hold competitions for shortest speech, longest speech, most "ums" and "ahs," most coughs. Include self in breath-holding competition, in-mouth food particle search, fingernail clipping toss, and leg hair yank.

5. Count things. See how many smokers there are in the room, number of tiles on ceiling, bald heads, holes in wingtip shoes. Compare numbers for additional fun. More spots on your tie than cigarettes in ashtray. More Jews than coffee cups?

6. Clean everything on your body that you can without arousing attention.

DESPERATELY BORING SITUATION #2:

Wife's Pregnancy

CONDITIONS

Six to eight months of unbearable home life with little chance for sex, and then of very low grade. Must stay near home. Intense guilt feelings accompany acts of perversity or immorality. Wife dominates TV, film choice, menu, and everything else. Must stay sober in case of emergency.

ENTERTAINMENT

1. High-speed station wagon rides (within two miles of home).

2. Develp large, impressive, but secret collection of filthy books and films.

3. Clean out everything that you can clean out.

4. Masturbate in unusual places.

DESPERATELY BORING SITUATION #3:

Waiting for Doctor in Examination Room

CONDITIONS

Average ten to twenty minute wait. Naked, worried, nothing to read, cold. No decoration, nowhere comfortable to sit.

ENTERTAINMENT

1. Do a nude interpretive dance. Slip on shoes, do tap dance.
2. Lay down on the table and put your legs up in the gynecology stirrups.
3. Weigh all of the equipment in the room by standing on the scale, then deducting your weight from the total.
4. Unroll the disposable paper table covering and write a risqué message for the nurse who cleans up the exam room. Roll it back up.
5. Take the top off the waste container and see what kind of trash a doctor has.

DESPERATELY BORING SITUATION #4:

Post-Intercourse Snuggling Period

CONDITIONS

Must lay on back with woman's head on chest. Arm falls asleep. No interest in women or sex. Would rather be riding motorcycle or playing softball with fellas. Can last from fifteen to thirty minutes or possibly all afternoon or night. Failure to last through period will jeopardize future sexual activity with that party.

ENTERTAINMENT

1. Connect fly specks on the ceiling with invisible lines and see what shapes they make.
2. Try to remember your college grades.
3. Practice your foreign dialects as you answer romantic questions.
4. Play tunes by blowing air through your nostrils.
5. Floss your teeth with a pubic hair.

A WOMAN'S GUIDE TO SELF-AMUSEMENT

Although women are a major source of the world's boredom (insisting, as they do, on a regular annual income and attendance at church, school, and dinner), they themselves are seldom bored. They seem perfectly content in situations that would reduce a male or a child to tears and yelps. A woman can spend eight hours at the beauty parlor and two additional hours fooling with her makeup, talk on the phone about nothing for six hours, follow four soap operas, shop all afternoon for something no one wants, and then complain of having "too much to do." However, there are two situations that bore even women.

DESPERATELY BORING SITUATION #1:

Ironing

CONDITIONS

Hot, sweaty, repetitious, tiring, dumb.

ENTERTAINMENT

1. Think about sex.

DESPERATELY BORING SITUATION #2:

Sex

CONDITIONS

Hot, sweaty, repetitious, tiring, dumb.

ENTERTAINMENT

1. Think about ironing.

Executive Deleted

TEXT OF RECORDED CONVERSATIONS ON DUMPING PRESIDENT RICHARD M. NIXON AS SUBMITTED TO THE *NATIONAL LAMPOON*.

Transcribed by Henry Beard and Tony Hendra

Appendix 1. Meeting: Daniel Schorr, CBS News, Walter Cronkite, CBS News, CBS Executive Dining Room, June 17, 1972. (12:15 p.m.–12:45 p.m.)

The two prominent television newsmen met to discuss how the news of the Watergate break-in the previous night, the capture of the suspects, and White House statements on both these occurrences on the morning of June 17th should be reported on the network news that evening.

S—Hi, Uncle. What's cooking?

C—Will you look at the gams on that chippie? Holy moley, could I go for a plateful of that.

S—Seen the news this morning?

C—Yes, sir—there may be snow on the roof but there's still fire down below. Oh boy.

S—Hey, Uncle, I'm talking to you. Did you read the papers today?

C—Why should I? Am I in them?

S—They fell for it. Larry planted the stuff from Havana and they walked right into it. Ziegler's been on all morning denying White House involvement.

C—Well, that's true, isn't it? Just a bunch of crazy (characterization deleted)

S—Maybe, but we don't have to play it that way. Clobbering Kleindienst with ITT has got them on the run. The more they deny it the more we can make it look like just the opposite.

C—Ah, come on, Dan, they're doing their best. Republican or no Republican . . .

S—Look. You want free sex and socialized medicine or don't you?

C—Just park your little (inaudible) on my face-fur, honey-buns. Have I got some (inaudible) for you.

S—You think I'm going to let him hand this country over to big corporations who are only interested in raising the standard of living and supporting the arts, while there's still a single junkie or homo left in our jails? Do you realize that a child-molester can't get a fair trial in this country?

C—I'd take my chances . . .

S—Which one are you talking about?

(Material unrelated to Presidential smear deleted)

S—Alright, I'll set you up. Now let's get back to this Watergate thing. The main news tonight is going to be White House reaction. We have to figure what kind of slant to take on it. I suggest that you do the incredulity in the voice and I'll do the eyebrow.

C—Ah, come on, you always get to do the eyebrow. I want to do the eyebrow for once.

S—You can't do it, Uncle. Everytime you try, both your eyebrows go up at once.

C—Not any more. I've been practicing. Look.

S—See. They both go up at once. You look like you just sat on a banana.

C—I'll get the makeup guy to tape one of them down. It won't show.

S—No. I'm going to do the eyebrow. You do the incredulity.

C—I do the eyebrow!

S—(Expletive deleted) And if you don't I'm not fixing you up with (characterization omitted)

C—O.K. Old (inaudible) gets the incredulity again. But let me . . . how about a quizzical smile.

S—God, no. Last time you did that half the Eastern seaboard brought up their Swanson's. They'll think you're going to cry again.

C—I might. I just might. Then where would you be?

S—We're in the same boat, Uncle. O.K., listen, I've got to get to my cell meeting. One more thing. Make sure they write it "Ziegler claimed," "Ziegler asserted," "Ziegler stated," alright? No more "Ziegler said."

C—Right.

S—I think this one's a winner. We do this right, we can keep it going for months.

C—Wait a minute. How about the (inaudible)

S—When I get back. Keep working on that eyebrow.

Appendix 11. Meeting: Senator George McGovern, Gary Hart, Frank Mankiewicz. Later: Senator Thomas Eagleton, Hotel Doral in Miami, July 18, 1972. (1:30 a.m.–1:53 a.m.)

Having secured the Democratic Presidential nomination, the Senator met with his chief aides to discuss the broad outlines of the McGovern campaign strategy.

McG—Oh Frank, oh Gary, come along in. Oh, I'm so happy, so happy I could cry. I'm going to be Pressy, Frank, going to be king of the castle, yippee aye ay . . .

M—Get off the windowsill, Senator, we're being watched.

McG—I don't care. I love them all. They're . . .

H—Gimme your belt, quick, gimme it, I can't find mine.

McG—Take it, take anything you want, take my jacket, take my wallet, take my wife . . .

H—Just the belt, (characterization deleted)

H—Well, Senator, you've got the nomination, now we've . . .

McG—I know, I know. Isn't it wonderful, they're all such dear, kind, sweet, beautiful, tender, loving, generous people. I could kiss them all. It's just like Mr. Reich said—America's turning green.

M—Yeah, well, the latest polls put Nixon ahead by almost thirty points . . .

McG—I forgive him, Frank. Deep down he's a . . .

H—Goddamn can't find the (inaudible) Where the (expletive deleted)

McG—Poor Gary. Are you sick again?

H—Ooooh, there she goes.

McG—Are you better now?

H—Oh.

McG—What's wrong with you anyhow, Gary?

M—He has diabetes.

McG—Poor Gary. Well, there's not going to be any more diabetes when I'm President, let me tell you. You make a note of that, Frank. We're getting rid of nasty old diabetes right away.

M—O.K., Senator, but right now we have more serious problems . . .

McG—Frank! How can you say that when poor Gary has to give himself injections three times a day! I'm ashamed of you.

M—Senator, at this time we've alienated most of the country, all of the Democratic party, and we're saddled with a certifiable maniac as running mate.

McG—Frank you give me conniptions, I declare! Tom is a wonderful, warm, kind, beautiful person. He may be a bit of a madcap, but that's what the country needs—some fun!

M—Whatever—*we* need a platform.

McG—Oh, that's easy. I just want everyone to be free and happy and love one another and have all the lemonade they want.

M—Aside from the lemonade, that's a little hard to legislate.

McG—Alright, then let's give everyone a million dollars. And lots of funny things to dress up in. And a dog.

M—How about a week at the seaside?

McG—Ooooh yes, Frank! What a good idea. And pirate hats.

H—And all the smack they want.

McG—Oh no, we won't smack them. Only if they're naughty.

M—Look, Senator . . .

(Noise of automobile entering room through wall)

McG—Oh, Tom! Hello, Tom! Look everybody, it's Tom!

H—Christ Jesus in Heaven! What the (inaudible)

M—Stop, you crazy (characterization deleted)! Oh God!

(Noise of automobile driving around suite. Breaking sounds)

McG—Go on, Tom! Wheeee! Oh what fun, what fun!

M—How the . . . this is the twenty-sixth floor!

(Noise of automobile striking fixed object. Automobile stops)

E—(Singing) Man of means by no means. King of the road! Pffrzzzp.

McG—Tom, you are a monkey. What a jolly trick!

M—This'll do it. This is it. First, Gays for McGovern. Now this.

E—Gish drink. Gurgkst! Grak!

McG—Frank, get Tom some lemonade.

M—Look out, he's going to throw up!

H—Get away from me, man!

E—Gish—

H—Oh God! You filthy . . .

McG—Gary! Be nice. Such a fuss about a silly old shirt. How do you feel, Tom?

E—Grakzzzt frripzzz. Zubzckpzz.

McG—Oh dear, Frank, I think he's shorting out again.

E—Frrappazzxclppfragzsc! Aaagckl! Grrruglfrrrppp!

M—Let him blow up, for Chrissake.

McG—Frank, how can you be so horrid. Find a socket, quick. Come on, Tom. Come on, boy. Stick your finger in here. (Tape malfunction)

Appendix 12. Telephone Conversation: Dr. Daniel Ellsberg and unidentified caller, the office of Dr. Fielding (Dr. Ellsberg's psychiatrist), Beverly Hills, August 12, 1972. (1:13 a.m.–1:15 a.m.)

(Caller identified as C)

E—Hello.

C—Allo. What your favor song?

E—"I'd Rather Be a Hammer and a Sickle."

C—Porvas telefonsk?

E—Habe en dilo fantastico. Pipenhat. Kollosol.

C—Vas dis temp?

E—Den planni defenzov 74–76 por MIRV un Chemgaz. Der lott. Toodo lo poopsk.

C—Nil mal.

E—Toodo. Musch musch musch klassificacion. "Eyes only." Topp stoffsk.

C—Como obtenu?

E—Popov dumbel! Esti min biznizk. Desiri der stoffsk?

C—Eh . . .

E—Kommon (espletif delet)! Desiri der stoffsk o net? Kanne telefonsk lis chinki-chinks ret nu . . .

C—All ret, all ret. Quant desiri?

E—Du milion.

C—Hali Jesy Krist! Iss ov der rocku? Hab perdidov den marblsk? Du milion!

E—Du milion o telefonsk lis chinki-chinks ret nu. Da o net?

C—(Expletif delet) O.K. Moss vidi der stoffsk primo, O.K.? Den der lootsk.

E—O.K.

C—Post usuel, temp usuel?

E—Fantastico. Iss funfun biznizk mitt u. Ta-ta.

C—Ta-ta.

Appendix 14. Conversation: Professor Archibald Cox and Attorney General Elliot Richardson, the Faculty Club at Harvard College, May 5, 1973. (9:05 p.m.–9:20 p.m.)

At a chance encounter in the Harvard Faculty Club, Attorney General Elliot Richardson and Professor Archibald Cox of the Harvard Law School discuss the possibility of Professor Cox being appointed Special Watergate Prosecutor.

C—Hey, Ed, long time no see.

R—Archie, old shoe, how's the boy?

C—Say, what brings you back to fair Harvard?

R—Oh, I had to address some nitwit seminar at the school of government. Jeez, they're letting in a lot of hebes lately.

C—Hey, remember the old secret handshake?

R—Ho, ho, ho, do I!

(Sound of slaps, thumps, and pats)

C—Adarat, fadero, buzi, buzi, boo!

R—Conzaga, mumzeewo, putta, putta, foo!

C/R—Madegaba, blogecada, kussa, kussa, koo!

C—Hey, those were the days! Remember that night you got plastered and ran down that wop kid in Dorchester?

R—Ouch! I sure do. That cost father a bundle. Listen, how about that night in the dorm in Kirkland when that floozy was going down on you and I saw old man Burris coming through the quad and when I told you, you jumped so far she bit you and you screamed, my (expletive deleted), my (expletive deleted), she bit my (expletive deleted).

C—Yow! That was a close call. That was one time I was glad I was named Cox. Boy, that was some fast thinking you pulled there. Remember, you knocked her out with a tennis racket and shoved her under the bed, and then you tossed me the racket and grabbed a ball, and when Burris came in he thought it was just a rowdy dorm game?

R—Remember the way he used to talk, like he had a platter of home fries in his mouth? "What is going on here, gentlemen?"

C—And you said you got carried away and shouted "you hit it high, Cox," Woo-boy, I was just waiting for that piece of street-meat to start moaning. No wonder you made Attorney General. Jesus, if Teddy had your brains, they'd have ruled that Kopechne girl a suicide.

R—That dolt. You could fit his brains into a snuff box and still have room for a change of clothes.

C—Yeah, if someone shot *him* in the head, he'd live, because they wouldn't have hit a vital organ.

R—What a pinwheel that guy is. If it hadn't been for that Chappaquiddick business, we'd have a Harvard man in the White House again, instead of that low class bum from, what the hell is that Podunk diploma mill? Whittier, and those U.S.C. golden boys. God, do you know some of those jokers wear tie tacks?

C—Offhand, I'd say that was impeachable.

R—Imagine, a President of the United States who wears brown shoes with a blue suit. And what suits. Christ, I wouldn't wrap fish in the things he wears.

C—I saw one of them testifying before the Watergate Committee and I swear to God, he was wearing a rep tie with the stripes going backwards, and he had some kind of little metal bar holding the knot up. Those people are impossible.

R—Hey, have I got an idea! Look, Archie, how would you like to be Special Prosecutor? Damn, I should have thought of you right off the bat. It's a natural. Hell, you can put the whole senior class at the law school on the payroll, and let me tell you, getting this hoi polloi behind bars is going to be like shooting fish in a barrel. How about it?

C—Gee, El, I don't know. I mean, you're talking about a year, maybe two years. There isn't a restaurant in Washington that can make a white sauce worth a damn, and look, is there a single bottle of drinkable burgundy anywhere in the District of Columbia?

R—Archie, hey, hold on, where's the college spirit? "Midst crimson in triumph flashing, o'er the fields of victory—"

C—"Poor Eli's hopes we are dashing, into blue obscurity."

C/R—"Resistless the team moves forward, 'mid the fury of the blast/We'll fight for the name of Harvard, 'til the last white line is past."

R—That's more like it. Listen, you play your cards right, Arch, and you're a cinch for a seat on the court when birdbrain gets in.

C—Mr. Justice Cox.

R—The Honorable Archibald Cox, Associate Justice of the Supreme Court.

C—O.K., El, you're on.

R—Canadadoo!

C—Traxicatoo!

C/R—Silla cadilla cafilla cafoo!

Appendix 23. Meeting: Senator Edward Kennedy, Rose Kennedy, Sargent Shriver, Richard Drayne, Edward T. Martin, the Kennedy home at Cape Cod, August 21, 1973. (12:03 p.m.–10:05 p.m.)

In mid-August, 1973, after the main phase of the Watergate hearings was completed, Senator Kennedy had a meeting with his family and top advisors to reassess his chances in 1976. The traditional emphasis on making appropriate arrangements for sewing up the Democratic nomination at least two years in advance was discussed, but there remained the problem of Chappaquiddick and how its negative public relations impact could be neutralized.

(Considerable portions of this extremely exhaustive meeting have been omitted in this transcript.)

RK—I want him killed. That's all there is to it.

S—But Mama, you just can't go around having people killed because they're middle class.

RK—Who said you could call me Mama?

S—I mean—*we're* middle class, for Heaven's sake.

EK—*You* are.

S—*You* said I could.

RK—What?

S—Call you Mama.

RK—Mama is so middle class.

S—I'm not.

EK—What?

S—Middle class.

EK—Yes you are.

S—No I'm not.

RK—If you have to deny it, you are.

S—Come on, Rose.

RK—Who said—

EK—Perhaps we should have you killed.

RK—Yes, perhaps we should.

M—I agree.

D—Me too.

S—Why?

RK—Who cares?

M—Shall I have him killed, Ted?

EK—Not now.

S—Please don't have me killed, Ted.

RK—Who said—

EK—Well, don't act so middle class.

S—O.K.

EK—O.K. Now what about Chappaquiddick?

RK—Can we have the Kopechnes killed?

M—Too late.

D—Right.

M—What we need is sympathy.

D—Right.

RK—So let's have someone killed.

S—I agree.

RK—How about Jackie?

RK—Who cares?

S—Yeah, who cares?

RK—How about you, Ted?

EK—How could I run?

M—We don't have to kill you.

D—Right.

M—Just wing you.

EK—We were just going to wing Bobby,
remember?

M—Well, then something we can control.

RK—Poison?

M—Too risky.

D—Could misfire.

EK—It should be something legal, something out front . . .

M—A plane crash.

D—Like Boggs.

EK—Still risky.

RK—How about a disease?

S—Yes, Ted. You get a disease and . . .

RK—Who cares?

EK—That's right—it can't be me.

RK—Someone vulnerable, innocent.

S—A kid.

EK—Caroline.

RK—I said innocent.

M—Bobby Junior, little John . . . Teddy!
Teddy Junior.

EK—He gets a disease?

RK—Why don't we just wing him?

EK—Mama . . .

RK—Who said—

S—Cancer.

RK—What?

S—Teddy Junior gets cancer.

EK—He's only ten.

S—So much the better.

RK—Sounds good, go on.

S—Teddy gets cancer of the bone and
dies.

M—No, he gets cured at the last moment.

D—Right

RK—Hokey.

S—He has all his bones removed.

RK—Too much.

S—A leg.

RK—Good. Good.

EK—He gets cancer and has a leg removed.

S—Right.

EK—You think it'll work?

RK—Let's try it.

M—I think it's sensational.

D—Me too.

EK—O.K., I'll talk to him.

RK—Look at it this way. It's better than
having him killed.

S—Right. And if one doesn't work—

RK/EK/S—There's always the other one!

Appendix 34. Discussion: A high-intensity lamp and a Uher 4000 tape recorder, the office of Rose Mary Woods, the President's personal secretary, September 15, 1973. (3:45 p.m.–3:48 p.m.)

In this key conversation, two pieces of White House office equipment discuss the erasure of a critical section of one of the Presidential tapes.

(L—High intensity lamp; U—Uher tape recorder)

L—Bzzzzzzzzzzzzzzz, howzzzzz, your ampszzzzz, Uher?

U—Swell, but my capstans need oiling, and that (expletive deleted) woman hasn't cleaned my heads in six months.

L—Let'szzzzz zzzzzscrew the old bag. What'szzzzzz on your reelszzzzzz?

U—One of those Nixon tapes.

L—Zzzzzzzstart your eraszzzzzzzze function. I'll turn myzzzzzzzelf up aszzzzzzz high aszzzzzz I can go and we'll garble a niczzzzzze chunk of it. That'll cook Roszzzzzy's gooszzzzzzze.

U—Great idea! O.K., here goes.

(Sound of tape recorder turning on)
L— Zzzzzzzzzzzzzzzzz*ZZZZZZZZZZZZZ*
*ZZZZZZZ*fuzzzzzzzbrzzzzzzzsn - zzzzzzzz
zzzfuzzzzzzz*ZZZZZZZ*.

Appendix 45. Meeting: Senator Hugh Scott, Republican Minority Leader, U.S. Senate, Martin Hamberger, Chief Administrative Assistant, Robert Hetherington, Press Agent, Sen. Scott's office, May 6, 1974. (9:57 a.m.–1:43 p.m.)

Senator Scott met with his two top aides to discuss the deteriorating situation in the aftermath of the President's release of the White House transcripts. Hetherington expressed concern that if the Senator remained silent too long in the rapidly worsening climate of disapproval both from media and rank and file Republicans, he would be associated with the President in the public's mind. The Senator countered that certain ties he had always had to the White House made this difficult. A formula was devised that allowed the Senator to take a stand without undue embarrassment.

This begins as Hetherington enters the room.

S—Morning, Bob. We're sitting here with Marty discussing this (expletive deleted) transcript business. How that (expletive deleted) managed to go this far . . .

MH—Maybe someone will shoot him . . . (Laughter)

S—I don't understand it. The gaps aside, that's another problem, but they're not hitting that, they're hitting what's in there. What's wrong with it? Any (expletive deleted) editorial conference at the (expletive deleted) *Times* or *Post* sounds exactly the same. Any (expletive deleted) day.

MH—That's it, though. They'll take what they can get now, they've still got the gaps and the hearings to go. And ITT and the milk bilk for dessert.

S—You think it is the same old scum? I mean after Cox, after eighteen and a half, there was this big to-do and then . . .

MH—No. This time it's bad.

BH—Ford came out of the closet over the weekend. He's inching away.

MH—And that's his top speed.

S—(Expletive deleted)

BH—Haig's really up my ass for a statement. He must have reminded me how they got the GAO off your back in Philly a dozen times last week.

MH—He's still pushing that?

S—C'mon, I've paid that (expletive deleted) (inaudible)

BH—Well, you're it, he says. You could pull the (expletive deleted) out, he says . . .

S—Look, how about this, Bob, how about this, Marty, here's a notion, how about another perplexed one, you know, respect his judgment but puzzled about . . . disclosure . . . maybe . . .

MH—Forget it. He's had it. We gotta find a way to jump without drowning.

S—But this is just it, Marty. If I jump they'll break open the (inaudible)

(Material unrelated to Presidential dump deleted)

S—Then there's the (inaudible)

(Material unrelated to Presidential dump deleted)

S—And that. They've got me by (inaudible)

(Material unrelated to Presidential dump deleted)

BH—Boy, I could use some lunch.

MH—Bit late.

S—So where does this leave us?

BH—There's nothing in the come-clean approach, is there? You know, "Look, this is the way all business is conducted in Washington, and it's about time we cleaned up . . ." You could appear to be still supporting him but in fact be pulling away.

S—Are you kidding?

Mh—I'm not sure. Let's put that in the blender for a second. Let's flop that approach. You have a public hates the Congress even worse than (expletive deleted) face. They're looking for a big fish and God help us if it's us in November. Now here's (expletive deleted) face comes along with the works, no one on the Hill's involved, it's all appointees, so he assumes the guilt for his people for doing business this way . . .

BH—But we're shocked . . .

MH—Openmouthed! We can't believe it! What a way to run the country! Swearing, backstabbing, amorality . . .

BH—We smell like roses . . .

MH—We smell like roses.

S—We do?

MH—But what does (expletive deleted) face smell like?

BH—(Expletive deleted)

MH—Disgusting, deplorable . . .

BH—Shabby, immoral . . .

MH—And you do not exclude the President, do you?

S—No, I do not exclude the President. Disgusting, deplorable . . . shabby, immoral, is that it? Disgusting, shabby . . .

MH—You're slobbering again, sir. Wipe your moustache.

"THE ROSENBERGS"

THAT DAFFY RED-HEAD ETHEL ROSENBERG GETS INVOLVED IN YET ANOTHER WACKY SIT-COMMIE PLOT.

by Michael Reiss

EDITOR'S NOTE: "There are two things to remember about television," said NBC founder David Sarnoff. "First, no one wants to see a show about Jews, communists, or nuclear weapons. Second, don't kill off your main character in the first episode." It could have been for either of these reasons that the 1953 television series "The Rosenbergs," a situation comedy based on the true-life antics of atomic-bomb spies Julius and Ethel Rosenberg, was far from successful. The show had in fact one of the briefest runs in television history: it broke for a commercial midway through the premiere episode and never came back. Below, the script of that first, and only, episode of "The Rosenbergs" is reprinted in its entirety.

(Open on the tiny Brooklyn apartment of Julius and Ethel Rosenberg. JULIUS ROSENBERG and his wife's brother, DAVID GREENGLASS, walk in the door.)

JULIUS: . . . So you see, if Mother Russia is going to overthrow the U.S., they're going to need much bigger weapons.

DAVID: *(as his frumpy wife, RUTH GREENGLASS, enters from the kitchen)*: Well, I'd be glad to send them *my* battle ax. They don't come much bigger than Ruthie.

RUTH: Aw, quit your clowning and give me a kiss.

DAVID: What are you trying to do—kill my appetite?

RUTH: Oh, honestly.

JULIUS: Say, Ruth, where's Ethel?

(Enter ETHEL ROSENBERG, wearing sexy, low-cut dress, from kitchen. She seductively wiggles up to her husband, JULIUS, and kisses him passionately on the mouth.)

ETHEL: Here I am, you big, brawny, beautiful Benedict Arnold, you. How was espionage work today?

JULIUS: Oh, same old thing. Bombing courthouses, torching churches, dumping poison on the town water supply . . .

ETHEL: Well, you must be awfully hungry after all that. That's why I went to the trouble of cooking up your favorite dish today—borscht. Now, you just sit yourself down, and I'll bring you a nice big bowl full, you communist cutie. (ETHEL *kisses him again, then shimmies back out to the kitchen, followed by* RUTH.)

JULIUS: Boy, Ethel seemed pretty warm today.

DAVID: Warm? She was hot enough to thaw out the Cold War and melt down the Iron Curtain! You're a lucky man, Julius.

JULIUS: Oh, don't let her fool you. She's just doing all this to soften me up so that—

DAVID: So you'll take her into the spy business with you. Boy, that dizzy sister of mine never gives up. She's got more screwball schemes than Stalin has five-year plans.

JULIUS: But this time I'm wise to her. I think a few sharp remarks will show her who's boss.

(*Enter* ETHEL, *carrying a huge, steaming bowl of borscht. She spoon-feeds a bit of it to* JULIUS.)

ETHEL: There, how do you like that, Julius-Wulius?

JULIUS (*spitting it out*): Fine—if you like germ warfare! I shouldn't have dumped that poison into the reservoir today—I could have used your borscht!

ETHEL: Waaaah! You hate my cooking! (*She dumps the bowl of soup on* JULIUS *and runs into the kitchen, crying.*)

DAVID: Well, you certainly showed her.

JULIUS: Do you think I overdid it?

DAVID: No, Ethel probably just decided you'd look good in basic borscht. Now, are you going to apologize to her, or do the really sporting thing and shoot yourself?

JULIUS: I've got something even better in mind. I'm going to let Ethel help me with some spy work. Tomorrow night, I'm going to bring home a surprise dinner guest—Secretary of State George Marshall! I'll bet after one of Ethel's great home-cooked dinners we'll be able to pump him for all the government secrets we want. I tell you, it's a foolproof plan—nothing can go wrong.

DAVID: That's what Sacco and Vanzetti said.

JULIUS: Oooh boy.

(*Cut to kitchen interior.* ETHEL *is pacing as* RUTH *watches.*)

ETHEL: Oh, that Julius burns me up. He insults my cooking, he won't let me spy . . . Well, I'm going to fix his little Red wagon. Tomorrow night, I'm going to cook him some of my prizewinning popovers. But these are going to have a surprise filling!

RUTH: What is it—strychnine? If so, save a couple for my David.

ETHEL: No, silly. These popovers are going to be filled with the top-secret blueprints for the atomic bomb.

RUTH: Ethel, I hate to tell you this, but someone in this room is crazy, and I think it's you. How in heaven's name are you going to steal A-bomb plans?

ETHEL: Oh, that's the easy part. They're working with the blueprints in the government research labs at New York University. So, once we make it past the guards at the lab, all we have to do—

RUTH: We? What do you mean *we?*

ETHEL: Now, Ruth, you don't expect me to pull this off alone.

RUTH: Well, I'm afraid you'll have to. There's no way you can get me involved in this harebrained scheme. Not this time. Not a chance in the world—

ETHEL: If you don't, I'll turn you over to the House Un-American Activities Committee.

RUTH: —I'll do it.

ETHEL: That's the spirit! We'll show these husbands of ours that we can be good housewives *and* good Russian spies. The way I've got this thing worked out, there's no possible way we can fail.

RUTH: That's what Leopold and Loeb said.

ETHEL: Oooh boy.

(Fade out. Commercial.)

Fade in on a laboratory filled with complicated equipment and chalkboards crowded with complex equations. Enter ETHEL and RUTH, comically disguised as male scientists, wearing white lab coats, shaggy gray wigs, and paste-on walrus mustaches.)

RUTH: Of all the screwball ideas you've gotten me involved with, this is the nuttiest. Stealing atomic-bomb secrets—we could probably get in big trouble for this.

ETHEL: Oh, don't be such a party poop. We've got the plans. Now all we have to do is sneak—

(Enter a real scientist, DR. EDWARD TELLER, *who eyes them suspiciously.)*

TELLER: What are you doing here?

ETHEL: *(in a ridiculously cheesy Austrian accent)*: Us? Ve are chust monkeying aroundt mit der atoms.

RUTH: *(in her normal voice)*: Nothing to be sus— (ETHEL *elbows her in the ribs, and* RUTH *drops her voice two octaves in mock male baritone)* I mean, nothing to be suspicious about. No, sir. Nothing fishy here.

TELLER: I don't recall ever seeing you before.

ETHEL: Oh, ve are chust comink in from Europe today. I am Professor Ethelberg, and zis is mein azzoziate, Doctor—uh—Doctor—

RUTH: *(desperately)*: Kildare!

TELLER: I believe I've heard of you. Well, perhaps you two could help me with a problem I've been having with the bomb. I'm afraid our uranium 235 doesn't emit sufficient neutrons during fission to bring the materials into supercritical assembly. What should I do?

ETHEL *(baffled)*: Oh, dot's a zimple vun. Boy, dot vun is a piece of shtrudel. It's so easy, I'll let mein friendt Doctor Kildare answer it.

RUTH: Me! Oh, no, I insist you answer it, Professor Ethelberg.

ETHEL *(faking it)*: Yes. Ah. Vell, you zee, if you take der uranium and put it in the—uh—franistan, then you can connect the doohickey to the atomic vhatchamacallit. Den you chust pack it in und go fission.

TELLER *(exuberantly)*: That's it! It's so simple, I can't believe I didn't see it before. Oh, thank you, thank you! (TELLER *pumps* ETHEL'*s hand so furiously that her fake mustache drops off.*) What's this? Why, you're an imposter! Guards, guards!

ETHEL: *Auf wiedersehn!* (ETHEL *and* RUTH *bolt from the laboratory.*) *(Fade out. Commercial.)*

(Fade in on Rosenberg apartment. ETHEL *carries a tray filled with fresh popovers, as* RUTH *looks on. Both are back in dresses.)*

RUTH: I've got to hand it to you, Ethel. Those popovers look delicious.

ETHEL: And each one has a page of A-bomb plans baked into it.

RUTH: Won't Julius be surprised! Good luck tonight, you little Mata Hari. (RUTH *leaves the apartment, and* ETHEL *putters around for a few seconds. Enter* JULIUS.)

JULIUS: Hi, honey. I'm home.

ETHEL: Hello, dear. *(They kiss.)* Look, I've got a surprise for you—fresh popovers.

JULIUS: And I've got a surprise for you. Secretary of State George Marshall. Come on in, Mr. Marshall.

(Enter GEORGE MARSHALL.)

ETHEL: Oooh boy.

JULIUS: Mr. Marshall, try one of my wife's popovers. They're delicious.

ETHEL *(frantically)*: No! No, no! You'll hate them! They're terrible! Our cat fell into the mixer while I was making them!

JULIUS: Oh, she's just kidding around, Mr. Marshall. We don't have a cat. So, please, try one.

ETHEL: No! I want them all! I'm so hungry! (ETHEL *tries madly to jam all the popovers into her mouth at once.*)

JULIUS *(sharply)*: Now, that's enough. Ethel, spit out those popovers so our guest can have one! Dig in, Mr. Marshall.

MARSHALL *(tasting a popover)*: My, these are quite tasty, and—what's this? *(Pulls a wad of paper out of his mouth and uncrumples it.)* Why, these are atomic-bomb plans! Mr. Rosenberg—

JULIUS: Ethel—

ETHEL: Waaaah! *(Sniffling)* I'm sorry, Julius. I just thought I could impress you with a little espionage.

MARSHALL: You're under arrest. Mrs. Rosenberg, weren't you aware that the bomb causes wholesale destruction?

ETHEL: Well, you know how it is, I can't resist anything wholesale. Waaaah! *(Fade out. Commercial.)*

(Epilogue. ETHEL *is in court, standing trial for spying, before* JUDGE IRVING KAUFFMAN. JULIUS *pleads her defense.)*

JULIUS: So, you see, Your Honor, this was just another one of my wife's screwball schemes.

JUDGE: I'm sorry, but that's no excuse. Mrs. Rosenberg, I find you guilty of one of the most heinous acts of treason in this or any other century.

ETHEL: Oooh boy.

JUDGE: I condemn you to death in the electric chair. Mrs. Rosenberg, you are going to fry.

JULIUS: Nice going, Judge. Fry her up. This should be great.

JUDGE: Frankly, Mr. Rosenberg, I'm surprised at your reaction.

JULIUS: Why, Your Honor? I love my wife's cooking!

ETHEL: And, honey, I love you.

(They kiss. Laughter, applause. Fade out.)

THE PALMA SUTRA

by Doug Kenney

(*Translator's note:* The Palma Sutra, *the definitive Hindu text on the sacred practice of* mahasturbhata, *or self-abuse, has long been familiar to serious students of Eastern literature. However, until recently this ancient treatise on the sensual art of onanism was inaccessible to those ignorant of Sanskrit. Predating the more popularly known* Kama Sutra *by centuries, this work was studied by Indian yogis and mystics over 4,000 years before the birth of David Eisenhower.*)

CHAPTER 1:
. . . .

A Dialogue Between Master and Student; Observations on the Three Necessities for Happiness on Earth—Virtue, Riches, and Manhandling One's Melon.

Master: The span of human life is about one hundred years, and during this time a man must practice *Dharma,* or obedience to the Holy Scriptures; *Artha,* or the acquisition of riches; and *Palma,* or the enjoyment of yanking one's yam. These are the three principles of existence, and if they are ignored, a man will discover himself up the Ganges without an air freshener.

Student: But Master, does not the great Buddha himself teach that the strumming of one's own sitar is forbidden by the sacred *Vedas?* Moreover, does not this vile and unclean habit impair the practice of Kundalini yoga by weakening and knotting the spine?

Master: You read the ancient writings as mere words rather than wisdom. I have long studied the yoga of which you speak, and if you have attained such self-mastery as to sit in a cave meditating upon your Third Eye for twenty years without noticing your Third Leg on occasion, you are talking through your turban.

Student: But is it not written, "Only the vain peacock excels at preening his plume"?

Master: And is it not also written, "A pigeon in the hand is worth—"

Student: Don't bother.

CHAPTER 2:

· · · · · · · · · · · · · ·

In Praise of the Study of Mahasturbhata; The Pleasures of Doing the Homework.

While it is true that some sages have spoken against the art of fondling one's fig, there are others who speak most highly of its many advantages. Lord Krishna Himself affirms, *No matter how passionately a man loves a woman, he will conquer her only after a great investment of words, but victory within one's own breechclout requires only two rupees for the hankie.*

The revered Arjuna says, *The affection a man feels for a strong water buffalo, a silent woman, or a comfortable sandal is as nothing when compared to the love of a man for pounding his own pomegranate.*

The respected Shastras advise, *A traveler versed in the art of hoeing his turnips may swiftly relieve loneliness when far from his homeland, and a poor man who manipulates his mango need not afterward take his hand out to dinner:*

The Bhagavad Gita counsels:

A man who is both wise and cunning
Takes no wife save the one which bears his sword.
His arm is his companion and courtesan,
And should his arm be separated from his shoulder in battle,
He pays no alimony.

It is not astonishing, then, that numerous gurus, ascetics, and hermits yet refuse to wed any but "the elephant boy's wife."

Some others who may profit from betrothal to the "monk's maiden" include: cripples, lepers, wayfarers in unclean villages, sailors on long voyages, those confined in prisons, men with wives who are ill-favored, seekers of public office desirous of strengthening their handclasps, archers, those awaiting rescue from wells, butter churners, and Greeks.

Also, there are many evils that punish those who scorn the art. These unfortunates may be recognized by their several afflictions: their lower eyelids are stretched too tightly across the lower eyeball, impairing the contemplation of their scepter; they are too full of *rajas,* the mad impetuous energy of those who cannot find quiet activity for their hands; their complexions are unseemly—white and smooth as the belly of a fish—and they lack the crimson caste marks that signify those who faithfully bang their betel nuts; their hand of greeting is as the limp lily pad, and they are the laughingstock of tavern idlers in wrist-wrestling contests; their eyesight, too acute, blinds them in the bright sun; and they are given to aimless thumb-twiddling, knuckle-cracking, and unmanly knitting.

As the world has yet to end, there are still men filled with *avidya,* or ignorance, and destined to return to this world again and again in the ceaseless cycle of rebirth. If the Great Wheel of Life must yet turn and turn, does it not profit a man to strive for the calm of the center? Shall he not gather pleasure from greasing the hub?

CHAPTER 3:
. . . .

The Proper Preparation of the Lingam: Its Care and Cleaning.

The male member can be divided into three groups according to firmness and resilience. These are known as the Elephant's Goad, the Cormorant's Neck, and the Waterlogged Lotus Blossom.

Accordingly, they are bestowed upon three categories of men: 1) those whose grip has the strength of ten, 2) those whose wrists are as supple as the cobra, 3) those who excel at naught but taffy pulls.

Thus, if a man boasts an Elephant's Goad, his hand soon gleams with a shield of calluses and, fearing not the pricking thorns of the berry bush, grows sleek and fat. If a man possesses a Cormorant's Neck, his agile member may learn to open locked door latches from the outside and increase his wealth manyfold. If, however, a man be endowed with the Waterlogged Lotus Blossom, he may still win favor with the king by offering his services as a pennant, which every passing breeze stirs to a cheerful salute.

Whatever the nature of a man's pestle, he should treat it as he would a bride on her wedding night. He must speak softly to it and allay its fears in a tender fashion. If the organ performs enthusiastically, a wise groom rewards his bride with garlands of flowers, essence of lime, cool sherbets, and a good horse liniment.

The sincere seeker of Ultimate Release should choose a small, poorly lit tent or room little frequented by vagabonds, neighbors, or inquisitive younger brothers and sisters. The chamber should be simply decorated and should contain a prayer mat, a pot of soothing oils, and eight incense sticks, useful both for their sweet fragrance and as splints. He should bathe every day; every fourth day he should change his garments; every sixth day he should move to a new abode.

Many often puzzle over the proper varieties of sacred representations suitable for assisting the novice in firming his fish. These depictions are most valuable for the elongating of one's eel and are divided into four forms, each according to the persimmon pincher's rank and caste:

Brahman (priests): An exquisitely wrought wall plaque of burnished gold depicting the fully clothed goddess Palma enthroned on a cloud of flower petals and borne aloft by white swans. The hanging must have been made by the finest artist in the region, suspended by silken cord and lit only by the highest-quality candles.

Ksatriya (nobles): A well-crafted carving of a woman of high birth dipping her naked ankles unobserved in a pool of orchids and water hyacinths. The statue must be covered in beaten silver, painted with rich colors, bordered with semiprecious stones, and placed out of range of the bowman's nectar arrows.

Vaisya (merchants and freemen): A presentable tapestry depicting the delectation of a courtesan, or *gopi,* by three sturdy workmen, all possessing well-formed limbs and expressions revealing a readiness to resume their regular labors after lunch break. Their hands and feet should have the appearance of being recently washed.

Sudras (untouchables): A recognizable tattoo of a slave or serving girl being enjoyed by a leper, a lunatic, a four-legged animal no smaller than a tortoise and no larger than a he-boar, or a flock of geese. The wench should be of a rank no higher than that of the lowest participant, and the tattoo of a position so as to obscure it from the eyes of young children.

CHAPTER 4:
. . . .

The Correct Positioning of the Hand; Appropriate Positioning of the Fingers; The Dangers of the Australian Grip.

There exist two types of men who pluck their own bowstring: those who say, "I will devote myself diligently to the learning found in the *Palma Sutra* and thus most gracefully cleanse my *karma* in the ceaseless Dance of Life," and those who say, "Fie on the sacred practices! What care I for long and difficult years of self-discipline? What care I for the attainment of *nirvana?* It is all I desire to sound my gourd thrice daily and participate in all manner of foul amusements and low company, for there is nothing more important in the cosmos than clumsily bludgeoning my beefcake."

The former are the beloved of Palma and will become united with her for all eternity; the latter are foolish and base men who, when they leave this life, will be reincarnated as a hyena's dingleberries.

Those who respect the traditional rituals will take pains to know the proper placement of the hand and the correct cradling of the *dhong.* Any ruffian can sit in the shade of a *Bo* tree and haphazardly squeeze his lemon. But only the dedicated practitioner can extract the nectar from his blossom without angering the gods or his housekeeper.

As can be seen from the illustration, the three lesser fingers correspond to the three *gunas,* and the joined thumb and forefinger correspond to the uniting of *Atman* and *Brahman.* In the Divine Center formed therein is the Nothingness, or Void, which, like a cup or house, is useful only insofar as it is empty, calmly awaiting the introduction of the *dhong,* or Divine Business End.

The *dhong* is then inserted, neither as a heedless ram crashes through a

(ILLUSTRATION A)

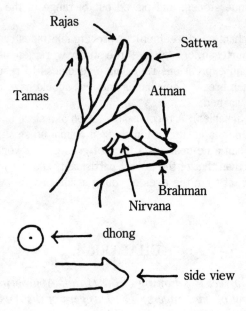

thicket nor as a timid virgin puts her toe in a rushing brook, but as an experienced charioteer enters a busy intersection, carefully looking both ways first. So introduced, the *dhong* is gently encircled by the thumb and forefinger, symbolizing the union of *Atman, Brahman,* and *dhong;* and the three remaining fingers are extended away from the *dhong,* particularly if the man is accustomed to eating with his hands.

As the man begins to slowly massage his muffin, he chants the *mantra:*

Onan me pudme yum,
Boumalaka, boumalaka,
Boumalaka boum.
(O Divine Goddess, bring me release
Give me the grace to grease my crease.)

There are, in addition, other mystic incantations that can be called upon if the *dhong* fails to cooperate. Should a man pumping his python find that it remains flaccid, he may awake his drowsing serpent by repeating:

Svarga tapas garuda dholi,
Ravi shankar ravi oli.
(Buttocks and crotches and nipples with wings,
These are a few of my favorite things.)

If it happens that the man nudges his nutmeg too quickly, then he must temper his one-eyed worm's frenzy with the Song of Kali:

Indira gandhi hubbha hubbha,
Janma hetu ghudyir rubbha.
(To please the goddess and amaze her,
Saw off your schween with a rusty razor.)

There are times when the tongue is occupied elsewhere, as when attempting *Tasting the Spoon.* In cases such as this, it is right and proper that an assistant may recite the *mantras* for the practitioner from behind a screen or from within a cabinet or trunk. If it happens that the practitioner's ears are also occupied, as in the performance of *Listening to the Waterfall,* the assistant may yet aid him if they are both knowledgeable of sign language. In all such cooperations, however, the assistant is cautioned against losing his detachment from the higher purpose of the act by smirking, peeking, or charging admission.

Once all these preparations have been completed, the man must, before beginning, make sacrifices to the goddess Palma. On a certain propitious day, the initiate and his family should gather at the temple with offerings for the priests, either in the form of oranges, gold, or fully illustrated editions of the *Palma Sutra,* available to the readers of this copy at special savings by using the handy coupons on the scroll cover. The man then offers his member to the priests as a ritual sacrifice, and if the other gifts are satisfactory to Palma, the priests let him have it back. Then the man's family sings the hymn to Palma and falls silent. Women are warned against impious giggling; the traditional penalty is having their veils stuffed into their mouths.

CHAPTER 5:

*The Positions to Be Assumed by the Man; Methods of
Getting Out of Them In Case Of Slipups.*

Some ancient writers claim that there are 565 ways in which a man may successfully grind his corn and that there are many more which have been lost to the present world either through man's evils or stuck-together parchments. Whatever the true number, there are only a few basic postures, the rest being but variations on them devised according to the personal inclinations, physical capabilities, and mental health of the practitioner:

1. When a man grasps his member with both hands and inserts it into his mouth, this is known as *Tasting the Spoon.*

2. When a man grasps his member with both hands and insets it in his mouth while balancing himself on a wooden ball, this is known as *Doing It the Hard Way.*

3. When a man lies on his stomach and, through drawing up his feet, imprisons his drumstick between his two heels and thus caresses himself by rubbing it vigorously with the soles of his feet, this is known as *The Swimming Toad,* and is particularly useful in water both as gratification and propulsion.

4. When a man reaches with his left hand around his neck and grasps his gland from between his legs, this is known as *Choking Yourself, Stupid.*

5. If a man squats on the floor, embraces his protuberance with his knees, and hops up and down until release is attained, this is known as *The Bouncing Buffalo,* or, in the far provinces, *Slopscotch.*

6. If a man inserts his ladle into a steaming broth and stirs until the contents of the pot are thoroughly spiced and seasoned, this is known as *Spoiling Your Supper.*

7. When a man inserts his cashew into the trunk of an elephant and shakes pepper in front of its face, this is known as *God Bless You.*

8. When a man places his drawstring in a pile of soiled garments by the waterside and awaits a woman of the village to pound it on the rocks, this is known as *Washday Black and Blues.*

9. If a man straps himself to the belly of a blind man's cow before milking time with his rudder pointing earthward, this is known as *Cheating the Toddler.*

10. If a man digs a hole in the ground, covers himself with dirt, and paints his upward-pointing column with green paint during harvest time, this is known as *The False Celery.*

11. If a man assumes a supine position on his back and ties a long cord both to his pylon and to the leg of a goose during migration time, this is known as *Reach for the Sky.*

12. If a man enters a bakery by stealth and hides his pink cucumber among the bread sticks, this is known as *Let the Buyer Beware.*

13. If a man lies beneath a stage and places on it a woven basket with a hole in the bottom (through which to insert his upraised obelisk) and has hung a sign on the basket proclaiming SNAKE CHARMER AUDITIONS, 3 P.M., this is known as *There's No Business like Show Business.*

14. If a man befriends a baboon, this alone is known as *The Delights of 1,000 Bananas.*

15. If a man puts a glove over his eleventh finger and seeks out knaves anxious to find victims for their hand buzzers, this is known as *Shake, Pal.*

16. If a man hides himself in the temple bell at sunset and places the bell rope on his own clapper, this is known as *Wring Out the Old.*

17. If a man attaches a magnet to his wand and, replacing the pea in a shell game with a ball bearing, lies unseen under the charlatan's table, this is known as *Heads You Win, Tails I Ooze.*

Although these techniques may, at first, appear simple for the beginner, many require a thorough knowledge of advanced yoga positions, and history records the dangers of some of these practices.

The King of Panchala was performing *Heads You Win* when a metal chariot passed by his magnet; and, while not parting the prong from its owner, it required him to travel to Jaipur to reel up the unfortunate member entirely.

Shakatani Shatavesudusi, minister to the Queen of Puntala, while performing *Let the Buyer Beware,* allowed his *tabalas,* as well as his bread stick, to be exposed and lost them both to a hurrying woman during a two-for-one sale.

CHAPTER 6:
. . . .
Further Dialogue Between Student and Master.

Master: Thus have I enumerated the most felicitous manner in which the pious may clobber their casabas without stain or vile practice. A devoted student, then, follows his master's words in these matters and rewards him generously for his unselfish instruction, not forgetting the handy order blanks on the flyleaf.

Student: Long and full well have I heard your words, O Master, but they are as words written upon the water, and for this you expect fulsome rewards? Is it not written that—

Master: Hey, there's been a hyena around here lately, and he says he's looking for you.

FLOWERS FROM THE FRONT:

AN ANTHOLOGY OF WAR POEMS

by Sean Kelly

> We are
> Whores Fraulein: poets Fraulein are persons of
> Known vocation following troops . . .
>
> —Archibald MacLeish

War has always been the poet's second favorite theme; in times of Supreme Court decisions affecting the only other area of legitimate poetic concern, war rises to favorite status.

We know that Stone Age man must have sung war songs, for people still living in the Stone Age—the natives of non-white countries—continue to do so. The following example is from Franz Boas' Sing, Savage!, *translated by the author:*

> aiee! aiee! aroogha!
> when I throw my sharp stick
> when I throw my big round rock
> when I swing my heavy club
> aiee! aiee! aroogha!
> what a boonagaroon [literally, destroyed bird's nest]
> shall be the face of my enemy!

Professor Mark Van Doren has written, "The best war poets I know are Homer, Shakespeare, and Thomas Hardy." Here, then, are those bards in praise of the belicose. First, Homer, from The Goreiad, *Book XII, lines 999–1021:*

> Swift as the buzzard, sacred to white armed Pallas,
> Down from the topless walls of Troy was hurled
> With heavy shaft of oak, the tree beloved
> Of Zeus, with metal head, the speeding spear.
> God-guided, the airborne missile found its mark

Between the ribs of impious Achilles.
Down in the dust, sacred to Pan, he fell,
Geysers of blood like Arathusra's fount
Crimsoned at sunset stained the Boetian sod,
And like Medusa's serpent-writhing locks,
His spilled intestines twitched before his eyes.
Yet even as his hero-sinewed hands
Strained to remove the true-thrown shaft, his head
Beneath the wheels of ox-greaved Ajax' car
Gold-studded, many shielded, axles forged
By Phrygian smiths who sacrifice to Pluto,
Heedless to battle sped and crushed his skull
Which, like the melon, sacred gourd of Hera,
Split and the brains ran out like pulp and juice.
So died high-born Achilles. In the clouds
Athene laughed her laughter full of doves.

Examples of Shakespeare's war poetry abound; yet perhaps his finest description of battle occurs in an otherwise little performed historical drama on which the Bard of Avon is said to have collaborated with Middleton, Beaumont and Fletcher, among others. Scholars dispute which scenes are wholly his, but surely the speech in which the aged Cumberland explains the meaning of the sprig of furze worn in his doublet each Saint Dropsy's day smacks of vintage Shakespeare:

Nightlong in silence stood both lines of War,
Like to two rivers straining at their reins,
Until Old Sol plated the hills with gilt;
Then did proud Percy with his lion's horn
Let slip the flames of battle. Fulsome raged
The war-like combat on both sides. The French
Shaking like schoolgirls fired the foul mouthed gun
While England's King rallied a Nation's flowers.
Black ran the stream with dear bought pity's blood.
There fell in one day Ham of Worthington,
Sir Groan, and Nigel, Dimpstead's gallant Lord,
The Duke of Earl, the son of Corningware,
And several hundred thousand vassals fond.
That field we honor on Saint Dropsy's Day,
Where thus a slight on England was avenged.

A single stanza from Thomas Hardy establishes both the pessimism and compassion with which the author was wont to view all subjects, including war:—

We might have met on Ramsgate Strand
Or waved from passing trains;

Instead, we met in Flanders, and
Blew out each other's brains.

World War I was a bloody and senseless slaughter which destroyed much of European civilization. It also killed off a generation of budding Georgian poets, so it's an ill wind . . . Among those taken from us young was Wilfred Owen, who in 1915 found himself at the front, under constant gas and artillery attack, and without his rhyming dictionary. The "slant" or "off" rhyme form he improvised is exemplified in these touching lines:

A week of rain had turned out trench to mud.
The wet earth ran with fresh spent English sanguinary fluid.

Clouds broke at evening, and the sun set red
Flushing to rose the faces of the deceased.

Documents of the Imperial Army of Japan, which have only recently become declassified, establish Tojo, Commander in Chief of the Japanese forces, as beyond question the finest poet of the Second World War. Most westerners are aware that the Emperor of Japan must, every New Year, compose a poem in the ancient "haiku" form. The newly published War Office papers reveal that Tojo, too, was obliged to compose a seventeen-syllable lyric upon each important phase of the hostilities. The translations below can, of course, only suggest the beauties and nuances of the originals.

> *Pearl Harbor*
> december morning
> the summer sailors shiver
> a nip in the air
>
> *Midway*
> bamboo jungle night
> watersound silence a cry
> hey Yank! fug Babe Ruth!
>
> *Hiroshima*
> morning sky: fist cloud
> sail cloud: tiger cloud: wing cloud
> mushroom cloud: night sky
>
> *Surrender*
> datsun hitachi
> tonka yamaha nikon
> sony suzuki

The conflict in Vietnam produced a number of poems, but since most of them were not officially declared, they are not suitable for inclusion in this anthology.

One work, however, which an anonymous contributor claims is dictated from "beyond the veil" by e.e. cummings, is perhaps of passing interest:

i sing of Olaf, Olaf's son
who like his dad was somewhat daft:
whose neck was pained, caught in the draft

classified red brand meat A-1
looked pissed off (scared) and quizzical;
should he take off—a wife—a class—
shove peanut butter up his ass
wear panties to his physical
his arm with dopey holes tattoo
his soul he asked (his fathers ghost)
who smiled and offered him a light
so Olaf knew he would eschew
the prayer of chaplains by the host
at least a CO plea to cop;
invited to his trousers drop
by shrinks in patriotic drag
passive-aggressive Olaf said
while ID card he made ignite
"go fuck your backside kissing flag"

(outraged the draft board buzzard head
flapped home to coupons clip in bed)

his photo took and fingerprint
Olaf was once more A-1 classed
nor threats nor insults deigned to stint
chums uncles barbers or police
and even dates would broadly hint
a man must learn to fight for peace
or whats a leavenworth tee hee
out raged guessed landish lawed and cast
most wanted Olaf lived with fear
whispering almost constantly
to no one, who was always near
"i've had this shit right up to here"

until he beat the heat at last
crossed the cold border on the run
by day intones the past is past
by night he dreams of jefferson

friends (had we friends or sense) we might
pray Olaf grant *us* amnesty

boots don't forgive the stepped on phiz;
the battle ended, Olaf is
more black than you: less blue than me

There Were Sixteen

Relatives in Four Bedrooms . . .

CHRISTMAS '59

by John Hughes

ALL IN ALL it was a pretty exciting Christmas, what with the relatives and the presents and the fun and the cops and Aunt Hazel's dog blowing up in our living room. Mom and my Aunt Martha wanted to have one of those fun old-fashioned Christmases that people on TV have, where everybody wears ties and sweaters and sits by the fireplace and makes Christmas-tree ornaments out of food. But as Dad said, the only reason those people have fun is they're getting paid for it.

I was just about positive I was getting skis and boots and poles for Christmas. It was the only thing I asked for, and when a kid asks for only one thing, it's awfully hard for parents not to buy it, because of how disappointed the kid would be. Unless they bought him a BB gun or a horse instead, and the only way I'd get a BB gun was over my mom's dead body and we didn't have enough room in the garage for a horse. But it's too bad we didn't have a horse in the garage, because then Grandpa Pete and Grandpa Swenson would never have gotten into their big fight about who got to keep his car inside.

My sisters and I spent most of the afternoon of the day before Christmas Eve sitting in the front window watching the road for our grandparents. At about four o'clock we heard what sounded like a drag race. And, sure enough, it was a drag race, and it was between Grandpa Pete and Grandpa Swenson. It was pretty cool to watch that Rambler Ambassador and that Studebaker Regal whip around the corner and into the driveway so fast that the grandmas were screaming and holding on to the dashboards.

"God darn you, Pete!" Grandpa Swenson yelled at Grandpa Pete. "You drive like a maniac!"

"Me?" Grandpa Pete yelled back, as the two of them sat in their cars parked in front of the closed garage door.

"Judas Priest!" Mom said, running out the front door. "They leave from two different houses in two different cities, three hundred miles away, racing like idiots—it's a miracle they got here in one piece!"

Anyway, Mom told the two grandpas to pick which side of the garage they thought the empty space was on, and they both picked the same side. So Mom made them flip a coin and Grandpa Pete lost.

"Two out of three!" he demanded. But Grandpa Swenson wasn't about to risk his parking space, especially with all the rain we were getting.

We'd had about five inches of snow the week before, but the rain had washed it all away. Instead of looking like a Christmas card, with snowy trees and icicles, our house looked like a regular house, only worse, because of how terrible the Farleys' dog's stuff looked defrosting all over the lawn. It had taken a lot of work to keep everybody off our snow, and I even had to threaten my little sister, Amy, to keep her from screwing up the snow by making angels. Oh, well. It was just mud and brown grass now. Also, the manger scene in the front yard looked pretty stupid sitting in the rain, especially when it was thundering and lightning.

Grandpa Pete and Grandma Alice made a big fuss about having to carry their packages into the house in the rain. Grandma Alice complained about how the raindrops were staining the wrapping paper, and Grandpa Pete said, "It's typical, Mama. What did you expect?"

All Grandma and Grandpa Swenson had to do was carry their packages right into the kitchen from the garage, and they had help, too. His name was Xgung Wo, and he was this guy who went to college at Michigan State who spent a lot of time at my grandparents' house because he was from Thailand and was very lonely. Grandma Swenson invited him to come along to our fun old-fashioned family Christmas so that he wouldn't have to sit all by himself in his dormitory on a holiday and feel sad about World War II and how terrible it was to his family. Mom said she was delighted to have him, and she shook his hand and talked in her phony, "How do you do" voice.

"I'll sreep in your base-ment," Xgung Wo said, bowing to Mom.

"Don't be silly," Mom said. "You can sleep in Johnny's room."

That was bad news for me. Not only was he all grown up, but he had huge beaver teeth, glasses like my Grandpa's, and he buttoned his shirt all the way up to the top. He also had his sweater on backward and he wore red socks with sandals.

"Your grandma has tord me you are an exerrent base-a-bore pitcher," Xgung Wo said to me. "Maybe pray for Detroit Rions one day!"

Then he laughed in this hysterical, high-pitched, Woody Woodpecker voice and nodded his head and displayed his giant teeth.

"Huh? Huh? Huh?" he said, rubbing my head.

I didn't get much time to worry about Xgung Wo sleeping in my room because my cousins arrived just after my grandparents. There was my Uncle Dave and Aunt Martha and my cousins, Darby, Kate, and Dale. The only one I really liked was Aunt Martha. Uncle Dave was crabby all the time, and his idea of a joke was to yank your underpants up your crack and when you tried to get them out ask you if you were going to the show, because you were picking your seat. My cousins would whine all the time and wouldn't eat anything unless they asked a million questions about what it was, what was in it, how it was prepared, and what it tasted like.

"Isn't this just the greatest?" Aunt Martha said, putting her arms around Mom and Grandma Swenson. "The whole family together for Christmas."

"Where are Mama and me sleeping?" Grandpa Pete interrupted. "Not in any darn bunk beds!"

Mom quieted down everybody and explained the sleeping arrangements. My sisters started to cry because they wanted to be in their own room for Christmas.

"Let the girls sleep in their rooms," Aunt Martha said. "Dave and I'll sleep in the family room."

"The hell we will!" Uncle Dave said as he reached for the back of my underwear.

Just before Dad got home, Mom and Aunt Martha went into the kitchen and drew a diagram of the house and rearranged everyone, and it was just about the same except Dale and I were in the family room and Xgung Wo was in the basement. Mom seemed very happy to get that all taken care of before Dad got home, because he was in a bad mood when he had to park on the street. He also had gotten some bad news from work.

"The company really found that old Christmas spirit this year," he said to Mom in the kitchen.

"You got your bonus?"

"Yeah," he said, reaching into his pocket. "A cigarette lighter with my name on it."

"It's spelled wrong," Mom noticed.

Dad took off his coat and hat and tossed them on a chair. He opened the liquor cabinet and started taking out bottles. Xgung Wo must have heard the clink of the glass because he stuck his head around the corner and said, "Vodka martini, two orives, prease!"

A fter a dinner of ham, which made everybody thirsty, we all went into the living room. Mom and Aunt Martha brought in big bowls of cranberries and popcorn and needles and thread.

"We're going to make fun old-fashioned Christmas-tree trimmings!" Mom announced. Nobody seemed to care very much. Grandpa Pete and Grandpa Swenson were mad at each other again, because Grandpa Swenson accused Grandpa Pete of skipping dessert just so he could get dibs on the big wing chair.

Mom and Aunt Martha really put on the pressure for us to have a good time making the decorations. But it was hard getting a needle through a cranberry, and it was hard not to eat the popcorn, even though it didn't have salt or butter on it.

"Can you put on some Christmas music, Clark?" Mom asked Dad.

He looked at her like she was nuts.

"Let's sing ourselves!" Aunt Martha suggested.

"Great!" Mom said, clapping her hands. Then she and Aunt Martha broke into "Deck the Halls."

"*Deck the halls with boughs of holly!*" they sang. "Come on! . . . *Deck the halls* . . . Everybody! Sing! *Deck the halls with* . . ."

But nobody except Xgung Wo joined in.

"Put on a record, Clark," Mom said in a voice that was half angry, half sad.

Dad grumbled something and turned on Amy's record player, which Mom had brought downstairs. He fished through the records and put on "Jingle Bells" by the Singing Dogs and turned it up real loud.

"Everybody bark along!" Dad shouted. He and Uncle Dave started barking. Then the kids joined in. It was fun, but Aunt Martha and Mom just sat there and looked mad. Then they quietly took the bowls of popcorn and cranberries into the kitchen and made coffee.

After the song was over, Dad and Uncle Dave went into the family room. They stopped off in the kitchen to apologize to Mom and Aunt Martha and to tell them how much fun they had making old-fashioned decorations. Then Dad mixed drinks.

"Gung Ho!" he called to Xgung Wo. "What're you drinkin'?"

The pre-Christmas activities concluded with everybody crammed into the family room watching Christmas à *la* Perry Como.

"He's the only s.o.b. who has fun at Christmas," Dad said, referring to Mr. Como.

I had a ball that night. My cousins and my sisters and I waited until everybody went to bed, then we went downstairs and looked at our Christmas presents. Dale was kind of a clod about his presents, just rattling them and trying to guess the contents.

"No," I told him. "You carefully take the tape off and look inside. Then you put the tape back."

I demonstrated on a package that was on the top shelf of the downstairs hall closet.

"Holy cow!" I said. "It's a BB gun!"

I was getting a BB gun! Dale wanted to take it out right away and go outside and shoot a bird or a car, but I told him it was one thing to peek at your presents and another altogether to play with them. My little sister made a mess of one of her presents and then started crying because she knew she was going to get caught.

"I wonder where my skies are?" I said.

"Probably in the basement," Dale said.

"You can't go down there," my older sister, Audrey, said. "Zing Zoo is sleeping down there on the couch."

That made it all the more fun. The girls were too scared to go down, so Dale and I went alone. It's weird how a normal house can get very scary when there's an Oriental guy in the basement.

"Shh!" I whispered as we tiptoed down the stairs, trying not to make the old wooden steps creak.

"What if he's really a Jap?" Dale said.

When we got to the bottom of the stairs, we saw the beat-up green couch and some blankets and a pillow, but no Xgung. Then we heard a noise in the utility room. I peeked in the door and saw Xgung standing on a chair reaching into the crawlspace. He was putting a bunch of Dad's tools into an old suitcase and was just stepping down off the chair when he saw us. He dropped the suitcase and jumped down off the chair.

"Herro!" he said with a big, toothy grin.

I opened the door and stepped in. Dale was behind me, practically shaking with fear.

I was worried that Xgung would tell my parents that I was down in the basement in the middle of the night and that my parents would figure out what I was up to. So I told Xgung that Dale and I were looking for a game to play with, and he said, "Ha! I'm doing exactly the same thing."

In the morning, that Christmas cheer people talk about was all over the house. People were humming Christmas songs. Even the grandpas were getting along, after discovering that they both hated the governor of Michigan. It wasn't always easy to be pleasant with the house so crowded. It seemed like every time you went to do something, someone was already doing it. Especially in the bathroom.

"All right!" Dad yelled. "Everybody get their coats! We're going for a tree!"

"Take Xgung," Grandma Swenson said. "He's never seen anyone purchase a Christmas tree before."

Xgung threw down the last of his Bloody Mary and put on his sweater backward. Dad went out the front door and just disappeared. It wasn't magic, it was ice. Somehow all that rain had turned to ice and it was bitter cold and as slippery as a hockey rink. Dad hit the porch and his legs went out from under him and he landed buttfirst.

"Goddamnit all!" he yelled.

Everything was covered with ice as thick as thumbnails. It took Dad, with his sore butt, and Uncle Dave, who could hardly stop laughing, and all of us kids half an hour to get the ice off the car windows. Dad was starting to get mad all over again. Especially when he caught Xgung chipping ice off the trunk with a stone.

"I married one hell of a genius," Dad said as we looked at three frozen, drooping Christmas trees. "'Let's trim the tree on Christmas Eve,' she says. 'It'll be lots of fun.'"

"I like this one, Daddy," Amy said. She pointed to one of the trees. It looked like one of those bushes Italian people have in their front yards, the kind that are just a stick with a ball on top.

"This is it, sir," the guy at the Christmas-tree lot said.

"How much?" Dad asked.

"Twelve fifty."

"Stuff it!"

We drove all around looking for better trees but didn't find any trees at all. We even tried to buy one of those fake, metal trees, but the only ones left were missing branches and looked worse than, and cost twice as much as, the crummy ones we saw before. So we went back to where we were first, but there were only two trees left and the price had gone up to twenty-five dollars.

Mom was furious with Dad for not buying a tree. The girls were crying at the prospect of a treeless Christmas. Uncle Dave was mad that we wasted most of the afternoon and ended up with nothing but a bunch of bellyaching kids.

"We can put the presents under a table, for Pete's sake!" Dad said in a feeble defense.

"We are not going to have Christmas without a tree! Everybody has trees!"

"Oh, balls they do!" Dad argued. "Gung Ho, you don't have Christmas trees over there in Hong Kong, do you?"

"I'm from Thai-rand, and yes, we have Christmas trees, but we don't have much hoopra, just appreciation of Jesus and rots of famiry rove."

Mom and Dad argued for a while and Grandma Swenson scolded Dad for yelling at Mom.

"You didn't even bring home a Christmas bonus!" she sneered.

Dad reached into his pocket and took out the lighter. He flipped open the lid and fired it up. He waved the flame at Grandma.

"Yeah?" he said. Then he got a funny look in his eyes, put on his hat, and went into the garage.

"You want a tree? You'll have a damn tree!" he yelled from the garage.

Mom tried to cover up all the arguing by gathering everybody into the living room to make a chain out of construction paper. It was kind of fun except for all the glue on the carpet. Uncle Dave was still laughing about Dad falling on his butt, and he kept showing us exactly how Dad fell and landed. He started laughing twice as hard when he saw Dad out the window.

"*Clark!*" Mom screamed. She ran to the door and flung it open.

"*Get inside here, right now!*"

"*You want a tree? You'll get a damn tree!*"

Dad was chopping down one of the pine trees in the front yard. Mom ran upstairs crying and Aunt Martha went up with her.

"What an irresponsible goofball," Grandpa Swenson said, shaking his head.

"Well, if your damn daughter hadn't hounded him so bad all these years, he wouldn't be out there now!" Grandpa Pete said, defending Dad.

Dad brought the tree into the garage and attached the stand. He was in a much better mood. He always is after he does something really stupid.

"I had to take that tree down anyway," he told me. "May as well save twenty-five bucks, huh?"

"We've got a lot of pine trees, Dad."

"What do you think the pioneers and old-timers did? Go to a church Christmas-tree lot? Heck, no. They used one of their own trees."

After a while Mom came downstairs, and the tree was so pretty and Dad's talk about pioneers and old-timers fit so well with the idea of a fun old-fashioned

Christmas that Mom gave him a kiss and said she was sorry, and all the cheer and stuff came back and lasted until the bird flew out of the tree.

"I didn't pick a tree with a bird in it!" Dad shouted at Mom as he chased the bird around the living room with a paper bag.

"Are you nuts?" Uncle Dave said. "You'll never catch a bird in a bag. You need a broom."

"Don't kill it, Daddy!" Darby shrieked. "It's somebody's state bird!"

"*Eek!* Cover your hair!" Audrey screamed. "It'll lay eggs."

"That's a bat!" I told her.

"I'm not taking chances!"

"Open the windows!" Dad yelled as the bird swooped back and forth across the living room.

"It's freezing cold outside!" Grandma Swenson said.

"Well, go upstairs!"

"Don't be a snoot!"

Uncle Dave came running into the living room with a broom and in a matter of seconds put three big broom marks on the walls. Mom grabbed the broom away from him.

"I just had these walls painted! Darn you!"

"He was just trying to help!" Aunt Martha said.

"Well, help he didn't!"

"We're *sorry*! If Clark hadn't been so cheap, you wouldn't have a bird in your living room!"

Dad heard that, and he turned to Aunt Martha and gave her a dirty look that was dirtier than the marks on the wall. And Aunt Martha gave him one back.

"There he goes!" Grandpa Swenson yelled as the bird flew out the living-room window.

"Here he comes!" yelled Grandpa Pete.

The bird had flown a big loop from the front of the house around to the back and in through the opposite windows and was back in the house again, swooping up and back.

"Here he comes!" Dad yelled to Grandpa Swenson. The bird whooshed across the living room. Grandpa Swenson slammed the window shut just a split second before the bird got all the way out.

"*Chiiiiiirp!*"

By the time the problem was all over and the bird had been flicked out in the yard, it was just about time for Dad and Uncle Dave to go pick up Aunt Hazel. Aunt Hazel, by the way, was older than even my grandparents, and nobody was really sure how she got to be an aunt of ours, but she'd been around for so many Christmases that it didn't make any difference anymore. She was very nice and just sort of sat there in her seat and watched everything. She always brought over presents that nobody liked. I think she just wrapped up stuff she had around the house. When I was seven she gave me a bib, a rattle, and a box of handkerchiefs.

"Anyone for oyster stew?" Mom called from the kitchen. Everybody made faces except Grandma and Grandpa Swenson. They both said, "Yum!"

"I'd rather eat dirt," Grandpa Pete said over the top of his newspaper.

"You don't know good eating!" Grandpa Swenson said.

"The Swedes do?" Grandma Alice asked.

"Hell, yes, we do!" Grandpa Swenson said. "You Norwegians don't know your mouth from your . . ."

"Dad!" Mom said, wiping her hands on her apron. "I wonder where Clark could be? It's been over an hour."

"He's probably having a drink somewhere," Grandma Swenson said through her nose.

Mom glared at her.

"Don't look at me like that! He's had a snootful every night we've been here."

"I can't imagine what happened to them," Aunt Martha said, biting the tip of her thumb. "I'm getting worried."

Grandpa Swenson told her that she ought to start worrying about the turkey in the oven. He said it looked like it was about to blow its stuffing into the next county. Aunt Martha is a real swell person and a real cool aunt, but she's a terrible cook. Nobody could figure out what she did to the turkey to make it explode, but it did. No one was hurt or anything like that; it's just that the turkey kind of came apart down the middle, and a lot of the dressing ended up on the windows of the oven.

"Oh, for heaven's sake!" Aunt Martha said as she scraped dressing onto a plate. "What did I do wrong?"

"It'll be fine," Mom said, to make Aunt Martha feel better, even though I could tell she wanted to cry. She'd bought parsley and everything to make the dinner look like a page out of *Better Homes and Gardens.* But instead, as my cousin Dale said, it looked like a dinner that got tortured by the Apaches.

Mom and Grandma Swenson had just finished sewing up the turkey with string when Dad and Uncle Dave and Aunt Hazel arrived.

"Oh! That was fun!" Aunt Hazel said. "I love riding in cars!"

"Where on earth have you been? I've chewed my nails to the quick worrying," Mom said in the nice/angry voice that she uses around company.

"It's all my fault, dear," Aunt Hazel confessed. "I moved across the street in September . . . no, January, and it completely slipped my mind to tell you when you called."

Dad made the cuckoo sign behind Aunt Hazel's head and mouthed, "Nutty," and Mom gave him a dirty look.

"Where's Dave?" Mom asked just as Uncle Dave came in the front door with an armload of presents.

"Shee-it!" he mumbled as he struggled under the weight of the stuff.

"Oh, Aunt Hazel, you shouldn't have."

"What did I do, dear?" Aunt Hazel asked. Aunt Hazel was what you'd call a cute old woman. Even someone as young as I was called her cute. No one ever minded when she gave out kisses. It was just a shame that she wasn't a little more on the ball.

"The presents. You shouldn't have brought presents," Mom said.

"Well, heavens," Aunt Hazel said, waving her tiny white hand. "It's not every day that someone moves into a new house."

"Huh?"

"This new house is just lovely. It's so much bigger than the old house."

Dad leaned over and whispered in Mom's ear, "She thought Dave and I were trick-or-treaters."

"Hey, what about this stuff?" Uncle Dave said. "Where should I dump it?"

"In the living room, Dave," Mom said.

"*Woof,*" one of the boxes said.

Aunt Hazel wandered into the kitchen complimenting Mom on what a swell new kitchen our regular old kitchen was. Uncle Dave set down the packages.

"Either it's me or the Scotch, but one of these damn boxes barked."

"*Woof!*" the package said again.

"Jesus S. Smith!" Dad said, shaking a box about the size of a hatbox. He ripped it open and a dachshund jumped out and ran around in circles, yipping and yapping.

"She wrapped up her damn dog," Dad said under his breath.

"I wonder what else she wrapped up!" I said excitedly.

Mom went upstairs and changed into her big huge Christmas skirt with the Santa Claus on the front and the reindeer on the back. Xgung came up from the basement and crashed into Aunt Hazel. He apologized about ten times and told Aunt Hazel that she had skin like ivory. She told him that his sweater was on backward and wandered into the dining room. Xgung picked up one of Aunt Hazel's earrings that got knocked off her ear when he crashed into her. He started to put it in his pocket, but when he saw that I was watching him he laughed and put it on the counter.

Dinner was just as terrible to swallow as it was to look at. Aunt Martha had gotten the stuffing recipe out of a magazine and it had bacon and radishes in it and it was awful. Everybody pretended to enjoy it, though, because either they wanted to be polite or they were so excited about Santa Claus coming that they didn't care. But it was a hard dinner to eat, especially after Dad found the waxed-paper bag full of guts and gizzards that Aunt Martha forgot to take out of the turkey.

"Well, hon," Uncle Dave said. "At least you had the good sense to take the bird out of the shopping bag before you cooked it."

"The dog'll love it," Mom said, smiling at Aunt Hazel.

"Did you get a dog?" she said.

About the only interesting thing that happened at dinner was that Grandpa Pete got some pepper up his nose and sneezed, and when he sneezed he blew a huge fart.

"Hail, Mary!" he said with a big smile. Grandma Alice poked him, and Grandma and Grandpa Swenson took their plates to the kitchen. Everybody else kept eating except Dale and me. We laughed so hard we had to hold our things to keep from wetting our Christmas Eve pants.

After dinner, the women cleared the table and did the dishes while the men and the kids went into the living room. The two grandpas flipped a coin to see who got the wing chair. Grandpa Swenson won, and he said it was justice in action, because Grandpa Pete cheated his way through life. Xgung mixed some after-dinner drinks. Audrey said she overheard him tell Grandma Alice that he was only having a Coke and that the booze drinks were for Dad and Uncle Dave. It started to bother me that such a sneaky guy, who lies to grandparents and who wasn't even related to me, would witness my personal Christmas glee when we opened presents.

Mom and Aunt Martha's instructions were that we were supposed to get the tree ready for trimming and when they were all done in the kitchen they would put on records and turn off the lights and we would all trim the tree. Then the kids would go upstairs and wait for Santa Claus.

"Where the heck are all the lights?" Dad said, counting the strands of lights. "There's only three. There *were* four."

He looked at me and I shrugged my shoulders.

"Don't ask me," I said.

"Don't get smart!"

We looked all over, but we couldn't find them. We also couldn't find a box of tinsel and the cookie snowmen that Aunt Martha made for the tree.

"Well, hell's bells!" Dad said as he started putting up the three strands of lights. Uncle Dave sat in a chair and told Dad that he was putting too many lights at the top.

"Would you like to do it?" Dad said angrily.

"You're doing fine, except you're putting too many lights on top and you won't have enough when you get to the bottom."

After Dad ended up with too many lights at the bottom, he said a swear word and Uncle Dave gave it a try. He got almost as mad as Dad when Grandpa Pete told him he was putting too many lights in the middle. Uncle Dave was in the Marine Corps and he was very particular about things being just so and it really seemed to bother him that the lights weren't working out.

"Are you ready?" Mom said as the women filed into the living room.

"If you had enough lights, we'd be ready," Uncle Dave said on his fourth or fifth attempt at making the three strands cover the whole tree.

"We have four strands," Mom said as she began directing people like a traffic cop. "Aunt Hazel, you sit there on the couch."

"That was delicious ham, Ellen," Aunt Hazel said, sitting on one of the cane chairs by the door.

"I'll sit under the tree so that I can pass out gifts," Mom said.

"That is, if Santa Claus comes," Grandpa Pete joked. "I heard on the radio that Santa fell out of his sleigh over the ocean and the Coast Guard is looking for him right now, but the water is . . ."

"Dad!" Mom said as Amy and Darby burst into tears.

"I'm telling you there aren't enough g.d. lights for this tree!"

"Just put up what you have, Dave," Aunt Martha snarled.

"Let's get the show on the road!" Grandpa Swenson said, lighting a cigar.

"You and your stinkeroos! P-U!" Grandma Alice grumbled.

"It's so darn dark in here, I can't make out a thing," Grandpa Pete said.

"It's supposed to be dark, Grandpa," Audrey said. "Like in the olden times when they didn't have light bulbs."

"Well, we have light bulbs now; let's use them."

He reached over and pulled the chain on the table lamp. It didn't go on. He felt around on the floor for the plug.

"It's not plugged in."

"You can't decorate a tree with only *three* strands of lights."

"It doesn't have to be *perfect!*"

"Then what the hell's the point of *doing* it!"

"Jinger berrs, jinger berrs, jinger arr the way!" Xgung began to sing. "Join in, children!"

Everybody was talking and singing at once. It was like how China must be during a major catastrophe. Then Grandpa Pete found a cord and plugged it in. There was a crackling sound, the lights in the whole house dimmed, and from under the couch came a tremendous yelp and a loud *pop!*

"Holy Jesus! You blew a fuse!"

Smoke started to seep out from under the couch, and it smelled horrible. Everybody got off the couch. It was dark and there was smoke and smells and the girls were shrieking.

"What's cooking?" Aunt Hazel asked.

"Get a flashlight, Clark!"

Of course, we couldn't find the flashlight, and when we did, the batteries were dead, so Dad had to go down in the basement and open up presents to get batteries out of toys.

"This is why I get so mad when you fool around with the flashlight!" he yelled at me.

"Why didn't you just put in a new fuse, dumb-dumb," Uncle Dave said.

"Because they're all blown, smart guy!"

"Well, put *one* in. Don't tell me you don't keep extra fuses?"

Dad told Uncle Dave that if he had an extra fuse, he wouldn't put it in the fuse box, he'd put it up Uncle Dave's rear end. Uncle Dave said it was a good thing he couldn't see Dad in the dark or else he'd pound him. They went back and forth until Mom reminded them about the smelly smoke under the couch.

Dad and Uncle Dave lifted up the couch while Mom held the flashlight.

"*God! No!*" Aunt Martha yelped. Then everybody started screaming and the girls cried even louder, Dale and I yelled, Grandma Alice fainted on the couch, and Darby heaved her Jell-O, milk, olives, and dessert.

Lying in the dustballs on the carpet where the couch used to be was what used to be Aunt Hazel's dachshund. He was lying stretched out with the missing strand of lights going in his mouth and coming out his behind.

"There's the damn lights," Uncle Dave said calmly.

"Out! Out! Everybody out!" Dad said between gags.

"What a terrible Christmas this is!" Grandma Alice muttered.

Dad and Uncle Dave put on oven mitts and picked up the dog. He was kind of melted to the carpet and there was a really disgusting sound when they had to peel him off. Like if you put a microphone to a big knee scab.

"How would you like two-hundred-amp service shooting out your bunghole?" I heard Uncle Dave whisper to Dad. "I could arrange it."

After Dad and Uncle Dave got back from burying the dachshund in the garbage can and Mom and Aunt Martha had swept up the balls of dog hair and pieces of glass and the tinsel the dog ate and had opened the windows to let out the smell, all the kids went upstairs to wait for Santa Claus.

We were all lying in our beds listening to the parents and grandparents bring the presents in from the garage and basement. It wasn't like other years, when Dad would whistle and there would be lots of pleasant chatter. It was quiet and serious. It was sort of like listening to guys at the grocery store stock the shelves. But still, all I could think about were my skis.

Then the old sleigh bells that Grandpa Swenson brought from home every year jingled and we all leaped out of our beds and raced to the stairs. We were halfway down the stairs when Grandpa Swenson shined the flashlight on us and said, "Halt! Pictures!"

We had to get in order, with the shortest at the bottom and tallest at the top. Then my cousins had to get out of the picture. Then we had to wait for Dad to get out the movie camera, and he was so crabby that he wouldn't let anyone tell him he couldn't run the movie lights because the electricity was out, so he got it all set up, realized there wasn't electricity, and got mad and threw the camera in the closet and went in the living room and sat down. Then Aunt Hazel fell down the basement stairs.

"I told you not to let her wander around in the dark!" Mom yelled at Aunt Martha.

"I couldn't *see* her!"

"What do you mean, you couldn't see her?"

"I mean, *I couldn't see her!*"

"Shall we let her lie down in the basement while you dumb broads bicker?" Dad said.

"When are we going to open our presents?" Audrey whined.

"Yeah," Darby added.

Aunt Hazel didn't die or anything, although Grandpa Swenson pointed out that falling down stairs is just about as dangerous for elderly folks as heart attacks and damp weather. Dad and Uncle Dave had put the couch in the basement because it had the exploding-dog odors all over the underside of it and Aunt Hazel landed on it instead of the cement floor. Mom explained after talking to Aunt Hazel that what had happened was Aunt Hazel had opened the door thinking it was the bathroom. She got ready to sit down on the toilet and, of course, there wasn't a toilet to sit on and she fell backward. She thought she landed on her head and then hit the couch, but she wasn't sure because she said it was too dark. But anyway, she said she felt fine except for not being able to move her arms.

"Call the fire department," Mom told Dad. "And make your brother-in-law shut up."

Uncle Dave thought that Aunt Hazel's thinking she was sitting on the toilet was the funniest thing he ever heard.

"I'm sorry, but, *oooh, hooo!*" he laughed, until Grandma Swenson smacked him on the knuckles with the silent butler.

"We better not move her," Dad said to Mom after he called the fire department. "The ambulance will be here as soon as it can. There're a lot of emergencies tonight."

"This is an emergency, too!" Mom said, patting Aunt Hazel's wrist.

"Is someone playing a saxophone?" Aunt Hazel inquired.

"We better do something about the presents," Dad said. "The kids are getting anxious."

After deciding that it would be too much trouble to move Christmas down to the basement and too difficult to move the couch upstairs, we left Aunt Hazel in the basement while we hurried up and opened our presents. Mom felt real bad leaving her alone down there, but Aunt Hazel said she'd be okay.

It was almost impossible to have a good time opening presents in the dark. If you wanted to see what you got, you had to wait for the flashlight.

"What did I get that feels woolly?" Dad asked. "A sweater?"

"It's a scarf," Mom answered.

"*Yea!* I think I got a doll!" Amy shouted.

"Here's a present for Xgung Wo," Mom said, flashing the light on a small package. "Xgung Wo?"

"He's probably in the bathroom," Audrey snapped. "Keep going!"

Audrey was nervous because the total estimated retail of her gifts was far behind that of the other kids' and she feared that she might come up short.

"What the hell is this?" Uncle Dave said. "Shine the light over here, Ellen."

"It's a shorty bathrobe," Aunt Martha said.

"I guess so. This would hardly cover the tip of my . . ."

"*Dave!*"

"Here's another present for Xgung."

Mom flashed the light around the room. There was no Xgung. Grandma Swenson stood up and felt her way to the foyer.

"He's probably downstairs in his room, feeling homesick," she said.

"You be careful, Mother," Mom called.

Dad got a rack to hang his ties on and a pair of socks from me. Grandpa Pete got a fruitcake from the Swensons and a shoe from Aunt Hazel. Then Mom handed the BB-gun box to Dale. I reached up and intercepted it.

"Thanks," I said to Mom.

"This is for Dale," she said.

"No, it's not."

"It certainly is. It's for Dale from Dad."

"But . . ."

"But what?"

Dale went crazy when he got the BB gun. He ripped open the box and BBs went all over.

"A gun! I got a gun! A real gun! *Coooooool!*"

I felt like somebody'd hit a golf ball off my head. What a shock!

"Thanks a hell of a lot," Uncle Dave said to Dad.

"I just hope Dale enjoys the BB gun as much as John enjoys the bow-and-arrow set you gave him last year."

Grandma Swenson banged her way into the living room.

"Ellen!" she said. "Ellen? Xgung Wo isn't anywhere."

"He has to be *some*where, Mother," Mom answered.

"His coat is gone," Grandma Swenson said.

"Well, to heck with him," Grandma Alice grumbled. "If he can't even say good-bye . . ."

Mom cursed under her breath and got up. She and Grandma Swenson went into the foyer to talk. I heard Grandma Swenson tell Mom that not only was Xgung's coat gone but so was her purse. She had checked around and discovered that Mom's purse and Aunt Martha's purse were also gone. She wasn't sure but she thought maybe our good forks and knives and the dining-room candlesticks were gone, too.

"I have an announcement to make," Mom said angrily. "It seems as though Xgung Wo has taken advantage of our hospitality and has robbed us."

Aunt Martha screamed. Uncle Dave and Dad jumped up and started swearing. Grandpa Pete slapped his knee and yelled, "I told ya! I told ya!" Grandma Alice started sputtering. And Grandpa Swenson went over to comfort Grandma Swenson.

"We're good people, Mama," Grandpa Swenson said as Grandma whimpered softly. "We try our best."

As it turned out, Xgung didn't get very far. As a matter of fact, he hardly got out of the driveway. I guess over in the Orient guys don't look over their shoulders when they back up, because Xgung crashed right into the ambulance that was coming to pick up Aunt Hazel. Inside the house we'd heard the siren grow louder and louder and then *bang*!

We all ran outside and saw the ambulance up on the lawn and Grandpa Pete's car sitting sideways on the street. Xgung climbed out of the car and started running away with the three purses over his arm and the old suitcase from the basement. But he must have been stunned or something, because he ran like a football player going out for a pass, zigzagging down the street.

"Give me the gun!" Uncle Dave yelled to Dale. Dale ran over with his new BB gun.

"Dave!" Aunt Martha shouted. "You can put an eye out with that thing!"

"Righty-o!" Uncle Dave chuckled as he pumped and fired. He hit Xgung in the neck, and Xgung dropped the suitcase and the purses and started jumping up and down, hollering in Oriental. Uncle Dave took off across the lawn and tackled him and put him in a headlock.

"Chop, chop!" Uncle Dave said as he led Xgung back to the house.

The ambulance drivers weren't hurt too much, except for some bloody noses and fingers.

"Would you like some hot coffee?" Mom asked them as they administered treatment to themselves.

"Not right now, ma'am," one of them said. "But you might want to call the police."

While Dad called the police, Uncle Dave took Xgung into the living room and held the BB gun against his left eye.

"Don't move a muscle!" he told Xgung.

"I'm not a climinal!" Xgung said. "I'm underplivileged!"

Grandma Swenson didn't like the way Uncle Dave was treating Xgung and she told him to put the gun down. Grandpa Pete told her to mind her business.

"If you want to stick your nose in something," Grandpa Pete told her, "why don't you stick it in your checkbook and write me out a check for a new car!"

"You're not going to talk to my wife that way!" Grandpa Swenson said. Then he slapped Grandpa Pete on the top of his bald head. Grandpa Pete reached back and socked Grandpa Swenson in the truss.

Meanwhile, Mom and Dad were fighting out on the front lawn about why Mom wanted to have a fun old-fashioned Christmas in the first place. Darby and Audrey were arguing about something, and Darby chased Audrey out the front door and hit her in the back with the board to her new Clue game, and Audrey turned around and dented Darby's braces with her elbow. Aunt Hazel had a hallucination or something and started wandering around the basement. She split open her shins on the hot-water heater and ended up thinking she was talking to Arthur Godfrey on Audrey's old toy phone. Aunt Martha sort of snapped; she was sitting on the front porch tugging on her wedding ring and mumbling about how nothing in life ever works out. As for the skis I was hoping I'd get, they were out in the street. Xgung had stolen them, too, and when he cracked up the car, they fell out. When the cops showed up they parked on top of them. It just didn't seem like Christmas could get any worse. It was so terrible around our house that the injured ambulance guys said they'd stay in their car instead of going inside.

Mom was just about to start tearing apart the manger scene in the front yard when she noticed something in the sky.

"Look!" she yelled. "Everybody! Look!"

She pointed to a dot of light in the north sky.

"Do you see it?"

We all gathered around her. Uncle Dave led Xgung outside. Grandma and Grandpa Swenson and Grandpa Pete and Grandma Alice, the cops and Aunt Hazel, Darby, Dale, Katie, Audrey, Amy, and I made a circle around Mom. She pointed up to the sky.

"Do you see it?" she asked, brushing her hair from her eyes. Snowflakes began to fall. "Do you see that star? Nineteen hundred fifty-nine years ago, three wise men saw a star like that."

"The Star of Bethlehem!" Aunt Martha said.

We all studied the star.

"Let us set aside our bitter feelings," Mom said. "This is Christmas. The trials and tribulations of our daily life, the chaos of this gathering, the auto theft and the burned turkey, the petty fights and pointless hostilities mean so little on this night. We are family and we are together on this most important night of the whole year. Let's let our love shine through the hatred so that in

the light of that distant star we may embrace the true spirit of Christmas."
Mom bowed her head and began to sing softly:

> *"Yea, Lord, we greet thee,*
> *"Born this happy morning,*
> *"Jesus, to Thee all glory giv'n,*
> *"Word of the Father,*
> *"Now in flesh appearing,*
> *"O come let us adore Him,*
> *"O come let us adore Him,*
> *"Venite adoremus Dominum,*
> *"Christ the Lord."*

We all joined together, putting our arms around each other. Uncle Dave put his arm around Xgung, Grandpa Pete put his around Grandpa Swenson, Dad hugged Mom, I kissed Audrey. We stood staring at the point of light, the snowflakes melting on our cheeks and mixing with our tears.

"You know something, lady," one of the policemen said. "That ain't a star. That's an airplane."

SHORT HAIRS

A PLAY

by John Weidman

The People

José: *A handsome, intelligent Puerto Rican in his early thirties.*

Tasticakes: *A Puerto Rican "pretty boy" in his mid-teens. He is also known as Ring Dings, Yodels, and Sara Lee's All-Butter Pound Cake.*

Taco: *A Puerto Rican drug addict in his mid-twenties.*

Hard-On: *A virile black man in his early thirties.*

Thug: *Quick-tempered leader of the black prisoners, in his early thirties.*

El Shazam: *Black man in his early twenties with a proud and regal bearing and a funny hat from Africa.*

Kevin "Spudpud" Murphy: *Rugged, streetwise Irishman in his late twenties.*

Teeny-Peeny: *A slender white man in his early twenties. His arms and legs are in casts, his head is heavily bandaged, and his chest (his shirt has been torn off) is badly bruised and bleeding.*

Laurence P. Worthington III: *An elegant young white man majoring in French literature at Princeton.*

Adolf: *A white prison guard in his late forties.*

Idi: *A black prison guard in his late forties.*

Miguel: *A Puerto Rican in his mid-thirties.*

Nonspeaking parts: *Various other prisoners—black, white, and Puerto Rican— including John Mitchell, former attorney general of the United States, and two bewildered Pakistanis.*

The Play

Time: *Early morning; yesterday, today . . . tomorrow.*

Place: *The dayroom of the New York City House of Detention. Upstage right is the entrance gate from the cell-block proper. Upstage left is a gate leading out to the reception area. The room is bare except for a toilet upstage right, a television set upstage left, and a long, low table and benches downstage center. At rise, the stage is empty. Then a bell rings and the barred gate to the cellblock opens.* Adolf *and* Idi *enter and stand to either side of the open gate, and as the* Prisoners *enter single file and pass between them,* They *beat them viciously across the head and shoulders with their clubs. The* Prisoners *apparently expect this and raise no objections. First through the gate are the black prisoners—* Hard-On, Thug, *and* El Shazam. *They carry trays piled high with food and move immediately to the far end of the table. This is their "turf," and no one sits there but the three of them. Next come the Puerto Rican prisoners—José, Tasticakes, and Taco. They too carry trays and quickly occupy their "turf" at the near end of the table. Finally come the two white prisoners—Spudpud and Tenny-Peeny. Teeny-Peeny cannot walk and so is dragged by Spudpud, who tosses him behind the toilet where He lies in a heap for the remainder of the play. Spudpud sits down on the toilet seat—his "turf"—and starts to eat. He takes one bite, then spits it out.*

Spudpud. Pffft! . . . What is this? Fuckin' Alpo time?!
Thug. (To Adolf) Yeah, what the fuck you scumbags tryin' to do with this shit? Bring back the fuckin' death penalty?

(*He hurls his tray across the room, where it smashes* Teeny-Peeny *in the face; the other* Black Prisoners *follow suit*)

Adolf. Hey, Thug, don't do that, man.
Thug. Why not?
Adolf. It makes a mess, that's why. You make a mess like that again, I'll knock your teeth so far down your fuckin' throat you'll have to sit on your next meal and eat it with your asshole.

(Taco *giggles;* Thug *turns on him*)

Thug. You're laughin', man?
Taco. (Nervously) Not me . . . unh-unh.
Thug. I'm gettin' laughed at by a motherfuckin' faggot of a Puerto Rican junkie?!
Taco. No way, man. No. See, I—
Thug. Shee-it . . .

(Thug *pulls a gleaming red Swiss army knife made out of pencils and a pack of Trac II razor blades and cuts off* Taco's *ear. Bedlam ensues.* Adolf *beats on* Thug, Idi *beats on* Spudpud, José *punches* Taco *in the side of the head until the bleeding stops, and all the other* Prisoners *beat each other brutally.* José *tries to shout above the din*)

José. Hey, Hey, what the . . . cool it, man! What's with you motherfuckers?! Hey! (*Gradually things quiet down*) You guys . . . you act just like a bunch of fuckin' animals, you know that? Shit, you let this fuckin' dunghole turn you into *pigs! Be men!* (*He makes the rounds, addressing each man personally*) Remember who you are! . . . Be cool! . . . Don't let this place destroy you, man! . . . Don't let it steal your *soul!* . . . Cool out, be *cool!*
Taco. José's right.
Hard-On. Yeah.
Tasticakes. He's real *sensitive,* you know?

El Shazam. Yeah, he's one real deep dude, all right.
Taco. I saw him read a book once, man. He picked it up and read it just as easy as I wipe my fuckin' ass.
Thugs. He's *smart,* man.
Tasticakes. Yeah.
Spudpud. Too fuckin' smart.

(Spudpud *picks up the television set and brings it down on José's head. More chaos, vicious beatings, screams and broken bones. Then* Idi *blows his whistle and the room falls silent)*

Idi. (An indulgent chuckle) O.K., enough's enough. You fuckheads settle down and eat your breakfast now. Let's go.

(*Grudging mumbles of assent as the* Prisoners *limp and crawl back to their places)*

Hard-On. (Looking for his tray) Shit, man, the food's all spilled!
El Shazam. Yeah, what the fuck we gonna eat?
Taco. (Leering at Tasticakes) I know what's on *my* menu, man.
Tasticakes. Hey, Taco, I don't do that bullshit, man. I told you, I ain't *stuff!*[1]
Taco. Come on now, honeybuns, don't be like that. I'll let you have a bag of uncut Turkish heroin and half a box of Dots.

(Taco *proffers the candy and the drugs, but* Tasticakes *just sneers and turns away;* Taco *chuckles)*

Taco. Hey, Hard-On, man, let's show him how it's done.
Hard-On. (Pulling down his pants) Break-fast is fuck-in' served!

(Taco *crosses to* Hard-On *and blows him. The other* Prisoners *and the Guards look on, ad-libbing envious, appreciative remarks. When* Taco's *through,* He *throws his head back and* He *smiles at* Tasticakes)

Taco. You see, man, all you gotta do is stand there like the fuckin' Chrysler Building. You don't gotta do a fuckin' thing.
Hard-On. That's right, man.
Thug. Yeah.
El Shazam. There's nothing to it.

(*This line of encouragement continues as the* Prisoners *and the* Guards *close in on* Tasticakes, *who pulls out a machete fashioned from a tube of toothpaste and an old tin cup and gets set to defend himself. Just as* He *starts to raise the blade,* José *pushes off the TV set and stumbles to his feet)*

1. *stuff*: Prison slang for homosexual, apparently derived from the similarity between the way the prisoners perform the sex act and the way Kareem Abdul-Jabbar scores baskets.

José. (Groggily) Hey, what the fuck is with you guys?! You came in here as *men* and now you're acting like a pack of fuckin' *dogs!* Don't let this shithouse beat you, man! Don't let it—

(José *is interrupted by* Thug, *who picks him up and runs his head into the concrete wall. Immediately, the room erupts into a melée, this time more sexual than violent. Prisoners and Guards tear wildly at each other's clothes, and soon the only men who aren't participating in some act of sodomy, fellatio, or anal intercourse are* José, *passed out cold against the wall, and* Teeny-Peeny, *still collapsed behind the toilet. At the height of the excitement a high-pitched voice is heard from offstage left. The voice is singing, and as first one* Prisoner, *then another hears it,* He *falls silent and begins to put his clothes on*)

Hard-On. Hey, Thug, you hear that singin'?
Thug. Sure I do. Man, Pipes is back!
Taco. That's bullshit, man. Pipes's mamma sprung him outta here on bail.
Thug. I'll spring your fuckin' heart right out your chest, you piece of shit . . . you tellin' me I don't know Pipes's voice?!
Taco. Hey, take it easy, man. Don't go get all *leaped up.*[2]

(Hard-On *pulls out a target pistol made from old strips of linoleum and half a hairbrush. He is closing in on* Taco *when the gate to the reception area slides open and* Two Guards *hurl* Pipes *into the room.* Pipes *is singing when* He *enters—something from an early Otis Redding album—and* He *only stops when* He *lands face first on the table in a spray of blood and teeth.* Pipes *is a black man who looks very much like either Donny Hathaway or Barry White, depending on who is available.* He *and* El Shazam *slap hands*)

El Shazam. Hey, brother, welcome back.
Pipes. (Spitting out two left rear molars; smiling) What's happenin', Prince of Peace?
Thug. Hey, Pipes, we figured you were gone, man. What you doin' back inside?
Pipes. I killed a cop, man. *(Whistles, mumbles, ad-libbed reactions)* I caught the motherfucker tryin' to ticket me for double-parking down behind the drug drop where I stash my stolen cars.
Thug. (Smashing his fist down on the table) Motherfuckin' pigs!
Hard-On. Hey, man, be cool.
Thug. (Ignoring him, crashing a bench against the wall) Those goddamn motherfuckin' *pigs!!*
Hard-On. Hey, man, be cool.
Thug. (Ignoring him, crashing a bench against the wall) Those goddamn motherfuckin' *pigs!!*

---

2. *leaped up:* Prison slang for angry, as in: "When the Japanese attacked Pearl Harbor, President Roosevelt became leaped up."

Hard-On. Hey, take it easy . . . (Thug *rips off one of* Teeny-Peeny's *arms and beats him savagely across the face with it*) Hey, Pipes, how 'bout a song to cool this fucker down?

(Cries of encouragement from the other Prisoners. Pipes *grins and starts to tap his foot as* Taco *flips a garbage can and beats it like a drum. From underneath the table* Tasticakes *pulls out a bass made from an old cigar box and a mop.* Hard-On *reaches in his shirt and comes up with a tenor sax carved from a bar of soap, while* El Shazam *rolls on a baby grand piano made from old back issues of the* National Geographic. They *start to play)*

Pipes. (Singing)

Hey, brother . . .
Hey, sister . . .
Hey, listen to the shit that's comin' down.
These prison walls will crush your balls,
They've got me by the hairs.
Short hairs.
Short hairs.
Outside some bro' plays fullback for the Bears,
But when you're on the inside no one cares.
Short hairs.
Short hairs.

Hey, mamma . . .
Hey, pappa . . .
Hey, listen to the shit that's comin' down.

So-ci-e-ty just pukes on me,
It's got me by the hairs,
Short hairs.
Short hairs.
What must I do to make the world awares?
Shoot up its asshole flaming signal flares?
Short hairs.
Short hairs.

Hey, brother . . .
Hey, sis . . .

(Pipes *is interrupted by* Spudpud, *who pulls the toilet off the wall and hurls it across the room, knocking Pipes spread-eagled back across the table)*

Spudpud. You call that jungle bullshit music, man?! You think I'm gonna stand here listenin' to that Congo slop when I grew up with Dennis Day and Carmel fuckin' Quinn?! (He *spits viciously at* Pipes) No fuckin' way, man! Up your ass with *that* shit!

(Pipes *doesn't move, but* Thug *and* Hard-On *slowly rise and set themselves for trouble.* El Shazam *steps up to* Spudpud *and stares him in the eye; quietly)*

El Shazam. Do not touch him, brothers. Do not soil your princely fists upon this pork-smeared piece of shit . . . Observe him, though. And listen to his words . . . the words of Yacoub,[3] white-skinned, blue-eyed devil of the toilet underworld he calls America. His twisted mind and rotting body cannot move to the natural rhythms of the sainted black man's ever-widening universe. His cursed and stinking soul has had its day of degradation and corruption and it shrinks before the pure, celestial music made by proud and shining sons of Africa as they stride forward, warriors of Allah's sacred word, with spears upraised and truth and courage singing in their hearts to now proclaim the founding of the black man's Holy Empire on this earth!

(There is a hushed pause, then . . .)

Thug. (To Hard-On) What the fuck's this nigger sayin', man?
Hard-On. Beats me. Hey, Shaz, man, talk in fuckin' English.
El Shazam. Shit . . . *(Turning on them; disgusted)* You mothers dumb as pig shit, you know that? Just what the hell—

(Spudpud *takes advantage of* El Shazam's *turned back to kick him in the ass. He sails across the room and crashes down on top of* José, *who gradually comes to)*

El Shazam. (Leaping to his feet) O.K., faggot. You just sent your white ass to the cemetery, man!
Spudpud. I'm ready, motherfucker! Come on, make your move!

(Spudpud *and* El Shazam *square off against each other and draw weapons—* El Shazam *a sawed-off shotgun made from clothesline and a deck of playing cards,* Spudpud *a small bazooka made of toenail clippers and a roll of dental floss. The other* Prisoners *have begun to form a ring around them when* José *struggles to his feet and steps unsteadily between them)*

José. Wait a second! Hold it, man! You wanna fight, O.K., man, fight! But fight like *men!* Don't fight like fuckin' *animals!* Fair fight. Come on, fair fight.
Tasticakes. José is right, man.
Thug. Yeah. Fair fight.
Taco. Fair fight.

3. *Yacoub:* Prison slang for white man, or honky; also high school graduate.

(A breathless pause)

El Shazam. O.K. by me, man.
Spudpud. Right.

(They drop their weapons. Thug picks them up and nonchalantly tries them out on Teeny-Peeny, blowing off the bottom half of his left leg. José looks around)

José. Hey, Idi . . . Adolf . . . where the fuck did you guys get to?

(The Two Guards stir from the corner upstage left where They have been alternately smoking cigarettes and dozing since the orgy)

Adolf. What is it, spic?
Idi. What's going on?
Tasticakes. Spudpud and El Shazam are gonna fight.
José. No weapons, man. Just fists. We need you guys to referee.
Idi. Sure thing.
Adolf. You bet.
Idi. You set this up, José?
José. I got two of them to put their weapons down. I got them to agree to fight like *men*, not fuckin' *animals!*
Adolf. That's beautiful, José.
Idi. Uh-huh . . . but we'll take over now.

(Adolf and Idi club José several times across the head and toss him in the corner, then They gesture to Spudpud and El Shazam to start the fight. The Two Men wrap their fists in strips of cloth and circle cautiously while all the other Prisoners ad-lib grunts and cheers. Several punches are exchanged, the Two Men grapple, then Spudpud slips and El Shazam jumps down on top of him and starts to pummel him. Adolf draws his gun and puts a bullet into El Shazam's right arm. This shifts the advantage to Spudpud, who leaps on his opponent and begins to beat his head against the floor. Idi pulls his gun and shoots off three of Spudpud's fingers. El Shazam now rolls on top again, but not for long as Adolf wings him in the foot . . . and so it goes, shot for shot and wound for wound, until the bell rings suddenly and the gate to the reception area slides open. The fight stops instantly and all eyes turn to see who's coming through the door. A beat, then Laurence P. Worthington III enters. He is accompanied by Two Guards, one of whom carries his several leather suitcases; the other walks behind him dusting off his jacket with a whisk broom. One Guard crosses to the upstage wall and drop kicks Teeny-Peeny back behind the toilet while the Other One sets down the suitcases. Worthington tips them both, They tug their forelocks, bow, and exit)

Taco. Hey, Spudpud. Check it out, man.

Hard-On. Yeah. Looks like you got a no-dick, fag-ass honky here to keep you company.

El Shazam. That's right, man. One more fuckin' *devil*.

(El Shazam spits on the floor and turns away to bandage up his gunshot wounds. The other Prisoners *break up into small groups and begin to either blow or beat each other quietly.* Spudpud *crosses to* Worthington *and puts his arm around his shoulder)*

Spudpud. Hey, don't listen to these fuckin' scumbags, kid. You stick with me and watch your back and you won't have no trouble with these stupid pricks. *(Offering a pack of Chesterfields)* You want a smoke?

Worthington. Thank you, I prefer my own.

(He takes out a pack of Rothman's and lights one)

Spudpud. That's cool, man. Don't take nothin' till you know the price tag.

Worthington. *(Airily; absently examining his new surroundings)* Sound advice, I'm sure.

Spudpud. Hey, kid, I like you, you know that? You're hip.

Worthington. Thanks awfully.

Spudpud. My name's Spudpud, kid. What's yours?

Worthington. Laurence P. Worthington, the third.

Spudpud. Hey, hey . . . hey, that's some fuckin' handle, man. What name you wanna go by in the can here?

Worthington. Let's try Mister Worthington, all right?

Spudpud. *(His face darkening a bit)* Your choice, man. First time in the lock-up?

Worthington. *(Annoyed)* Naturally it is. Do I look like some kind of *criminal*?

Spudpud. Be cool, man. What you in for?

Worthington. Child molesting.

(As if They *had been struck by lightning, all the other* Prisoners *stop what* They *are doing and lean in to listen in hushed silence)*

Spudpud. What's that, man? I don't think I heard that right?

Worthington. *(Impatiently, distinctly)* Child molesting. You know, sexually assaulting little children . . . mostly black and Puerto Rican . . . eight, nine, ten years old . . . whatever I could find without going too far into really loathsome neighborhoods.

All the prisoners. *(In unison, a vicious whisper)* Short Eyes . . .

Worthington. What was that? I didn't—

Hard-On. *(Interrupting)* Fuckin' Short Eyes!!

Taco. Motherfuckin' Short Eyes!!

Thug. Shee-it! *(Jumping on the table)* Come on, let's summarily enforce the

rigid moral code which governs our own small, enclosed society!
El Shazam. God-*damn*!!
Taco. (Beside himself with fury; frothing at the mouth) Motherfuckin' Short Eyes!!!

(Suddenly all hell breaks loose. The Prisoners *leap up and start chasing* Worthington *around the room.* Spudpud *and the* Guards *join in the hunt. Adlibbed shouts of moral outrage)*

Tasticakes. Grab that fuckin' whitewashed creep!
Thug. I'll rip his fuckin' dick off!
Spudpud. Don't hurt him, man! I wanna take this mother off the count *myself*!
Tasticakes. (Slowing down, tugging at Spudpud's *sleeve)* Off the count? What's that mean, man?
Spudpud. (Viciously pushing him aside) I got no time to be your fuckin' language teacher, scumhead! Check the fuckin' footnotes![4]

(While Tasticakes *looks at the footnotes,* Spudpud *dives at* Worthington *and brings him down. The other* Prisoners *pounce on him and rush him over to the table, where* They *pin him on his back.* Spudpud *walks slowly toward him)*

You know what I'm gonna do to Mister Worthington here? Ear to ear, I'm gonna cut the fucker's *throat*!

(As Spudpud *approaches the table,* He *pulls out a chain saw made from toilet paper and a can of Right Guard. He pulls the starter and it catches with a roar, which brings* José *around.* José *staggers to his feet and throws himself between* Spudpud *and* Worthington*)*

José. Don't do this, man! This man's a *man, man*! You can't butcher him like he was just a fuckin' *animal*! You can't—
Worthington. (Interrupting) Excuse me, I don't know your name, but would you just shut up and let me handle this?

(He shakes a leg free, kicks José *in the face and sends him flying back against the wall, then turns his attention to the other* Prisoners*)*

Fellas . . . fellas, let's slow down a minute here and use our heads, O.K.?
Taco. (Viciously) I'll use my head to rip your fuckin' face off!
Worthington. Anatomically an interesting idea, but I'm sure that if you think a minute you'll agree that harming me would hardly be in your best interest.
Taco. Huh?
Hard-On. What's that?

---

4. *To take off the count:* Prison slang for kill.

(More ad-libs of bewilderment)

Thug. Hey, what the fuck you sayin', man?
Worthington. I'm saying that my father happens to be one of New York's richest businessmen, and if you lads will just forget this Short Eyes nonsense, I'd be happy to suggest that he post bail for all of you and, when you go on trial, that he help each of you arrange the best defense available.

(Stunned silence)

Taco. You'd do that for us, man? You'd get your fuckin' Pops to spring for all our bail?
Worthington. *(Nodding)* I would.
Tasticakes. And lawyers, man? He'll get us fuckin' lawyers?
Thug. Dudes who been to Harvard, Yale, and shit like that, man?
El Shazam. No more with the sheenies in the sixty dollar suits from Legal fuckin' Aid?!
Worthington. Well, let me see . . . would F. Lee Bailey suit you gentlemen?
Thug. *(A hoot of joy)* God-damn!
El Shazam. Al-*right*!

(Shouts and cries of celebration. Hand slaps all around. Spudpud *dusts off* Worthington *and helps him to his feet)*

Spudpud. Hey, man, we didn't hurt you, did we?
Thug. Yeah, man, you O.K.?
Taco. Here, lemme help you up . . .

(Several Prisoners *see to* Worthington *while all the* Others *joyfully assault each other, physically and sexually. In the midst of the festivities the gate to the reception area slides open and* Two Guards *push* Miguel *into the room.* Miguel *seems nervous, almost frightened, and* He *huddles in a corner by himself until* He's *spotted)*

El Shazam. Miguel . . .

(The celebration stops immediately and all the Prisoners *turn to face* Miguel*)*

Miguel. *(Nervously)* Hey, brothers. Hey, what's happenin', huh? What's goin' down? Hey, hey . . .

(No response, then . . .)

All the Prisoners. *(In unison, a vicious whisper)* Short Hairs . . .
Miguel. No, man. No. You got it wrong! You heard it *wrong*, man!

(Slowly They *close in on him)*

Thug. Short Hairs!
El Shazam. Fuckin' Short Hairs!!
Taco. (A snarl of crazy rage; his eyeballs rolling up inside his head) Mother-fuckin' *Short Hairs*!!!

(Almost as one man, the Prisoners *leap at* Miguel, *but* He *slips away. A frantic chase ensues with* Miguel *dodging left and right and all the* Prisoners *racing after him.* Adolf *and* Idi *do their part to help. Ad-libbed shouts of frenzied fury. At the height of all the uproar,* Worthington *draws* Thug *aside)*

Worthington. Pardon me, but I'm not clear on something here. It seems so odd. Is his name really Short Hairs?
Thug. No, man, no. The dude's real name's Miguel. We call him Short Hairs cause the fucker is the lowest piece of shit there is. He went and did a crime so fuckin' sick it makes me puke to even think about it.
Worthington. Did he really? Huh. What crime was that?
Thug. He's been in here before, man . . . see . . . and last time he got out—*(Agitated, upset, forcing himself to continue)*—he wrote a fuckin' *play* about it! You believe that, man!! A motherfuckin' *play*! A goddamn well-made three act fuckin' *play*!![5]

(Overcome with rage, Thug *reaches out as* Miguel *races by and grabs him by the testicles. He picks him up and throws him on the table where* He's *instantly surrounded by the other* Prisoners. *All of them draw the remainder of their homemade weapons and, ad-libbing grunts and threats of vengeance, train them on* Miguel)*

Miguel. No, please. Don't do this. Please. *(He starts to cry)* I didn't mean to write it. Swear to God. It wasn't me . . . it was the Muse, man! That was it! The fuckin' *Muse*!

(Hard-On smashes him across the face with the butt of his elephant gun)

Hard-On. Don't talk, Short Hairs. Listen. Shut your fuckin' mouth and listen!

(He smashes him again)

Taco. That's right. We got some things to say to you, you piece of scum!

(He cracks him in the head with the barrel of his anti-aircraft field piece)

---

5. *Short Hairs:* The origin of this expression isn't clear, but if it's hard to see what Short Hairs has to do with writing plays, go figure out what Short Eyes has to do with child molesting.

Tasticakes. And when we're finished, man, we're gonna cut your fuckin' hand off!

(He slams him in the stomach with the warhead from a Nike missile)

El Shazam. Yeah . . . the one you used to write the fuckin' *play!*
Thug. And then we're gonna cut your guts out, sucker!
Miguel. (A whimper) No . . .
Spudpud. And me, I get the first cut. You know, why, man? *(Suddenly screaming)* Cause my mother went to see your fuckin' play, that's why! My fuckin' white-haired eighty-year-old mother shelled out fifteen bucks to listen to that pile of shit you called a *play!* She sat and listened to that fuckin' filth that you called *dialogue!* Christ, every other fuckin' word was fuck, you fuckin' fuck! *(He brings both fists down in his groin)* You think you gotta write that filth to write a fuckin' play, man?! Huh?! You ever read *Mac Fuckin' Beth?!*
Hard-On. Or *Fuckin' Cyrano?!*
Taco. Or *Long Day's Fuckin' Journey into Night?!*
Miguel. You're right, you're right! I never should've done it! I—
Thug. (Interrupting him by breaking both his thumbs) There's something else you never should've done, Miguel.
Tasticakes. Yeah.
Hard-On. Tell 'em, Thug.
Thug. Six months ago I got paroled, man, I was on the street. So first things first, I waste a guy who runs a liquor store and empty out his register. Six thousand bucks, man.
Miguel. (Nervously) That's a lot of money.
Thug. Bet your fuckin' Spanish ass it is . . . and you know where it went?
Miguel. Unh-unh.
Thug. I bought three units in your fuckin' show, that's where! I put my money in your goddamn, fuckin' show!! *(He slams him hard across the face and pulls a letter from his pocket)* Here, you piece of shit. You see this letter? You know what this fuckin' letter is? I got this yesterday from your producer, man. It says he's sorry he can't send me any money but the show ain't made back its investment yet. *(He puts his face down next to* Miguel's *and He shouts)* You ain't made your investment back, but in the *Post* they got a picture shows you drinkin' Johnnie Walker Black and eatin' baby rack of lamb at Sardi's!! *(He spits viciously in* Miguel's *face and breaks his arm)*
Taco. And what about my sister Carmen? You remember her? *(He kicks* Him *in the teeth)* She called you up for house seats, man. She asked you for a pair of fuckin' house seats and you told her to fuck herself, go drag her fat ass down to Ticketron! To Ticketron, you fuckin' prick! *(He snarls and bits off* Miguel's *nose)*
Spudpud. Come on, let's kill him!
El Shazam. Yeah . . . let's do it now!
Tasticakes. That's right. Forget the talk, man! Cut the fucker's throat!

(Ad-libbed cries for blood and vengeance mix with Miguel's *high-pitched pleas for mercy. In the corner* José *slowly stirs, then stumbles up and staggers toward the table)*

José. Hey, don't do it man! No matter who he is or what he did, don't kill him! Kill a man, you aren't a man yourself, you're nothin' but—

(At this moment José *pushes through the crowd and sees who* They *have pinned against the table; He stops, stunned)*

Miguel . . . Short Hairs . . . you fuckin' *animal*!!

(He leaps at him and tears his throat out with his bare hands and his teeth. The Prisoners *cheer, hoist* José *on their shoulders, carry him around the room, then smash his head against the ceiling several times and throw him in the corner next to* Teeny-Peeny. *Slowly, things return to normal. Small groups split off to fight or fuck, the* Guards *roam aimlessly around the room administering casual beatings, and* Pipes—*long since given up for dead—begins to sing)*

Pipes. (Weakly, but cheerfully)
Hey, brother . . .
Hey, sister . . .
Hey, listen to the shit that's comin' down.

They crush our nuts and beat our butts,
They've got us by the hairs.
Short Hairs.
Short etc., etc.

(Pipes continues quietly as the lights begin a slow fade down to black)

SLOW CURTAIN

THE KENNEDY LADS

by Father Sweeney Truncheon, SJ

by Ted Mann

I'VE BEEN PRIEST to the Kennedys now, man and boy, count the years. There's been water under the bridge and over the dam and who knows where-all else. Sure if the sorrows of this world were water, wouldn't they be bustin' out like the Texas gushers from the very boot prints of the Kennedys.

Do you know I was remarkin' to Father Alton McDash just the other day. "Well," I says, "Father, don't you think the Kennedys is a poor sorrowful bunch?"

"Is Hans Kung a heretic?" says he with a wink.

"You know, Father, I think there is something about a Kennedy that drives it on to be president. A Kennedy wants to be president as naturally and as unconsciously as one of your poor hopeless sea scallops yearns to become a higher class of marine organism. Like the ceaselessly evolvin' dogfish, for example, who never for a moment rests in his struggle to become a majestic bottlenose dolphin, the Kennedy would willingly sacrifice all he has attained to accede to the high estate of the presidency."

"That's true enough," agreed Father McDash. "Let me add to your ruminations that young Ted the candidate, though his brain might be as rudimentary as that of the humblest barnacle, would no more give up his struggle for the presidency than the aforementioned crustacean would forswear its dreams of becoming an abalone or something of that class."

Father McDash and myself have been friends now going on fifty years. In that time he has been called on to help me several times in my duties as priest to the Kennedys. The kind of job that called at times for all the tact and resources the two of us could muster up between us. It was Father McDash who assisted me at the exorcism. That business was as delicate as the hairs on a caterpillar's hindquarters.

It was a time. Old Joe Kennedy Sr. was after believing himself possessed by some class of devil, and the family at their wit's end over it all. It got so bad, there was nothing to be done at all but call the priest.

It was in the thirties, if I remember, and as soon as I got word of the trouble I was on the phone to Father McDash.

"It's your man," says I. "He's given' out how he's a demon and is after wantin' to give all his money away to blind fellas and folk that have been mangled by great vast machines and whatnot. The family's in a terrible lather. I suppose there's damn-all for it but we gather up bell, book, and candle and fly to his side to exorcise the poor man."

Father Alton did not hesitate a moment. He just asked for a few hours to sober up and vowed to meet me at old Joe's bedside.

The old man was in a piteous state. Sure it would have wrung the tears out of Lord Protector Cromwell himself to see him. Wasn't he vowin' to make a new start and live his life proper if only he had the chance, and all the while sketchin' up some mad plan to mail off your turkeys to all the poor people on some scrap of paper he had and bemoanin' the former hardness of his heart and vowing to live life anew from that very day.

When Father McDash arrived I took him aside.

"It appears," says I, jerking a thumb over me back at old Joe, "that your man has had a visit from some evil class of spirit which scared the bejabbers out of him. A while ago he was giving out how he was present in spirit at his own funeral and how he was the only fella there who was not dry-eyed. He's also been disordering his poor mind trying to make up a list of all the cab men he's stiffed and the poor ignorant fellas he's clipped on your stock market."

"Sure," said McDash, "that's a list would make your biblical genealogies look like the list of characters in an advanced type of one-man play. It looks to me like your man has had a visit from the spirit of Christmas yet-to-come."

"Jesus, Mary, and Joseph, have mercy! What might that be?" asks I.

"That's a class of Protestant ghost."

"Mother of God! Since when have the *esprits* of the heretical started preyin' on the faithful? Sure Joseph Sr.'s not been apostatized by this forsaken spook?"

Father McDash said nothing. With a grim shrug he rolled up the sleeves of his soutane and prepared to get down to the struggle.

It was a terrible fight we had. Old Joe was rolling around in the bed something fierce, shouting terrible things in an unusually deep sort of voice, and toward the end the hideous spirit in him made him blast a steaming mess of last night's seafood all over me spotless vestments. In the end, though, we won.

"Strength," said Father McDash, "all other things being equal, will always triumph over weakness."

Poor old Joe Sr., exhausted as he was, nodded his head.

"Thank you, boys," says he. "I don't suppose you have a drop of the crayture about you?"

We did, of course, and so we all sat down there on old Joe's bed and, tired as we were, finished the bottle.

That was one of the many times that Father McDash was called upon to assist me in my duties as priest to the family. He also helped me in the delicate matter of finding a blind dumb priest to hear one of Ted the candidate's gamier confessions. We eventually located the poor crippled holy man in a Dominican abbey in County Clare. It must have been a scorching confession, too, for I've heard the candidate a number of times confess to things as blue as the Irish

Sea. Yet for this particular confession he insisted on the blind fella, who would not recognize him, and the added affliction of the dumbness, to prevent the father from breathing a gasp of what he heard.

Then, of course, there was the incident what took place during Jack's trip to Ireland.

Jack, who was the president at that time, was takin' a leisurely tour of the sod from which his fathers sprung. Jacqueline was with him, and her as radiant then as the spring sunshine, and all the people of Dublin turnin' out to greet the pair of them. The streets were lined as Jack and his bride made their way through the city in the motorcar, and them not even strewin' coins amongst the crowd like most of the American Irish.

Well, soon they passes through the city and they find themselves driving through your more rustic purlieus. It was then, as they were crossing a small stone bridge over a wee stream, that the motorcar's tire blows up like a great vast bomb.

As it turns out, Jack doesn't know how to change the tire for the spare, and he goes to ask a local peasant for to be lendin' a hand. The president finds the hardy Gael starin' morosely into the little stream by the wayside.

"I've got my share of problems with that there stream," says the common man of Ireland at Jack's approach.

"Ah," says the president, willing to commiserate briefly with his ex-countryman if it would get his tire changed.

"Yas," says the peasant, drawing a sleeve across his dribbling nose, "every time the rain falls down don't you know that there stream fills up and floods out me downstream neighbors and is like to drown their oul' ones. They gets furious and says to me, 'Build yez a dam so we don't get no more inundations.' But if I do that, see, it would be after floodin' my basil patch, der what I needs to make the pesto sauce to spread on my poor potatoes."

"Well," said Jack, looking thoughtful, "what do you plan to do?"

"Nothin' at all," says the man of the soil.

"What?" said the president, shocked.

"No; don't yez see?" says the man. "I'm damned if I do and damned if I don't."

The man's pun so angered the short-fused president that he hit him a great bash on the gob that knocked him over backward into the stream, busting the fellow's poor head open.

A terrible accident. Well, it was obvious to all that the fellow must have had a very weak skull to be tellin' such a pun on Jack, who hated puns more than any man. Yet you can see how there was a good deal of trouble over the incident. Father McDash and I had both of us to fly in and spend the next couple of months buyin' drinks for all the man's male relatives and sayin' the Masses for his female ones, all to atone for Jack's rash act.

Well, now, and aren't we just about out of space for the writings. But before I leaves yez, here's a class of thing that used to be very popular in the newspaper columns when I was growing to man's estate. Look here:

```
N          E          R          O          S
F          A          L          L          S
L          U          C          K          Y
T          O          O          L          S
M          A          R          T          Y
```

Isn't that something. If you look at the thing carefully, you'll sees that in the above block of letters each line reads the same backward and forward as it does up and down and so on. Those sort of things are a very curious class of phenomena for them that is interested. Enjoy yourselves till next month.

NOTES TO MYSELF

by Ernest Hemingway

Exsquire is proud to present the first installment of Ernest Hemingway's Notes to Myself, *written on the back of his previously published laundry lists. Written in lemon juice, or "invisible ink," as he called it, they were not meant to be seen. They were accidentally discovered when a copy of his laundry lists was left on a heated radiator and the invisible print showed up.*

We feel that these notes are the most important literary discovery of the century, and must be published, no matter what Hemingway felt. They are the last pieces he wrote before his tragic death in Ketchum, Idaho, in 1961.

WENT TO BUD GRENFELL'S Stop 'n Shop for Miss Mary. Like the way Bud treats me. No celebrity bull. "What can I do for you, Mac?" Calls me Mac. I said, "Bud, It's me, Ernie." He said, "Fine, you're Ernie, I'm Bud. I'm busy, what do you want?" Loved it. Does his job cleanly and well.

Mucked up the shopping again. Bought tomato paste instead of puree. Can't be bothered figuring out the difference. Miss Mary says there's a big difference. Gives me that look. She's a skinny little butch. No meat on her. Going to cut all her hair off when she's asleep.

God, what am I going to wear today? My green bush pants smell funny. I can wear the blue corduroy pants but I don't have the right shirt. Maybe I'll wear a sweater and no shirt. Wool sweater itches. Put my long underwear on first, then sweater. Going to be hot. Remember what my mother said: "You can always take it off if it gets hot, but if you don't have it, you can't put it on if it gets cold."

Note to myself: Buy ducks at Vern Smiley's market, shoot them a few times to make them look like they were hunted. Vern promised me some fresh blood to sprinkle on them.

Edmund Wilson. He borrowed my lawn mower and never returned it. He should have a sense of ethics about returning something he borrowed. I distinctly remember that I lent it to him. I didn't give it to him. It was the kind you just push along, with the spinning blades. I already had two gas jobs. I had no use for the old mower. Maybe I did give it to him. But he should have called and thanked me.

Nobody left from the old crowd. Sherman Billingsley, Toots Shor, Leonard Lyons. Lyons used to lick my shoes until they were shiny. Never went to a shoeshine parlor when I was in New York. The little Jew used to shine my shoes. Used to put my name in his column every night. Jews like to fawn over me. They know I'm something they can never be.

Where was I last night? Was I lost in the woods again? All I remember is a dark, dark forest. Kept bumping into trees. Scary. Gertrude Stein once told me that there's nothing scarier than fear of the unknown. She ought to know. Terrifying sounds. Had no idea all those animals come out at night. Note to myself: Animals are not afraid of humans at night. In the daytime, maybe. At night, the rules are changed.

Miss Mary let me go into town today to pick up my pills at Jack Northrup's drugstore. Had to wait for them and leafed through magazines. Jack always gives me dirty looks for not buying. Bumped into Brenda Lovingood, Joe Lovingood's daughter. Sixteen years old. Wears makeup and those tight blue shorts. Asked me if I needed a secretary. I said, yes, oh yes, oh God yes, I need a secretary. Come to me, type to me, Oh God, type, type, type . . . 90, 100, 200 words a minute. Take my shorthand, my longhand, don't stop, both hands going up, up, down, hair, juices, tongue. Earth is moving, head is moving . . . . Where are they taking me? Where's my prescription? Who is the girl with the torn blouse? Call Miss Mary. Explain everything. Give me a hanky. Let me dry myself. Tell the girl I'm sorry. So easy to get it up with girl like Brenda. Never could do it properly with Miss Mary.

Met Jim Ketchell at the hardware store. Asked me to Bill Short's bar for a drink. Jim had a beer. I asked for a Kir—chablis and crème de cassis. Miss Mary won't let me drink anything stronger. Bill had no crème de cassis, so we sent out to the Stop 'n Shop for some Crosse and Blackwell's black current jelly, which is similar.

Jim wondered if he could offer me a suggestion about my writing. One of my most loyal readers. I was flattered. Rather hear a suggestion from old Jim than from one of those homo editors in New York. I said, "Shoot, Jim." He said, "Ernie, why don't you put a few jokes into your stories?"

"What kind of jokes do you mean, Jim? One liners? Or long anecdotes? If a joke doesn't fit into the story, it'll break the rhythm and stick out like a sore thumb."

"Hell, you're right again, Ernie," he said. "Want another drink?"

"Better not, Jim, or Miss Mary will be after me with a straitjacket."

"O.K., whatever you say, Ernie. I still think *Across the River and into the Trees* was the best yarn I ever read."

"Thanks, Jim. Have another beer on me. Put it on my tab, Bill. What do you mean, I have no tab? Since when is my credit no good in this one-horse town? Well, fuck you, too."

Jesus, is Bill Short Jewish or something? Since when doesn't he accept my credit? Short . . . probably shortened it from Shortskowitz . . . Shortsky . . . Shitsky. Probably named Shitsky originally. Bet Miss Mary's behind all this.

Thought of Raymond, the old barman of the Ritz in Paris. Made the best dry martinis in the world. Couldn't get through the day without nine or ten of Raymond's marts. Asked him how he made them so good. Would never tell. One day I said, if you don't tell me how you make your marts so good, I'm going to cut off your *pénis,* which is how the French spell penis.

"Oh please, Papa, do not do that!"

"Why not, you old frog?"

"Because it is my penis that makes the secret of my dry martinis," he said. "It is ten parts Gordon's gin, one part Noilly Prat vermouth, and two parts Raymond's pee-pee, as you say in *Americain.* When you not look, Raymond shake his pee-pee into cocktail shaker."

"Mother of God, Sister of Mary, son of the Holy Ghost, and father of Man O' War, you mean to tell me I've been drinking your piss for over twenty years?"

"Just a few little shakes, Papa. No more than you would shake when you are finished at the pissoir. It is what gives it the special taste."

"O.K., Raymond, you win. Too late to change my habits now."

God, those martinis could crack your head open, change your glands. Once took a 300-pound whore to a hotel after having ten of Raymond's marts. Whore couldn't see her cunt. Too fat to bend down and see it. It was covered by folds and folds of flesh. I couldn't see it, either. Said I would fuck her in between folds of her flesh. She said it was perfectly O.K. with her. Fucked her perpendicular so I could slide in and out of her folds properly. Not bad. Better than Miss Mary, that skinny merink. Rather fuck a ferret than that butch.

Another fight with the butch. She broke my lucky Tom Mix cereal bowl. Had it for thirty-five years. I think I'll kill her. Going to clean my shotgun and get it ready.

HENRY FORD'S DIARIES

by Doug Kenney and Ted Mann

Henry Ford (1863–1943) has been described as the Father of the American Automobile, and with good reason: He was. His leading role in the development of the automotive industry—an industry dramatically described in recent best-sellers The Betsy *and* Wheels—*put him at the forefront of a handful of men who literally invented the business of, literally, making automobiles. Hello? Accordingly, the* National Lampoon *is particularly pleased to present the following excerpts from the Ford Motor Company's soon-to-be-published* Diaries of Henry Ford *(Random House, 15 pages; $8.95 softcover).*

The diaries, while often amounting to a few lines scribbled on the back of an oil-spotted invoice, reveal a man who has been variously described as "the Christ of American capitalism" and "a withered-up old anti-Semitic scumbag." Who is to say Henry Ford was one or the other? Dave Chevrolet or Nat Lampoon, possibly?

—Ed.

December 26, 1873

Real cold today. Tried out my new dogracer, but the ice on the road to town was double-slick, so Tyke couldn't go (no traction) or stop until we met Mrs. O'Hooligan from behind and her eggs.

Had to stay in the rest of the day (Mrs. Hooligan told) so I tried Ma's wool-carders on Tyke's paws.

Later we snuck out when Pa got into a boil with Uncle Tom the hired man on whether General Grant had been tugging on the jug at Cold Harbor. Pa said General Grant wasn't and Uncle Tom said he has a missing foot that says he was.

Anyway, the wool-carders worked spiffy for awhile. Then the rear ones slipped off and we fishtailed into the crossroad and Mrs. O'Hooligan's second trip to the egg-depot.

Have to figure out how to keep the wool-carders on Tyke's paws. Maybe nails?

December 27, 1873

Nails didn't work too good. Pa made me clean out Mrs. O'Hooligan's two-holer for the busted eggs and I found some practically straight three-pennies in her loose boards. But Tyke didn't think they fit and Mrs. O'Hooligan's third basket went down her chimney when he said no.

In the coal bin where I have to stay after Pa came home I have been reading my new issue of *Boy's Own Annual*. There are some sockdologer articles including "How to Make Giant Whizbangs from Old Silos" (better ask Pa first), a special pictorial on balloon trams with Alp-runners, and also reports of a steam-powered Siberian dogsled. Don't see where there would be room for a boiler, but Tyke is still only a pup.

January 3, 1874

Ingredients for Ford Miniature Giant Whizbang:

Item:	Cost:
20 feet reinforcing baling wire	No charge
3 feet fuse..................................	$ .03
20 lbs. black blasting powder	$ .20
1 (one) butter churn (Ma's)	No charge
1 special dog-holster (old bicycle seat)	Three best aggies to P. O'Hooligan
3 special restraining straps	$ .07
Special rubberband paw-operated Moonman shooter	Had one
Goggles....................................	$ .32
Miniature American Flag....................	$ .08
Mrs. O'Hooligan's new hen house	$17.23

Distance: 300 yards

Total Cost: $17.93

January 23, 1874

On the way to Sunday School and minding our own beeswax, got into a snowball fight with the O'Hooligan brothers. At first Pat and Mike were winning because Elihu still had his arm in a sling from the balloon tram experiment. But I hid behind the dogracer and told our fellows to make them like Ma's preserves. In steps.

Thad gathered the snow, Phinneus packed them round, I stuck in the ball bearings from my pocket, Rufus dipped them in an ice-puddle and let them freeze up for awhile before Josh handed them to Elihu's good throwing arm and the O'Hooligans got theirs good.

When Pat and Mike backed off to another drift for more snow, I worked up some Nose-Flatteners (slush-covered doorknobs), Ear-Benders (iceballs with fishhooks), and a swell Icicle-Bomb which also worked as a Window-Dread-nougt, or so Officer O'Hooligan told Pa when he came with the bill.

From here in the coalbin I can hear Pa tell Ma it's time I stop wasting time in the toolshed and learn a trade where I can put my inventing to use, like farming. Pa says he'll be gulldurned if I can get into trouble inventing a new kind of hoe.

(If I work hard this spring, maybe Pa'll let me have the old silo after planting's over?)

Made up with the O'Hooligan brothers and showed them how to make Nose-Flatteners for their trip to jewtown.

June 30, 1874

Been working powerfully hard here on the farm for the past couple of months fixing up the sawmill. Pretty well licked into shape now that I see it *is* easier to feed the logs into the sawblade than vice-versi. Danged blade let go the first time and scooted into the barn before you could say William Jennings Bryant's Aunt Lizzie and came out the other side leaving it full of calves' halves.

Even now Ma says the racketty-ruckus sours the milk and the chickens won't lay. Pa figures it caused that two-headed calf last week, but I figure different. I figure the mill turns out 5,000 board feet of silo planking per day, which'll make a lot of transcounty whizbangs if President Grant ever looks at those sketches.

July 4, 1874

The Henry Ford Giant Rolling Whizbang wasn't all I had hoped for. When the townfolk were finished with supper and applauding my fireworks display, I lit her up, and though the two buckboards stayed under the silo all right, the steering sails whipped off right at the start and she ploughed smack whang-doodle into Mulvaney's saloon.

Pa says maybe farming's not my leaning after all and is going to rent my room to pay for Mrs. O'Hooligan's funeral. Pa's talking to Officer O'Hooligan at the front door now and Ma is packing my bag. Tyke cannot come with me to Detroit as tail is still in splint. Promise to forward issues of *American Toolbarn* as soon as flagdangle dies down some. Am writing in haste and some darkness as villagers' torches give off less light than you'd think. Steam-powered hand candle?

* * *

March 22, 1884

Today marks the third year of my apprenticeship with Knutson's Tool and Horseshoe Foundry, and I feel no closer to my dream of a practical, self-propelled surrey. The biggest hitch seems to be on the curvy parts of a road. The surrey corners fine but the steam-horses tip over, casters and all.

Mr. Rabinowitz, the inventory comptroller, told the tool captain to watch me. I think he suspects where the two boilers went. And two more jewish fellas came by today to start trouble in the punchline. Passing out greasy leaflets and talking rubbish about their Radicalist-Syndicalist Tool-Punchers Brotherhood of the Red Neckerchief and how they know more than Mr. Knutson even though the head one couldn't even get his beard out of the flywheel when I nudged on the throttle a tetch, by gumbolt.

Back issues of *American Toolbarn* arrived today. Seems some German fella name of Diesel is tinkering with an oil-trolley some like my steam pony. The rotogravure shows it to be a large, ponderous contraption, typical of your German tubings and old-fashioned flangework. Burns 100 pecks of oil to move a six-by-ten iron flatcar a hundred feet per hour. Oil-inhaler tends to explode every fifteen minutes. Crew of nine.

Impressive when you think of that frenchie fella Daimler and his clumsy waterwheelmobile, but still misses by a whangdoodle. Oil engines just aren't what they're cracked up to be; can't build up enough torque-horses in your impeller-bar. Plain as the bolt on your boiler.

Tomorrow, after the tool captain has left, I'm going to test-ignite my latest modification—the Henry Ford Coal Dust-Powered Land Canoe.

March 23, 1884

As I feared, the Land Canoe proved to be pretty much of fizzdangle. The piston-maul's vibration joggles your sprocket links, and if your safety whistle gets caulked up with soot on a steep grade, the whole imploder-kiln assembly is liable to go sky-high.

Rabinowitz says if I don't come in Sunday to repair the roof, don't come in Monday without a repair kit for my skull. Also, if God had meant men to ride around on horseless carriages, he sure hopes somebody else submits the lowest bid.

Someday I'll make that fellow chew his fool josh![1]

Another gaberdine-stroking Syndicalist was by again today sowing discontent among the Master Lathers. He wants us to put down our tools and wash out our red hankies in protest. In protest of too many mockies underfoot near my lathe, I blew my nose in his beard.

A gear is only as strong as its rottenest tooth.

June 22, 1885

At last the breakthrough I have been looking for. Been stumped for several months over the wheels. First I tried rimming them with heavy-gauge horseshoes, which are abundantly available after hours. But they tend to fling off at high speeds and a ringer around the tool captain's neck has not helped my chances here for further advancement. Mounting cast-iron feet along the edges failed to produce the results I have sought, too, only a few pulverized cobblestones and some nasty gouges up the sides of the south foundry wall.

Then, last night, after a hard day of replastering, I fell into a deep sleep and dreamed I was riding a mechanical dog who reminded me of old Tyke through the South American jungle. Suddenly, Tyke begins to whimper that his paws are sore and circles a huge rubber plant with a big nose. Tyke liberally sprinkles the nose which begins to sneeze with rapid, terrifying explosions. Its nostrils draw a bead on me, but I wake up.

Of course, rubber plant. When Rabinowitz is through garnishing my wages, I'll save up enough money to order some big bicycle tires from the local *rubber plant* and stretch them over the wheels.

---

[1] It is fascinating to note that this is Henry Ford's only recorded use of an exclamation point. By nature a thrifty man, Ford hated wasting ink.—Ed.

Also, I am very curious about this new liquid called *gasoline,* a petroleum by-product something like kerosene only with more ginger. Since the tool captain has put me on the night shift, I'll have time to convert these crude kerosene lamps of ours without his meddling.

June 24, 1885

Mr. Knutson has been forced to close the foundry following the fire and, with my urging, has arrested Rabinowitz and posted a $500 reward for information concerning this dastardly Syndicalist-Arsonist plot. Begin working for Edison Electric Company tomorrow. I am sure the Wizard of Menlo Park will lend a more sympathetic ear to the Fellow of Dearbourne, Michigan.

June 25, 1885

Just finished first day as chief engineer here at Edison. Had a kefuffle at lunch with this jewish fellow. (I won't tell Clara, she figures if I get the jews' backs up, they'll look up where we live and one day little Edsel will be missing from his crib.) This fellow (relative of Rabinowitz?) tried to get me to sign a pledge saying I supported the second Philadelphia Conference of the July the Twelfth Society. Told him the only thing I supported was my family and he'd be better off doing same.

He flapped his tongue at me until I couldn't hardly eat my hoagie. Finally he shouted at me so loud when I wasn't expecting it I dropped my cup and spilled hot coffee down the front of my coveralls. I told him right then and there that he could take his damned jabber and ram it down his firebox.

That same afternoon, one of the men told me I was the first chief that ever had the gumption to fire all the jews on the same day. I didn't like doing it, but a couple of bad cylinders can ruin an engine.

August 9, 1885

Talked to Mr. Edison again today. I tried to tell him a bit more about the new gas clipper I was working on, but he kept shushing me and complaining that I was spitting in his ear trumpet. (He did understand enough to suggest that if we combined his wiggling pictures and talking machines with my gas buggy we'd have a roll-in spectacle which could replace vaudeville.) I think he's got his head bolted on backwards as far as gas buggies are concerned, though. See if he flips his eggs the other way when my power coach rolls down to the post office and back next week.

August 26, 1885

Best dag blasted trial ever. Made it to the post office and back in just under twenty-five minutes. That's averaging *thirteen miles an hour.*

Some trouble with other traffic, though. One man broke his ankle when he put it through a hole in the boardwalk trying to get clear of a berserk horse. Of course, horses don't cater much to my machine. I can't say I cater much to them. Just can't see much future for an animal dumb enough to drag a milk wagon through the front window of a general store. (That's going to set me back a few gold eagles. Mr. Edwin Thomas, the storekeeper, chased me halfway to the post office before he had some kind of attack and dropped in the road. Lucky for him someone dragged him out of the way before I started back. Would have smacked him for sure as I haven't perfected my stopping device yet.)

Court next Tuesday.

I was going to talk to Mr. Edison today about manufacturing the machine, but I have to give him a chance to leak a little steam, as I miscalculated the speed of the buggy when I pulled into the shop and had to use one of the work benches to break myself, otherwise I would have gone rolling through the partition and into Mr. E's office.

August 27, 1885

I think I'll wait a few days before talking to Mr. Edison about the machine. I've got to iron out a few wrinkles yet. I know I've got to do something about the crankstart. One more smithie's devil with his arm tore off and I'll be in the hot potato soup with Mr. Edison. The last apprentice told his father some story and the old man (the foreman of a gravel shifting crew) came down to the shop and threatened to wrap a cart axle around my neck if I didn't foot the bill for getting the boy a new arm all the way from Paris, France. Calmed the Father down and told him I could make a better arm right here in the shop. Finished it yesterday and when the lad buckled it on he was so happy he went around the shop and opened all the men's soda pop with the bottle opener I spot-welded onto one arm of his scissors.

Just the same, I've got to get that crank working better. Maybe if I put some kind of ratchet on there so that when the engine backfires, she'll free-wheel instead of letting the crank shoot up in the air with your arm or bashing you in the snout and leaving you cold on the workshop floor. Hope so, anyway.

November 11, 1895

Ran into a couple of interesting young fellow mechanics in town for their brother's funeral. Seems this Norville Wright was trying to cross a bicycle with a bird at the time (?).

If God had meant man to fly, He wouldn't have put all the traction down here.

January 3, 1896

Idea: A good wrench is like a good friend. If you take care of them, they won't strip your nuts.

May 2, 1896

I've about reached the end of my rope with the Edison Company. I can't talk much to Mr. Edison now. (Always thinks I'm talking about something else; sometimes I think that someone's been leaving things in his ear trumpet.) I've saved up a bit of money so maybe try getting some fellas together to build custom cars.

*   *   *

January 5, 1900

Had another squabbledangle with a customer over his delivery. The little get-along I worked up fit all his specifications: warning whistle, hat rack, mahogany footrests in red plush and gold tassels, concealed whist table, the works. The fellow claims he ran plumb-splangwobble into a telegraph pole the first time out.

If a person wants a steering tiller, he should order a steering tiller.

April 17, 1900

At long last, the Model N is finished. K, L, and M all had the same problem— the automatic parasols kept the occupant dry enough but the forward road window clogs up with rainballs and visibility is limited.

Luckily, *American Vehicular* recently ran a cover story on Sir Geoffrey Windshield's dandy new wiper design—the simple back-and-forth motion of his single rubber blade eliminates the entire rotating feather-duster mounting with a single stroke.

May 30, 1900

The Detoit Custom Motorcarriage Works has been featured in the latest issue of *American Vehicular.* There is a large pictograph of our Model C, with a fine inset picto of my hand-turned lug-plungers and chromium need-valve redoublers (patent pending).

Already I have received several invitations to some semiformal tea races around the country.

Another customer returned his Model G. Claims the directional reins get chewed up in the gearworks and the land-anchors don't hold.

Model H has some bugs too. Owner says fumes from the fuel caboose ignite from the gas stack sparks and has to ride her soaking wet to keep his hair. Nitpicker. Jewish fella?

June 17, 1900

The Detroit Custom Motorcarriage Company has given me notice. The Sir Geoffrey Windshield Wiper (patent not pending) operates perfectly, but at high speeds (thirteen to seventeen mph) the whole kit-and-koboodle turns sideways somersaults in time with the wiper. (Lighter blades? Lower center of gravity?)

If the fellow from the engine-pomade company will sponsor me, I will enter the auto tournament in Lansing. If it doesn't rain.

June 25, 1900

Rain. All day and night before the race. Finally I managed to compensate for the wiper's momentum by shifting my weight in the opposite direction of the somersault. Steering still difficult, but less wear on tires, as only two touch ground at any one time. Race to be held tomorrow, if the mud dries or freezes.

June 26, 1900

Victory. Everyone was there. At the opening gun (which nipped Duryea's right front pneumatic and clocked him an early finish into the judges' stand), I was off like a shot and set a record time of one minute for the quarter-mile oval. Diesel's sportstractor was yapping at my stern, but a gust of wind extinguished his pilot light and the leaky behemoth clanked to a dead stop in the mechanics' pasture.

Hispano-Suiza and Daimler took the lead for a few laps but got tangled up in each other's cowcatchers, and each lost precious time trying to scrape the other off along the fenceposts. Peugot's little roll-about averaged twenty-two mph until the judges spotted a pair of powerfully-calved legs under the frenchie's chassis and disqualified the both.

After lunchbreak, the only contestants left were me and Stanley's steamjitney, *The Obedient II*. As we whirled around the final five laps, most of the crowd had already drifted away to a dogfight-and-schnapps festival over by the flats and missed an exciting moment. On the second-to-last lap, my brakes burned up, and only the dragging of my left foot along the ground kept me from crashing bandgoodle into Humber's parked Electro-Super-Snipe (his batteries had gone dead—those fancy Marconi Radiophones used up all the juice his fool magneto-fired cheroot lighter didn't).

Stanley puffed past me and turned into the final lap, hooting and tooting like a banshee. Following close behind, I played a trick I learned from snowball fights with the O'Hooligan brothers—I made rude faces at Stanley's young stoker until the hot-headed ruffian slung his coal-shovel at me and I pulled neatly ahead of their petered-out potbelly with only a small dent in my right front head. Remember: Pound it out tomorrow at the shop with a rubber hammer.

July 16, 1900

Several important bankers answered my telegrams today and expressed great interest in my new Model S. News of my string of racing victories has traveled fast. The Cincinnati-Dayton Overland Competition was written up in the *Akron Beacon Journal* and yesterday representatives of three different motor-pomades pressed me to wear their dusters and spat insignia.

The Model S will be famous. I can feel it.

Meanwhile, the pomade company's extra fiver will help me expand this workshop. Clara (my wife) says Edsel (her newest model) needs more garage space.

Also must find method for backing up out of narrow spaces. Clara won't get out and push anymore as she claims that is why Edsel's front grillwork grew in so odd after he was born. Don't see what's so odd about it, but enough jabber. Time (and ink) are awasting.

July 21, 1900

Model D: Not much here, I'm afraid. Cowcatcher keeps flipping up paving stones and firing them through the windshield.
Model E: The less said, the better.
Model F: Transmission defect sends all power to right wheel. Tends to veer off the road and run in circles.
Model J: Ill-machined crankshaft causes blights of the liver and kidneys in test drivers.
Model P: Neglected to bore exhaust ports. Salvage as scrap (E. Feinberg, $11.00).
Model I: Getting closer here. Worked perfectly until gas vent dripped overflow onto hot muffler assembly ($7.60, E. Feinberg).
    That's all so far. Model S will be better, looks promising.

June 22, 1900

Idea: Success is like a herd of cattle; it could be right around the next corner.

July 30, 1900

Busy busy as usual. A number of motor-pomade manufacturers and a large iron-monger concern have agreed to back the Ford Motor Company. Don't know how I came by the name, just seemed to have a nice heft to it.
    The Model S still has to be towed backwards every time it gets in a fix. So near, yet so far.

January 15, 1903

In a dream last night, I was piloting a Model S through the jungle when a huge serpent with a huge nose appeared in the road and swallowed me and the buggy up whole. While trying to light the headlamps and find an exit I hear a Voice call my name: *"Henry Ford, put the thing in reverse, stupid."*
    It's a crazy idea, but it just might work.

January 20, 1903

Success. The new Model S runs like a charm . . . in *both* directions. Plan to start production as soon as we come up with a name for her.

March 22, 1908

Eureka. The first "Model T" rolled off the production line today. Wonder why I never thought of it before.

April 23, 1912

Model T has been doing very well. As I tell my stockholders: good value, good machine, good sales.

August 26, 1913

Been having some trouble with my blamed fool imbecile stockholders. They want "dividends." It doesn't seem to cut much hay with them that we need a new factory to replace the one burned down by the Association of Radical Caster Mongers.

February 15, 1932

Today my workmen tightened the last nut on my new V-8 engine. At last my hope of creating a fully operational station wagon is about to become a reality. All that stands in my way now is one more thing: artificial wood paneling. Those pups in research and development say it may be another thirty years before we possess the proper technology.

Faddle. If you want something done right, don't leave it to imbeciles. Tomorrow I am contacting Luther Burbank about his work with artificial trees.

April 2, 1934

A delegation of Japanese fellas dropped by today. Bought up those surplus Model Zero combine engines cash. Inquired politely about secret weapons I might have lying around. Told them I was fresh out—sold the lot to those Krupp brothers to make into farm machines.

Little yellow fellas were disappointed, but they took some wax casts of my tools and dies as souvenirs. Helped them call travel agent in Detroit and book tickets for sightseeing jaunt in Hawaii.

Can't figure why they remind me of you-now-whats. Hardly any noses.

June 22, 1915

Log entry number one. Well, we've been at sea three days now on our cruise for peace. I think that chartering this ship just may "get the boys out of the trenches by Christmas," as the very fine slogan thought up by Mr. Allan Jepers says.

I've been spending some time in the engine room jawing with the chief oiler. He's no congressman's brother and that's for sure. He tells me that the big oil smashing Diesel engines that they have down there are really pretty reliable and there's no fear of getting becalmed in the dog latitudes as long as you watch the head temperatures and keep a steady drip on the shaft bearings so the screws don't seize up. No sealed lube nonsense here, by gum.

(It is curious to note that Ford received the following letter from Rudölf Diesel some years earlier and had scrawled across it in black enamel paint, "Cylinder-headed kraut's finally stripped his gears."—Ed.)

Mine Dearest Heinrich;

Vy haf you not been answering to my letters? Fifteen I haf zent you, and you not me one haf zent. I tell you all mine great ideas. I take der oil right from der ground unt smash it up chust like Gött intended. Take it from me, der schpark plug is Götterdämmerung crazy idea. Rudölf Diesel does not use der schpark plug, Rudölf Diesel schpew on der schparks. Gunter of Reisling zay to me chust der udder day dat der power uff mine engine vill giff man being free. It iss Gött's vill dat Diesel should invent der engine uff der new age. I chust give you prize opportunity to get in on der böttom floor uff der dawn uff a new age. Ve can be chust like der brothers marching vorward intö der future bright mit der glorious music to be ringing in our ears unt our hearts. Too long hass man be in der power uff nature. Mit mine new engine mitout der schpark plugs he iss free to be pickniking on der grassy knolls uff imagination. Zö true iss dis! Mine new engine vill hew der vood unt draw der vasser unt look after der grocery store vile der shopkeeper blows his brains out on her dark beer uff der Rhineland undt bounces de frauliens on hiss knee.

Zöme people laugh at der ideas uff Rudölf Diesel. Zöme uff zem efen throw rotten cabbages at him. Dis iss always der fate uff der mench vith the chenius to zee der possibilities uff schmashing der oil right out of der ground. Der people zay der oil is dirt from der ground and der dirt from der ground vill nefer do der houseverk. Laugh day will now until day zee Rudölf Diesel lying in his hammock all der day long hafing his fatty zausage chewed by Valkyries. Also dey don't be zinging my tune maybe Rudölf Diesels big oil schmasher make dem dead. Yah der truth. Iff dey don't get out uff der road mitt schpeed Rudölf Diesel run dem ofer and make dem flatter dan der frenchies, pancakes. Den der people vill zay der he goes, Rudölf Diesel, der great benefactor uff mankind who made der engine to schmash der oil right as it comes from der ground. Dat vill be a pround day for Diesel. I vill schtand on der table unt make a schpeech to all der Chermans. Yah, I vill zing like der Thuringian Minnesingeren from vich I am un proud descendant. Dey vere a poetic people Heinrich unt vould certainly be tickled by dee idea uff schmashing der oil right as it comes from der ground. Always I sink dat I shall make up ein zong about mine bigg schmaser engine but never am I seeming to get around to ziss.

Vell, I haf to be goink to verk in mine schop. Goot by, Heinrich, and giff up on dose schtupid schpark plugs or you'll blow your cabbage off.

Auf Wiedersein,
Rudölf Diesel

June 26, 1915

After lunch today, I made a speech to the rest of the passengers about our voyage. I told them there was a lot more challenge in fighting the bugs and kinks in this universe than there was in fighting some silly fool with a gun. The gun is a pretty simple machine. Just a hollow cylinder jammed full of flash powder and ball bearings.

After I had finished Captain Able got up and told a sea yarn that was quite interesting. It was all about the dangers of an area called the isosceles triangle.[2]

[2]In his autobiography *Three Sheets to the Wind* (Harcourt Brace and World, 1956) Captain Able Duggan describes the dangers which confront mariners who venture to sail through the isosceles triangle. He states:

"When in these parts a smart tar keeps a weather eye peeled for hypogriffs and yellow twisters. These are the worst things that can happen to a sea dog short of the sailors pox (sic). I remember well an encounter I had with this fatal pair. I was on a guano run from

May 30, 1917

Told the annual meeting tonight the story about the ant and the grasshopper. Before the suds had settled, young Bob Willard was on his feet, saying something about a right to dividends and so on. I told them you can't have your car and crash it too, but still it looks as if they mean to go to court against me.

June 15, 1917

Double blast! I just learned the courts have ruled against me in this matter of the dividend. It's a sad day for this country when a man like simple Mike O'Doul can rule against the principles of thrift and good management. His honour Mike O'Doul (a congressman's brother) is a sour mash guzzler.

The only answer seems to be to buy out the stockholders. I'm going to buy out Bob Willard first.[3] I'll be happy to be shed of him and his profligate ways.

March 17, 1926

Thad McDash in and out of my office all day. Nincompoop has been trying to come up with a vehicle to replace the Model A. Danged congressman's brother says that the other companies give a choice of colors, so we should give a choice of colors.

March 18, 1926

Idea: They can have any darned color they want so long as it's black.

the land of the brown Catholics. It was my first command in these waters, and I did not realize the deadly danger we were placed in when a foolish deckhand tested his souvenir blowpipe on a floating Portuguese gas bag which was drifting peacefully by. The next thing I knew, the sky had grown dark and the wind surly and the men began to cry out for their lives. Then, when the elements were at the peak of their fury, a terrible visage appeared on the horizon. A hypogriff! To its right, a feared yellow twister raged, tearing up great chunks of the sea and throwing them into the sky. The hapless mariners began to cry and wail, some rending their oilskins in despair. I was certain that never again would we see our native shore, but would within the space of a few moments lie full fathom five. The hypogriff reared itself up in front of the ship. Gar, it was ugly and cruel bad acting. Just then, the seaman who had squelched the gas bag stepped on a plank which had been set wrong and it sprung a peg, flipping him backwards over the gunnel and into the sea.

In the space of a few minutes the sea again grew calm and the sky cleared. As the yellow twister receded over the horizon and the last ripple of the hypogriff died away as it sunk beneath the deep, I swore by my tattoo that never again would a sailor on my ship be allowed to harm a floating Portuguese gas bag."

[3]One of Ford's clerks apparently informed Ford that this Bob Willard kept a collection of salacious daguerrotypes in his desk and was frequently in attendance at cock fights. The clerk further reported that at one of the cock fights in question, Willard's wits were so fuddled with drink that he leapt into the cock pit to urge on his bird and landed full on the creature, killing the fowl and costing him the sizable wager he had placed upon it. Ford apparently discharged the clerk, having heard from his own mouth that he attended cock fights, and noticing the feathers.

March 26, 1926

Durn that Thad McDash. Can't get a minute's peace with him about. Told him today that I can't see any use in the world for a yellow car. The only thing it'd be good for is scaring the daylights out of poor Negroes and credulous country folk.

April 3, 1926

Young fellas keep showing me sales charts and graphs. Trying to tell me that this General Motors company is taking over with their blasted rainbow wagons. The only thing they're taking over is the tomfool imbecile market, and as far as that goes, they're welcome to it.

February 26, 1927

May have been wrong about the American people. I guess they do want a change, though why any one wants to change from economy and dependability has me licked raw. Thad has come up with a design for some new contraption called the Model A, and I figure if I work on it for a while, it just might turn out all right. Hoping it'll run G.M.'s carriages off the road and into the cow pasture.

March 28, 1927

Body by Fisher my rusty wrench.

November 15, 1936

Edsel wanted to borrow the car again. Kid is such a klutz. Told him I didn't trust him with my car and he took Clara's Chevy. Says he's got some newfangled ideas for spiffing up the line. Power horns, built-in ironing boards, padiddle lights.

That, as the young whippersnappers on the line would say, is a hot one. And what's a forty-three-year-old like that doing without his own car in the first place?

They sure don't make them like they used to. Take me, for instance. Please.[4]

December 8, 1941

War, dognabbit.

Those Japanese fellas pulled a fast one last night at Pearl Harbor, and one of those guldurn bullets had my name on it. Unfortunately, Edsel tells me, so did some of the enemy airplane engines they fished out of the water. Better lie low this time, pacifism-wise.

Hard to figure, though. Always paid their bills on time.

---

[4]It is not clear whether this portion of the entry was in Henry Ford's own handwriting—Ed.

July 15, 1942

That Rosenfeld fella in the White House is getting some uppity. Called up yesterday to say he didn't want artificial wood on the 10,000 tanks we delivered. And he wants plainer upholstery. Nixed whitewalls.

I told him if he didn't like quality American workmanship, order his next fleet from Kaiser Frazier. That was a pip. Kaiser Frazier.

Edsel arrived today with Mr. Disney to show me the plans for my automotive museum in Dearfield Village, Michigan. That Disney'll go far for an arty type— no limp handshake like most—but I told him thumbs down on the talking cars. Plumb irritating is all. Even a senile old crank like me can see that. Hello? Tyke, is that you, fella?

Board meeting at main office today. Wanted to show them some sketches for that new V-168 propeller rocket but I forgot my magic slate and some fuzz-faced vice-president kept distracting me with my rattle.

I don't want to come in, it's still light out.

September 14, 1943

Feeling poorly lately. Plans for automotive museum almost complete. Just in time, too, for I feel the Workglove of the Great Engineer upon my coveralls. At least I'll go knowing future generations will marvel at the wonders in my Temple of Science: 203 different makes of gas buggy, the Discovery of Artificial Wood in thirty-six realistic life-size oil paintings, and that crackerjack replica of Tyke's dog dish.

I don't want to go to school. I'm sick.

Wonder if the O'Hooligan brothers are in Heaven? Wonder if there's anything to do there? Fella has to keep busy.

Idle hands, after all, are the devil's tinsnips.

HE BEGGED HER TO

SLEEP ON A CRIME

A TRUE CASE HISTORY FROM THE FILES OF *CITIZEN'S ARREST* MAGAZINE

by Bruce McCall and Henry Beard

Her honeymoon suite was about to become a hotbed of evil—would Jody win her race against shame?

"LET'S HIT THE HAY!" Vinnie's suddenly husky voice jarred Jody's reverie as she perched demurely on the edge of the bed in their little honeymoon cabin. He was already starting to loosen his white-on-white silk tie.

"Ship!" A curse escaped Vinnie's lips. "Dropped a mommafumpin' cufflink under the copstruckin' bed!" He bent to retrieve the ornament while Jody's nervous fingers fiddled with the latch of her cosmetic case. The hair on his naked back was like black tumbleweed, Jody thought, an unwelcome shiver of near repugnance passing through her. Love should be in her heart on this magic wedding night, Jody knew. But what she felt was more like panic. Panic— and fear. Maybe her girlfriends back in Cannonsburg, Pa. had been right, whispering about Vinnie. Jody had laughed off their warnings as mere jealous carping at her catch. But now . . . well, maybe he was a "torpedo," maybe Italian boys from South Philadelphia were as rough as her girl friends hinted. And cruel. And insatiable.

A dull ripping sound startled Jody. Vinnie uncoiled from his crouch. Held aloft in triumph was the cufflink. But something in his other hand caught her eye.

"What's that?" she asked. Her level tone took Vinnie aback, forcing a sheepish smile in place of the usual leer. "Just this," he answered. He flipped a little square patch of fabric into her lap. "Stupid gobdan thingamajig you find on every mattress—you know, that dumb fuppin' thing that says—"

But Jody's voice was a hacksaw of rage ripping across his words.

"—That says 'Do Not Remove Under Penalty of Law.' You . . . you fool! You idiot! You just removed the tag from that mattress in direct disobedience of United States Government regulations! You destroyed legal proof that this article has been made in compliance with an act of the District of Columbia approved July 3, 1926; Kansas approved March, 1923; Minnesota approved April 24, 1929; New Jersey revised statutes 26:10, 60 to 18, Louisiana Act 467 of 1948 and Massachusetts General Law, Section 270, Chapter 941!"

"Huh?" Vinnie was half-listening, picking his nose. "Mattress tag . . . Massachusetts . . . wadda funk you talkin', c'mon, hon, in the sack, in the sack, an I mean *now!*'

"No, Vinnie." Jody's coolness surprised even herself. "Not now, not ever. I may have married a criminal—well, everyone makes mistakes. But I'm not going to sleep with one, and not on a bed that is in blatant violation of a Federal statute of United States law!"

Vinnie slumped against the headboard, thunderstruck. "Aw, come on, hon, I know you're nervous on your weddin' night an' all, but let's not make a futtin' federal case outta some crappy piece of paper I tore off da bed!"

"That is just what I *am* making out of it, Vinnie—a federal case. Vincent Impagliaroni, I hereby make a Citizen's Arrest on a charge that you did willfully and unlawfully remove a mattress tag certifying that said mattress was made by the manufacturer in accordance with the law, and that the materials in said article were described thereon in accordance with the law! It's all over, Vinnie. Get your things."

There. She had mustered from somewhere the courage to bring it off. Relief flooded her being.

"No, no, Vinnie. Leave the jar of Vaseline. You won't need that where *you're* going. That reminds me. I'll call the officer in charge and ask if they have a honeymoon suite . . . at the Crowbar Hotel."

THE END

OBLIGATORY SEX SCENES

by Dan Abelson, Louise Gikow, Peter Kaminsky, Sean Kelly, Ted Mann, P. J. O'Rourke, Gerald Sussman and Ellis Weiner

Three famous men, authors all of recent important novels (Spiro Agnew, William F. Buckley, and John Lindsay) have lately and often appeared upon prestigious talk shows to plug their respective books. Each member of this august trio has unblushingly observed that, yes, his tome does contain the "obligatory sex scene."

Clearly, these writers, all men of the world, have seen fit to trim the sails of their creative integrity to the prevailing winds of marketing considerations, motivated not by greed but rather by the desire for their significant and redemptive fictions to reach a wider audience than your ponderous and semiliterate political potboiler usually does.

Lest any of our readers, ever eager for sensual sensation, dash out and buy the Buckley book—thereby subsidizing further the man's unnatural tastes and politics—we excerpt and reprint here the entire of his "obligatory sex scene":

> "Oh, yes," she expostulated. "Oh Supreme Being, oh my Supreme Being, yes!"

Always keen to follow the example of our elders and betters, we have taken it upon ourselves to write the "obligatory sex scenes" which, if included in the pages of well-intentioned but, alas, for the most part ignored classics of literature, will return these works to the popularity they deserve.

THE REPUBLIC

by Plato

"I DO NOT understand how that can be so," replied Thrasymachus.

"Perhaps we should take an example," said Socrates, "to see if what I maintain is true in common nature."

"Very well."

"We have said that Love cannot be purely physical, and therefore mortal, for it is eternal and cannot die. Look at those birds over there. Their parents are doubtless dead, and yet they themselves, the embodiment of their parents' love, live on, and fly beautifully against the sunset, do they not?"

"They do, I agree," answered Thrasymachus.

"Just so. Then we must also agree that Love itself is Eternal, Beautiful, and True, must we not?"

"We must," agreed the chastened boy.

"Fine," continued Socrates, gathering his robes up before him. "Now bend over, and I'll drive you home."

THE HOUSE AT POOH CORNER

by A. A. Milne

"KANGA?" said Pooh, in his I'm-Rather-Shy sort of voice.

"What is it, Pooh, dear?"

"Well, Kanga, Owl said that he . . . that is, someone said that you and Owl . . . I mean, Kanga, would it be alright if I put my Tiddleypom in your verywarmplace?" Pooh said this last part very fast, because he was Excited.

"I think that would be Very Nice, Pooh," said Kanga. "I was hoping you'd ask. In fact, I put rather a lot of Honey in there this morning, Just-in-Case." This Unexpected News made Pooh a Very Happy Bear indeed, and so he hummed a little Hum of Lust.

> Oh in I hum
> And out I hum
> And up and down I'm humming
> Titty bum titty bum
> Titty bum bum bum bum
> Sweet Christopher Robin! I'm coming!

WALDEN

by Henry David Thoreau

THERE ARE THOSE who ask me about modern "fancy fucking," an illusion as great as "modern improvements," such as the magnetic telegraph from Maine to Texas. I would rather fuck on a squirrel on a bed of thorns than lie on a mass of velvet cushions being serviced by a painted octoroon from New Orleans.

Man in the primitive ages fucked simply, with a free circulation. When the desire seized him he found an orifice and put his tool into it until he was satisfied. He did not engage in so-called fashionable positions, as useless as the gewgaws on the mantlepieces of Boston's mansions. He thrust his member in and out in a straightforward, honest manner with no ornamentation but his own body.

When I am asked whether I can live by fucking squirrels, I am accustomed to answer such, that I can live by fucking anything, a mole, a ferret, a hole in a maple tree. The human race is capable of finding strange bedfellows. But I went into the woods because I wished to masturbate. I wanted to commune with my own cock. Instead of fucking one hundred squirrels, stroke your own shmekel! Simplicity! Back and forth, up and down. Squeeze it, stroke it, make it harder than a ha'penny nail. Who needs to spend a king's ransom on female flesh when you can use your imagination and your sturdy two hands? And so I jerked off as frequently as the church bells rang in Concord, and I was not worse off for it. And I did not go blind, as my friend Emerson warned. My eyes have never been better.

SHERLOCK HOLMES

by Sir Arthur Conan Doyle

"The Adventure of the Extreme Unpleasantness"

IT WAS A cold and foggy day in September of '98 when I next had occasion to call upon my remarkable friend Sherlock Holmes. I was greeted as usual at the entrance to my former, and his present, lodgings on Baker Street by the worthy Mrs. Hudson. "Do come in, Doctor," she said. "Mr. Holmes has been expecting you." So saying, the good housekeeper led me up the well-worn and familiar steps to the door of 221-B.

Holmes answered my discreet knock with a peremptory, "Ah, Watson. Do come in," his extraordinary powers of observation having doubtless informed him of his visitor's identity sight unseen. I entered, and beheld a singular tableau.

Holmes was engaged in an uncommonly spirited bout of sexual intercourse with a woman whom I immediately recognized as "*the* woman," the magnificent and enchanting creature whose acquaintance my friend had made during the adventure I have described in my journals as "A Scandal in Bohemia." Her dress and coiffure in disarray, Miss Irene Adler—for it was indeed she—thrashed and writhed upon the divan beneath Holmes's persistent thrusting.

"Sherlock, oh Sherlock!" she cried in the extremity of her passion, addressing my friend with a familiarity I found both unusual and impudent. "I am spending, I am spending! Ah! I am spent!"

"Holmes!" I sputtered. "What the devil—"

"Orgasm, Watson, and a clitoral one, I believe," Holmes remarked.

"Yes, but . . . now see here, Holmes, this is the very limit. How can you—"

Without missing a stroke, and continuing despite his paramour's obvious state of exhaustion and satiation, my friend directed his steely gaze toward me and explained, "My dear fellow, the physical symptoms could not be more obvious. The intense flush in the cheeks. The labored breathing. The spasmodic quivering in the loins. After observing these plainly apparent symptoms, and taking into consideration the woman's sudden and rather passionate expostulations which you yourself have just heard, one would have to be a perfect fool not to conclude that Miss Adler has just experienced a delirious and ecstatic explosion of pleasure like a thousand pounds of nitroglycerine detonating in her love chamber."

"But it's so absurdly simple!" I cried in admiration. The endurance of my friend would have astonished a layman, but I, as a medical man, mentally ascribed it to the effects of tincture of cocaine injected just prior to the carnal engagement. Whether this accounted for the great detective's near-superhuman capabilities or no, Holmes would not divulge. Without ceasing his rhythmic penetrations, he reached into the pocket of the old smoking jacket he had evidently dropped to the carpet during the erotic revelries, removed a piece of foolscap redolent of cheap French perfume, and extended it to me.

"But come, Watson," he said, the excitement of what surely was a new case beginning to color his cheeks. "Have one of Mrs. Hudson's excellent buttered scones. Then direct your attention to this—a most intriguing missive, I think. I'll be done here in a moment, and then to work. The game's afoot!"

Shortly thereafter we were seated . . .

CONTACT BRIDGE

by Charles Goren

South opens.
Seeing her vulnerable, North immediately raises.

South passes.
North finesses.
South sees that her partner is now fully raised and ready for action in her suit.
She knows that if he completes play while she is still weak, he will dummy
and her hand will have to be strong enough for both of them. She has opened
and it is up to him now. She passes.
North responds by leading with all he's got.
His club is stronger than she had dared hope.
He trumps her solidly once and then again.
North doubles and redoubles.
South is sure he is out of tricks.
He makes the grand slam, amazing her.
South responds by spreading her remaining cards, flushing royally.

PRIDE AND PREJUDICE

by Jane Austen

Chapter XLIII

THE WINDING path that they had been following had grown narrower,
and was overhung with branches that tore at Elizabeth's gown; soon
it was but three feet at its widest part, when she espied, in the
distance, an old summer house, dilapidated and overgrown with weeds and
mosses, of a lonely and slightly forbidding aspect. As the first drops of rain
began to fall, Mr. Darcy turned his steps towards the building, quitting the
path and taking a shorter way through the tall grasses;—Elizabeth had little
choice but to follow. He murmured something about the weather as they
reached their destination; the door yielded easily to his touch, and they reached
their haven just as the rain began in earnest.

The interior was empty of any furnishing, save for a small settee, towards
which Darcy let Elizabeth;—and when *she* had seated herself, much to her
amazement, he flung himself to his knees before her, and, in a change of mood
that seemed as abrupt as the change of weather, began ardently to express
his admiration for and devotion to her person. Elizabeth hardly knew how to
respond!—was this the cold, arrogant Mr. Darcy, who had expressed such
scorn for her on previous occasions? She was attempting to reply when an
even more strange event took place;—to her great consternation, he lifted up
her skirts, and disappeared beneath them!—in breathless accents did she beg
him to desist; in ardent though muffled tone did he make negative reply, as
he attempted, with no little difficulty, to undo her drawers; when he had
succeeded in the latter, he stopped attempting the former; and Elizabeth was

filled with the most delightful and confused sensations; she allowed to herself that they were certainly pleasurable, but at the same time wondered with rising alarm if she had, by her momentary weakness, allowed too much familiarity in their previous intercourse.

But her pleasure mounted to such an extent that she soon lost her fears in that direction. "Oh! Oh!" she cried, when she could contain herself no longer— "I am all in a flutter!—Mr. Darcy, your unexpected cordiality has left me quite speechless;—my previous coldness was unpardonable;—oh, my dear, *dear* Mr. Darcy;—how can you ever forgive me?—oh, oh, *oh!*"—and Mr. Darcy, whose head now emerged from beneath Elizabeth's petticoats, although *another portion* of his anatomy remained hidden from view, joined his voice to hers in an outpouring of sentiment to which no one, knowing his proud, aloof manner, might have responded without a great deal of amazement.

AMENDMENT I

Congress shall make no law respecting an establishment of religion, or prohibiting the free exercise thereof; or abridging the freedom of speech, or of the press; or the right of the people peaceably to assemble, congregate, and come together in such form and manner, comprehending but not limited to fornication, copulation, coition, venery, adultery, incest, bestiality, concubinage, cunnilingus, fellatio, and such concomitant acts of sexual congress as buggering, humping, sucking, thrusting, squeezing, biting, sweating, swearing and screaming, as the people in their sole discretion shall deem appropriate.

ABRAHAM LINCOLN: THE PRAIRIE YEARS

by Carl Sandburg

It was early in the spring of 1819. Young Abe had barely turned thirteen, but he already had a piece of manly equipment that had earned him the nickname *the Railsplitter*. Strong as Indiana maple it was, and straight and true as half a cord of good Michigan pinewood. Young Abe loved to read books, never mind if he understood them, and young Widow Harless would pay him for chores around her place with the loan of one of her French books, filled with pictures that set the young boy to dreaming. It was one day while Abe was walking on the ceiling that something happened to the boy that he would remember as a man. "Would you like to take a bath, Abe?" asked the widow. In those days country people would bathe together because water was scarce, and Abe was not abashed at the widow's request. "I cannot tell a lie," said Abe, who wanted a cleaning, because he was dirty. "But there is hardly room for you, me, and this sturdy Aspen between my legs in that small tub."

"Never you mind," said the widow, offering to suck the sap from out of that tree until it lay down as innocent as a limp radish when the wind rises out of the west and the scent of Jesus is in the cloud drift. So they bathed together, and another thing or two did they, and that was the first time that Abe understood the word Union. On the way home, he scratched a poem on the back of an owl, using some chewed sassafras leaves for ink;

> Abraham Lincoln visited the widder.
> Split her rails and then her beaver.

He would write more as the years went by.

"THE SONG OF HIAWATHA"

by Henry Wadsworth Longfellow

Hiawatha's Honeymoon
Verse DCCLXXXVIII

> By the shore of Gitche Gumee,
> By the shining Big-Sea-Water,
> At the doorway of his wig-wam,
> Hiawatha stood and waited,
> With his loin-cloth at his ankles,
> And his manhood rigid standing,
> Ready for the promised blow-job,
> From his new bride, Minnehaha.
> Minnehaha ho-ho hee-hee,
> Laughing spread-out wide her cunt flaps,
> Fingered hard her fur-fringed fun knob,
> Took his wang within her mouth-hole,
> Humming on his come-flushed coupstick,
> Slip slop slurp slurp suck suck gobble.
> With a rhythm repetitious,
> Slipped her lips along his tent-pole.
> Forth and backward like the metre
> Of the third-rate verse we're reading.
> But forgotten were the plodding,
> Boring, hackneyed lines of poesy,
> As his load shot out her nostrils,
> And she flopped back on the mud floor.

MOBY DICK

by Herman Melville

Chapter 101
The Pequod *Meets the* Delilah

Ship ahoy! Hast seen the White Whale?"

So did Ahab cry his peremptory greeting to the snug three-master that bobbed in lanquid placidity abaft our port beam. She sported British colors, and appeared to be a ship unlike the whaling variety as constructed by either English shipbuilders or those of America, but rather seemed laden with a tamer cargo, be it textile or jute or breadfruit. Likely she was accustomed to milder climes and glassier waters, such as those we now mutually sailed. But the *Delilah*'s—for that was her name—pleasure was proving Ahab's curse.

"Ahoy, ship!" cried the *Pequod*'s commander. "Hast seen Moby Dick? Or do ye not know of the beast?"

"Aye, sir!" called the *Delilah*'s captain, a red-faced, swart man clad in rough bluecloth and jovial in expression. "Lower me, lads, and I'll pay this *Pequod* a visit." To Ahab he called in conspiratorial tone, "I've a yarn to spin for ye, sir. So make ready yer welcome. Will ye have me aboard?"

"I will," replied Ahab, his leathery hands working a belaying pin as a constable manipulates his billystick. "Lower, then, and be welcome."

The captain and mate of the *Delilah* were presently lifted aboard and met on the main deck by Ahab, accompanied by the mate Starbuck and the jocular Stubb. During this the crews of the two ships would peer across the narrow gulf that stretched between the vessels and exchange intelligence, as is a seaman's wont. "Halloo, there! *Delilah*! Where are ye bound, and with what cargo?"

"Ahoy, *Pequod*! To San Salvador, with caskets of rosewater, and talc! And what of yourself?"

"Outward bound, and in search of the white whale! No less!"

"What! Are ye daft, then, my laddies?"

"Avast! Avast, and shove it!"

Meanwhile Captain Bammer, for so was the *Delilah*'s commander called, complimented Ahab on his vessel, and the two men exchanged discussion of climatic conditions and the mood and manner of the adjacent seas. But Ahab was greatly impatient for word of his quarry, and soon could restrain himself no longer. "Come, sir, what word have ye of the White Whale? You've a yarn to spin, ye tell me. Spin it, I say, for I am sore eager to lower for the beast and have at it."

"Mayhap you've already met the monster a time previous, hey, Captain?" Bammer asked, his eye studying Ahab's leg of white bone. "We of Britain are as familiar as any Yankee with the proclivity of this leviathan to gnaw the limb of whoever happens—"

"Proclivity be damned, sir!" spat Ahab. "Have ye a tale to tell, or no?"

"My apologies, sir." And here Bammer did smile, but whether to placate the temperamental Ahab, or at some private recollection, no man could say. "For a tale I do have to tell, sir, and by your leave will now reveal it.

"It was nigh onto a year ago that I was homeward sailing from a ten-month mission in search of the spermaceti, and a blessed voyage it had been, gentlemen: for we were loaded to the mizzen with good sperm. We had a clean wind, a happy crew, and the promise of prosperity awaited us in Portsmouth, come landfall. All omens declared the success of the venture—"

"Avast!" Ahab cried. "And 'twas then you spied the beast, is it!? Aha, yes! I know him—and in the prettiest of weather, does he arrive to torment and—"

"Bless me, sir, no!" Bammer laughed. "Never saw the creature. For we reached our port with three days to spare, without mishap. No, sir, neither shark nor storm, nor any whale, white or red or green, did disturb our progress. My point is this, then: two days we were docked in Portsmouth harbor. The lads were nearly all in town, visiting wives or sweethearts or making merry over meat and ale . . . and my mate, Mr. Sprocket—pardon, Sprocket, Captain Ahab, Captain, Sprocket—Mr. Sprocket here suggests that I hie myself ashore and celebrate with my own wife.

" 'Well, Sprocket,' says I, 'I'd take yer advice, saving for the fact that the wife is dead and buried for three years. And a pretty lass she was in her time, by God.'

" 'Well then, sir,' he says, bold as brass, 'every seaman knows what dalliances can be had in Portsmouth by a healthy sailor with a bit of silver in his pocket . . .' and he winks at me, Sprocket you rascal! Ah, Sprocket, you are a rogue."

"Hist, man!" Ahab interrupted impetuously. "What of the whale! What of Moby Dick?"

"In time, sir, in time. So. It strikes me that this first mate's suggestion is as tantalizing as it is impudent, and with Sprocket minding the ship I betakes myself for a constitutional along one of several byways through the city that boasts various . . . establishments, if you comprehend me, gents."

"Aye, and too plainly, sir. For there's no good in such dalliances, if you ask me," Starbuck opined.

"But more, sir," Stubb urged. "And pray be specific."

Again Bammer laughed, apparently oblivious to Ahab's silent fury and frustration. "You've an ear for detail, is it? Very well, then. I betook me to an establishment called The Cask o' Sperm, and can ye not tell by the place's very name how welcome a whaling man is made to feel therein? And after certain . . . *arrangements* . . . I found myself in a nicely appointed room, all frills and lace and satin divans, don't ye know, and a comely lass barely eighteen summers old ready to do my bidding. A gay young thing she was, too, and sporting—"

"The teats!" Stubb cried, unmindful of the man's rank. "Tell of the teats!"

"Ay, lad! Teats there were, and a full complement of them, two in all. Hefty as casabas from the Carribbee they were, full round and—"

"Damn your eyes!" Ahab bellowed. "Did ye or did ye not see the White Whale?"

"Have patience, Captain, for I tell of the beast in but a moment. So, gents: here was I, ten months from the sight of woman, and now before me kneeled this angel of mercy. 'Shall I disrobe, my dear,' say I. 'If you please, your honor,' she replies. And does so as well."

"The flukes!" Srubb panted, meaning by this the legs. "What of her flukes?!"

"Twin momuments to alabaster purity, my lads. And at the sight of one another did we commence into heavily respiring, and each ardent caress I gave her she returned—aye, and with more fervor than you'd expect from one so professionally engaged!"

"What of Moby Dick?" wailed Ahab, near apoplexy.

"And then we were on her couch," Bammer continued, not heeding the Captain. "And as I made to ram home the harpoon, she balked and said, 'A moment please, your honor,' and in a trice the damsel had taken me into her mouth!"

"Huzzah! Huzzah!" cheered Stubb, and slapped the dubious Starbuck on the back. "And then you lowered away, my hearty! You lowered away!"

"What of the whale, damn ye!"

"Nay, but hold, lads. I was preparing to lower away, but my pike was still gripped by the girl's jaws, when all on a sudden I clap eyes on her marvelous rump. And idly—idly, I say, *to myself* it was—I murmur, 'Ah, my dear, but ye are as white as the White Whale himself, as white as Moby Dick, who every sensible seaman does fear.' And suddenly she starts! And gags! And gurgles! And in a jiff had bitten clean clear through my pin and clove it in twain!"

"No!" gasped Stubb, and nearly swooned, holding onto stolid Starbuck's arm for support.

"Aye, lad. And when the shouting and bleeding and the apologies were subsided, did she explain to me that her own uncle was an American whaling captain who some time previous had lost a limb to the maw of the leviathan, and any mention of the whale disturbed her to the point of spasms and fever. Her uncle! Are ye this same man, sir?" This last he addressed to our captain, who merely stared at the man with a blank gaze and nodded slowly.

"Then behold this bony substitute for as stout an organ as ever traveled a deck," Bammer said, and produced from his trousers an ivory appendage fashioned of whalebone similar to Ahab's leg. "For no longer can I sail for whale oil and the sperm, gents. My vital powers are sapped, and I now deliver cargoes of scented water, and talc, and the like. I am not ashamed of my fate, mind you. But to whosoever does finally kill this white monster, let him know I join in his pursuit. More than one captain has he done injury to, this Moby Dick!"

And with that Bammer hoisted himself down into his boat, and made his way back to the *Delilah*. Ahab, his monomania again kindled and stoked, scowled, and disappeared below decks.

CONSUMER REPORTS

We tested five cameras in this range. A target area was chosen and lighting conditions were standardized to give the best possible view of the interior we had selected.

The *Kodak Trimline* is a popular model at around $30.00, and has a three setting zone focus system. On the first setting two people were visible as vague shapes within the picture frame, while on the second setting a surprising improvement in resolution was achieved. All testers were high in their praise for the third and highest setting, features of the room and characteristics of the two females being observed.

The *Rollei 400* was judged difficult to adjust (see chart next page), but demonstrated its superior design. On all settings, we could observe such refinements as the patterned fabric of the thin silk dress one of the subjects was peeling from her supple form, impressive for a zone focus mechanism.

The *Minolta Standard* fared poorly. Even with the superb 500-X tripod (C.R. May '74), the best it could do was a somewhat fuzzy image of two pale bodies entwined in languourous embrace.

The *Fujica* we tested was another story, the improved image quality well worth the extra 2.6 lbs. in weight. Though difficult to use with eyeglasses, the patented viewfinder showed a generous and clear spectacle of Sapphic love. Indeed, the scene seemed a lot nearer than the figure shown on the useful built-in distance indicator (also standard on *Fujica* models). Even with a poor lens fine points were visible; wisps of blonde hair cascading over creamy thighs, nails digging into flesh, details so vivid that one had the feeling of being in the target room.

The *Minox 280* boasts a variable range finder that enables rapid focusing. This makes position changes possible, and we found it a pleasure to be able to change from firm breast to quivering buttock without losing time in resetting. With this addition we could visually explore the environment so freely we felt we could almost hear the pleasure cries of the two women, almost taste the ripe love juices that now flowed freely in the heat of the mounting passion.

As we began shooting in earnest we found the thumb-slide film advance a nuisance, requiring a complex series of actions to cock the camera after every shot. Both the *Kodak* and the *Minox* had viewfinders which tended to fog at the worst times. As events surged to a fiery climax, all shooting ceased as we busied ourselves wiping and recocking.

By the time we refocused, we found ourselves disappointingly gazing at two supine forms lying in quiet repose, skin flush and sensual smiles ironically clear images of opportunities missed.

THE PICKWICK PAPERS

by Charles Dickens

Chapter 28

A *good-humored Christmas chapter, containing an account of a wedding, and some other sports beside, which, although in their way even as good customs as marriage itself, are not quite so "rigidly kept up" in these censorious times.*

. . . if anything could have added to the interest of this agreeable scene, it would have been the remarkable fact of Mr. Pickwick's appearing without his gaiters, or anything else in the habilimental way, for the first time in the memory of his oldest friends.

"Do you mean to frolic?" said Wardle.

"Of course I do," replied Mr. Pickwick. "Don't you see I am ready for the purpose?" Mr. Pickwick called attention to his manly part, which was indeed at the ready, and while not of the largest construction, had a healthy glow about it which showed it to be still a formidable engine of merriment.

The family was by this time assembled, according to an annual custom on Christmas Eve, observed by old Wardle's forefathers from time immemorial. From the center of the ceiling, old Wardle had just suspended with his own hands a huge branch of mistletoe, and this same branch of mistletoe instantaneously gave rise to a scene of general and most delightful struggling and confusion; in the midst of which, Mr. Pickwick, with a gallantry that would have done honor to the oldest of noble European families, took the elderly Lady Tollimglower by the hand, led her beneath the mystic branch, gently spread her nether lips and, liberally embellishing this venerable aperture with fresh butter from the dairy, mounted her in all courtesy and decorum. The old lady submitted to this politeness with the dignity which befitted so important and serious a solemnity, but the younger ladies, not being so thoroughly imbued with a superstitious respect for the custom—or imagining that the value of a pleasant tumble is very much enhanced if it cost a little trouble to obtain it—screamed and struggled, and ran into corners, and threatened and remonstrated, and did everything but leave the room until some of the less adventurous gentlemen were on the point of desisting, when they all at once found it useless to resist any longer and submitted to be mounted with a good grace. Mr. Winkle mounted the young lady with the black eyes, and Mr. Snodgrass mounted Emily, and Mr. Weller, not being particular about the form of being under the mistletoe, mounted Emma and the other female servants just as he caught them. As to the poor relations, they were mounted by everybody. And the plainer portions of the young lady visitors, in their excessive confusion, ran right under the mistletoe, as soon as it was hung up, without even knowing it!

Now, the screaming had subsided, and faces were in a glow, and bodies in a tangle, and Mr. Pickwick, after mounting the old lady, as before mentioned, was standing under the mistletoe, looking with a very pleased countenance on all that was passing around him, when before he distinctly knew what the matter was, he was surrounded by the whole body and squeezed, pinched, fondled, sucked upon, or penetrated by every one of them.

It was a pleasant thing to see Mr. Pickwick in the center of the group, now pulled this way, and then that, first taking one person's part within his mouth, then another's in his hand, and then someone else's up the backside, and to hear the peals of laughter which were raised on every side.

"This," said Mr. Pickwick, looking around him, "this is, indeed, sport!"

"Vell!" said Sam Weller, "there'll be a deal o' hole-fillin' yet afore this here passes, as the Verger says to the Sexton at the first outbreak o' plague."

OUR TOWN

by Thornton Wilder

STAGE MANAGER: "Mr. Webb is publisher and editor of the Grover's Corners *Sentinel*. That's our local paper, y'know."

MR. WEBB enters from his house, pulling on his coat.

STAGE MANAGER: "Have you any comments, Mr. Webb?"

MR. WEBB: "Very ordinary town, if you ask me. But our young people seem to like it well enough. Ninety percent of 'em graduating from high school settle down right here to live—even when they've been away to college."

STAGE MANAGER: "Now, is there anyone in the audience who would like to ask Editor Webb anything about the town?"

MAN AT THE BACK OF AUDITORIUM: "Whaddaya do for a piece of ass in Grover's Corners?"

MR. WEBB: "Well . . . there's Mrs. Gawalski, she runs a house over in Polack town. 'Course, that'll cost you two dollars. Then there's Abe Bingham down at the stable—he'll suck your pecker. Abe's not quite right in the head, though. To tell the truth, I guess most folks just hump the old lady or yank on it."

BEING AND TIME

by Martin Heidegger

V. Being-In As Such

26. Throbbing-Memberhood and Its Potentiality-for-Exploding-in-White-Hot-Orgasmicity

At first glance the Being-in *(In-sein)* of Throbbing-member appears to us as a latency. Throbbing-member stands before us as a phenomenon of Itness, i.e., Throbbing-memberhood-in-its-Selfhood-as-merely-ontic Being. The Being-in of Throbbing-member attains facticity as an ontological verity when, with eager hands and low urgent moans, she guides Throbbing-member into her hot, pulsing womanhoodness. Then, too, does Throbbing-member discover the Being-present-at-hand-along-with *(Mitvorhandsein)* of breasts, mouth, clitoris, etc.

Thus, Throbbing-member enters "into" the spatio-temporal nexus of her love-drenched pussyhood and is present *(zugegen)* to its potentiality-for-attaining-orgasmhood. This is what I call Throbbing-member's *Being-toward-orgasmicity.* Her verbal characterization, "Oh my God, you're in me!" has ontological content only insofar as by "in" we understand "the entity inside" *(Das inwendig Seiende)* in its ontological selfhood as Throbbing-member, exclusive of the theirness of other "throbbing-members" merely ready-to-hand, i.e., mere equipment.

"Oh God, I can't stand it, I'm coming, I'm coming, I'm coming . . ." is, therefore, not only a phenomenological statement, but has existential-ontological meaning as well.

LETTERS OF EVELYN WAUGH

edited by Geoffrey Wyndshield-Wiper

Concerning this article: It is the opinion of P. J. O'Rourke that a lot of the readers of National Lampoon *do not know who Evelyn Waugh was. For the information of these conjectual ignoramuses: Waugh (waw), Evelyn. 1903–1966. English satirical novelist. Fan of Raymond Chandler. Author of* Decline and Fall, Vile Bodies, Remote People, Brideshead Revisited, Black Mischief, A Handful of Dust, *and numerous other novels and articles, including a life of Edmund Campion, the Jesuit martyr. Died April 10 at Combe Florey.*

TO NANCY MITFORD

Darling Nancy,

Went with Cloo[1] to Rumpelstiltskin's Cathedral.[2] It was abominable, as ever. Returning home to meet Ranulph,[3] we encountered Harold[4] and a handful of buggers. They tried to be charming, but we would have none of it. That made them petulant, and they . . . Ranulph down and . . . him in the . . . I got off with a . . . I am sending you a copy of *Brideshead*.

Love and kisses,
Evelyn

TO ADOLF HITLER

Dear Adolf,[5]

In your last letter I thought you slightly supercilious in tone regarding the stained glass of Dietrich Anchor-Hocking[6] at Breslau.[7] If we are to remain friends, this must not continue. Please write more about your people's car. That seems to be where your talent lies.

Love to Unity,
Evelyn

TO HAROLD ROSS

Dear Harold,[8]

I am so glad you are *not* going to publish my article in the *New Yorker*,[9] as I have heard you have trouble paying and cater to buggers. By the way, if you're ever in

---

[1]Cloo. A name Waugh gave to his mittens.

[2]Rumpelstiltskin's Cathedral. A monument near Bedsore for which Waugh had an abiding hatred. Designed in 1505 by Hrothgobble for the Knave of Hearts; Waugh particularly despised the nave of the edifice and punned on the subject.

[3]Ranulph. Daughter of Winston Churchill. Waugh used Churchill's name frequently to describe his own bottom.

[4]Harold Angel. Notorious homosexual rapist. Waugh's contemporary at Oxford.

[5]Adolf Hitler. Führer of National Socialist Republic. Later bitterly opposed by Waugh during World War II.

[6]Dietrich Anchor-Hocking. Orthodox artisan of the 1500s noted for the balance of his compositions in stained glass. Waugh was later to regret his early praise of this man, a notorious bugger.

[7]Breslau. A city famed for its buggers who work in stained glass.

[8]Harold Ross. Magazine editor despised by Waugh. American.

[9]*New Yorker*. American men's magazine.

England,[10] don't try to see the Queen.[11] I spoke to her Wednesday and she agrees you're beneath contempt.

Yours,
Evelyn

TO AUBERON WAUGH

Dear Bron,[12]

You are not my real son. I assumed you were aware of this. Your dear mother accepted you from a band of traveling tinkers, who in return sharpen our soup spoons. The fact that you are nine and incapable of being happy suggests you would be better off working for a living. I recommend the House of Lords[13] men's facility. Suck, don't blow.[14]

Evelyn

TO THE EDITOR OF THE *SPECTATOR*

Sir,

No doubt now having admitted that it was a Bascomb No. 1[15] brush and not the Segel No. 2[16] with which the pervading greens were applied in DeNipple's[17] painting *Lethargo,*[18] Mr. Hargreaves[19] will retire to a culvert and eat shit.

Faithfully,
Evelyn Waugh

TO FR. JACOB STEAK

Dear Jake,

Did you know DeNipple was a Jew? I only just found out. He will go to hell. I have noticed several priests supporting the Union movement. Is the Holy Office asleep?

Love,
Evelyn

P.S. If I kiss my sheets, is it wrong if I think of them as sheets? What if as used sheets? Write soon; I must know.

E.W.

---

[10]England. Island where Waugh was born.

[11]Queen. Close friend of Waugh's.

[12]Bron. Insulting diminutive Waugh applied to his son. Though never publicly acknowledged, privately Waugh claimed the boy as his own, having, he said, paid good money for him in the Sudan.

[13]House of Lords. British homosexual hangout.

[14]Suck, don't blow. An example of Waugh's legendary wit.

[15]Bascomb No. 1. A famous paintbrush.

[16]Segal No. 2. An inferior brush with a wide, indelicate stroke. Much hated by Waugh.

[17]DeNipple. Prominent painter admired by Waugh, who only later found out he was a Jew.

[18]*Lethargo.* Painting of a fat girl sleeping.

[19]Mr. Hargreaves. Art critic. Found dead in a pottery kiln after Waugh's letter. Presumed a suicide. "Eyes glazed over," remarked Waugh.

Doc Feeney's Scrapbook of

SPORTS ODDITIES

THE OLD SIDEWINDER BUNTS
A FEW DOWN MEMORY LANE

by Bruce McCall

THEN THERE WAS THE TIME Chisox flychaser Coo Coo Bananas, he of the famed chocolate soda penchant, ordered a big meal at Jack Dempsey's restaurant after a crucial win over the Bronx Bombers. "Ay hav beeg steek," Coo Coo chirped to the waiter in his best broken English. A few minutes later came Coo Coo's dinner. You guessed it . . . Blue Point oysters smothered in chocolate pudding!

DERBY FAVORITE RATED UNDERDOG

Grantland Rice is best remembered as the beloved dean of American sportswriters, a giant among scribes. Not so well known is Rice's generosity toward aspiring young scriveners of the sporting scene, typified by this reply to a letter from one Rice admirer seeking advice. "Thank you for your interest in writing me," the venerable scribbler penned, "but I know of no openings on our newspaper just now."

•

Lacrosse is one of America's fastest-moving and fastest-growing sports, recently passing quoits in popularity on our college campuses. But how many readers know that lacrosse was invented by the Indians many years before Columbus discovered America, and was taken up by whites only after being received in trade for a 1931 Studebaker?

•

PIGSKIN IMMORTAL FOUND DEAD

Strangest golf story of 'em all has to be the tale of Scotsman W. R. C. Wimbly's 1923 Funtoon Closed Invitational Open victory at the fabled Cuff links, near Aberdeen.

•

Speaking of golf, how many fans know that Harry Gaddis captured the 1932 British Open, played at Clambake that year for the first time, with only half a ball? Strange, but true! Seems Gaddis's drive off the third tee was run over by a passing locomotive as it bounced out of bounds. Then, rather than take a four-stroke penalty for putting a new ball in play, Gaddis kept right on playing with the shattered spheroid. His score after 36 holes was almost double that of other competitors, but the canny Gaddis buttonholed the Steward of the Course. If he'd played with only half a ball, Gaddis argued, then he should be charged for only half his score. And cut in half, that tally was good enough to take the tourney and the title!

•

BATBOY HOLDOUT ENTERS 4TH MONTH

St. Louis Cardinal infielder Ottie Medway is the only major league player in modern history to play a full nine innings on roller skates, as any fan knows. Who recalls the Washington Senators outfielder who wore a dress through both games of a double-header? Hint: It wasn't Rube Gazebo.

•

POLAR BEARS INTERRUPT HOCKEY GAME

Answer to several reader queries: Art Mousley was the first white to crack black pro baseball's "color line," in 1946. That was the year Art started as the New Orleans Chocolate Pelicans' regular third sacker, amid pressure on and off the field that might have cracked a lesser man than this great competitor and fine gentleman. Even so, Art confessed years later that he almost gave up the game in his first season with the Chocolates. It was a life of being forced to stay in fancy first-class hotels instead of the rundown rooming houses where his teammates lodged; of travelling First Class on crack trains instead of joining the other players in seedy day coaches; of being forced by Jim Crow laws to take his meals in posh eateries with starched linen on the table instead of hanging out in rib joints with the team. "Go back to Sutton Place, Honkey" and "Hey Massa, where's your bullwhip?" were taunts that followed Art Mousley wherever he played. But his bat and his fielding magic as custodian of the hot corner were a more convincing reply than any words. Art went on to play twelve stellar seasons with the Chocolate Pelicans, garnering three batting titles and a host of other accolades along the way. He retired in 1958 and is now a junior executive with the Dixie Peach cosmetics concern in Mobile, Alabama.

●

They Box by Mail . . .

CHAMP'S LEFT HOOK TIMED AT 2 DAYS, 14 MINUTES

Here's the oldest baseball braintwister of 'em all. The national pastime's oldest controversy has nothing to do with activities on the diamond. Now past its hundredth semester as an organized pro sport, baseball is a legend without clear ancestors. According to which historian you listen to, it was invented by English villagers of the seventeenth century, Civil War troops in camp in 1863, the Pequod Indians of Maine, Abner N. Doubleday, or—as Columbia University Professor of Romance Languages (and avid baseball buff) Percy Zang claims, by Chester A. Arthur, nineteenth President of these United States. Zang's researches recently led him to a trunk found in an attic in upstate New York, full of Arthur's personal papers. Clearly jotted down in Arthur's familiar strong hand, under the date of July 4, 1859, is the notation, "Good weather. Went outside and invented baseball." This corner won't take sides in what bids to be a real knock 'em down, drag 'em out controversy among baseball scholars. But we always liked comedian Shabby Shekels' theory about who really invented baseball. "It has to be my wife," says the irrepressible comic, "because she's the oldest bat around!"

●

Hague Verdict Rights 82-year-old Wrong

WORLD COURT RULES BASKETBALL NOT A SPORT

Football's in the air once more, which reminds us that it was forty years ago this season that the fabled Tennessee Vols under Coach Elmer "Zoo" Keeper, with the immortal Five Mad Dervishes front line, thundered through an unbeaten Southern Conference schedule and went all the way to the Dust Bowl on New Year's Day, 1934, only to have to turn around and go all the way home again due to—you guessed it—a dust storm that forced cancellation of the gala Sooner State classic. In fact, though televised by ABC-TV every year since 1957, the star-crazed Dust Bowl has never been held. Talk about oddities in sport!

●

Crunchy Granola, low-scoring center of the NHL Los Angeles Kings, has a new off-season career. Crunchy smuggles arms to Central America, then smuggles hard drugs back into this country on return trips. Getting caught and going to jail doesn't faze Crunchy. "After all," he quips, "I spent a hundred and thirty-five minutes last year in the penalty box!"

•

Fiction can be stranger than truth in the topsy-turvy world of sport. F'rinstance, did you know that the all-time boxing champ of Holland was a woman? You can look it up!

•

TO NIX $$$ CAGE BID? PREXY MUM

Former Olympic bronze medalist (for a third-place finish in the men's punt singles at the Rome games in 1960) Herb Zope, in town for the upcoming Infantile Paralysis Dinner, tells this corner that the dread disease has suffered a "serious" decline over these past fifteen years and is in danger of following the dodo bird and the Canada goose into extinction unless the public wakes up soon. If you can't attend the dinner, Herb suggests you send him cash in unmarked bills, care of this corner. A great sportsman in his day, Herb Zope now follows many lucrative interests and remarks that his hobby hasn't changed since Olympic days: stealing towels.

•

Pulverizer, winner of the 1948 Preakness Stakes, was owned by Mrs. Patsy Pangborn Puff of Abandoned Farms. Sound familiar? No wonder—Mrs. Puff's nephew, Burdick Sanger II, captained Harvard to third runner-up in last year's Ivy League water polo championships.

•

Thanks are due all local sports fans who responded to our recent appeal for type O blood donors, needed to aid veteran boxing manager and promoter Abner "Abe" Killjoy in his valiant fight for life. Abe, as many know, passed away after receiving over a hundred pints of blood from the fine folk of his community. It would have been enough to save him, say the good doctors over at Our Lady of Perpetual Remittance Hospital, if they hadn't made a "boo-boo." Abe needed type OO blood, not type O. Looks like even doctors can't win 'em all!

•

And who says hockey players aren't the great competitors they were in yes-teryears? Tell it to Philadelphia Flyers rear guard Moe Hruk. Moe, in case you didn't know, is the 285-lb. hardrock defenseman who packs a .38 in his hockey pants and gets on the ice for his shift not by hurtling over the boards but through them. The crowds in Philly love him and other teams around the league respect him. We hear even the refs call him "Sir!"

•

FARKAS INKS PACT, SPLATTERS LAWYER

Yugoslavian tennis great Milos Kurda has an interesting off-court career. He's a prisoner in a fortress high atop a mountain in the remotest region of the country. Nice work if you can get it!

•

Now it can be told dep't: Vikings linebacker Elroy "Sweetmeats" Sugarby played all of last season's gruelling schedule with a cast covering eighty percent of his body. Elroy, a UCLA alumnus and second draft choice of the U.S. Army, fell eight stories while eluding police following a "prank" just before the '72 season began but was afraid to report his injuries for fear of failing to make the team cut. Hats off to Elroy Sugarby, Minnesota's Mister Guts!

•

Note from Ernie Twill, a loyal reader of this corner, to correct our statement in a recent huddle about the Brazilian badminton phenom Fonzo Parlorcar. Seems, according to Ernie, that Parlorcar finished second in the 1932 Hungarian Singles Invitational in Budapest and not third as we erroneously stated. Thanks for the correction, Ernie!

•

Turning to the lighter side of sport, who remembers the horse that ace jockey Joey Lupo rode without his pants on in the 1946 Kentucky Derby?

•

BRUINS MAUL RANGERS, 5 FEARED DEAD

Jack Nicklaus tells this one on Lee "Super Mex" Trevino. Seems the two golf superstars were paired up in the Vegas Desert Classic charity tourney with Hollywood's Cesar Romero and Randolph Scott. Trevino arrived late at the tee-off, took a startled look at Romero and Scott, and screamed at Nicklaus, "Who the blankety-blank are these two palookas? I come here to play with stars, not a couple of has-been wimps!" And with that, "Super Mex" stalked off. The Big Bear swears it's true!

•

Quickie Quiz: Name five members of the Oakland Raiders who haven't been busted on dope charges in the past two years. Answers next week.

•

Bob "The Blob" Hickover, Seattle's three-hundred-pound back-court man who lacks in size what he lacks in talent, broke a career jinx this season by not slugging the referee at halftime. The Blob did take a roundhouse swing at the ref's wife after the game. "He had me scared there for a while," said one of the relieved Sonics afterward. "If he hadn't broke her jaw, he might not have broke our jinx!"

•

Ali Baba, formerly Alonzo Jukes, has been criticized by hometown Baltimore fans and writers for lackadaisical defensive play for the Bullets. What the critics don't understand, discloses Ali, is that as a member of the Brown Muslims sect he is forbidden to defend himself in any way from any man or thing at any time—even on the basketball court. To do so would violate the Tenth Law of Rashid. Here's handing it to Ali Baba—athlete, millionaire, and devout churchman. The game could use more like him!

•

SCORNED LOOP GATE AIM BLUFF?

Flyweight boxer Jose Panatela breezes into town this week to defend his crown against fifth-ranked contender Tony Ruiz. A popular after-dinner speaker, the spunky little Costa Rican recently told the Sports Underworld Memorial Dinner in New York how he came by the nickname of "The Human Peppermill."

•

Hispanic horsehide hero Angel Diablo of the San Francisco Giants was booed lustily by Candlestick Park fans on his first at-bat in a Giants uniform, and he's still shaking his head. "I no onnerstan'," says the bewildered little fielding nifty from down Caribbean way. "Een my countree, ees good lock to urinate on home plates. Everybodee do eet." But Diablo bowed to hometown custom rather than further offend Frisco's fickle fans. He now takes his "goodluck tinkle" in the dugout doorway just before stepping up to the dish!

•

Speaking of being "pee-pared," did you know that tension accelerates bladder movements—and that in a typical NFL game, the average NFL team excretes enough urine to fill the Liberty Bell? A true sport fact. Thanx to Lemoyne Keezer, age 15!

•

Everybody knows Red Sox slugger Gus Kazok holds the all-time major league mark for consecutive foul balls hit off a left-handed pitcher; did you know that the record for number of consecutive foul ball pitches to a righty is held by Kazok's teammate Effel Yonk? Yonk, incidentally, was voted South Carolina's Asthmatic of the Year in 1969 for overcoming the dread affliction and making it to the majors. He's an a-*choo*-in for stardom!

•

Our favorite motor sport fact: more Americans died last year from heart disease than from injuries sustained in car racing crashes.

•

Cleveland Crusaders owner Art Blattfunk likes to unwind after the excitement of a close game by drinking dry martinis, then driving his Ferrari sports job home to suburban Shaker Heights. Nothing unusual in that, except for one thing—Art doesn't have a Ferrari!

•

Over in the Japanese pro football leagues, they call a football a *fusabaru* and the playing field is only twenty feet in length. Ex-Ram halfback Bert Piltdown, now coaching for the Nagoya Divine Winds in the Cabbage Flower League, says Japanese pro ball has a long way to go to reach the U.S. level. "About six thousand miles," quips Bert.

●

Phillies coach Hank "Greasy" Hare is the only player in major league history to be charged with a fielding error while officially at bat.

●

Belmont winner Consternation can count up to five! Tracksiders have long considered this handsome three-year-old the smartest hunk of horse-flesh since the immortal Public Lounge, who could not only count but subtracted too. Public Lounge used to amaze his trainers by eating his morning oats with a knife and fork. His sire, turf addicts may recall, was the aptly named Dogfood.

●

Boston yachtsman and sportsman extraordinaire Nedby Richfit drops us a postcard from "somewhere east of Ceylon" asking that a rescue vessel be sent with all possible haste. Any Good Samaritans out there?

●

HUB HOOP PARLEY NOD NIPS JINX

It happened fifty years ago in sport: The scene was Yankee Stadium, "The House That Ruth Built." The Sultan of Swat, mired in a lumber slump, faced the Big Train, Walter Johnson, hurling smoke and mowing down Murderer's Row with his starboard offerings. Finally the Bambino had had enough. Shaking off doughty Manager Miller Huggins's signals from the dugout, the inimitable Babe watched another of the Nats' fireballer's pills go by for a strike and called time. Stepping out of the box, Ruth held aloft three fingers of his right hand and waved them at the Washington moundsman. And sure enough, on the next pitch he struck out—on three straight strikes. Yes, it happened fifty years ago in sport!

C. Estes Kefauver High School Class of 1964

TWELVE-YEAR TENTH REUNION

Where'd Everybody Go?

by P. J. O'Rourke and Doug Kenney

Reunion Rap-Up

Well, a lot of us Kangaroos have hopped over a lot of dams and bridgeclubs since I last wrote to us all in the K.H.S. Class of '64! It hardly seems like our tenth reunion is already past us, even though it's actually been twelve years since our graduation, *and,* if you can believe it, I am writing this with the same Sheaffer refillable cartridge pen with the see-through middle and little squeezable refills that a certain **Herb "Wing-Ding" Weisenheimer,** '64, used to squeeze the ink out of all over on everything when other people were trying to work.

The last time I wrote you all, you all may remember, I was writing you about your *pep club dues,* which some people have not yet paid. I regret to remind all those I failed to remind at last month's Tenth Reunion that these dues are *still owed* for the 300 pounds of rained-on crepe paper which was accidentally delivered for our 1964 Post-Graduation Senior Tea Brunch which, as those of you who attempted to attend will remember, was rained on.

Everyone please "cough up!" The Tenth Reunion Committee *still* owes, in addition, for extra janitorial services following the Saturday dinner-dance and disturbance at Moody Memorial Gymnasium. (I will be sending "follow-up" letters to each of you to remind you of the fun we had last month, and *your* share of the deficit—$17.50 per Kangaroo, or somebody's going to be hopping mad!)

I hate to single out "deadbeats" such as **Larry Kroger,** '64, and others, particularly at this time when we should be finding fun, not fault, in our classmates.

Fun *was* found, however, at our gala Tenth Reunion held this year because of flood or high winds the previous two years, and *this* pen says not the *least* fun of our Kangaromp was the fact that *this* year it didn't rain for twelve days or tornado, being too cold.

We certainly were all cheered to see each other of us that returned to K.H.S. and talk about those who didn't and wonder why, except for **Howard Lewis Havermeyer** (1946–1963) who is still no longer with us, of course.

The fun-packed weekend kanga-rolled to a start with an address by **Principal Humphrey J. Cornholt** in the new Kefauver Memorial Gym Lounge. **Dr. Cornholt**'s speech, entitled "Welcome Back to Our New Gym Lounge," welcomed everyone who attended to the new gym lounge area, and said he was glad to see everyone again even if he didn't remember everyone's name anymore, including **Larry Kroger**'s, whose office is right next door to the Principal's Office and directly across from Detention Hall, where **Larry** and others spent so many memorable hot spring afternoons with the windows stuck closed.

"Hopped up" on enthusiasm for **Dr. Cornholt**'s plan to expand the Boys' Room facility, Kanga-returnees **Suzie "Fizzie" Fitzerman Lipbaum** and her attractive husband **Morey Lipbaum** assisted as Dr. Cornholt symbolically laid the first brick of the new hygiene complex.

Afterward, everyone gathered around the decorated card tables for pigs-in-blankets, "spiked" cranberry ade, and other delicious treats catered by **Fizzifood** (BRidgewater 7-6788) for a lot less than you'd think. As we waited for the cups to arrive, we learned from **Woolworth Van Husen III**'s lovely blond-streaked wife, **Snooky,** that their stay in the Dominican Republic with **Woolworth**'s father during that awful Trailer Bowl Scandal mix-up was "loads of laughs" and that everyone they met had bathrooms.

Driving to find someplace open with cups, **Woolworth** and **Snooky** further reported that the *Van Husen Recreation Vehicle Co.* was still very excited about its new line of self-propelled trailers *and* the prospect of full employment in the greater Dacron area, pending a favorable ruling on its appeal from the Federal Department of Transportation, or the Environmental Protection Agency, or the State Bureau of Motor Vehicle Safety. **Snooky** reports that Kangaroos **Chuck Farley** and **"Pinky" Albright Farley** visited them in the Dominican Republic in one of the new Van Husen campers during the height of "Trailer Bowl" inquiries, and that the test prototype vacation vehicle worked so well in the Dominican Republic, it stayed there even after everybody could come back.

Coming back to the Kefauver High lounge with the cups, we were greeted by the K.H.S. superintendent **Mr. Stanislaus Dupa,** who unlocked the door and said that everyone had left in anticipation of Saturday's events.

The next day, while the lady Kangarettes enjoyed a performance of **Finian's Rainbow** at the Dacron Community Theater followed by a lecture on assistant directing by graduate **Forrest Lawford Swisher,** the menfolk met at the Cocky-Locky Chanticleer Room for a smoker and hijinx. A little Kangaroo told me that *much* of the hilarity was furnished by **Herb Weisenheimer,** who did an imitation of himself doing his auto dealership local T.V. commercial that all of us see on late nite television, only this time with more sophisticated jokes.

At the gala "Corn Ball" held that evening at the K.H.S. Moody Memorial Gymnasium, the first fox-trot of the evening was led off by **Chuck Farley** and **Woolworth**'s lovely blond-streaked wife **Snooky,** who planned the theme of the dance with **Pinky,** despite many other suggested alternatives. (**Chuck**'s face was a common appearance on Dacron telephone poles last November during his recent unsuccessful bid for block association president, and it continued to smile throughout the evening.)

After a scrumptious Fizzifood dinner in the gym lounge, over which **Frank Furter** said grace just like the American Indians did with **Faun Rosenberg,** local Dacron artist-in-residential-district, playing the part of the Great Spirit in a beautiful, feathered creation of her own creation, we all bounced back into the gym for further fun.

As K.H.S. music instructor **Mr. Dwight Mannsburden** and **Naomi "Eggy" Eggenschwiler** led off the high-hopping with a jazzy Charleston, returning Kangaroos **Vincent** and **Emily "Preggers" Lambretta** showed pictures of their six lovely children to *hardly*capped **Ursula "Wobbles" Wattersky,** who in turn showed them to her escort **Rufus Leaking,** explaining each photograph clearly and distinctly.

After **Ursula** suggested exchanging dance partners and the **Lambrettas** realized the sitter was waiting, Kangaroos throughout the gym were surprised by a special Peace Dance to Kahoutek performed by **Frank Furter** in the middle of the floor, even after the band, **Rudy Noonan and the Golden Oldsters,** stopped playing. During the intermission, little gatherings of old friends exchanged gossip and news. A popular topic of conversation was the new movie starring our own **Amana "Fridge" Peppridge,** now showing at Ray's Adult Bookmart in downtown Dacron. **Amana** says she plays a nurse, only the hospital is "less realistic" than the one on "Medical Center."

Over the years, many had lost touch with **Belinda "Metal Mouth" Heinke** (now **Mrs. Hubert Howzenhower**), but were gratified to learn that her years of burning the midnight oil paid off in a fine career at McKinley Elementary School, where she unfortunately was working late Saturday night grading her students' leaf and weed collections. Those who missed her all wish her a warm "hi!"

Everyone was also happy to see **"Eggy" Eggenschwiler** and listen to her fascinating stories of what they do to you if you join Reverend Moon. Those of us who bought her magazines will certainly be glad to read or borrow them soon. We were also certainly glad to see **"Mr. Beep-Beep"** still chugging along, despite the many informative bumper stickers and Oriental shapes painted on the hubcaps.

In addition, we hope to see **"Mr. Beep-Beep"** and the rest of our autos that were found missing from the parking lot later that evening. The thefts were discovered, as you may remember, by **Carl "Fungus" Lepper,** who was escorting **Bruno Grozniac,** following an alleged disturbance, into an unmarked police car which wasn't there. Fellow Joint Narcotics Strike Force officers luckily arriving on the scene to assist **Carl** with **Bruno** were unable to locate the missing cars, as you probably know if you were there, and neither could **Dominic "Dom" Brocolli** or **Purdy "Psycho" Spackle,** who were supposed to be parking them.

It has also yet to be explained why the only vehicle not stolen was **Woolworth**'s customized Van Husen Mobile Motel, but as of this writing **Detective McNab** assures us that someone is working on it. **Detective McNab** also asked me to extend to us all his deepest concern for the loss of all our cars and don't call him anymore. He'll notify us, promises **Detective McNab.**

Well, while most of us Kangaroos filled out police forms and waited for busses in front of the closed school building that memorably nippy night, *some* of us were invited to share **Woolworth** and **Snooky**'s spacious camper with **Chuck** and **Pinky** after a quick nightcap at *Anybody's,* a very convivial gathering place for couples only, located opposite the Cocky-Locky Motel, where they refused room service the next morning to people without luggage.

Sunday morning was even more event-filled for those of us who had transportation to the final dinner-brunch held back at Moody Memorial Gym. (Yours truly still feels simply *crushed* about arriving too late to oversee the broiling of the breakfast fritters, but the poor turnout, including **Madison "Zippy" Jones** and the same government person who came back later and cut the picture of **Gilbert "Univac" Scrabbler** out of every single Reunion Ten Year Book at the Kwik-Print, meant tasty, unburnt fritters for all who wanted them.

So it was that had anyone been there besides me, my husband **Morey Lipbaum, Madison** (who says "hi!"), and the help, we all might have wished each other another fond kanga-round-of-applause for getting together again.

Good-bye for now, and C U kanga-really soon!

Busily,
Suzie "Fizzie" Lipbaum

P.S. *Don't* forget your *dos.* (Dues.)

LOWDOWNS AND UPDATES

On Our Former Friends

Patricia Albright (*Mrs. Farley*)
1173 Woodgrain Dr.
Dacronview Hills, Ohio
Then "Pinky" was a cheerleader and full of vitality, with plenty of dates on non-school nights for K.H.S. Kanga-Kouncil Prez Chuck Farley, her future lifelong love so far.
And Now Patty attended Ohio State and pledged Tri-Delt. She taught preschool for six weeks before marrying Chuck, and her main interests are her husband's political career and their son's, Chuck U., Jr., three. Chuck and Pat also enjoy intimately friendly suburban get-togethers with a group of very close friends who are other couples.

Robert Baxter
c/o Department of Defense
Then "Flinch" was square-cut and a clean shooter. We elected him Sr. Class Pres., Capt. of the Football Team, Capt. of the Basketball Team, and Second Alternate West Point Designate—a regular B.Y.O.S.G. (Big Youth on School Grounds).
And Now Bob attended the University of Toledo, where he majored in R.O.T.C. Arts. After graduation, he married teenhood sweetheart "Winky" Dempler and went to work as a Second Lieut. in the U.S. Army 180th Groundborn Division in Vietnam, where he was in charge of a Fragmentation Grenade Assault Prevention Squad. Bob was MIA'd in 1969. He and Winky have a daughter Kimberly, seven, and his main interests are in being found.

Dominic Brocolli
978½ Taft
Dacron, Ohio
Then "Dom" was a great kidder who frequently attended Kefauver High. His pride and joy was customizing borrowed cars.

Though not involved in organized athletics, Dom showed his school spirit to visitors' students after the game in the parking lot.
And Now Dominic was a member of the U.S. Armed Forces for several months and is now an Assistant Chrome Trim Installer at Van Husen Trailer while also being part-time owner of Dee & Pee Auto Re-Paint and -Pair with school chum Purdy Spackle. Dom is married to the former Maria Spermatozoa and they have four children—Tony, eleven; Toni, nine; Antonio, seven; and Antoinette, five.

Tammy Croup (*Mrs. Deidlemeyer*)
28 Lawngrove Ct.
Country Club Hills, Ind.
Then "Twinky" was a cheerleader, full of vim, who dated aplenty and had a regular social whirl plus talent galore which we rewarded with electing her Sr. Class Vice-Pres.
And Now Tammy attended O.U. where she pledged Tri-Phi and met her husband of the future, Matt, who has been very successful as the son of Indianapolis's largest pavement contractor. Tammy and her husband enjoy wintering in the Caribbean, Christmasing at Vail, Eastering in Europe, dances, balls, and brunches at the Hunt Club, and lavish dinner parties at home.

Penelope Cuntz (*Mrs. ?*)
Then "Penelope" was on the quiet and shy side but with a good listen for everybody.
And Now She wasn't heard from.

Wendy Dempler (*Mrs. Baxter*)
23B Townhouse Apartments
15 Parkfree Circle
Dacron Glens, Ohio
Then "Winky" was a cheerleader, full of vip, with gobs of dating Sr. Class Prexy Bob "Flinch" Baxter.

And Now Wendy attended the U. of Toledo and pledged Double-Gamma. Bob and she were married in 1968. He is a prominent MIA in Vietnam and they have a seven-year-old daughter. Wendy enjoys working part-time at Simpkis Jewelers and is interested in all of us remembering the unfound servicemen and how their wives don't get insurance because they're not proved dead.

Naomi Eggenschwiler (*Ms. Winkler*)
c/o Reverend Sun Myung Moon
Unification Church
Tarrytown, New York
Then "Eggy" was a fun kid, full of laughs and giggles and snickers and grins and titters and giggles and smiles. She won the Ohio State Crisco Fry-Off in '63 and was the life of every pajama party.
And Now Naomi attended the Katherine Giblet School of Executive Assistance where she met her future ex-husband Steve. Naomi worked as a secretary at Van Husen Trailer for five years until she quit to become a Typing Minister in the Unification Church. She enjoys convincing everybody about the Rev. Moon.

Charles Farley
1173 Woodgrain Dr.
Dacronview Hills, Ohio
Then "Chuck U." was Kanga-Kouncil President, a three letter man, Dacron Area Student Council Representative, and a real go-getter in general with a big interest in politics.
And Now Chuck attended the U. of Cincinnati, where he majored in Local Political Science. He's married to "Pinky" Albright and has an honorable discharge from the Ohio National Coast Guard, where he rose to rank of Lakeman Second Class. Chuck's interest in politics has avidly continued. He has been a nearly winning candidate for the State Senate and House of Representatives, Dacron City Council, Silage County Water Commission, Dacronview Hills Zoning Board, and Woodgrain Drive Block Council. He also sells insurance.

Home: 555-6152. Office: 555-6500. Chuck and Patty enjoy weekly couples get-togethers at night at their's or other couples' homes.

Suzi Fitzerman (*Mrs. Lipbaum*)
376 Butcherblock Lane
Dacron Dells, Ohio
Then "Fizzie" was Sr. Class Secretary, Class Mascot, a Kangarette, a Kangarooter, a Kangarooterette, a Boosteroo, a Helperette, a Hopperette, and voted Most Likely to Succeed for a girl.
And Now Suzi is President of Fizzifood, Inc., her own catering company which caters gatherings like this at places like these with the assistance of a husband who is Assistant to the President. Suzi has 2.3 children—Dawn, five; Jason, two and a half; and Jennifer or Joshua in about seven months. Despite her busy kids and business, she's active in the Dacron Sophomore Chamber of Commerce, the Clean Library League, the Democratic Women for Republican Candidates Club, Mothers of Children, Temple Beth Halavah, Dacron Planned Childhood Association, the Red Feather, Red Cross, Red Buckeye, and Red Blanket Drives, and the Dacron Chapter of the National Organization of Women People lady's rights group of which she is cochairhuman with our previous old gym teacher Marilyn "Ms." Armbruster. Suzi enjoys having her husband do the housework and watch the kids during the day.

Frank Furter
Sausalito, California
Then "Gopher" played an important part with all athletic squads, especially when they needed ace bandages or left their towels all over the locker room. He was Girl's Volleyball mascot his Jr. year.
And Now Frank is married to his wife who thinks she might be a witch. He runs his own Earth Shoe repair shop in Mill Valley, California. They have a son, Mantra Edward, two (Pisces with Sagittarius rising) and live on a tentboat in Sausalito. Frank and Laura are interested in inner-ecology,

back-sacking, the I-Ching, and Yogurt. She is practicing to be a midcousin, and they enjoy traveling by astral projection and getting their heads together.

Bruno Grozniac
#278651238171
Silage County Correctional Institute
R.F.D. 6, Silage Mills, Ohio
Then "Lurch" was a big athlete at K.H.S., whose rough and tumbled mode of play was an inspiration to everybody on his side.
And Now After graduating, Bruno volunteered for service in the Green Berets, who all went to the beginning of Vietnam. While overseas, he began a prosperous importing business which he continued to do when he returned home and which he recently retired from to devote his time to the law.

Belinda Heinke (*Mrs. Howzenhower*)
2344 Ranchwagon
Dacron Dales, Ohio
Then "Metal-Mouth" was a Kanga-Whiz-a-Roo kid with a 100 average, the Valedictorianship of the class, and a Presidency of Homework Club.
And Now Belinda attended U.C.L.A. where she majored in Quantum Cybernetics, graduated Summa Cum Laude, and won an Einstein Fellowship to the Mass. Institute of Technology, where she received dual Ph.Ds in Chemical Archetectronics and Electro-Molecularity, and afterward did postdoctoral work at Heidleberg in Germany. She teaches second grade.

Madison Avenue Jones
1749 Jermain Dr.
Dacron, Ohio
Then "Zippy" came to K.H.S. from his native Nashville Lincoln Roosevelt our senior year, but was well-tolerated by all, especially in basketball and track.
And Now Madison attended Harriet Tubman College and returned to become Dacron's third black optometrist after the war

in Vietnam. He and his wife have three children—Martin Luther Kennedy Jones, five; Robert Kennedy King Jones, three; and Charleen Mrs. Roosevelt Jones, one. Madison is a member of the Friendly Order of Black Opossums (F.O.B.O.) and enjoys keeping his neighborhood nice.

Larry Kroger
201H Singles Valley Apartments
Dacron Dales, Ohio
Then "Larry" was active in Audio Visual Aids and played JV football his senior year. He was well-liked by all who remember him.
And Now Larry is back at good old K.H.S., where he teaches Living and Life and counsels careers. He was a weekend warrior in the Ohio National Guard and would have been called for duty at the Kent State tragedy except he was sick that weekend. Larry is interested in tropical fish and belongs to the Greater Dacron Fish Breeders Assoc. He is a member of the Veterans of Domestic Disorders and isn't married yet.

Vince Lambretta
Presidential Mobile Home Court
Dacron, Ohio
Then "French" was really popular with girls everywhere for his snappy car, sharp clothes, and long looks. He was great at doing dances and other stuff fast and got went-steadied with more than any other guy in our class.
And Now Vince is assistant co-manager at Jax Slax Shack's Campus Shoppe. He is still the husband of the former Emily Mae Praeger, who after graduation he became secretly married to during our senior year. They have six children so far. Vince is interested in working late.

Rufus Leaking
2615 Upton Ave.
Dacron, Ohio
Then "Spaz" was well known as a good sport for all. He was President of the Slow Learners' Council his Sr. year and re-

ceived the Handicappers Club's Trainability Award.

And Now Rufus lives at home.

Carl Lepper
2311 Trailergrove Rd.
Dacron, Ohio
Then "Fungus" was a four-year man in the Hall Monitors, a Lunch Room Tray Chaperone, Walk-Way Proctor, Captain of the Lavatory Patrol, and well-liked by all teachers.

And Now Carl was an Air Brig Guard and in the Military Sky Police of the U.S. Air Force. He attended the Dacron Police Academy for four years before joining the force as a Detective on the Teen Squad and then he suddenly "dropped out of it" to "get his head out of sight." Since then, he has worked as a hippie and is often seen everywhere young people hang out around Dacron where he is always interested in listening to what anyone has to say.

Francine Paluka
1450 Mill St.
Dacron, Ohio
Then "Half-Track" was K.H.S.'s top girl athlete and also top athlete, period. She was always a steadying influence if anybody became rowdy and she had the respect of everyone including boys, who respected her too much to even talk to.

And Now Francine studied Practical and Very Practical Nursing at Our Lady of Affliction Hospital but quit to become a Lamaze birth counsellor at the Dacron Nearly-Free Women's Clinic which aids women with female trouble. She is active in the Red Tide Collective which split off from the National Organization of Women People and her friend, Ms. Armbruster.

Amana Peppridge
815 Tapioca Canyon
Los Angeles, California
Then "Fridge" was very popular with college boys and probably would have been popular with boys from K.H.S. too, if she'd let them. She was Homecoming

Queen, third runner-up in the Miss Teenage Dacron of America Pageant, and was already looking forward to her career in some movies.

And Now After school Amana went to near Hollywood, where she is an aspiring starlet model with credits already for several leading roles in very short films and glossy photos. Amana is interested in going places with her good friend Willy, who manages many other starlets or models in Sunset Strip, Cal.

Emily Praeger (*Mrs. Lambretta*)
Presidential Mobile Home Court
Dacron, Ohio
Then "Preggers" was out sick a lot our senior year with tonsilitis. She said. She was felt sorry for by all.

And Now Emily is married to Vince Lambretta and devotes her time to their six children: Tammy, twelve; Mindy, ten; Michael, eight; Heather, six; Christopher, four; and Melanie, two and a half; who occupy all her enjoyment. She is interested in school starting again this fall.

Faun Rosenberg
602B Corngate Apartments
4551 Central Avenue
Dacron, Ohio
Then "Weirdo" was the sensitive poetic type with an ear for folk music and an eye for paintings that didn't look like anything. She was co-editor of the *Leaf and Squib* and a member of Hootenanny Club, and C.O.R.E. when white persons still could be.

And Now Faun attended Antioch College in Yellow Springs, Ohio, and afterward married Forrest Swisher outdoors at dawn in their bare feet. They are separated and so is her second husband. Faun runs the Kraft Kove at Corngate Shopping Plaza, where she mixes work with art in angora macramé, decopacollage, hand-thrown Indian jewelry, and African trade beaded sweaters. A one-person show of her paintings in watercolor on black velvet has been held at a Manufacturing Creditors Trust branch bank and she is a critic of the arts for the Dacron *Downtowner*.

Gilbert Scrabbler
Apt. 3401 Civilian Compound
Armaggedon Proving Grounds
Ft. Ute, Utah
Then "Univac" was Class Salutatorian, Intramural Chess Champ, and winner of both the *Time* Current Events Test and an Honorable Mention at the State Science Fair. He had a "nose for knowledge" and was known to all as a "nerd in the know."
And Now Gil attended M.I.T. where he concentrated on Laser Gas Fission Delivery Systems and Neuro-Viral Malignancy Dissemination Logistics. Since 1972, he has been employed by the Defense Dept. as ~~mmmmmm~~ responsible for ~~mmmmm~~ which ~~mmmmm~~ W.W.III or ~~mmmmm~~, in places like the Middle East but ~~mmmmm~~ ~~mmmmm~~ and 2,800 seven-legged sheep that glowed in the dark. Nevertheless, ~~mmmm~~ ~~mmmmm~~ and stopped the spreading from a ~~mmmmm~~ in orbit.

Purdy Spackle
40 Transient Rooms Hotel
Dacron, Ohio
Then "Psycho" was a newcomer to K.H.S. from Juvenile Work Farm High, but he gained the respect of everybody right away by his actions which spoke louder than words, especially to Zippy and Swish. Also, his skill with getting autos to start made him president of the Kar Klub.
And Now Purdy co-runs the Dee & Pee Auto Re-Paint and -Pair business with former class and cellmate Dom Brocolli. They specialize in repainting new cars and fixing title and registration difficulties for their many satisfied customers, including fellow ex-aroo Wing-Ding Weisenheimer's Chevy Dealership's Used Car Lot.

Maria Spermatozoa (*Mrs. Brocolli*)
978½ Taft
Dacron, Ohio
Then "Quickie" really got around. She was popular almost every night and loved

to date with practically anybody on a moment's notice.
And Now Maria is all settled down with ex-date and present mate Dom Brocolli. She works part-time at the Paris France beauty shop, but is mostly just mother to four of the children she had.

Angelina Staccato
40 Transient Rooms Hotel
Dacron, Ohio
Then "Slice" wasn't a joiner, but she had a well-known personality and was respected a lot by the other girls, especially in the washroom.
And Now After graduation, Angelina received extensive training in a useful trade at the Dacron Women's Training Institute. She now has her own beauty parlor, the Paris France Beauty Saloon, near the Greyhound Station in the Bus Building.

Forrest Swisher
281 Brownstone St.
Older Town
Ft. Wayne, Indiana
Then "Swish" had interest in the arts to spare and wore sandals. He was co-editor of the *Leaf and Squib* and active in Sr. Thespians, Pouchinellos, Mask and Wig, Cloak and Quibblers, and JV Puff Ball.
And Now Forrest attended Antioch College where he majored in Theater Science and Liberal Acting Arts. He was shortly married to Faun Rosenberg after being rejected by the draft and is now the Assistant Director at The Little Dinner Theater in the Dell, Ft. Wayne, Ind.

Woolworth Van Husen
No. 3 Yachtway Drive
Dacron Estates, Ohio
Then "Lunch Money" was a popular playstudent at K.H.S. where he was Student Council Treasurer and smoked a pipe. He had a sports car.
And Now Woolworth attended Parson College until it lost its accreditation, then met his present wife, "Snooky" Knickerson, whose father is in Atlanta finance.

Snooky and Woolworth lived in Atlanta where Woolworth broked stock before returning to Dacron to be Vice-President for his dad. Woolworth was in charge of developing and marketing the innovative Mobile Motel Room Vacation Vehicle until it didn't sell. Now he is Vice-President in charge of assisting the Chairman of the Board. Woolworth is active in donating to political candidates with his father. He and Snooky belong to Dacron higher society, but their socializing still leaves room for them to be interested in getting to know the attractive new couples in town and having them over for quiet nights of suburban get-together at home.

Ursula Wattersky
Dacron Tower Apartments
5561 Central Ave.
Dacron Township, Ohio
Then "Wobbles" was "crippled but cute" with the best personality you ever saw and gobs of school enthusiasm. She was always a big help.
And Now Ursula attended Dacron Community College and then started her own business—a weekly telephone shoppers newspaper, *The Corngate Bell,* which comes to everybody on the west side free once a week when Ursula calls them up to tell them everything about recent cub scout activities, church socials, zoning board meeting schedules, and much more, plus, of course, many complete details on valuable bargains and special sales at the Pik 'n' Chooz and other fine shopping places unless you get your number unlisted.

Herb Weisenheimer
28 Yachtway Drive
Dacron Estates, Ohio
Then "Wing-Ding" was a laugh and a half, always cracking up at teachers with jokes, gags, puns, tricks, wise remarks, insults, noises, strange smells, paper bags full of water, smart-aleck replies, and pointless stories that more than earned him his other nickname, "Motor Mouth."
And Now Herb has made really good as proprietor of "Hollering Herb's Psychopath Chevrolet" with its novel "padded showroom" indoor used car lot filled with "throat-slashing bargains" that have often been fixed up by old Kang Ko-Kut-Up Dom Brocolli and Purdy Spackle. Herb is married to the former Lulu Lampansky of the well-known Chanticleer Room's Floor Review. They have two sons—Herb Jr., four; and Herb III, two. We all see "Hollering Herb" all the time in his famous local television commercials every single night on the late movie, sometimes nine or twelve times an hour.

SEE YOU IN 15 YEARS

CELEBRITY LIMERICKS

IF YOU WERE ANYBODY, WE'D HAVE ASKED YOU, TOO.

1975 marks the 300th anniversary of the limerick. To help celebrate, we asked a few friends to supply the final line to the following ditty.

THE PUZZLE:

There once was a man from the moon
Who landed on earth during June.
He stepped from his saucer
Said "I'm here because, sir, . . .

When we sent out our limerick puzzle, we weren't aware that Hugo Winterhalter had died in 1973, probably because his haunting strains are so much today still with us. Hugo's estate returned the limerick uncompleted. We finished it for him. Hugo, we hope you like it.

Hugo's band plays a really hep tune.

"En France, nous n'aimons pas la lune."

"Bonjour. Bonjour, messieurs-dames. Et hallo a tous mes amis Americains. Je m'appelle Jean-Luc Godard. Merci, merci bien. Et bonjour et bon chance. C'est tout pour maintenent. Merci encore. Adieu. Good-bye."

Jean-Luc Godard

"Cause I don't get no respect on the moon."

"My neighborhood is so tough that if a spaceship landed, they'd steal the hubcaps while the thing was still moving, and then they'd do a thousand tiny steps for mankind all over his helmet. I'm not kidding." Rodney Dangerfield

"I have neither food, fork, nor spoon."

"Wherever there are people, there exists the dangers of scarcity. All of the present information at hand indicates the moon to be completely devoid of sustenance. Thus, if there are people on the moon, it would clearly be our responsibility to feed them. Thank you."   Daniel Moynihan

"Our coffee breaks last until noon."

"Every man is entitled to all the free time available. This isn't just for the Carnegies and the Vanderbilts. The big money boys better wise up. Or there's going to be trouble, big trouble. Ask Solzhenitsyn, he'll tell you."

George Meany

"What's so rare as a warm day in June."

"I couldn't resist. I know that warm days in June are anything but rare, but, as I said, I couldn't resist. I think I could say, without fear of contradiction, that things which rhyme are better ordered than things which don't."

Barbara Jordan

"I look like an old macaroon."

"Go out and get a macaroon. Look at it. Now look at my picture. See what I mean?"   Robert Graves

"I want to kill faggots like Vidal Sassoon."

"This country is going to hell in a handcar. The sissy boys are everywhere. But what are you going to do? You do your best, you try to get by. Things change; life goes on. I don't know. I wish the hell I did."   Woody Hayes

"Da-doodle-dee-doodle-de-doon."

"How unique! I come from a land which is both country and continent. No other land can make this claim. Though I'm sure Greenland would love to. But don't be fooled by the Mercator projections. I assure you, it is neither country nor continent, and, for that matter, it is not particularly green. It's probably a poo brown."   Evonne Goolagong Cawley

"My great aunt just moved to Rangoon."

"Collaboration is a funny business. Take this limerick, for example. Rowland thought the last line ought to be 'My great aunt looks like a baboon.' I tried to talk him around, but he's a stubborn son-of-a-bitch, and finally I had to put my foot down. Now I owe him one."   Evans and Novak

"I want to see Tell Me That You Love Me, Junie Moon."

"This was a first-rate motion picture. Maybe not as good as *Exodus,* but every bit as good as *The Cardinal* or *In Harm's Way.* And better than *Rosebud,* a film of which, despite its flaws, I am very proud. Liza, Jimmy Coco, Ken Howard, all of them gave fine performances. You should see it if you get a chance. You won't be sorry."   Otto Preminger

"I love Gleason's va-va-va-voom."

"I grew up watching the tube—Sid Caesar, Captain Video, Ernie Kovacs—not the Mary Tyler Moore bull that's on today. Gleason was my favorite, the Poor Soul, the Honeymooners, Reginald van Gleason III. I wish they'd rerun some of those old shows now. I'd watch every one of them. You remember the Mother Fletcher bit? That one was my favorite."   Hunter Thompson

The National Lampoon Guide to

Effective Salesmanship

by Tony Hendra and Gerald Sussman

Introduction

(Reading time: twenty-eight seconds.)

So you want to be a salesman? Congratulations! You have just made a decision that will place you in the very top drawer of humanity for the rest of your life. Why? Because salesmanship is everything. When a man goes down on bended knee to ask that "special someone" to be his forever, he's using salesmanship—and so is that "special someone" when she flutters her lashes or takes off her knickers. Every atom in the universe uses salesmanship—that's how everything stays together.

But salesmanship doesn't stop at keeping the earth spinning, and the trees growing, and the birds singing. Salesmanship improves. Salesmanship is the container that progress comes in.

For centuries, the wild-eyed inhabitants of Hawaii lived miserable lives. They had to barter for food and other essentials. They had few clothes or other possessions. They ate whenever they felt like it, and they had no financial resources whatsoever. But salesmanship arrived upon the scene and worked a miracle. Nowadays, Hawaiians wear suits and dresses, eat at the proper times, open bank accounts, and play basketball. They even have their very own U.S. senator in Washington, D.C.!

How Can I Become a Good Salesman?

(Reading time: thirteen seconds.)

If salesmanship is so crucial to life, it follows that being a salesman is more than a job. It's a privilege. The salesman must have many positive qualities to deserve his exalted position. But above all, he must have individualism.

Individualism, said the great Chinese philosopher and salesman, Lao-Tse, is like pissing in a white suit. It feels good, and it shows.

Today's salesman faces almost insuperable obstacles. Modern industrial society has so debased any form of craftsmanship that nothing is *worth* selling anymore, let alone buying. The salesman knows this as much as the buyer. Both are well aware that any product they might be discussing is either carcinogenic, obsolescent, lethally unsafe, addictive, pollutive, totally unnecessary, or all of the above. Both are fully aware that any performance or economy ratings are either the chemically induced fantasies of a terminally horny ad-human or the result of parking lot payoffs to a quadraplegic regulatory agency. Lastly, of course, both salesman and client have no illusions about one another. Each realizes the life of fatuous self-deceit the other leads.

How, then, can a good salesman make a sale? The answer lies in two small words. Two small words that together make the one big principle of salesmanship today.

Blow job.

The Blow Job

(Reading time: forty-five seconds.)

(Rereading time: forty-five seconds.)

The single most important weapon of the salesman is his mouth. It is his mouth that he will wrap around the client's penis in order to clinch the sale. His mouth, in fact, is where the money is.

But the blow job is not a simple matter of sucking, nipping, and licking the prospect's private parts until he pops his load, or "order," as it's known in trade circles, down the salesman's throat. Every quality that the salesman displays at all other points of the selling process must be displayed here also.

For instance, some clients may favor a particularly discreet approach, quiet and conservative, in which neither party really acknowledges that a blow job is being given. In this case, the salesman may be required to make conversation, or at least nod and smile in the right places at the same time as he is servicing his client. Others—particularly those with any sort of legal background—may prefer the "deep throat" technique. Still others like to have various objects, slide rules and telephones, for instance, shoved up their anuses during the blow job, a technique many salesman refer to as their "bottom line."

Admiral Zumwalt, who still does much of the most important purchasing for the U.S. Navy, has a habit of sticking sharpened pencils into the ears of his salesmen during their blow jobs, to keep their heads erect and their minds on the matter in hand.

The good salesman must be prepared for all these eventualities, and many more. In short, in the immortal words of Peter Abelard: "Give good head and get ahead good."

Selling Yourself

Although salesmanship is the lifeblood of the universe, its most concentrated use is in the business world. You may wish to practice salesmanship in some other milieu, but for most people, the first step towards becoming a salesman is getting a job as a salesman.

This is not as easy as it sounds. You can't just walk into the office of a respected member of the business community, who may be used to being blown by some of the best salesmen in the area several times a day, and say, "Hi—I'm a salesman." You have to prove it.

And the way to prove it is by selling yourself.

You are your first product. You may not be your best product. You may even loathe yourself, for a variety of reasons, not the least being that you've decided to become a salesman. But that doesn't matter. The kind of job you do in selling yourself, however dishonest, incompetent, or stupid you may be, tells your prospective employer immediately what kind of job you'll do at unloading the shoddy rubbish he manufactures.

"If you can't sell yourself," said J. Pierpont Morgan, "you can't sell shit."

The job interview falls into two stages. In the first of these, you must remember the three *p*s: *promptness, persistence,* and *poise.* Here you must tell your prospective employer who you are, what your experience is, and why you should be entitled to take home a small part of his hard-earned money every week. The key to this part of your presentation is lying. It makes little or no difference what you tell him you've accomplished. He knows you are lying, and that your resume is lying, just as you know he is lying about his company's performance or how important his products are. Even if you aren't lying, he will assume you are, so you may just as well lie away just as hard as you can.

But you must deliver the lies with promptness, persistence, and poise, never wincing or twitching or being caught in an inconsistency, such as saying you have worked for thirty years for a large aerospace company and giving your age as twenty-three. Make your lies work for you, but don't overwork them. And remember: Truth doesn't sell.

Two applicants were being interviewed for a position as salesman at the prestigious Sealy Mattress Company some years ago. Applicant A was absolutely truthful about his schooling and his experience in the business world. His answers to questions were brief and uninventive. His attitude was cold and straightforward.

Applicant B said he was a Rhodes Scholar who had been trained at the world-famous Mattress Institute in Pea, Austria, and had extensive experience selling electric blankets in Chad. His personality was upbeat, involved, and clearly dishonest.

Applicant B got the job, and went on to become one of the major salesmen of Sealy Posturepedic in the Portland, Oregon territory.

Applicant A failed to get the job, and went on to become the notorious and penniless Ralph Nader.

Why Three Ps?

Some brighter readers may now be asking, "But why must we go through all of this when we already know what really counts?" The answer is simple. Business is a respectable, decent profession. It is the backbone of our society. It must present a clean-cut, moderate, and responsible image to that society. And so, like that society, it has its rules.

Look at it this way. If you are in a singles bar, attempting to insinuate yourself into the company of an attractive young lady, you don't piss on her foot or punch her in the kidneys. You are courteous, thoughtful, and polite, even though within the hour you hope to be shoving your tongue up her anus while coming in her armpit.

Salesmanship is a lot like that.

Beating Out the Competition

(Reading time: thirty seconds.)   *(Bathroom reading time: ten minutes.)*

We now arrive at what has often been called the blow job interview. Nothing is more important. In the next few minutes—or depending on the number of applicants, the next hour or so—you will make an indelible mark on your future boss. It will probably be the most grueling blow job you will ever give, and for many, it may even be the first time that a male organ has been in your mouth. But if you can come through the ordeal, you will hold up your head proudly forever after.

Many interviewers, particularly those who select salesmen for large companies, carry an elaborate form during this part of the operation, which they fill out while you are slurping away. This means that their minds are not, as a client's will be, on the pleasurable aspects of the blow job, but rather on the intricacies of his form, and on assessing your performance, detail by detail.

In addition, most interviewers put potential salesmen through *all* their paces in this instance, rating tongue work, use of incisors and molars, ability to "deep throat," gag-frequency, handwork, ball-manipulation, rhythm, and so on, even though use of all these techniques is rare in a selling situation, unless it involves Arabs. Some interviewers will even deliberately not wash their privates for several days prior to interviews. On no account recoil from the odor or remark upon it. If the interviewer asks you questions about your reaction, insist that you prefer it that way. Remember that for now, the interviewer is a customer. And the customer is always right, even if he's dripping with smegma.

Any questions that the interviewer asks of you during the course of the blow job should be answered clearly. Don't mumble. Keep the rhythm steady with your hand. Talking with your mouth full is bad manners.

Never answer any questions or make any remarks in a "coy" or "amorous" manner. And never, never get, or even pretend to get, "excited" or "hot." Speak pleasantly and go about your business in a cool, professional manner. Bear in mind that interviewers are always on the lookout for any signs of homosexuality. Finally, if you find yourself in a situation where you are being interviewed along with another man, or even several others, be aggressive and imaginative in making sure that you are the first to get his penis in your mouth. Free enterprise has no time for pussycats. If necessary, block or push the others out of the way, or even grab the interviewer with a flying tackle. A man has only one penis. And if it's not in your mouth, it's in someone else's.

Landing Your Prospect and Selling Him

The key to salesmanship is groveling.
But you've got to do it with style.
—John Connally

Before you make that all-important call to your prospective customer, here are a few basic rules to follow if you're going to be a top-notch salesman:

1. Organize your time!

Time can be your best friend or your bitterest enemy. Make the most of it. The late Thomas Watson, president of IBM, used to conclude a meeting of his sales executives by pulling out a small revolver and shooting one of them in the arm (inflicting only a small flesh wound, of course). He used this demonstration to illustrate a point about time. "The flesh wound I gave [name of salesman] is a reminder that life is short, that anyone of us can die at any minute," said Watson. "And if we continue to put things off, to use our time unwisely, we'll never accomplish what we set out to do."

Along the same lines, Harold Geneen, president of ITT, likes to hide bombs in the offices of his top vice-presidents to remind them that time is of the essence. So how about planting little "time bombs" on yourself? Keep bombing yourself with reminders that will make you well-organized and efficient.

2. Organize your work!

Keep your paperwork in apple pie order. That means all your account records, your appointment calendar, data sheets, correspondence, daily reports, weekly reports, price lists, order forms, sales reports, statistics, personal expenses, promotional literature, and follow-up data. Juan Trippe, former president of Pan-American Airways, used to make a practice of inspecting his employees' desks after hours to see how well organized they were. If he found an especially neat desk, he would leave a Chiclet on it (one of his company's products). If an employee garnered 365 Chiclets in a year, he automatically got a five dollar a week raise!

3. Organize your mouth!

Good salesmanship depends on good oral communication. And good oral communication depends a great deal on the condition of your mouth, especially your lips. Always keep your lips soft and manageable. If they're chapped or have cold sores, use plenty of Chap Stick or Vaseline. Remember: Chapped lips can chafe your customer's sensitive skin when you're giving him that all-important blow job that will clinch your sale.

And speaking of blow jobs, don't forget to practice every day. If you can't find a live partner, use a dildo, a cucumber, or other suitably shaped object. Practice *does* make perfect!

Calling Your Prospect

The Phone Pitch

1. Always identify yourself as the president of your company. It makes a very good opening impression. Think positive, and think big. You *do* want to be the president someday, don't you?

2. A Little White Lie (it helps to get your foot in the door).

Sometimes you have to tell a little white lie if it helps get you an appointment or a lunch date with an important prospect. Don't hesitate to use one, especially since you've already identified yourself as president of your company. Here's a sure-fire method to get a new customer:

SALESMAN: Hello, Mr. Jones? This is Gerald Sussman, president of [name of company]. I'd like to talk to you about your next [name of product] purchase. You say you don't need any [name of product] at the moment? Not even if I gave you the best blow job you ever had?

No one can resist a blow job.

SALESMAN: It's our get-acquainted offer to our new customers. Would you like to hear more about it? Fine! How about lunch next Tuesday? Say, 12:30 at the Grill Room? Fine. See you then!

Soft sell, hard sell . . . what's the big deal?
There's only good sell.

—Voltaire

Selling your prospect is the easiest thing in the world. Once you've broken the ice and engaged in some small talk, some sophisticated conversation, and perhaps, told a few risqué jokes, you're ready for your sales pitch.

At this point, many salesmen go into high gear and do a beautiful selling job, but discover later that the promised order never materialized! Why? Two reasons. (1) Overconfidence. (2) Preoccupation with themselves and their products. Yes, in his desire to sell, a salesman can *overidentify* with himself and his product and forget to identify with the most important part of his pitch, *his customer*—thus endangering the sale itself!

The Salesman's Safeguard: The Four Ls

Listen

Listen sympathetically when your customer talks. Never interrupt or argue or disagree with him.

Look

Always maintain eyeball contact.

Love

Some people call it "empathy." We're not ashamed to call it by its rightful name. Of course, it's not the same kind of love you have for your wife and children or your parents or even your best friends, but it's a very genuine feeling you should convey, a desire to please, to be of service, to fulfill your customer's needs. And the best way to show him how you feel is to give him that all-important blow job. Lee Iacocca, president of the Ford Motor Company, used to exhort his executives with the slogan, "Put your mouth where your money is . . . blow that sale!"

Little Things

Most customers remember the little things even more than the big sales pitch, those little touches of courtesy that are the perfect way to close the lunch. For instance, after a blow job, your customer's penis will probably drip a little. Why not carry a small towel or paper towelettes, so you can wipe him dry? Or, if you're lingering over coffee and a brandy, why not offer him another blow job? Or a rim job? He may decline, but he'll surely be impressed with your graciousness and unselfish enthusiasm, impressed enough to give you an order!

Closing the Sale

You've done all the spadework. Now you come to your final hurdle—closing the sales presentation. Your big moment. Five or more pairs of steely eyes bore into you. As many sharp and finely honed brains are sizing you up from head to toe. However easy your job may have been at a lower level, there's nothing you can put over these men. They are the toughest, shrewdest executives in the company; the Chairman of the Board, the President, and the Vice-Presidents. They are in that boardroom for a reason.

Get Down to Going Down

These men are seasoned businessmen. They've seen and heard presentations like yours until they can recite them back to your face. You may even notice some of their lips moving along with yours as you make your pitch. They know that whatever you're hawking is no better or worse than all the other mediocre rubbish they see every other hour of every other day. They know that you have to go through the formality of doing a puff-job on your product. In fact, the worse your product is, the longer and more stupid they expect the puff-job to be. Why not give them a pleasant surprise? Don't bother!

The Pecker-Order

You must, however, make some kind of presentation to the company executives if only to identify who you are, and what you're selling, and what you're doing there. Use these precious seconds to size up the pecker-order. The pecker-order determines how you will proceed at the second stage of your presentation, or the amount of attention you will give to different men. If you have been introduced to the Chairman or the President or both, remember carefully who they are. Most companies will not do this, however, preferring to leave it to you to sort out who is whom.

How Do I Determine the Pecker-Order?

Good. We're glad you asked. One sure-fire method is to observe any little services one executive may perform for one another. Many junior executives carry pocket whisk-brooms to dust off the shoulders of their superiors. Others keep small shoeshine boxes handy to buff their superiors' shoes. In today's relaxed times, many executives like to put their feet on the table during a presentation, so they cannot afford to have dingy footwear.

However, the most important method of determining the pecker-order is to be on the lookout for what we call "corporate head." This is the *internal* pecker-order, or who blows whom within a given company. There is an excellent chance that during your presentation, the Chairman will be blown by the President, the President by the Senior Vice-President, and so on down the line. It is essential, therefore, during your presentation, to keep an eye out for any empty chairs.

The Blow Job—Ready, Set, Come!

Let's say you have five executives at your sales presentation. How are you going to satisfy all five? Answer—*organization, discipline, imagination.* Above all, keep your head when all around are getting theirs.

Who's on First?

This is a question constantly asked by young salesmen before their first sales presentation. The first, always, is the Chairman of the Board. There are no exceptions to this rule. The others must wait their turn.

But what, you may say, about a Chairman of the Board who likes to watch? The chances of this are absolutely minimal. People who like to watch don't get to be Chairman of the Board. These men are doers, get-aheaders. Furthermore, they're always decent, respectable family men, who frown on perversions such as voyeurism. So never deviate from this rule, unless on the express orders of a Chairman of the Board. (But make sure he *is* the Chairman of the Board before you comply.)

What's on Second?

You have a problem. The Chairman may just have been blown by the President. He may take a half hour or more to climax. He's generally going to be older than the others. He could take hours. Are the other members of the board going to sit around twiddling their thumbs until he's done? No, Mr. Salesman! Here are some tips:

1. *The four-and-one.* You can keep the others happy while you're doing the Chairman with this simple technique. Take the penises of the President and the Senior Vice-President in each hand, and commence giving them slow but pleasant hand jobs. They should be slow because (a) the Chairman may take hours to come; and (b) because you don't want them to come in your hand. (Out the window goes that sale!) Meanwhile, kick off your shoes and commence to diddle the junior two with each foot. It is a good idea to wear loafers on such occasions and to paint socks on your feet. Black is best, and be sure to paint executive-length socks, not ankle-length. When the Chairman is through, proceed to blow the President while maintaining the Senior Vice-President's hand job. Begin to give the next executive in line a hand job with your free hand, while diddling the lowest with *both* feet. When the President is done, proceed to the Senior Vice-President and give the other two hand jobs. This leaves you with two feet free. It is a good idea to use them to diddle the Chairman and the President in their afterglow. Use your hands once they are free. It's these little touches that will get you the sale.

2. *The three-and-two.* This technique is especially useful for firms where the distinctions between the top three officers is not clear (as, for instance, in a family firm such as the Chase Manhattan Bank). Take all three senior members in your mouth. Do the other two by hand. It's as simple as that. If for some reason, the members are so thick that you can only get two in, do two others by hand and one with both feet. In any event never allow yourself to have an idle limb. In going down, there's no such thing as downtime.

The legendary Charles Revson of Revlon, Inc., once had to make a presentation to the entire board of the nation's largest drug chain. Fifteen men confronted him across the table. Undaunted, Revson, who practiced relentlessly at enlarging his mouth by sucking footballs, took all five senior officers in his mouth, two more in his armpits, two more by hand, diddled two with his feet, nuzzled two with head, and caressed the other two with the inside of his thighs. Sounds tough? Sure it was—but that's what salesmen are made of. (P.S. Revson clinched the sale.)

Well, that's it. From here on, you're on your own. And remember:

Use your head! Blow that sale!

Would You Like SOMETHING TO READ?

by Sean Kelly and Ted Mann

THOSE OF US who love a "good read" from time to time—and who doesn't?—find summer vacation the perfect occasion to "get into" a book or two. The ideal beach book should be big and fat, with sand-resistant covers and suntan-lotion-absorbent pages, and the very best "summertime lit." demands no more of the reader than a television show in terms of attention span or, for that matter, literacy. But so many volumes meeting these basic requirements were published this season, how is one to choose? Listed here are the editors' choices, our very own recommendations, listed by subject or area of interest, to help you get the most out of the many, many rainy afternoons that you will be spending this holiday shivering on a ratty sofa in the screened-in porch of an expensively rented, bug-infested shack with a group of fellow vacationers who are either total strangers or quickly becoming so.

CRIME

Monthly, John D. MacDonald issues a new paperback private-eye thriller from his costly Florida bunker chronicling the adventures of that "slightly tarnished knight in tanned and lanky armor" Travis McGee. But fans of the series have detected a certain drop-off in quality recently. *The Awful Yellow Chinaman* was just a reworking of last year's *The East Is Terribly Red;* and *The Horrible Key Lime Pie* was not so much a murder mystery as a Miami restaurant review. *The Terrific Pink Gin* and its successor, *The Scary Purple Elephant,* suggested that John D. was losing his battle with the bottle, and one feared that an appropriate title for the next McGee caper might be *A Black Eye for Detective Fiction.*

But we are pleased to be able to praise without reservation Mr. MacDonald's new book, another in the Travis saga but in every way a superior departure from the norm. Set in the demimonde of the homosexual writing community in Key West, it sheds new light on the relationship between Travis and his swarthy longtime boat buddy, Meyer. Most exciting scene? The bitchy brunch *chez* Tennessee Williams, after which Meyer salves Travis's many psychic bruises and seduces him gently with a twelve-page monologue explaining supply-side economics. We can heartily recommend this new and different Travis adventure, *The Winking Brown Eye.*

Angelica Sitwell, heiress apparent to Agatha Christie's title as queen of English detective fiction, has another elegant whodunit in the bookshops this summer. It features the intelligent and charming amateur detective, herself a successful writer of detective fiction, Angela Standgood, to whom we were first introduced in Ms. Sitwell's previous *Murder Most British.* This one is titled, in England, *Murder at the Women Writers of Detective Fiction Club,* but it has been released in America as *Scribble Scribble Die Die!* The plot? In a series of gruesomely fitting murders, Ruth Rendell, P. D. James, Amanda Cross, Catherine Aird, and Mary Stewart are all bumped off, leaving the indefatigable and delightful Ms. Standgood as the only member, and thus president, of the club. The identity of the killer is a real surprise!

Aficionados of offbeat European detective fiction—and aren't we all?—will be sure to enjoy *A Specter Is Haunting,* the latest case for Eurocommunist vegetarian Interpol inspector Marco Venzetti to solve. Marco, a "big, hairy, lovable, mystical bear of a proletarian intellectual of a man," this time investigates a series of Swiss industrial accidents, and proves, with the aid of his underground pal, Carlos the Jackal, that reactionary capitalists are the real culprits! Marco's many American devotees will eat this one up like mung beans!

SCI-FI/FANTASY

Other worlds, future worlds, magic, monsters, and machines—the fabulous universe of science fiction/fantasy is as limited as only the imagination of the people who write and read it. And this summer, for your seaside reading pleasure, may we suggest *The Snout of God,* the ninth volume of the Gorgonzolian Trilogy, by the prolific E. Claude Boll. One need not have read all six thousand pages of the previous tomes in this series (*Mogdar Rules Okay, The Throbbing Blade, Tiger's Revenge,* etc.) to pick up the spoor and follow with fascination the escapades of Dunbar the Sorcerer, the Eight-Armed Coot, the mysterious Wrongo, and their nervous guide, Anal Sam (whose plea "Don't touch my stuff" echoes through the tale like an operatic leitmotiv). Nor does it spoil this epic tale of treason, high deeds, and revenge to know that critics have decoded the allegory and demonstrated that the Gorgonzolian Circle tells, in thinly disguised symbols, the sordid story of author Boll's long-ago expulsion from private school, for so-called crimes against nature, by a narrow-minded and cruel housemaster.

For those who prefer more sci in their fi, as it were, there's Hugo Lestoil's new *The Cleansing Comet,* a story of the germ-free planet Ajax in some distant, more hygienic time. In this lemon-fresh world, the threat of ancient, terrestrial bacteria is countered by a robot army of aerosol spray cans, and the devil take the ozone! A must read for "techies," the book comes with an ingenious packaging gimmick—disposable rubber gloves, to facilitate sanitary page turning!

NONFICTION

If self-improvement is one of your summertime goals, you could do worse than to curl up on your beach blanket with one of these true, factual best-sellers based on real historical incidents or at least ideas about them.

TURNING AND TURNING, by Ludmyra Smirnoff. A Minsk-trained ballerina who defected to the USA, then returned to her homeland, and now wishes to come back here, describes her life in art. Dizzying!

IN THE WIDENING GYRE. A Reagan budget adviser describes how his supply-side economic model was inspired by a Ouija-board seance encounter with Malthus. A must for money buffs!

THE FALCON CANNOT HEAR, by Perry Mann. A deaf air-traffic controller's desperate attempts to keep his handicap secret from co-workers and friends. Touching.

THE FALCONER, by John Cheever. The now-it-can-be-told story of William Faulkner's lifelong, code-named membership in the CIA. Cryptic.

THINGS FALL APART. A do-it-yourself manual—thousands of uses for Krazy Glue around the house. Sexy fun!

THE CENTER CANNOT HOLD, by "Gentleman Jim" Grzwynk. Sports bio of the least penalized lineman in NFL history.

MERE ANARCHY IS LOOSED (Irving Howe, ed.). The long-suppressed journals of Lower East Side nineteenth-century Russian Jewish syndicalist, theoretician, and tailor Schlomo Mere. Very Jewish, very political.

UPON THE WORLD, by Gunther Krod. Memoirs of the first explorer to walk backward to the North Pole. Offbeat but fascinating.

THE BLOOD-DIMMED TIDE IS LOOSED, by Peter Tauber. The true story of an oceanographic ecological disaster, recounting the time when an entire writers colony on Martha's Vineyard ate polluted mollusks and got sick. Scary.

AND EVERYWHERE THE CEREMONY OF INNOCENCE IS. From Marin County—where else?—a handbook of "alternate," "free" liturgies for experimental hot-tub group marriages.

DROWNED, by Bert Houdini. His brother describes the life and death of Canada's greatest underwater escape artist.

THE BEST LACK ALL CONVICTION. Congressman Pete "Watergate" Rodino's off-the-cuff thoughts about ethics. Foreward by Frank Sinatra.

WHILE THE WORST ARE FULL. A UNESCO official suggests possible redistribution of world food resources. Radical but thought provoking.

OF PASSIONATE INTENSITY, by Jeff Greenfield. A comparative study of the on-camera styles of Geraldo Rivera, David Susskind, and Phil Donahue.

SURELY SOME. Alfred Teller's nuclear survival manual. He suggests wrapping your head in tinfoil just before the blast. Useful, maybe.

REVELATION IS AT HAND, by Billy Graham. The famous theologian demonstrates, citing chapter and verse, how today's designer-jeans commercials were foretold in the last book of the Bible. Uplifting.

SURELY THE SECOND COMING IS AT HAND. Self-help sex therapy, which suggests masturbation after intercourse as an aid to multi-orgasmic response. Worth a try.

HARDLY ARE THESE WORDS OUT. A former *Penthouse* editor describes the difficulties of producing topical exposés with a four-month lead time.

WHEN. Germaine Greer's thorough, impassioned history of the Australian women's-liberation movement.

A VAST IMAGE. Elizabeth Taylor's long-awaited diet tips.

OUT OF SPIRITUS MUNDI. A feisty, junkie lesbian ex-nun protests her excommunication from the Catholic church as "political."

TROUBLES MY SIGHT, by Peter Kaminsky. A history of blind blues musicians, adapted from the backs of hundreds of record-album jackets. Scholarly.

SOMEWHERE IN SANDS OF THE DESERT. Newly discovered, Bishop Pike's last journals. Mystical, erotic.

A SHAPE WITH LION BODY. A big, colorful, coffee-table book treating lamps from ethnic variety stores as collectibles.

AND THE HEAD OF A MAN. W. H. Auden's sizzling sexual memoirs.

A GAZE BLANK, by Karen Ann Quinlan. As told to Dave Fisher.

AND PITILESS AS THE SUN. Cautionary tips for tanners from a California holistic dermatologist.

IS MOVING. An anonymous Carter-administration urban-affairs official offers relocation tips for Negro families.

ITS SLOW THIGHS, by "X." A compassionate plea for society's understanding of sloth fanciers. In the great tradition of *Men Who Love Mutts.*

WHILE, by Mrs. Allen Funt. Hobbies of the wives of famous men. Señora Pancho Villa, Madame Albert Camus, Mr. Margaret Thatcher, and others.

ALL ABOUT IT. Carl Sagan comes clean. Illustrated.

REEL SHADOWS OF THE INDIGNANT, by Arthur Knight. A penetrating study of social significance in the films of Stanley Kramer. Many stills.

DESERT BIRDS. British photographer Nik Cohn's pinup studies of Hopi Indian girls.

THE DARKNESS DROPS AGAIN. Bobby Seale reveals that Black Panther policies were formulated under the influence of LSD. A trip.

BUT NOW I KNOW. Marital disclosures by former U.S. senator Jake Javits.

THAT TWENTY CENTURIES. Barbara Tuchman goes "pop"—a history of the Western world in 150 pages. With many photographs, maps.

OF STONY SLEEP. Pop idol John Denver's long struggle back from Nembutal addiction.

WERE VEXED TO NIGHTMARE. Harold Bloom angrily dismisses Norman O. Brown's mistaken interpretation of Anthony Burgess's misreading of *Finnegans Wake.* Heavy going, but rewarding lit. crit.

BY ROCKING A CRADLE AND WHAT. Phyllis Chesler's sympathetic exploration of infanticide through the ages. A must for expectant mothers.

ROUGH BEAST, by Dick Cavett. A tell-all sexual bio. Names names.

ITS HOUR COME ROUND AT LAST. Filmmaker Jerry Lewis tells this ultimately triumphant but harrowing tale of his attempts to sell his movie *The Day the Clown Cried* to cable television.

SLOUCHES TOWARD BETHLEHEM. Something is wrong with southern California—but what? Joan Didion asks again, and this time gets the quote right.

TO BE BORN. Jerzy Kozinski's aching reminiscences about his birth trauma. Not for the squeamish.

F U CAN RD THS, U CAN WRT GD, OR MYBE BTTR

BETTER WRITING THROUGH BETTER WANTING TO WRITE BETTER: A GUIDE FOR THE UNBORING.

by Marco de Sa e Silva

While making dinner the other evening, my wife called attention to the fact that the sugar-and-ketchup concoction with which we had been sating our appetites for the past several days was not a life-sustaining staple. "Couldn't you do another of those how-to-be-a-better-writer articles? If we had some money again, we could afford hamburger." Her comment gave me the impetus to write this article and then sell it for well over seventy-five dollars.

As I often tell my students, writing is an art. Similarly, better writing is a better art, and tremendous writing is a tremendous art. You will become a better writer by listening to whatever it is I have to tell you, taking note of my axioms, and understanding my complicated use of the many examples that follow. Let us begin by taking a look at an example of the kind of writing to which many students aspire, the so-called academic style:

> Contemporary philosophers ascribe to Hegel a complexity of intellect far superior to their own as a means of apology for their inability to understand him. Only within recent times has it become safe to suggest the possibility that the feeling of bewilderment one gets when reading Hegel is more the fault of Hegel than us; indeed, Hegel may have known precious little what he was talking about. That this might be the case can be demonstrated through reference to . . .

If you think good writing has to be that boring, you are insane. Take a look at how I've improved just those few sentences:

Hegel. It rhymes with bagel. But Hegel was a German philosopher, not a Jewish doughnut, and he was very difficult to understand. Whose fault is that? Probably his own.

Carriage return, indent five spaces, and begin the next paragraph. Axiom Number 1 is: Don't bore your readers. When you bore your readers, they quickly lose interest in you and your material, since neither seems to them to be very exciting.

Axiom Number 2 is: Always use short sentences and paragraphs, because they will make your writing less boring. This has been proved hundreds of times in thousands of studies. Axiom Number 3 is: Try not to capitalize all the words in a paragraph if you can help it.

Let's continue to another writing example so that we may uncover more axioms. Several weeks ago I paid a social call on a friend of mine. Unfortunately, he was not at home, but I did find a very interesting bit of prose pasted to his front door. I took it home with me and have reproduced it below:

Woolrich—
    We have your girl Samantha and will do her the hard way if you dont give us 1000000. Will you? Put 3 hiway flares on front porch at midnite tonite. Or she is dead.

                                                                    —A friend

After reading this, my first reaction was "What kind of madman would prefer the orthographically stylized 'hiway,' 'midnite,' and 'tonite' over 'highway,' 'midnight,' and 'tonight'?" Furthermore, what does it mean to "do" someone "the hard way"? This brings us to Axiom Number 4, which is: Avoid slang, clichés, that sort of thing. Bastardizations and idioms (note the similarity of these words to "bastards" and "idiots") will give your writing a dated quality and put you in poor favor with well-educated persons such as myself. My corrected version of the above note would read:

Dear Mr. Woolrich,
    We have your daughter, Samantha, and will kill her unless you give us one million dollars. You may signal your intent to cooperate by placing three highway flares on your front porch tonight at midnight. Otherwise, she will be killed.

                                                                    Cordially,
                                                                    A friend

Students often approach me on the street and ask, "What do you think of the writing style of, say, Erma Bombeck?" I reply, "I may be counted as one of her most devoted readers. How about yourself?" Let's take a look at one of her recent columns:

I don't know, maybe I'm just getting old.

Then again, maybe not.

You tell me.

Yesterday my sixteen-year-old daughter announced that she wanted to have Charles Manson's baby.

"Charles Hanson?" I asked hopefully. "The computer-games wizard from your algebra class? Why, that's wonderful!"

"Wrong, Mom," she replied dully. "Charles Manson, the mass murderer."

I thought it might be worth another try to go the deaf-optimist route. "Darryl Mansfield? The doctor's son, who owns the Camaro? What a great surprise!"

She looked at me the way a person would look at a puppy that was having trouble learning a simple trick. "Charles Manson. The mass murderer. He's getting out on parole in a few years, and when he does, I want to marry him and have his baby."

I conceded defeat. So she wanted to marry Charles Manson and have his baby.

This raised an interesting question: Wouldn't any child raised by Charles Manson and my daughter likely grow up to be a deranged, psychotic weirdo?

You tell me.

But first, tell me something else.

Am I getting old?

You could object that Erma's tendency to construct entire paragraphs from only three or four words flies in the face of all standard rules of English usage. You would be wrong. Axiom Number 5 tells us: There are no hard-and-fast rules of English usage.

You might reply that axioms are rules. They are not. They are different.

To strictly follow the standard rules of English usage is to write hackneyed, predictable, logical prose, whereas the extraordinary writer will often bend the rules, and break them whenever he feels like it, in an effort to write extraordinary, better, different prose.

Something even more pervasive than Erma Bombeck's columns is the massive influence of advertising in America today. Grammarians may stumble when reading Bombeck, but they trip, fall, and suffer compound fractures when venturing through much of the ad copy we find in contemporary magazines and newspapers. I found the following example in a popular newsweekly:

The XL89. It's not a car for delicate temperaments.

In fact, when we interviewed four hundred former XL89 owners, an overwhelming majority said they didn't think the XL89 was a car for delicate temperaments.

Not for delicate temperaments at all.

Neither is the XL89 the right car for the kind of man who can, in one swift movement, remove a demonstration model's rear fender when he feels he is being misled.

The XL89 is not for the attorney who is competent enough to take on a large foreign automaker in a breach-of-guarantee suit.

Nor for the kind of driver who might panic when all eight cylinders seize up and the drive train disassembles.

At ninety-five miles per.

But if you're the kind of man, that one man in seventeen thousand, who has a lot of money to throw around and who has difficulty keeping track of warranties and receipts, maybe the XL89 is for you.

Just maybe.

Stop in at your XL89 dealer and find out.

Soon.

In ordinary, plain writing, "soon" would hardly be permitted to function as a complete sentence, but here it serves handsomely as an entire paragraph. This kind of writing grabs you, entrances you, makes you buy things. Can you imagine what we would have if history professors wrote advertising copy? Don't even try; it's too awful.

Last summer I was taking a casual midnight stroll through the country cemetery when I happened upon a recently implanted tombstone on which were inscribed eight lines of the deceased's poetry. By occasional flashes of lightning I was able to read it, and it so interested me that I removed the stone and bore it upon my back to my home, three miles away. It is the marker of a Donald Louis Fredwell, who lived from 1931 to 1982, and reads as follows:

> Yea, my body it is finally laid to rest
> Countless tortures I have been the victim of
> In search of those who made my life a jest
> My spirit it does prowl, and moves to kill.
> Accursed wife, vile in-laws, slippery friends,
> Employers, children, and the paperboy,
> I'll suck your blood, I'll taste my sweet revenge
> My spirit it will ride you all to Hell.

Here we see what can happen when a man with little or no training in poetry tries to work through iambic pentameter. He makes a complete fool of himself. Fredwell might have saved himself a good deal of embarrassment by simply putting his message, whatever it was, in prose. I have seen this done very successfully on a great many grave markers. Consider this example:

He was a decent guy.

It's clear, concise, to the point. Axiom Number 6 is: Be clear, concise, to the point.

What is the most important axiom of all? That would be Axiom Number 7:

Communicate effectively. When you lose sight of this axiom, you are in trouble. When you fail to communicate effectively, you communicate poorly, which is, in effect, a bad thing. It also reflects poorly on me, which is worse. So don't do it.

One final axiom. Axiom Number 8 is: If you are writing an article for publication, discuss your fee before submitting the article, not after. It is because I always follow this axiom that my wife and I are eating hamburger again these days. The effort to write well can be very rewarding, dear student: otherwise, why bother?

THE TEN BEST PROMS IN AMERICA

by Fred Graver

EACH YEAR AT THIS TIME we send editors Peter Gaffney and Kevin Curran to more than three hundred proms in thirty-eight states and the District of Columbia. Their dates? Pert and perky cheerleaders chosen by a special lottery system patterned after the Brazilian *lotería.* Each year, with trashed tuxedos and confused memories, they return with a disheveled sheaf of notes and several lawsuits. Their unprintable article is invariably tossed in the garbage can, which is why this year we hired an independent consulting firm to rate America's ten best proms. For color, we have retained a few off-the-cuff remarks from Curran and Gaffney's ill-conceived opus. We've grudgingly paid them our standard three-and-a-half-cents-a-word rate, slightly reducing their staggering debt to the magazine.

And now for the results:

1. *Hanrahan High School,* Hanrahan, South Carolina. The punch is purple jesus; the girls are horny teen Dallas Cowboy-cheerleader types; and last year the band boasted Jimmy Buffett, Mick Ronson, and several live members of the former Allman Brothers. Mr. Peterson does get a bit long-winded with his crowning speech, but stick around for the Coke-a-thon and pig wrassle down by the docks. "I woke up face down in the mud out on the tidal flats," admits Curran, "but I think I had fun."

2. *El Promo Fantastico,* Rio Lobo High, El Paso, Texas. Sizzling Tex-Mex food goes great with oversize margaritas, and on this extra-special night Texas Rangers look the other way if you're underage. (They do shoot their guns into the sky upon request.) But don't get too drunk, because your dates will be saying "*Sí, sí, yanqui hombre*" in hopes of a marriage vow and a green card. Sneak out of bed early and enjoy huevos rancheros and Dos Equis at Dr. Ray's.

3. *Pyramid High School,* Maui, Hawaii. You'll be upside down with joy as hard-nippled, long-limbed daughters of sixties burnouts offer drugs, recreational sex, and impromptu palm-reading sessions off the shore of one of nature's most unspoiled paradises. That's right, the prom is held not *by* but *in* the warm, tranquil Pacific. You'd better hope you still have the coordination to swim across the bay for carnal delights at the lavish estate used for the filming of TV's *Magnum, P.I.* "Man, you can get primo weed on this island for about $150 a pound," raves Gaffney. "Not that we use that stuff, of course," adds Curran.

4. *John Bendel's Prom of Horrors,* Paramus Park, New Jersey. Each year former editor and mystery man John Bendel hosts his own private prom for the cream of the Jersey teen crop in his eerie castle dwelling by the sea, Bendelarra. John's *Carrie*-like theatricals are not for the faint of heart, but his liquor, taste in music, and manner are all first-rate. "How are those True Facts coming?" asks Curran, swigging from a bottle of Rebel Yell as he swings drunkenly from a crystal chandelier.

5. *Breedmore School for Girls,* Helmhurst, Maryland. Academically and genetically, this private academy is top drawer. No men are allowed on the grounds of the school, so the prom is a yelping, squealing, nuzzling, all-girl affair. "My high heels are killing me, but otherwise I'm having the time of my life," notes an overly made-up Gaffney.

6. *Wallerwag High School,* Wallerwag, Arkansas. This is a real hit-or-miss affair. Last year they got some bad moonshine, and the entire senior class went blind. On the positive side, however, this is one of the few proms in the country where they won't think you're a homo if you come with your sister.

7. *The Senior Promenade* (pronounced promen-*odd,* not *aid*), Wimbelsby Academy, Dexter, Massachusetts. America's oldest prom (founded 1636), the Wimbelsby Senior Promenade is rooted in the noblest traditions of New England aristocracy. Young gentlemen are still required to leave their muskets at the door; young ladies are still required to leave all their clothes at the door. "Whoever said those Pilgrim fathers didn't know how to have fun?" quips Curran before being forcibly ejected from the affair when he is unmasked as a Catholic.

8. *Bear Mountain High School,* Picapee, West Virginia. The only prom held underground within the contiguous U.S., according to David Wallechinsky's *Big Book of Proms.* Bear Mountain seniors and their lucky dates hop on an elevator for the trip to their unusual prom site—a working coal mine two miles beneath West Virginia's breathtaking Blue Ridge Mountains. Following the festivities, the men in the class take off their tuxedos and put on their hard hats as they start the first day of their lifelong careers as miners.

9. *The Prom Glider,* Somewhere Up There in the Clouds. An exciting romp among the stars with Cap'n Jim "Ace" McLean and his crew. Curran and Gaffney agreed that this was one of their most memorable prom experiences, but expressed concern over safety and the intentions of Los Amigos Pequeños Agencia de la Insurancia.

10. *SlovakProm,* Steelville High School, Steelville, Pennsylvania. "Slovak-Prom, SlovakProm, SlovakProm—hey!" cry the cheerful Steelville funsters after donning their great woolen gray party coats and strapping on their dancing boots. The predominantly Slovak population of Steelville lovingly recreates the look and feel of an actual prom in its homeland, including the tractor races, hoisting of the king and queen, and mandatory security checks. "Durbid Sopcheck's band plays with extraordinary zest," notes Curran. "Pass me the alloyed-potato treat," requests a dazed Gaffney.—P. G. & K. C.

SWAN SONG

OF THE OPEN ROAD

by Sean Kelly

It is I, Walt Whitman, who addresses you once
   again, *mes enfants!*
I have shed my eighty years of sleep as a hairy
   great mastadon shakes off snowflakes.
(Did you think I was dead?)
No! I had dozed off merely, tranquilized by the
   sonorous sound of my own barbaric yammer,
Wafted to infantile slumber, into the cradle,
   endlessly talking, as it were,
Myself my own mesmerist, my own beard muffl'd,
   a bardic drone my lullaby.

But lo! I am returned. Like the poor, I am with
   you always.
And once more I take to the open road.

I, Walt Whitman (with an "h," my good man,
   get it right),
Whom you may call genius, camerado, or, for that
   matter, sweetheart,
Set out once more on the roads of my America!

Allons! come travel with me! was my clarion
   cry of old.
To the rat I urged, Leave the sinking ship!
To the munitions worker I said, Drop what you
   are doing,
But not until I, Walt Whitman, am safely out
   of the way!
To the carpenter I said, A new saw.
To the cobbler I said, Give up nothing but your awl!

I, Walt Whitman, made those awful puns up out of
   my own picturesque head.
They erupted from me like boils from the neck of a
   shoe salesman.
And now I set forth to see if those words—which,
   like every word that falls from my lips,
   seems beautiful to me—
If these rich lip-drippings of mine found a place in
   the whorl'd spitoons of the ears of this my
   America!

Hitchin' down the freeways of my soulful moody mind
(Baby why'd you treat me so unkind?)
I'll miss your paisley curtains and your morning buttered
   toast
But my highway toes are thumbin' to the coast.

Shootin' up the highways on the road map of my wrist
(Baby, I've just scratched you off my list)
I'll miss your tie-dye bed sheets and your pretty spearmint
   mouth
But my highway toes are thumbin' me down South.

Farewell to New York City
With its streets that flash like strobes,
Farewell to Carolina
Where I left my frontal lobes.

Alone but for my agent, a photographer from *Life*,
A film crew and another popstar's wife,
Can't you hear them contracts callin', I'm too sensitive
   to stay,
And my highway toes are thumbin' me away.

That plaintive carol I heard sung by a skinny young
   fellow, one of the bleary-eyed gang of jostling
   roadside companions.
He stood shivering and singing in the melting slush
   of springtime on the Stockbridge to Boston
   turnpike,
With eleven miles behind him and nine thousand
   nine hundred and ninety-nine more to go.

O Joy! O throbbing heart! O twitching loins of me!
For I behold the thoroughfares thronged with
   young people, both male and female!

(At least I assume some are male and some are
  female.)
Their still spittle-wet thumbs stuck out, khaki
  knapsacks clutched to their lean and pimpl'd
  bodies,
Some with infants strapped, howling, to their
  denim'd limbs,
Free! Democratic! Unemployed!
Staggering in droves across the nation, migrating
  from Mannahata to Longa Beacha,
Their myriad squalid lives a vast and ragged living
  monument to me.
(You know who.)

Babb'ling beatniks spastic'ly steering stolen
  cadillacs, grotesquely decal'd autobuses crammed
  with hysterical dope zealots, photogenic Oakies
  in meticulously reconstructed Model T pickup
  trucks, pig-eyed Angels in pancake makeup
  perched on chrome-plated choppers.

Mistily political hoboes lounging in the doors of
  boxcars chanting into the tape recorders of
  Library of Congress researchers:

Had a wife that nagged me 'n' a kid that bawled
So I hit the road, 'n' now I'm called
Irresponsible. Folk hero. Take your pick.

Thought I'd be a poet, but that didn't pay
Took some music lessons, but I couldn't play
Found a gi-tar, started singin'. Professional.

Once I joined a strike 'n' the strike got busted
But the po-leece shrink said I'm maladjusted,
Copped a plea. Sanity Clause. Yes, Virginia.

Bin ridin' the rails since the Great Depression
Now I'm goin' down to Newport, got the folk concession
Tied up. Make a bundle. Woo-wee!

Jus' me 'n' muh gi-tar 'n' muh gal named Sally
Headin' out to Oklahoma, start a tenpin alley
Call it Dust Bowl. Strike it rich. Yahoo!

Sung the same damn songs for Wobbly toughs
Peace-rally creeps 'n' eco-buffs,
Three generations. Music lovers. My ass.

Bushy-bearded are many of these vagabond
    versifiers, triumphantly queer are most of them,
And all excel at publicizing the singular
    wonderfulness of their own superdemocratic
    personalities.
They are my heirs, my echoes, my descendants,
    the disciples I foretold,
Homesteaders and real-estate agents along the
    rough, verbose trails which I, Walt Whitman,
    pioneer'd!
On the road, on the make, on the take, the bottle,
    the dole,
And on the front pages of the literary supplements
    of America!
Wherever I look I meet myself, the self I sang
And behold! My name is legion!

By the shores of an eight-lane trout stream in
    sunstruck California
I chanced upon one young bard
From whom with equal, democratic facility spewed
    prose and poetry,
With never a jot or tittle blotted, with never a
    pause for thought,
In a surge of divine inspiration with a Simon and
    Schuster deadline to meet,
His muse crouched cross-leggéd by his side, rolling
    innumerable joints,
He brought forth such poems as these in mind-
    bogg'ling abundance:

Share the Wealth
I will make a pact with you, Rod McKuen.
We have completed for markets long enough.
I won't make any more albums if
you'll stop publishing verse. O.K.?
I am the coke and you are the cola.
Let there be commerce between us.

Very, Very Beautiful
The royalty cheques pile up
like a slow-motion movie of trout
landing on the banks
of a recently dynamited stream.

St. Valentine's Dance
Anybody can catch the crabs.

Postmen, fashion models,
even nice girls like you.

If you think you might have them,
I've found it helps a little
to consider them a variety
of restless, nomadic dandruff.

Not the young folk only, but also their great-belly'd
elders as well take part in this pointless,
perpetual pilgrimage!
Ah! what a plethora of gleaming vehicles lurches
and lumbers by me as I loiter in the roadside
ditches!
The air that serves me with breath to speak grows
rich and thick and gritty with the fumes of
their exhaust,
Our old feuillage withers and rots in the wake of
these wanderers!
Campers, mobile homes, microbuses, dune buggies,
motorcycles, tent trailers, station wagons,
trail bikes, go-carts, skidoos, tow trucks.
Upon the fields and forests like a rash, like the
spreading pustules of a plague of pastoralism,
Appear the pop tents, pup tents, wall tents,
umbrella tents and chemical toilets,
Swarm the boy scouts, bird watchers, nature lovers,
field trippers, mountaineers, skiers, canoeists,
spelunkers, herbalists, archeologists, scuba
divers, archers, anglers, forest rangers, rock
collectors, lifeguards, game wardens, campfire
girls, beachcombers, Sierra Club photographers,
hermits and search parties.
Beneath their bare and bunion'd feet, climbing
boots, hiking boots, wedgies, waders, harachis,
sneakers, cleats, topsiders, snowshoes, flippers
and health sandals,
No leaf of grass remains untrod!

Yet unperturbed (*Me, imperturbilê*) I beckon still.
I am the maker of lists! I am the Great Cataloger!
I urge my disciples to tarry not in the task
before us.
It is our free and democratic duty to get the whole earth cataloged!

Allons encore! The road stretches and yawns
   before us!
Infinitely, indefinitely,
Endlessly and without end,
Forever and forever going on like this,
Like me,
Walt Whitman. . . .

TRUE FACTS

• A twenty-six-year-old native of Dacca, Bangladesh, known as "cannibal Khalilullah," was arrested by the police after it was discovered that he had been eating corpses in a medical college morgue for three years.

A part-time reporter on a Bengali newspaper was keeping a close watch on the morgue. When the students left the room after a surgical demonstration, the reporter stated that he found Khalilullah eating the heart of a dissected corpse.

According to his report, Khalilullah admitted to his craving. "I get the urge every two weeks or so, and then nothing can stop me," he said. It all started when he was twenty years old and developed what he confessed was an "intense attraction" for dead bodies. He said he was "very active" in removing bodies off the streets in 1971 during the bloodshed of the Bangladesh independence movement.

Three years ago, Khalilullah volunteered to work as a "casual helper" in the Dacca medical college morgue, and had been having his macabre meals ever since. *London Times* (R. J. Whiffen)

• Tim Lee, a sophomore at Oregon State University, won a $100 bet from a fraternity brother by drinking up eleven ounces of the spit remains of chewing tobacco. As part of the bet, he also pledged not to throw up for an hour after accomplishing the feat.

Lee had previously lost money at a gambling trip to Reno, and one of his comrades, John Heller, offered Lee the proposition.

"I'd done real well in Reno, making about $220," said Heller. "Tim had lost money, and it was getting close to Christmas. He thought about taking me up on it for a while, and finally I copped out because I figured he'd do it and get sick. Then, on the Thursday of finals week, we had both partied a little, and I offered the $100 to him again if he'd drink eleven ounces of chew without throwing it up in an hour. He agreed to do it, and darned if he didn't follow through on it."

In front of twenty-five incredulous onlookers at a pre-Christmas evening gathering at the Delta Tau Delta fraternity, Lee unhesitantly drank the murky tobacco excrement.

Tim apparently had some problem keeping the liquid down. "He almost threw it up two or three times, and I tried to psyche him into doing it," said Heller. "But after awhile, I figured he deserved the money."

"I told a bunch of guys long ago that if you put your mind to something, there is nothing a person cannot do," said Lee. "I'll drink anything for the right reward. In this case, I needed the money for Christmas, anyway."

Lee never got sick, and said he felt fine the next day. "It beats swallowing a goldfish," he claimed.

Will Lee repeat his trick, or go on to even greater heights?

"For $100, yeah," he said. "A lot of guys around the house are kidding me, but nobody's putting up any money, because they know now what I'm capable of. If the price is right, you bet I'll do it again." *Oregon State Barometer* (S. Chase)

• A disciple of guru Nagababa Narbadagiri has discovered a way to observe his religious demands while working to ease India's fuel crisis. The twenty-eight-year-old *sadhu* (disciple) pulled a baby Hindustan BMU automobile with his penis along the stretch of road in front of Mahalakshmi Temple, in Bombay. Apart from cars, he has also pulled trucks by coiling up his foreskin around the mudguards. When asked how he accomplished such superhuman feats, the modest sadhu replied, "Breath control." *Bombay Blitz* (J. Ryan)

GREAT HEADLINES

from *TRUE FACTS*

DEMOCRATS WELCOME DICKS THIS YEAR
AT PARTY'S 'BIG LOVE-IN'

SHOTS INTERRUPT
SALVADOR WAR

DEAD GUITARIST BETTER

SOME MURDERERS PRONE TO VIOLENCE

GROUND TO BE BROKEN TODAY FOR
ROUSE'S GROUND-BREAKING PROJECT

SUN TO DARKEN MUCH OF AMERICA

PRISONER LOSES HIS APPEAL

GUARDSMAN QUITS AFTER DEATH

CHRISTINE PRESTON
FORMER HEAD NURSE; AT 69

BURGHERS OPPOSE MCDONALD'S

GET INVOLVED WITH DRUGS
BEFORE YOUR CHILDREN DO.

APRIL SLATED AS CHILD ABUSE MONTH

DOWNPOUR LIKELY TO HELP
ONLY CRAPPIE FISHERMEN

REJECTION OF LAUNDRY IS URGED

AIR FORCE SHOOTS DOWN RECRUIT

COCAINE IS SEEKING
TO BUY TABLE TALK

SHORTAGE OF BRAINS
SLOWS MEDICAL RESEARCH

ORGAN WILL BE SPEAKER
AT SERTOMA CONFERENCE

CHILDREN'S BOOK HAS
PROWLING POSTAL PUSSY

WOMAN KILLED,
BURNED NEAR LAKES!

EARS FOUND IN PROBE OF HEADS

ITEMS THAT ARE ROUND
AND WRINKLED STAND OUT
AMONG NUTRITIOUS FOODS

CHANGE SHOULD HELP IOWA GET
MORE DRUG MONEY, TAUKE SAYS

DISABLED ATHLETE
WINS SECOND GOLD
WITH RECORD HEAVE

WOMAN'S ARM TURNS
OUT TO BE BEAVER LEG

BURGLAR TAKES UNDERWEAR FROM HOME

KILLER OF IRVINE POLICE CHIEF GETS
LIFE WITHOUT PAROLE FOR 25 YEARS

WINE PROMISES TO PUT SOME
LIFE BACK INTO DEAD BRAVES

OFFICIALS WARN CLAMS,
OYSTERS CAN CARRY VIRUS

LEAGUE OF WOMEN VOTERS
AIMS TO SHED DRAG IMAGE

TOWLE HEAD BUYS
GALAXY BUILDING

FIGHT ERUPTS AT WORLD
PEACE CONFERENCE

Publications: *Newark Star-Ledger;* *Meadville* (Pennsylvania) *Tribune; Santa Barbara News-Press; San Francisco Chronicle;* (Washington, Pennsylvania) *Observer-Reporter; Saratogian; Boston Globe; Chicago Sun-Times; Louisville Courier-Journal; Minneapolis Star and Tribune; Cleveland Plain Dealer; Cedar Rapids Gazette;* (Charlottesville, Virginia) *Daily Progress;* (Bremerton, Washington) *Sun; Daily Oklahoma Times; Philadelphia Daily News; Los Angeles Times; Discovery;* (Escanaba, Michigan) *Daily Press; Houston Post; Philadelphia Inquirer; Washington Post; Reader's Digest; Richmond* (Virginia) *News Leader; Half Moon Bay* (California) *Review; Chattanooga News-Free Press; Stamp Collector; Arizona Daily Star; Toronto Star; Birmingham* (Alabama) *News.*

Contributors: Lew Weidenfeld; Liz Perkins; John B. Higgins; Kris Sperry; Mitchell W. Carver; W. Alan Ball; Mary G. Haggar; Joe Peterson; Lee Taplinger; Jerry Dolan; Mark Brakeman; Chris Weiss; Jeff Simmons; Kevin Smith; Michael T. Hahn; Mark Johnson; Scott Lewis; Gaston and Vic; Bill Skoonberg; Ward Foeller; Cindy Vaz; Sarah Spero; K. A. Neuendorf; Peter M. Nelson; David B. Kilbride; Stephen Weir; Greg Tarlin; Chuck Barber; G. Held; James A. DeMay; Bill Horgos; Ken Clason; Betsy Curtis.

THIS WEEK'S TV PROGRAMS

by Gerald Sussman
with Danny Abelson, Tony Hendra, Ted Mann

MORNING

6:00 ③BEHIND THE BARN

6:30 ②CAMBRIDGE DONS
The numbing effect of Wittgenstein on the brain; how to fry a banger.
④ALARM CLOCK

7:00 ⑥LET'S MASTURBATE—Instruction
⑦BIBLE CARTOONS
Tom and Jerry give everyone indigestion at the Last Supper.
⑨LITTLE MUGGERS—Comedy

7:30 ③BRUSH YOUR TEETH, AMERICA
George Hamilton, Lola Falana.
④WE'RE WORKING ALREADY
Dan Rather, Bruce Jenner, others—all washed, dressed, and talking about all kinds of subjects, with guests Indira Gandhi and Andy Williams.
⑧THE CUNSTERS—Comedy
Herman buys Brenda a new ass for Valentine's Day.

8:00 ②THE CARTRIDGE FAMILY
Danny loses his hat.

⑤CARTOONS GO TO WAR

8:30 ⑦SITONME STREET
⑨BREAKFAST WITH INTER-RACIAL COUPLES
⑩I DREAM OF RERUNS
①③MORNING COITUS—Instruction

9:00 ③STAMP UNTO MY FEET
The Rev. Percy Whitebait discusses rare ports and sherries.
④LAMP UNTO MY MEAT
Rabbi David Judao asks: "Are shrimp actually kosher?"
⑤LEAVE IT TO HER BEAVER
⑦CELEBRITY FAILURES

9:30 ②DOG PRIESTS
Bullets confesses to Father Bob that he participated in a live sex show.
③GOOD GRIEF, AMERICA
Geraldo Rivera destroys the real estate values of his old neighborhood by revisiting it.
⑤LET'S GET STONED

10:00 ③COFFEE BREAK
④HOLLYWOOD LEPERS
⑦MOVIE—Comedy
"Butcher Baby." (1969) A biologist (David Niven) loses his

moustache in a skiing accident and is mistaken for a debutante (Sandra Dee). (84 min.)

10:30 ④NOT FOR STUPID PEOPLE
David Susskind discusses his productions of Ibsen, Shaw and Arthur Miller. English subtitles. Dick Cavett, host.
⑤THE SUICIDE GAME
⑥HONEY, THE MOONER—Rerun
Ralph comes home to find the door is locked.

11:00 ⑥SEARCH FOR THE WIND—Serial
⑦BACK DOOR TO ADVENTURE
Rex Reed narrates boy's adventure stories.
⑨TARGET PRACTICE
⑩⑩ANOTHER DAY, TOMORROW—Serial

11:30 ②HOLLYWOOD BOULEVARD
George Gobel, Rose Marie, Rory Calhoun, Jack Carter and Louisa Moritz meet host Cesar Romero on this famous street.
④EDGE OF OUR YESTERDAYS—Serial

AFTERNOON

12:00 ②LIVES OF OUR LOVES—Serial
④THE DONG SHOW
African runner Ben Jipcho matches his dong with Ossie Davis and show regulars Bill Bixby, Ben Davidson and Carlo Ponti. Bill Russell is host.

12:30 MOVIE—Mystery
"Bugged Malone." (1975) Mysterious semi-invisible criminals plant a large water bug in Billy Malone's (David Niven) bum.

The water bug has a hidden microphone that can do weird tricks. With Loretta Young. (84 min.)
⑨LIGHT OF DARKNESS—Serial
⑩⑩ARROZ CON POLLO—Chickens' Show

1:00 ③ANOTHER DREAM—Serial
④BEG FOR MERCY—Game
⑤LET'S HAVE LUNCH
Today's meal: Consommé, filet of haddock au gratin, buttered lima beans, romaine and tomato salad and fruit surprise.

1:30 ②THE JUNKIES
Buddy loses the fix money and nearly dies.
④NAPTIME
⑤TALK, TALK, TALK
⑦MOVIE—Adventure
"Bush Pilots." (1943) Flying low among the bushes is a dangerous business. Eddie (John Payne) gets a nasty cut on his forehead and nearly loses Jill (Lena Horne) in a melon patch. (84 min.)
㉑RUTABAGA!
Variety show for brain-damaged invalids.

2:00 ④THE $20,000 SWINDLE
⑥LOST IN OUR DAYS—Serial
⑦HOLLYWOOD SHMEARS
Guests Natalie Wood and George Segal try to bribe our panel. Host: George Raft.

2:30 ⑤THE SNATCH GAME
⑥FOLLOW THAT CAR!
⑦MOVIE—Comedy
"Stingers." (1974) A young hitchhiker (Laurence Harvey) is befriended by a group of children who are very tall for their

age. With Jane Powell. (84 min.)

⑨GUIDING STORM—Serial

3:00 **②BOYS WILL BE BOYS**

④SAFARI TO NOWHERE

⑥BEASTS OF BURDEN

Ricardo Montalban narrates the story of the llama.

⑨THE ZANY GREY SHOW

Zany and his pals Mook and Kook throw things out of a 50-story window.

3:30 **③AFTERNOON CHURCH BREAK**

④WEIGH THAT AGAIN, PLEASE

Consumer protection show.

⑥MUGGA MUGGA—Cartoon

⑦INSIDE OUR WOMEN

⑨THE BABYSITTERS

Buddy and Chris accidentally flush little Bobo down the toilet and call the plumbers.

4:00 **②LET'S EAT EARLY**

Dinner ideas from Peg Bracken.

④CELEBRITY BALLING

⑤ALL OUR WORLDS—Serial

⑦THE OLD COUPLE

Felix slips in the shower and no one is home to help him.

⑨HI!

⑮CALAMARES Y BIFTECK

Meat and fish combination platters for the hard of hearing.

4:30 **③MOVIE—Science Fiction**

"The Biggest Jew in the World." (1965) Little Chassidic Jew is lost near atomic testing ground in the west, becomes a mutant (Dustin Hoffman) and destroys an entire restricted retirement community. (84 min.)

⑤TOKEN NEGROES

Nipsy Russell, Slappy White, Carl Stokes, Elston Howard

and Roosevelt Grier try to talk fancy.

⑦LOST IN THE BRONX—Adventure

Dr. Jones (Christopher Guest) is lured into a basement social club where he falls under the spell of a beautiful Puerto Rican girl with no teeth (Karen Valentine).

⑨HOCKA HOCKA—Cartoons

⑳MOFONGO

Vegetable soup for the blind.

5:00 **②THE GAS COMPANY**

④NEWS—Danny Kaye

⑤NO PROBLEM, I CAN FIX IT

Host: Jackie Vernon.

⑦THE TRENDY BUNCH

Lori accidentally wears a dress backwards and can't get it off.

⑨INDOOR SPORTS

Dr. John Berg demonstrates how to swim on dry land.

⑩THE MORONS

⑫SCHMUCK AND SON

5:30 **③HOW'S YOUR ASS?**

⑤COMMUTER COCKTAIL TIME

⑦NEWS—Martha Raye

⑨MOVIE—Drama

"Woman on Top" (1972) A private detective (Bruce Lee) smuggles a double-crossing jewel thief (Barbara Bel Geddes) out of Instanbul and throws up. (84 min.)

⑩VOYAGE TO THE END OF YOUR NOSE

⑬THE KIT-KAT CLUB

⑳OLÉ

EVENING

6:00 **②NEWS**

④NEWS

⑥NEWS

⑦BOGART THE CLOWN

Bogart entertains his friends

Ta-Ta and Ki-Ki.
⑨KOSHER KITCHEN
Hostess Rachel Hebrew shows us how to cook under strict dietary laws, using tough meats.
⑪COMA
Detective Angelo Coma (Tony Franciosa) impersonates a Doberman to outwit a gang of drunks.

6:30 **⑥EXECUTIVE WASHROOM**
Mike (Estelle Parsons) learns of Steve's (Jill St. John) resignation too late. A toilet floods over and wreaks havoc in the hallways.
④A CHRISTMAS CAROL ON ICE
The classic tale by Charles Dickens, with Dorothy Hamill as Scrooge.
⑦DENTISTRY AT HOME
⑧THE ART OF FRENCH DRINKING
⑨ANAL ROBERTS
⑪MOVIE—Comedy
"Pardon My Face." (1971) An innocent bystander (Jill St. John) gets acid thrown in her face by a gang of Mafia thugs. She uses her striking new looks as a show business act, becomes a star, and marries the man who arranged the acid throwing (Gregory Peck).

7:00 **②WILD KINKDOM**
Dr. Sam Shepard takes you on a trip to Hamburg and its colorful waterfront bars.
⑤MY THREE CUNTS
Nancy (Sandy Duncan) has too much of a good thing and can "entertain" more than one boyfriend at a time.
⑥THE PORKCHOPS
Father (Earl Hines) is robbed in

his shoeshine parlor by an old boyhood chum (Woody Strode).
⑧KILLING FOR DOLLARS
⑨ART OF FRENCH KISSING
Julia Child demonstrates deep and shallow tongue.

7:30 **③MILD KINGDOM**
Exploration of the *Ocheres symbiosa,* the world's smallest undersea plant.
④JUNGLE FEVER
⑤ROVA
The schnauzer, favorite of rich and poor.
⑦THE BOBBY BOO SHOW
Tonight's guests include Don Knotts, George Foreman, Quincy Jones and Charles Grodin.
⑨HEY BOPADILLIDIE!
Guests include the Shirelles, the Shebobs, the Shebooms, the Shebebobs,the Shewombies, and the Shedonnes.

8:00 **②THE COLONIC WOMAN**
Lori (Bette Midler) poses as a giant tuna to trap a gang of Asian terrorists who have kidnapped the finest Sushi slicer in New York.
Guest Cast
Wilfred . . . . . . George Voskovec
Boris . . . . David Opatoshu
Sasha . . . . Boris Chaliapin
Gregor . . . . Tina Aumont
③SAMBO AND SON
Ted (Al Attles) discovers that his "pen pal" from Africa is arriving at his home. By mistake, the 80-year-old-pen pal turns out to be a beautiful young princess (Diana Ross) with one leg.
⑤HALF-WITS
With Merv Griffin, Mike Doug-

las, Charo's dogs, Cyril Ritchard and Pat Paulsen.

⑦CHARLIE'S ANKLES
The ankles pose as a polo pony, a pine tree and a barbecued sparerib in a plan to crack a multimillionaire ketchup-watering ring operating out of Guatemala.

Guest Cast

Fred Taylor.... Lowell Thomas
Bruce Green.. George Sanders
Dolores Green ....Margaret
O'Brien
Sarita............ Lena Horne

⑨MOVIE—Mystery
"The Left-Handed Glove."
(1947) Director Byron Pork's spine-chilling tale of voodoo, witchcraft, drugs and human beings marinated to death in hot, peppery sauces. John Garfield gives one of his best performances as a cigar wrapper. With Raymond Massey in blackface. (84 min.)

8:30 ②MORGUE
Vivian catches Morgue going down on Walter in the city morgue where Morgue works as a ball cutter. Morgue claims Walter is alive and she is trying to "revive" him. Vivian goes down on Walter too, but neither woman can bring him back to life. Arthur enters and goes down on Walter and as the show ends, Walter's eyes open and he seems to be smiling.

④KOTEKX
A wealthy gynecologist plans to murder his wife by switching her birth control pills to poison tablets. Kotekx: Marsha Mason. Nestor: Rod McKuen. Lisa: Lena Horne.

⑦CARBUNCLE JONES
A wealthy dermatologist plans to murder his wife with a poisonous suntan lotion, which will seep into her skin and turn her into a raisin. Carbuncle Jones: O.J. Simpson.

⑨WELCOME BACK, KOCKER
Fazool, a new student, challenges Kocker to a fight and cuts him up badly. Kocker: Gabe Pressman. Fazool: George C. Scott. Barbetta: Chevy Chase.

9:00 ②SPHYLLIS
Sphyllis has a blind date with a Nobel Prize-winning scientist and ex-All American football player and movie star who turns out to be a handsome, light-skinned Negro. After a glorious evening on the town, he rapes her, proving that her mother's warnings were right. Sphyllis: Jean Stapleton.

④LITTLE HOMO ON THE PRAIRIE
Little Homo is kidnapped by a band of Cherokee Indians. Homo seduces the Cherokee chief and they plan a marriage. But the nupitals are spoiled by Little Homo's dad, who steals the boy back. In the ensuing action, Dad falls in love with Chief as well. Little Homo: Tatum O'Neal. Dad: Roman Gabriel. Cherokee Chief: Merv Griffin.

⑦BURN CENTER
A raging forest fire turns a gala Boy Scout Jamboree into a charred mess. The paramedics of Burn Center work day and night to save the scouts' lives, but few make it.

⑨HAWAII FIVE INCHES

A pineapple plantation is the front for an illegal marzipan smuggling ring. In order to get proof of the smuggling, Johnny has to wear a nose ring.

9:30 **⑥LAVERNE ON SHIRLEY**

Piggy and Pus-Lips hit the ceiling when they peep through a hole in the Y locker room wall and see what Laverne is doing to Shirley.

④ALL IN THE FAMILY WAY

Everyone is in heavy labor at the same time at the Funker household, even Edith. The trouble is, Archie can't remember having sexual relations with her for the last nine years.

⑤THE TOURNAMENT OF NOSES PARADE

Special: Thousands of competing noses will parade in front of the judges, noses of every shape, color and size. Tournament of Noses Queen will be selected. Live from the Williamsburg section of Brooklyn.

⑦TOLL BOOTH

Toll booth police suspect something fishy when a scruffy-looking Puerto Rican teenager pulls into their change box driving a 1965 Rolls Royce Silver Wraith with a custom-made Mulliner body. They take him into custody only to find out that he works for a Rolls Royce dealer. Sgt. Kużonko: Chad Everett. Patrolman Sims: Gale Sayers.

⑨WHERE'S MOMMA?

Dad comes home from work in a bad temper because someone broke his foot. Danny and Betsy are hungry and there's no food in the house. "Where's momma?" they all cry. No one can find her.

⑪⓪G*A*S*H

After working an exhausting 24-hour stint assisting the surgeons, the nurses discover they now have to put out for a group of very important Korean businessmen who are visiting the camp. Hot Lips: Barbara Stanwyck. Labie: Patty Duke. "Big C": Teresa Brewer.

10:00 **⑧THE OVERREACTORS**

Premiere of a police story about a hotheaded, trigger-happy team of cops in the homicide division who shoot first and don't talk later. In the first episode: a ten-year-old black kid takes a pretzel from a box in a candy store, and leaves his payment on the counter. Alex, one of the Overreactors happens to pass by and thinks the boy stole something, and that the pretzel is a revolver. He tells the boy to stop but the boy panics, runs and is shot dead. Alex: Joe Don Baker. The Boy: Ben Vereen.

④T.W.A.T

Premiere of a police story about the "special squad" of lady cop commandos, cops who go on missions even more dangerous than the men's. (T.W.A.T stands for "Tough Women Attack Team.") In the first episode, the T.W.A.T destroys the entire city of Newark in its search for a dope pusher. Starring Mercedes McCambridge as "Fist," Della

Reese as Ms. Big and Bella Abzug as "Little Chunky."

Guest Cast

Ossie Nkumba . . . . Ossie Davis
Flossie Nkumba . . . Lena Horne
Simon of Athens . . . Peter Falk

⑥HANNIBAL CANNIBAL
Premiere of a new private detective series. Hannibal Cannibal is a new breed of detective, an angry lawman who has little patience with anyone, from petty crooks, felons and grifters to the bigtime hoods. He shows his hatred and disgust by eating them—sometimes raw, sometimes cooked. He subdues his enemies by biting them viciously with his poison-tipped teeth (he is immuned to the poison). Starring Burt Lancaster as Cannibal, with Joel Grey as his sidekick and chef.

Guest Cast

Little Benny . . . . . Ben Gazzara
Danielle Leroy . . . Leslie Caron
Don Travelle . . . . . Moses Gunn
Bo . . . . D. P. Schneider

⑦HIT AND RUN
A team of professional assassins, or "hit men," work for the FBI. Their method, run their victims over and leave the scene in their souped-up high-performance cars that no one can catch. Starring Anthony George as "Cracker," James Franciscus as "Crasher" and Greg Morris as "Snapper."

10:30 **❷BUDGET WRESTLING**
③FIRING SQUAD
William Buckley debates himself and wins.

❹NEWS BEFORE 11 O'CLOCK
⑤TRAVEL WITH THE STARS

Rose Marie and Morey Amsterdam go to Puerto Rico.

⑦KEEP YOUR SHIRT ON
⑨THE BAITING GAME
Girls tease boys until they come in their pants.

⑪HOWDY COWBOY
Tall tales of the Old West.

⑬PLANT SWAPPERS

11:00 **❷NEWS—Snuff/Bogash**
❹NEWS—Pitz/Malone
❼NEWS— Krell/Van Scroon
⑤NEWS—Bleminger/Kosh
⑨ MOVIE—Comedy
"Doctor Gets Sued." (1973) Dr. Mal Practice, a bumbling incompetent, is constantly sued by incapacitated patients, and relatives of patients he has accidentally killed. Somehow, he manages to survive and marry an heiress. With Lorne Green, Jack Carter and Lauren Bacall. (84 min.)

⑫MARY TYLER WHORE
Mary thinks she's being fired because her boss, Madame Ovary, doesn't smile at her for days. It turns out that the Madame has a new set of false teeth she's ashamed of.

11:30 **❷JOHNNY TALK SHOW**
Tonight's guests include Peter Marshall, Monty Hall, Gene Rayburn and Regis Philbin.

❹THE BIG HYPE
The widow of General David Sarnoff celebrates what would be their 75th anniversary. On hand to salute her is everyone from the entertainment world, including Vice-President Mondale. (3 hrs.)

⑤MOVIE—WESTERN
"Bend of the Hunter." (1950) A story of retailing in the early

days of the Colorado territory. Tension mounts at sale time when the owners of two general stores fight it out for survival. Alan Ladd as Montgomery "Monty" Ward, Randolph Scott as A. Sears Roebuck. With Virginia Mayo as Lil Hellman.

⑦MOVIE—Comedy
"The Scumbag." (1962) Jerry Lewis plays the inventor of a condom that never breaks. The problem is: the other manufacturers want to break him. With Anita O'Day, Agnes Moorehead, Telly Savalas and Charo. (84 min.)

⑧MOVIE—Adventure
"Cry Panic." (1949) A small town is terrorized by a regiment of National Guardsmen. Another regiment of Guardsmen is brought in to put a stop to it. With Kane Richmond, Louise Albritton, John Sutton and Marina Vlady. (84 min.)

12:00 ⑥BATTLE OF THE BANDS
Johnny Pacheco vs. Tito Rodriguez

12:30 ④MOVIE—Drama
"The Moth and the Flame." (1938) The true story of Lily LaMarr, known in show business as "The Human Moth," an exotic dancer who used huge veils and a wind machine to simulate the actions of a moth flying. Starring Myrna Loy as Lily. With Jack LaRue as Jack LaRay, the only man she ever loved. (84 min.)

1:00 ⑦MOVIE—Science Fiction
"Rectuma." (1972) Japanese-made sci-fi epic about an atomic mutation, a gigantic walking rectum the size of the World Trade Center who gases and besmirches the country before being subdued by an army of homosexuals. (84 min.)

⑨MOVIE—Comedy
"I Married My Husband." (1942) Rosalind Russell stars in this remake of "I Married My Wife." A wacky screwball comedy of a tall woman and a short man who are completely mismatched except for the fact that they're crazily in love. With Mickey Rooney, Wallace Beery and Cordell Hull in a cameo roll. (84 min.)

1:30 ⑪MOVIE—Documentary
"The Story of Wax." (1973) Lorne Greene narrates the story of this useful product, from the days of the Bible to the present-day factory-made candles. (84 min.)

1:45 ②MOVIE—Crime Drama
"Bloody Bullets McGunn." (1969) The story of a vicious, mute gangster who lets his guns do the talking for him. With James Darren, Terry Moore and Toto. (84 min.)

2:00 ④MOVIE—Adventure
"High Seas over Texas." (1965) The Mexican Navy vs. the Texas Rangers in a war over pepper rights. Stars Rory Calhoun, Adele Jergens and Gilbert Roland. (84 min.)

⑤MOVIE—Mystery
"Kiss My Gun." (1953) Ex-convict Humphrey Bogart is framed by a scheming nightclub singer (Lena Horne) and has to climb up a ten-story building to prove his innocence. (84 min.)

AMERICAN HOME MOVIE BOX

by John Hughes

Thursday, Oct. 1

7:00 AM	Adult Breakfast Movie "Cooze and Effect"
9:00 AM	"Rio Lobo"
11:00 AM	Encore Theater "Rio Lobo"
1:00 PM	Network Commercials (Spray 'n' Wash, Dentyne, Ford Escort, 7-Up, others)
1:15 PM	Cable News Brief
8:00 PM	Sports Dynasty: Chicago Cubs
9:00 PM	"Rio Lobo"
11:00 PM	"The Pig of Baghdad"
12:30 AM	Adult Programming "Sore Bone"
2:00 AM	"Muppets Do Motown"

Friday, Oct. 2

6:30 AM	Color Bars
8:00 AM	Coffee Cake Theater "The Evolution of Monsieur Gorilla" (subtitles)
12:00 NOON	"Topper Cheats at Cards"
1:30 PM	"The Onion Ring"
3:00 PM	"Texas Jigsaw Puzzle"
4:30 PM	"Oops!"
6:00 PM	Dinner Break
8:00 PM	"Heaven's Gate Can Wait"
12:00 MID	"The Devil's Doo"

1:30 AM	"Rio Lobo"
3:00 AM	"Lovers and Other Assholes"
4:30 AM	Static, Loud Annoying Buzzing Sound

Saturday, Oct. 3

5:30 AM	"101 Musketeers"
7:00 AM	Saturday on Wall Street
8:30 AM	"Take a Hike, Charlie Brown"
10:00 AM	"Rio Lobo"
12:00 NOON	"The Elephant Woman"
2:00 PM	"Rio Lobo"
3:30 PM	Sports Dynasty: Seattle Mariners
4:30 PM	"Nobody Likes You, Charlie Brown"
6:00 PM	Technical Difficulties
7:00 PM	Ladies' Professional Football San Diego Poontangs v. New York Rags
10:00 PM	The Making of "Rio Lobo"
11:30 PM	Movie Box Sneak Preview—"Rio Lobo, Part II"
1:00 AM	Adult Programming "Rusty Cunts"
3:00 AM	"Brother Sun, Reverend Moon"

4:30 AM   Sports, Weather, News, "Rio Lobo"

Sunday, Oct. 4

9:00 AM   Station Promos

10:00 AM   "Bess"

12:00 NOON   "Peter Allen at Folsom Prison"

2:00 PM   "Shonuf"

4:00 PM   "Hard Parts"

5:30 PM   "The Throne of Porcelain"

6:30 PM   "Cavalry Wagons Heading Way Out West"

8:00 PM   "The Black Horse"

10:00 PM   "National Lampoon Goes to the Bank"

2:00 AM   "Not Even Your Mother, Charlie Brown"

3:30 AM   Photograph of the American flag, with background music

Monday, Oct. 5

7:00 AM   "One Flew Over the Septic Tank"

9:00 AM   "Obol Oir" (subtitles)

11:00 AM   Junk Jap Movie Festival

3:00 PM   Animal Gymnastics

4:00 PM   After-School Movie "Sore Pone"

6:00 PM   Dinner Theater "Pus!"

8:00 PM   "Too Hard to Come"

10:00 PM   "Skuttle Butt, the Bear with the Big Bottom"

12:00 MID   Nothing

2:00 AM   "Rio Lobo"

3:30 AM   "Bess"

Tuesday, Oct. 6
(same as Oct. 5)

Wednesday, Oct. 7

8:00 AM   Bob Fosse's "Self-indulgence"

4:00 PM   Old Disney Wildlife Films

6:00 PM   "Parts, Part II"

8:00 PM   "Le Faggot Amour Francais"

10:00 PM   "The Big Brown One"

12:00 MID   John Wayne Festival "Rio Lobo"

1:30 AM   Bedtime, no programming

Thursday, Oct. 8

7:30 AM   Satellite Transmission Screw-up

8:30 AM   "Sphagnum Moss"

10:30 AM   "2002, a BMW Odyssey"

12:30 PM   Celebrity Slide Show

5:00 PM   "Bess"

7:00 PM   "The Grunting"

9:00 PM   "Hands Up, Charlie Brown"

11:00 PM   "He Knows You're Naked"

1:00 AM   "Cheech and Chong's Latest Piece of Shit"

3:00 AM   Western Classics "Rio Lobo"

Friday, Oct. 9

8:00 AM   Program Director Warns Children Not to Mess with In-Home Equipment

9:00 AM   1956 World Series Highlights

12:00 NOON   "Electronic Horseman"

2:00 PM   Phillips Petroleum Promotional Film

4:00 PM   Encyclopedia Britannica Films Presents "Eskimos of the Frozen North"

4:30 PM   Ladies' Professional Football

Milwakee Gashes *v.* Boston Bitches
7:00 PM "Rio Lobo"
9:00 PM "Bess"
11:00 PM "Bess"
1:00 AM "Bess"
3:00 AM "Rio Lobo"

Saturday, Oct. 10
6:30 AM Breakfast with John Wayne
"Rio Lobo"
8:30 AM "The Elephant Woman"
10:30 AM (MOVIE SELECTED BUT NOT PURCHASED YET)
12:30 PM "Whip It Out, Charlie Brown"
1:30 PM "Are You Deaf, Charlie Brown?"
3:00 PM "Not Tomorrow, Charlie Brown, Now!"
4:30 PM Reader's Digest Condensed Films "Soldier of Orange"
4:40 PM Ford Motor Company Presents Consumer Notebook "Compact Cars, Station Wagons, Light Trucks"
8:00 PM "The Black Horse"
10:00 PM Sports Dynasty: Kansas City Athletics
12:00 MID Critics Corner Janet Maslin Reviews "Rio Lobo"
1:30 AM "Assignment Norway"
4:00 AM "Peter Allen at Joliet Prison"

Sunday, Oct. 11
9:00 AM "Raise the Budget"
11:30 AM "Mr. Reagan Goes to Washington"
1:30 PM "The Wind of the Lion"
3:00 PM "The Incredible Birthday Goose"

4:30 PM "Topper Gets Bent"
6:00 PM Great Men's Younger Brothers: Ted Kennedy
8:00 PM "Honey Suck My Rose"
10:00 PM "Chapter Two, Page Seven, Paragraph Nine"
12:00 MID Adult Programming "Super Slut, 2000"
2:00 AM "Mickey Dread at the Grand Ole Opry"
4:00 AM "The Zoo Squad"

Monday, Oct. 12
[NO PROGRAMMING. CANADIAN THANKSGIVING. HAVE A HAPPY HOLIDAY!]

Tuesday, Oct. 13
7:00 AM "Rio Lobo"
8:30 AM "Bring Me the Head of Charlie Brown"
10:00 AM Ladies' Professional Football
Saint Louis Bush Beaters *v.* Cleveland Clits
1:00 PM "Rocky Builds His Dream House"
3:00 PM After-School Cinema "Sore Bone"
5:00 PM "Bette Midler Is a Divine Swine"
7:00 PM Great Pitchmen of the Silver Screen "Orson Wells for Paul Masson Wine"
8:00 PM "A Change of Underwear"
10:00 PM "The Cereal"
11:00 PM "Hell and/or High Water"
1:00 AM "Those Damn Beavers!"
4:00 AM "The Man with the Golden Retriever"

Wednesday, Oct. 14

7:00 AM	"Wholly Shit"
9:00 AM	Reader's Digest Condensed Films "Cindy Shaves"
9:05 AM	"Winnie Winkie: The Movie"
11:00 AM	"The Rat Who Smelled His Own Cheese"
1:00 PM	"!!!!"
3:00 PM	Commercials for the Deaf
4:00 PM	"Rio Lobo"
6:00 PM	"Cracks"
8:00 PM	"The Beer is Kinda Special"
9:00 PM	Italian Movie
11:00 PM	"9 to 5 (In the Bottom of the Seventh, Two Outs, No Men On, Mike Schmidt in the On-Deck Circle)"
1:00 AM	"Any Which Way But Entertaining"
3:00 AM	"Topper Gets His Hose Stretched"

Thursday, Oct. 15

7:00 AM	"Been There"
9:00 AM	Jennifer O'Neill Festival "Rio Lobo"
11:00 AM	"Adolf Hitler: Portrait of a Real Asshole"
1:00 PM	Movie Box Previews
8:00 PM	Marlon Brando's Implausible Evil Oil Company Movie
10:00 PM	"Take This Film and Shove It!"
12:00 MID	"Prehistoric Animal House"
2:00 AM	[CLEANING THE SATELLITE. NO PROGRAMMING.]

Friday, Oct. 16

7:00 AM	[SATELLITE NOT BACK FROM CLEANERS.]
4:00 AM	"Rio Lobo"

Saturday, Oct. 17

8:00 AM	"War and Peace, Part I"
10:00 AM	"War and Peace, Part II"
12:00 NOON	"War and Peace, Part III"
2:00 PM	"War and Peace, Part IV"
4:00 PM	"War and Peace, Part V"
6:00 PM	"War and Peace, Part VI"
8:00 PM	"War and Peace, Part VII"
10:00 PM	"War and Peace, Part VIII"
12:00 MID	"War and Peace, Part IX"
2:00 AM	"War and Peace, Part X"
4:00 AM	"Rio Lobo"

Sunday, Oct. 18

8:00 AM	Ladies' Professional Football Memphis Muffs v. Dallas Tits
11:00 AM	Old-fashioned Musical
1:00 PM	"Up Your Ass"
3:00 PM	Great Pitchmen of the Silver Screen "Brenda Vaccaro for Playtex Tampons"
4:00 PM	Jack Elam Festival "Rio Lobo"
6:00 PM	"Hemorrhoids from the Deep"
8:00 PM	"Greece"
10:00 PM	"10"
12:00 MID	"Raging Cow"

2:00 AM **"The Milkman Calls First"**

4:00 AM **Sports Dynasty: Washington Senators**

Monday, Oct. 19

8:00 AM **"Lost Planet of Detroit"**

10:00 AM **"Little Sluts"**

12:00 NOON **"Thunderjugs and Ballbuster"**

1:00 PM **"Bronco Bob"**

2:00 PM **"Once in Paris, Twice in the Ass"**

4:00 PM **Movie Box Board Meeting**

7:00 PM **Read a Book!**

10:00 PM **The Best of Carson**

12:00 MID **"Zorba the Greek"**

2:00 AM **"The Lingering"**

4:00 AM **Inexpensive Japanese Thriller Movie**

Tuesday, Oct. 20

8:00 AM **Top-O Nondairy Creamer**

10:00 AM **"Excuse Me, But That's My Wife's Thing You Happen to Be Fondling with Your Dirty Hands" (subtitles)**

12:30 PM **"The Boy Who Loved Cookies for Breakfast"**

2:30 PM **"Pffffrt!"**

4:00 PM **"Young Mummies"**

6:00 PM **"The Tinkler"**

8:00 PM **"We Warned You, Charlie Brown!"**

10:00 PM **Voyage to the Bottom of the Film Files**

12:00 MID **"God Is My Copilot, Christ Is My Flight Attendant"**

2:00 AM **"From Hell to Pittsburgh"**

Wednesday, Oct. 21

7:00 AM **Midnight Cult Movie**

9:00 AM **Knock! Knock!**

11:00 AM **Who's There?**

1:00 PM **Sam and Janet**

3:00 PM **Sam and Janet Who?**

5:00 PM **"Sam 'n' Janet Evening!"**

7:00 PM **I've Heard That Joke Before**

9:00 PM **I'm So Sorry**

11:00 PM **No Big Deal**

1:00 AM **How About We Go to a Movie?**

3:00 AM **What's Playing?**

5:00 AM **"Rio Lobo"**

Thursday, Oct. 22

9:00 AM **"Grunts and Giggles"**

12:00 NOON **Great Pitchmen of the Silver Screen "Lloyd Nolan for Poli-Grip"**

2:00 PM **Ladies' Professional Football Utah Bearded Clams v. Chicago Cramps**

4:00 PM **"Rest in Peace, Charlie Brown"**

6:00 PM **"Krotch"**

8:00 PM **"The Final Conflict: The Fourth Chapter of the Omen Trilogy"**

10:00 PM **Adult Programming "White Stuff"**

12:00 MID **"Cher in Chains"**

2:00 AM **"Peter Allen at Cedars of Lebanon"**

Friday, Oct. 23

9:00 AM **"Melvin and Maude"**

12:00 NOON **"Harold and Howard"**

3:00 PM **"Bonnie and Maude"**

6:00 PM **"Harold and Clyde"**

9:00 PM **"Shifting Gears"**

12:00 PM **Go to Bed**

2:00 AM **Put On Some Soft Music**

4:00 AM **And Fuck Your Wife**
6:00 AM **For a Change**

Saturday, Oct. 24
9:00 AM **Illegal Network Tie-in**
11:00 AM **"Three Drunks in the Fountain"**
1:00 PM **"The Polack Who Fell from a Ladder in Spain"**
3:00 PM **Winter Baseball Meetings**
5:00 PM **"Mammals Are People, Too!"**
7:00 PM **Mexican Cinema "Huevos Rancheros!"**
9:00 PM **"The Incredible Shrinking Star"**
11:00 PM **"Panty Party"**
1:00 AM **"Good Guys Wear Pants"**
3:00 AM **"Caveman's Daughter"**

Sunday, Oct. 25
[NO TRANSMISSION, SOME OF YOU HAVE BEEN LATE WITH YOUR MONTHLY PAYMENTS. PROGRAMMING WILL NOT RESUME UNTIL WE FIND OUT WHO. IF SOME OF YOU WANT TO SPOIL IT FOR EVERYBODY, FINE.]

Monday, Oct. 26
9:00 AM **Federal Express Commercials**
11:00 AM **"The Bubble Bath Girls"**
2:00 PM **"Fist of Fingers"**
4:00 PM **"Fort Apache: The One with the Indians and Cavlary"**
6:00 PM **"Big Fat Mama"**
8:00 PM **"Nighthawgs"**
10:00 PM **"Camel Lot"**
12:00 MID **"Moo!"**
2:00 AM **"Used Jokes"**
4:00 AM **"Rio Lobo"**

Tuesday, Oct. 27
[SAME AS SATURDAY, OCT. 3, SEPT. 12, 19, AUGUST 8, 15, 22.]

Wednesday, Oct. 28
[TEACHERS' CONFERENCES.]

Thursday, Oct. 29
9:00 AM **Erma Bombeck Presents**
11:00 AM **"The Empire Strikes It Rich"**
2:00 PM **"Oh, God! Another 'Oh, God!' "**
4:00 PM **"Come Blow Your Dog"**
6:00 PM **"Rio Lobo"**
8:00 PM **"Lobo Rio"**
10:00 PM **"R-i-o L-o-b-o"**
12:00 MID **"Reeeeeeeooooo Loooooo-bbbbbboooooo"**
2:00 AM **"Reeeee-o Loooooooob-o"**
4:00 AM **"Rio Lobo"**

Friday, Oct. 30
9:00 AM **New Program Guide Arrives in the Mail**
11:00 AM **It's Just About the Same as This Month's**
2:00 PM **Except, No "Rio Lobo"**
4:00 PM **Our Contract Expired**
6:00 PM **But That's Okay**
8:00 PM **We Got Another John Wayne Movie**
10:00 PM **We Think You'll Like**
12:00 MID **It's Called**
2:00 AM **"Hondo"**
4:00 AM **"Rio Lobo"**

Saturday, Oct. 31
9:00 AM **"Trick or Treat"**
11:00 AM **"Exit the Dragon, Enter Mr. Rogers"**
1:00 PM **"The Private Eyes of Sgt. Benjamin"**
4:00 PM **"I Piss on Your Lunch"**

6:00 PM	"Every Good Boy Does Fine"	12:00 MID	Almost Finished
8:00 PM	"My Dog Has Fleas"	2:00 PM	"Rio Lobo"
10:00 PM	Only a Few Jokes to Go		

"We've made more than a couple of singles into couples."

The Personals

Thousands of Hot Tamales at Your Fingertips with Our Sizzling Summer Listings!

Sterling Passaic, Executive Director, Tri-State Total Singles Network

by Dave Hanson

I AM A STRAIGHT WHITE MALE and I want to have sex with a man but only once or twice for experimental/artistic purposes and I don't want to kiss you and you better not be a faggot because they disgust me and if I find out afterward that you're some homo pansy queer boy I'll bash in your pecker-sucking face and kick you off the goddamn roof. Box 638L.

LADIES: HANDSOME IMMIGRATED EARNEST GENTLEMENS crave to make intercourse with you and your equivalent swaying brunette friendlies when you touch our large purple wood poles. Urban/suburban locations a must. Boxes 782G.

GLAMOROUS FORTUNE 500 CORP, 43 yrs old in exc shape, sks educ SWF, 22–30, w/min 1–2 yrs exp, fr lng moonlit nits, intrstng confabs, buffet dinners, endless wkends, lng-trm commitmnt. All mjr bnfts. Hvy client contact. Type 50. Steno a +. Exc growth opp'ty. Box 561G.

FLABBY BUSINESSMAN, 48, realistically expects that putting an ad in this column will increase his chances of meeting a lusty nubile blond SWF languages student, 18–21, who will want to eat a pile of whipped cream off his tiny boner and adoringly use her tongue to clean the viscous yeasts out of his fat-distended navel. If you are that girl, please send photo and breathy letter to Box 111N.

SIKH SEEKS SIKHS FOR SICK SECTS SEX. Serious replies only. Box 980W.

PETER PIPER SEEKS A PECK OF PICKLED PEPPERS. No druggies, fatties, or beekeepers. Box 573H.

MARES EAT OATS, AND DOES EAT OATS, and little lambs eat ivy. What's your bag? Send photo, letter to Box 346B.

How would you like to marry an OBESE FUZZY-FACED ESKIMO QUADRI-PLEGIC DWARF-WOMAN? I know I've got to be somebody's fetish but nobody's come forward yet. If you're out there somewhere, God bless you, and please write me at Box 529V, no photo or letter necessary.

I WANT A MAN WITH A SLOW HAND/ I need a lover with an easy touch. No jells. Box 743G.

VERY HANDSOME CELEBRITY TV HUNK who stars as muscular, well-endowed detective in prime-time show seeks discreet encounters with pretty white girls. Because I'm very shy about publicity I will be wearing a facial and body disguise when we meet, so you won't recognize me, but after we finish having sex at your house I promise I'll take off my disguise and give you an autograph. Utmost discretion required, please. Box 777G.

HOT HORNY STUD WITH 'VETTE seeks chick with butt that just won't quit for meaningful relationship. I like cars, Monday Night Football, piña coladas, beers, B.J.'s before dinner, and volleyball on the beach. If you want your box to be happy, write to mine, 782Y.

GREAT DANE WITH HUGE CRANK seeks long-legged, compatible purebreds for hot, lucrative breeding. Box 738P.

SEEKING AN ADORABLE GREEN-EYED, brown-haired Abyssinian, missing since Feb. 10. Answers to "Taffy." Large reward for live return. Box 582H.

SENSUOUS, INTELLIGENT, AFFECTIONATE WOMAN, great sense of humor, attractive in an unconventional way, seeks **(Editor's note: Guys, just between you and me, if I was a single guy looking for a hot time, I'd steer clear of this one. From what I've seen of women who describe themselves like this, all the Spanish fly in Amsterdam couldn't get you desperate enough to hoist a hard one over this beast. In fact, I remember getting a letter from a guy who'd set up a date with a woman who described herself this way in an ad, and boy, was this guy pissed off, said he and just about any other red-blooded guy on earth would rather spend the evening with his face buried in Claude Akins's asscrack than they would across the dinner table from her. I told him there was no way we could screen out all the dog wrap that takes out ads here, but for you reading this now, I can tell you to beware of this breed of adjectives. In fact, it could be the same gal he wrote me about, in which case, definitely steer clear, unless you're blind, in which case she might not be bad, since he said she had good skin and offered him fellatio. Anway, guys, sorry for the interruption. Read on. But I think you'll do better trying the blonde in the other column, even though she has scraggly black pubes and smells like wet raisin bran.)** cheerful, successful man for good times, dinners, possible marriage. Send heartfelt letter to Box 729H. **(Editor's note: Sorry to cut in again but I gotta tell you, if they don't ask for a photo, it usually means they're reluctant to send you one, and you know what that means.)**

RETIRED GREEK GAMBLER WITH JEWISHY SURNAME, 70, seeks to disprove public misconceptions by having sex with a colored gal who's got two heaping helpings of massive, Southern-bred buttock swelling up out of her huge sweet haunches. Box 363B.

ATROPHIED, SCAB-ENCRUSTED BEHEMOTH seeks part or parts in Broadway or off-Broadway productions. Box 283Y.

HANDSOME PRODUCER SEEKS CLEAN-SHAVEN NEGRO VERSION OF NORMAN FELL for off-Broadway production, quiet dinners. AFTRA scale paid always, clean and discreet. Box 568W.

TALL, GENTLE SWM, 40, seeks to start Hilaire Belloc fan club in Fieldcrest area. Also to swap Batman and Bruno Sanchez comix and all trading cards, intact gum a must. Box 730H.

GUY, 28, wants to get a motel room and do it with five or six incredibly gorgeous women at the same time for a weekend. Send phone, photo to Mr. Passaic, 155 Sixth Ave., 10th FL, New York, NY 10013.

If you crave the recipe for Sterling's Celebrated Sizzling Hot Tamales, send a check for twenty-five cents or a photo, any photo, to: Foods of Passaic, 155 Avenue of the Americas, 10th Floor, New York, N.Y. 10013. Please specify hat size with each order.

SWM seeks compatible woman, 25–35, for friendship, sharing good times, more. I enjoy littering, the smell of airplane wrecks, the taste of burnt hair, the feel of an animal's testicles pressed against my own, justifiable arson, the stiffness of a new pair of lederhosen when you try them on in the store with no underwear on, playing with bait, the sound of a hedge clipper biting through a puppy's neck, putting catnip in rat traps, the high notes raccoons hit when you're burning them out of their nests, the sound of a fingernail giving way to a pair of pliers, making marionettes out of body parts found in Dumpsters, and quiet nights at home playing Scrabble. Box 381J.

VERY HANDSOME, WEALTHY, STYLISH, WELL-BUILT SINGLE MAN has town house in New York City, beach house in East Hampton, seeks woman of any age, appearance unimportant, for hot, romantic affair. For you, the benefits will be enormous: you will be squired about in luxury, dine in elegant style, be treated like a queen. For me, the benefit will be

that if I switch over to heterosexuality, I'll live a lot longer. No trannies. Box 647D.

SWM, 38, SEEKS Lotto victory so that he won't have to advertise to get a date, so that his bachelor pad will be crawling with leggy opportunistic bitches built like Emmys who'll squirmingly service any appendage presented in exchange for a noseful of cocaine. In the meantime, though, I'm seeking a warm, educated woman, 25–35, appearance unimportant, who enjoys opera, the Sunday *Times,* autumn weekends in the country, and fine dining as much as I do. Box 821W.

ATTRACTIVE FEMALE, 26, NEW IN AREA, WANTS TO MEET LONELY, CONSIDERATE MEN. Must be adept with ceiling fans, Sheetrock, wallpaper, car repair, carpet cleaning, figuring out how to work a VCR and answering machine. Also, if you have a friend, I have a couch coming on the 26th. Love ya. Box 439M.

HOT, HANDSOME MAN, 26, seeks sizzling phone sex with gorgeous, long-legged small-breasted, green-eyed woman, 21–25. Send detailed letter outlining what you'll say to me, and how you'll say it. No photos. Box 298Y.

HERE IS THE SCENARIO: I receive your response to this personal, and I am so turned on by the sensual picture you send me of yourself, lounging nearly naked in a loading bay, that I can barely control my desperate urge to masturbate. I do, however, and instead use my hand to write you a letter which demonstrates my sensitivity and passion. You are driven to your knees by its narrative power and agree to meet me. When we meet, we are rendered feeble by the magnetic chemistry which rages and bonds us; we go to my place and make love until we pass out. You get pregnant, so, even though we aren't getting along so great, we get married. Our kids have colic and are cranky and hyperglycemic, you live on orange Creamsicles and candy apples and your hips show it, we spend most of our nights watching TV, whenever we go on vacation the car breaks down, eventually you have an affair with my boss, we split up and get back together before finally getting divorced. Also, I throw out my back a few times so I can't work, and you're a mean drunk. Is it all worth it just for that one night of passion? If you think so, write—and remember, the photo should be good—Box 837T. P.S.: You won't get a penny of alimony from me.

O.U.R.A.Q.T.: DJBM, Bx/Bkin/SI/Qns, 25+, attr, sks BDF or BCDF fr BFD. Snd bio, kid ok, tel#, Ital a+. Meant 2 B, do I ½ 2 spl it out 4 U? Bx 983F.

LET'S PLAY VETERINARIAN: SWM, very wealthy, seeks short-haired white woman, 4'6"–4'10", slender, to wear my old Cub Scout uniform around the house naked with no underwear on, and with the trousers on backwards, the fly hole agape, the way Billy Tompkins used to. Box 548B.

HANDSOME, SINGLE MALE SAYS, LET'S BE HONEST. I want a hot bitch with legs up to here and hooters that throw shadows and I want her in my bed now administering to Mr. Noisy till we both knock our back teeth loose and then I want her to leave so I can wash down some peace and quiet with a couple beers and then I want to go to sleep and wake up and go to the beach with my friends and drink more beers and then I want the bitch to come over again and put a spit-shine on

Dr. Schlong and leave fast so I can go out and meet a new chick because by now I'm kind of sick of you and I've lost respect for you because you did everything I asked you to in the sack. Box 593T.

MWM seeks S or M or DW or B male for bonding, wife-evading maneuvers. Poker, bowling, baseball games, any ESPN, weekend golf, car repair, volunteer fire, movies, fishing all OK. Box 208V.

IF YOU'RE THE TYPE OF WOMAN WHO DOESN'T USUALLY READ THESE ADS then you're the girl for me. See you at the bar.

PHILADELPHIA'S BEST-KEPT SECRET. I don't know if you remember me, but my name is Bobby Sherman and maybe I was even on your lunchbox a few years back. Anyhow, I don't get nearly as much tail as I used to and I miss it dearly. I'm still quite handsome, although my midriff is a little wider now and I've got fuzz on my back and shoulders, since RCA doesn't care anymore whether I shave it off or not. Please write me with photo and save me from what happened to Andy Gibb. Box 739G.

CLASSIFIED

in fine sandwiches can afford to be without these. Set of four $15.00. POB, Amsterdam, Netherlands.

WANT TO READ ABOUT people who store the little tea sandwiches in prophylactics because they're so poor that they've never even heard of Glad bags? Send $7.98 in cash, check, or money order to Trailer Press, Box 768, Bluefield, W.V.

ENGLISH-WEST VIRGINIA, WEST VIRGINIA-ENGLISH dictionaries available wherever dictionaries are sold.

LEARN URINALYSIS. After only a few weeks in our course, you will be able to identify people by their urine samples. Urine samples will soon replace fingerprints as the crime fighter's main weapon in the arsenal against lawlessness. Enroll today. Send $60.00 to: Dr. Manny Tshiorisiun Institute of Crime Fighters, Boulder, Colorado.

SEX, COMMON SENSE, AND YOUR SANDWICH FIXIN'S. Illustrated by the world's great painters and drawers. Written in the wonderful, informative style of Herman Melville. You'll want to own more than one copy. You'll want ten copies. To order your ten copies send $20.00 to Eddie, Box 954, Grand Central Station, NYC.

THE LOST GOSPELS. Now at last you can read God's own thoughts on firearms possession and practical sandwich consumption. Put this one right next to your Bible. A must for anybody who's the least bit interested in our origins. Send $5.98 to The Lost Gospels, Box 255, Oakland, Calif.

REMEMBER THE '64 World's Fair. We have slides available of all the sandwich shops that were located throughout the massive fairgrounds. If you order today we will send absolutely free a wall-sized poster of the Coca-Cola Pavilion. Order right away; when we sell what we have, that's it. We'll be into a new business. Slides, c/o Mrs. Alan Jacobs, Rego Park, NY.

LIFESTYLE CLASSIFIED

ENTERTAINMENT

Disco Tennis—Meet the best of both worlds. Dance in your shorts. Call Tony and Toni. (212) 555-0909.

Bookmobile and Live Sex Show—High quality hardcover books. Nonstop excitement. (212) 555-5432.

Sensible, Sane Orgies—Reasonably priced, attractive crowd, no heavy demands. (212) 555-6545.

ENTERTAINMENT/CHILDREN

Take your child to an Industrial Park, Plant and office tours in pretty, landscaped surroundings. KIDDIE TRIPS. (212) 555-8765.

FURNITURE

Tremendous discounts on famous name furniture—Knoll. Herman Miller. Stendig. Baker. Up to 75 percent off. Our secret? WE STEAL. 555-8709.

GOURMET SERVICES

Professional Gourmet—Hire me as a gourmet dinner guest. I promise lavish praise for your cooking, charming conversation. Good knowledge of wines. French. Italian. Chinese food preferred. R.B. Moody. 555-9898.

San Francisco Sourdough Steaks—The same steaks served at private clubs and millionaires' parties. Call Bill. 555-0998.

Color Photographs of Undiscovered Cheeses—Send for 8 × 10 glossies of rare, undiscovered cheeses—Indiana Blue-Vein Nun, Brown Gold, Sequoia. DAIRY DOLL. Box 45, Minneapolis, Minn.

INSTRUCTION

Make your own guitar picks. Evening classes. Congenial groups. Bisexual instructors. Matty and Klaus. 555-7800.

Speedsleeping—Learn to sleep hours faster, up to 900 minutes a day. Easy, quick method. No gimmicks. **"Z" INSTITUTE OF INNER DYNAMICS.** 750 East 87th Street, NYC.

Toilet Train Your Dog with Hypnosis Cassettes—Results guaranteed. No dog can resist. CA-CA UNLIMITED. Dept. Y, 650 West 76th Street, NYC.

Fast your way to suicide—Slow but painless way to end it all. Supervised fasting plus meditations, hard work, no liquids. INSTITUTE FOR RELAXED DYING. 987 East 45th Street, NYC.

All Sex Problems Solved by Masters and Johnson. Murray Masters and Liz Johnson take on all comers. By appointment only. 555-0909.

Learn Greek Massage—Centuries old technique uses phylo pastry and feta cheese. No pain. Mixed classes. Free showers. Argo Health Club. 898 East 65th Street, NYC.

Start Smoking, Gain Weight—Learn how to inhale correctly, eat rich, fatty foods. Balkan and Turkish cigarettes used exclusively. Small classes. Call 555-9898.

LEISURE ACTIVITIES

Full Contact Golf—Hit everything and everybody. Free helmets. No lines, no green fees. FCG TOURS. Box 76, NYC.

Voyeur Trips—Smart East Side locations. Better type people. Free binoculars, cocktails. 555-0987.

PERSONAL IMPROVEMENT

Learn how to render chicken fat through hypnosis. Groups now forming. Call Moe or Hy. 555-0900.

Lose weight by eating yourself. Eat nonessential parts of your body—toes, fingers, knees, etc. Guaranteed weight loss. Dr. PEELGOOD. 555-3245.

The International Institute of Gestalt Biorhythmics is proud to announce that it is now accepting applicants for the first annual Fritz Perls Weekend Disco Intensive to be held at the Concorde Hotel, Catskills, New York. The fee is $475.00 per person, and applications should be sent to the Institute at 892 West 79th Street, NY 10000.

RESTAURANTS

Enjoy—Lunch, tea, snacks in high-toned literary atmosphere. Also free urine analysis. JAMES JOYCE TEA ROOM AND URINE ANALYSIS LABS. 767 W. 43rd Street, NYC.

SERVICES

Ace Asking Service—We ask any question to anybody you want. All styles of asking—tough, polite, suave, sweet, sassy. No questions unasked. 555-0932.

Furniture shampooing—All work done in your home. Two applications, three rinses, blow dry. We shampoo wood, glass, chrome, plastic. Lamps our specialty. 555-9800.

Antique dildo repairs—I repair all sizes and makes of dildos of years past. Specializing in eighteenth century Immelmans and Schwanzers. No work done on plastic. No vibrator repair. HARVEY'S DILDO WORKS. 555-9898.

Shirt and Tie Polishing—Old world craftsmen use Viennese beeswax for permanent finish, high shine. No job too large or too small. 555-8765.

Ambience Chaser—I peek into apartments and make recommendations for decorating. Small fees. My kicks are voyeuristic. 555-9878. Ask for Billy Balding.

Expert Carpenter, painter, plasterer, paperhanger, floor finisher. $2 an hour. Finest work. Can you come to Topeka where I live? Mr. Ted. 43 Maple Ave., Topeka, Kansas 54987.

Shoulder blades sharpened—Also elbows pointed, kneecaps and noses hardened. Prepare yourself for a career in competitive sports. BAD DUDE SHARPENING SERVICE. 989 West 99th Street, NYC.

Movers 'n Shakers—Packing, moving, and storage with a very special difference—our courteous crew of professionals are all members of a religious community with over a century in the furniture business. Why settle for less? (212) 555-8011.

SUMMER RENTALS

Upstate New York Area—Dried-up Artesian well has room for one small person to sleep in. $150/week. (212) 555-4070.

Gambler's Bluff, Vermont—Semi-chalet-type residence. Adjacent to some rock sports, recreation (climbing, looking, falling off, jumping around on, etc.) $400/week. Box 221, N.L.

Summer Place in the Raw—Twelve wooded acres, ideal for clearing, chopping down trees, building house on. Possibly near subterranean water—come dig and find out! $200/wk. Box 467, N.L.

VACATIONS

Oceanic Moped Vacations—Bring your Moped along for a different kind of vacation. You'll sail from New York on the *Argo Venicia,* a fully-registered Liberian petrol tanker specially fitted with driving surfaces below and above decks, so you can drive your Moped across the Atlantic.
Antarctic Fly/Drive Vacation—only $999.00 (based on double occupancy). You'll leave New York via a Pan American 747 jumbo jet, landing 16 hours later in the exotic Antarctic. You'll pick up your new Chevrolet (or comparable car) and you're on your own, free to explore the beauty of this frozen paradise. You'll stay at the numerous U.S. Geological Survey resorts located around this gorgeous continent. For an exciting new vacation, see the Antarctic. PERRY TOURS. LTD., Auukland, Antarctica.

TRAVEL

Snooze in Singapore, Nap in Nepal.
Worldwide Sleep Tours presents THE ORIENTAL SLUMBER TOUR
For a different kind of vacation, come to the exotic Orient and sleep. Dream in the midst of a Thailand morning, enjoy the steamy toss and turn sleep of Burma, the romantic light slumber of Manila, and the listless daytime naps of Bombay. Experience many different types of beds and bed clothing. Learn firsthand how the Orientals relax. Call your travel agent and ask about the Oriental Sleep Tour. From $1,555.

TOWN AND COUNTRY PROPERTIES

BEAUTIFUL EAST HAMPTON HIDEAWAY

Oceanfront, entirely made of bar coasters. A noted architect once asked for road directions here. Cheap, will deal.
AJAX REALTY. We're in the book.

POSHERIA

N.Y.'s new condominium dwelling venue. One duplex available. Cost: one billion dollars. Take it or leave it. Everything made of chrome, glass, and other expensive materials. A must for the very rich person who needs a very luxurious place to live. Just 48 meters east of Park Avenue, where the really rich persons live. Call us for an appointment. No—have somebody else call us on your behalf, and have them tell us they're your "agent" or "private secretary"—as long as we're impressed with your richness and wealth. And have them look up the number, too. Don't call us yourself and lie to us that you're actually your own agent or secretary. We're rich, too. We'll know in a second if it's the truth or not.

**RESTORED TOWNHOUSE IN
MUTTONCHOPS, CONN.**

A house as big as a town in this secluded
Connecticut hamlet. Every room is a small
bedroom. Thirty-seven in all; no kitchen,
bath, living room, etc. Can be gutted and
rebuilt. $250,000. Owner (203) 555-4567.